EUROPEAN EMPLOYMENT
AND
INDUSTRIAL RELATIONS GLOSSARY:
GERMANY

EUROPEAN FOUNDATION
FOR THE IMPROVEMENT OF LIVING AND
WORKING CONDITIONS

EUROPEAN EMPLOYMENT AND INDUSTRIAL RELATIONS GLOSSARY: GERMANY

BY

MANFRED WEISS

SWEET AND MAXWELL

OFFICE FOR OFFICIAL PUBLICATIONS OF
THE EUROPEAN COMMUNITIES

1992

Published in 1992 by
Sweet and Maxwell Limited of
South Quay Plaza, 183 Marsh Wall, London E14
Typeset by Printset and Design Ltd., Dublin
Printed in Great Britain

British Cataloguing in Publication Data

A catalogue record for this book is
available from the British Library

Sweet and Maxwell, South Quay Plaza, London E14
ISBN 0421-44830-X

Office for Official Publications of the European Communities,
2 rue Mercier, L-2985 Luxembourg
ISBN 92-826-2605-9
Catalogue Number SY-70-91-006-EN-C

Publication No. EF/91/13/EN of the European Foundation for the
Improvement of Living and Working Conditions,
Loughlinstown House, Shankill, Co. Dublin, Ireland.

General Editor of the European Employment and Industrial
Relations Glossary Series

TIZIANO TREU
Professor of Labour Law
Catholic University of Milan

Revising Editor for the English language volumes

MICHAEL TERRY
Senior Lecturer in Industrial Relations
University of Warwick

Project Manager

HUBERT KRIEGER
Research Manager
European Foundation for the improvement of Living
and Working Conditions, Dublin

The present volume was prepared for the European Foundation for the
Improvement of Living and Working Conditions, Dublin

under the editorship of

MANFRED WEISS
Professor of Labour Law
University of Frankfurt

with the collaboration of

THOMAS KREUDER	JOACHIM WEYAND
Research Assistant	Assistant Professor
University of Frankfurt	University of Frankfurt

and with contributions from

BETTINA BEHNING	JÜRGEN GRIEBELING
JÖRG VAN LAAK	HANS SCHUBERT

STRUCTURE OF THE WORK

There are companion volumes of the Glossary (both national and international editions) already published for:

Country	National Team Leader
Italy	Tiziano Treu, Fondazione Regionale Pietro Seveso, Milan
Spain	Antonio Valverde, University of Seville
United Kingdom	Michael Terry Warwick University
Belgium	Roger Blanpain Catholic University of Leuven

Further volumes to appear will be:

France	Antoine Lyon Caen
Greece	Yota Kravaritou-Manitakis
Portugal	Mario Pinto
Ireland	Ferdinand von Prondzynski
Denmark	
Netherlands	
Luxembourg	

TABLE OF CONTENTS

USER'S GUIDE

This Guide is designed to help readers use the Glossary by providing an explanation of the contents and some of the conventions adopted.

This volume of the Glossary contains the following sections:

1. *List of Abbreviations*

This list comprises all the principal abbreviations used in the text, including those that form an entry in the Glossary. The latter abbreviations are cross-referenced to the relevant definitions.

2. *Foreword*

Written by the Director and Deputy Director of the European Foundation, the Foreword sets out the Foundation's aims in publishing this series of Glossaries.

3. *Preface*

A Preface to the series has been prepared by Professor Tiziano Treu in his capacity as Co-ordinating Editor. It serves as a background introduction to the Glossaries, explaining the origination of the material and the method of compilation and translation.

4. *List of Entries*

For cross-referencing purposes, the entries have been listed alphabetically in both German and English, with their relevant number in the text.

5. *Introduction*

The introduction provides a commentary and analysis of national characteristics, and highlights particular features giving an historical perspective to the background information.

6. *Glossary*

All the main entries are numbered and appear in **BOLD** upper case. They are listed alphabetically in German with appropriate English translations.

Cross-references are indicated in the text by, *e.g.* "see", "see also", etc. and also appear in **bold** upper and lower case.

The running heads refer to the first and last main entry to appear on each double page.

7. *Tables*

A selection of tables is included showing employment trends and other statistical factors.

8. *Bibliography*

A selective Bibliography of suggested further reading and source material has been compiled by the editorial team for each volume. The titles of all references appear in German, but other details have been translated where appropriate.

9. *Index*

The Index comprises two parts; an alphabetical index in English, followed by an alphabetical index in German.

All Index entries refer to the numbers of the definitions in the Glossary text.

LIST OF ABBREVIATIONS

ADGB	General Federation of German Unions (in Weimar Germany)
AFG	Employment Promotion Act of June 25, 1969, last amended on June 26, 1990
AngKündG	White-Collar Workers' Protection Against Dismissal Act of July 9, 1926, last amended on June 26, 1990
ArbGG	Labour Courts Act, as amended up to July 2, 1979, last amended on June 26, 1990
ArbSichG	Occupational Health and Safety Act of December 12, 1973, last amended on April 12, 1976
AuslG	Aliens Act of April 28, 1965, last amended on July 9, 1990
BAT	National Agreement for Public Sector White-Collar Workers
BBesG	Federal Career Public Service Pay Act
BBiG	Vocational Training Act of August 14, 1969, last amended (by decision of the Federal Constitutional Court) on May 14, 1986
BDA	Confederation of German Employers' Associations
BDI	Confederation of German Industry
BErzGG	Childcare Payment and Childcare Leave Act, as amended up to July 25, 1989
BeschFG	Improvement of Employment Opportunities Act of April 26, 1985, last amended on December 22, 1989
BetrVG	Works Constitution Act, as amended up to December 23, 1988, last amended on December 18, 1989
BGB	Civil Code of August 18, 1896, last amended on June 26, 1990
BPersVG	Federal Staff Representation Act of March 15, 1974, last amended on July 10, 1989
BRG	Works Councils Act of 1920
BUrlG	Federal Minimum Annual Holiday Act of January 8, 1963, last amended on October 29, 1974
CGB	Christian Trade Union Federation of Germany
DAG	German White-Collar Workers' Union
DBB	German Federation of Career Public Servants
DGB	German Federation of Trade Unions
DIN	German Standards Institute
EG	European Communities (EC)
EGB	European Trade Union Confederation (ETUC)
EGKS	European Coal and Steel Community (ECSC)
ESC	European Social Charter
EWG	European Economic Community (EEC)

EWGV	Treaty Establishing the European Economic Community (Treaty of Rome)
FDGB	Confederation of Free German Trade Unions (in the former German Democratic Republic)
GewO	Industrial Code, as amended up to January 1, 1987, last amended on December 20, 1988
GG	Basic Law for the Federal Republic of Germany of May 23, 1949, last amended on September 23, 1990
HandwO	Craft Trades Code
IAO	ILO (International Labour Organization)
IBFG	International Confederation of Free Trade Unions (ICFTU)
IG	industrial union
IHK	Chamber of Industry and Commerce
KSchG	Protection Against Dismissal Act, as amended up to August 25, 1969, last amended on December 18, 1989
LohnFG	Continued Wage Payment Act of July 27, 1969, last amended on December 20, 1988
MitbestErgG	Co-Determination Amendment Act of 1956
MitbestG	Co-Determination Act of 1976
MitbG	Coal, Iron and Steel Industry Co-Determination Act of 1951
ÖTV	Public Services, Transport and Traffic Union
RKW	Board for Rationalization of the German Economy
RVO	Reich Insurance Code of 1911
SE	Societas Europea (European Company)
SGB	Social Security Code
StabG	Stability Act of 1967
TVG	Collective Agreements Act, as amended up to August 25, 1969, last amended on October 29, 1974
ULA	Association of Executive Staff
WahlO	Electoral Code (First Order for Implementing the Works Constitution Act) of January 16, 1972, last amended on September 28, 1989
WGB	World Federation of Trade Unions (WFTU)
WVA	World Confederation of Labour (WCL)

FOREWORD

The Foundation believes that social dialogue at international level should provide, for all those taking part in it, a better understanding of the different contexts — for example, legal frameworks and traditions — in which dialogue about employment and industrial relations takes place. An essential prerequisite for such improved understanding is an awareness of the precise meaning of the terms used to describe the features of industrial relations systems in each Member State of the Community. This series of glossaries sets out to provide clear explanations of terms and the context in which they are used.

The Foundation hopes that the series will be of value to a wide spectrum of users. Novices in the field of employment and industrial relations will welcome a guide to the working of the system in their own country, whilst experts will seek the distinguishing characteristics of systems operating in Member States other than their own. By providing both a national glossary for each Member State and also an "international" edition, the Foundation believes it is providing an important aid to international understanding in the complex field of employment and industrial relations.

Clive Purkiss   Eric Verborgh
Director   Deputy Director

European Foundation for the Improvement of Living and Working Conditions, Dublin.

PREFACE TO THE SERIES

The idea to write a series of glossaries dealing with the industrial relations, labour markets and employment laws of the 12 EC Member States emerged gradually, out of the experience of expert academics and practitioners aware of the need to systematize and codify experiences in this important area. The development of a social dialogue, and the ever-increasing need for debate and discussion between the Member States, employers and unions, spurred by the prospect of full European economic integration in 1992, have given a fresh impetus to the need for clarity and mutual understanding in this vital subject. But these glossaries are not intended only as resources for such formal settings. Throughout Europe there are thousands of potential users of the glossaries: national and international administrators, academics and researchers, trade unionists and managers, and specialised journalists, among others. All these groups will increasingly need to communicate across borders in different languages, about a whole range of industrial relations-related topics. For them too, the need for greater understanding and clarity has become more urgent. The glossaries should become the standard tools for persons involved in meetings, formal and informal, of a whole range of interested economic and social actors.

The European Foundation for the Improvement of Living and Working Conditions immediately recognised the importance and usefulness of the proposal to compile a series of glossaries, and provided the funding for the first three; those dealing with Italy, Spain, and the United Kingdom. Later, it was to agree to provide additional funding for the remaining nine states, with Belgium, the Federal Republic of Germany, and France being the next three. It was agreed that the Foundation should provide resources for the translation of all the glossaries into English, for publication as a uniform series. It is now proposed to make the glossaries also available in electronic database form, which will greatly enhance the speed and flexibility with which they may be used. The glossaries for all countries are also available in their original languages, published domestically. In some cases these "domestic" glossaries are larger and longer than the English translations, since they have been designed as domestic as well as international sources of reference, and may contain material of little immediate relevance to the foreign reader.

Professor Tiziano Treu was appointed international co-ordinator, and he, in turn, worked to set up teams of experts in the first three countries, consisting of experts in all the disciplines involved in industrial relations, each team under its own co-ordinator. These teams were under instruction to provide comparable glossaries, covering the same range of topics. The intention was to produce volumes that would provide both definitions of several hundred terms of particular importance, and an insight into their relevance to the country concerned. The combined experience of all those involved in the project (academics, practitioners and others) was that simple translations of terms were insufficient, since they fail fully to communicate the substantive importance of the institutions and processes described. The products are designed to be of direct use both to the practitioner and to the academic student of the subject, so the glossaries have to be both technically correct and informed by relevant policy debate. The glossaries are intended to serve the practical needs of a diverse readership, of varying levels of knowledge and need, and to serve as an immediate reference or translation source or a starting-point for in-depth research. The audience will be a broad and diverse one; our researches have confirmed that the glossaries will be of interest to national, European and other international readers, given the worldwide interest currently expressed in European industrial relations.

Inevitably, we have had to be selective in our choice of terms. It was not the intention to produce an encyclopedia, but rather an annotated guide to key issues and concepts. In order to achieve this we sought both a degree of commonality in the terms to be covered (in order to ensure above all that the key concepts were dealt with in all the volumes) and a degree of differentiation, reflecting the national idiosyncracies that remain important aspects of the European scene. Our descriptions have had to be less than encyclopedic; the entries do not provide all the detail with regard to specific pieces of legislation, for example. Readers who need further precision will be able to make use of the reference works cited in the concluding bibliographies.

The glossaries all share the same format. An introductory essay covers the key features of the national system: the political-economic environment, the key actors, the role of law, and the current state of labour relations. This is meant to help the average user of the glossary (it is not particularly designed for a specialist audience) and it has been written in such a way as to be understandable to an international audience, and therefore to be as clear and "candid" as possible. The main body of entries follows, and the volumes conclude with sets of tables showing trends in labour markets, collective bargaining coverage, unionization and industrial conflict, with a brief guide to further reading. Those texts which have been translated into English also contain an additional index in the original language.

Certain conventions have been adopted in the translation. Wherever possible we have used English translations whose meaning is clear and which involve no specialized "jargon". But there are two other cases. First, where no English term in common usage exists and we have created our own translation. Here we have put the English term into double inverted commas, to indicate that it is not common English usage, but is simply an accurate translation. Second, in a few cases we have been unable to find a translation of less than a sentence for particular terms. Here we have left the term in the original language, and readers in English will need to read the entry to discover its meaning.

The process of writing and translating these glossaries has convinced the participants of the usefulness of the exercise. The European

Foundation has, in its usual way, sought the views of the social partners in the countries concerned, and their response has also been enthusiastic. The exercise has also revealed that beneath the superficial similarities of some terms there may lie significant differences of meaning and interpretation, but that, deeper still, lie important patterns of similarity and convergence and, above all, a keen interest in the consequences of an increasingly integrated and united Europe. We are confident that we have produced an instrument that will help forge a clearer understanding and, in its turn, a greater co-operation, in this vital area of social activity.

Acknowledgements

Many people have co-operated closely in the preparation of this series. This co-operation has been under the general direction of Hubert Krieger, the Foundation's manager for the project, and Tiziano Treu, the "rapporteur" who has acted as general editor.

The series is based on the dedicated efforts of the national teams, who have had the task of reducing formidable amounts of material to manageable proportions.

The task of editing the international (English-language) version has been particularly onerous. It is only fitting to acknowledge the exceptional contributions of Rita Inston, the reviser (of Cave Translations Ltd.) and of Michael Terry (Warwick University) who, in addition to having the main responsibility for the United Kingdom volume, has given invaluable advice on explanations in English of concepts peculiar to individual Member States. Professor Jon Clark (University of Southampton) made an important contribution to the editing of the volume for Germany.

With regard to general aspects of publication, the Foundation is grateful for the co-operation of the publishers and for advice from the Office for Official Publications of the European Communities, for the services of the Commission and those of Solon Consultants (UK).

Throughout the project there has been close co-operation between the research, information and translation services of the Foundation.

Professor Tiziano Treu

NUMBERED ALPHABETICAL LIST OF ENTRIES IN GERMAN

GERMAN

ENGLISH

	GERMAN	ENGLISH
1.	Abfindung	compensation for job loss
2.	Abmahnung	warning
3.	Abrufarbeit	variable working hours
4.	Abschlussfreiheit	freedom to conclude an employment contract
5.	Abwehraussperrung	defensive lock-out
6.	Acht-Stunden-Tag	eight-hour day
7.	AFG	AFG
8.	Akkord	piecework
9.	Aktiengesellschaft	public limited company
10.	Aktionär	shareholder
11.	Aktionsprogramm "Arbeit und Technik"	"Work and Technology" Action Programme
12.	Aktionsprogramm "Humanisierung des Arbeitslebens"	"Humanization of Working Life" Action Programme
13.	Allgemeine Ortskrankenkasse	Public Health Insurance Fund
14.	Allgemeinverbindlichkeit von Tarifverträgen	extension of collective agreements
15.	alliierte Streitkräfte	Allied Forces
16.	Altersgrenze	retirement age
17.	Altersruhegeld	statutory retirement pension
18.	Altersteilzeit	partial retirement
19.	Altersversorgung	old-age pension provision
20.	Anbahnung des Arbeitsverhältnisses	pre-contractual obligations in the employment relationship
21.	Änderungskündigung	dismissal for variation of contract
22.	Anfechtbarkeit des Arbeitsvertrages	voidability of the employment contract
23.	Angestellter	white-collar worker
24.	Angriffsaussperrung	offensive lock-out
25.	Annahmeverzug des Arbeitgebers	employer's non-acceptance of the work performance
26.	AOK	AOK
27.	Arbeiter	manual worker
28.	Arbeiterkammer	Chamber of Labour
29.	Arbeitgeber	employer
30.	Arbeitgeber-Arbeitnehmer-Beziehungen	employer-employee relations
31.	Arbeitgeberhaftung	employer liability
32.	Arbeitgeberverband	employers' association
33.	Arbeitnehmer	employee
34.	arbeitnehmerähnliche Person	person treated in law as similar to an employee
35.	Arbeitnehmerbeteiligung	employee participation
36.	Arbeitnehmererfindungen	inventions by employees
37.	Arbeitnehmerfreizügigkeit	freedom of movement for workers
38.	Arbeitnehmerhaftung	employee liability
39.	Arbeitnehmerkammer	Chamber of Labour
40.	Arbeitnehmerrechte	employee rights
41.	Arbeitnehmerschutz	employee protection
42.	Arbeitnehmersparzulage	employee savings supplement
43.	Arbeitnehmerüberlassung	hiring-out of labour

44.	Arbeitsamt	Employment Office
45.	Arbeitsbereicherung	job enrichment
46.	Arbeitsbereitschaft	on-call
47.	Arbeitsbeschaffungsmassnahmen	job creation schemes
48.	Arbeitsbescheinigung	certificate of employment
49.	Arbeitsbeziehungen	labour relations
50.	Arbeitsdirektor	employee director
51.	Arbeitsentgelt	remuneration
52.	Arbeitserlaubnis	work permit
53.	Arbeitserweiterung	job enlargement
54.	Arbeitsförderung	promotion of employment
55.	Arbeitsgericht	Labour Court
56.	Arbeitsgerichtsbarkeit	system of labour courts
57.	Arbeitsgerichtsverfahren	labour court procedure
58.	Arbeitskammer	Chamber of Labour
59.	Arbeitskampf	industrial action
60.	Arbeitskampfbereitschaft	willingness to take industrial action
61.	Arbeitskampfrichtlinien	union strike guidelines
62.	Arbeitslosengeld	unemployment benefit
63.	Arbeitslosenhilfe	unemployment assistance
64.	Arbeitslosenversicherung	unemployment insurance
65.	Arbeitslosigkeit	unemployment
66.	Arbeitsmarkt	labour market
67.	Arbeitsministerien der Länder	Ministries of Labour at Land level
68.	Arbeitsmotivation	motivation to work
69.	Arbeitsorganisation	work organization
70.	Arbeitspapiere	employment documents
71.	Arbeitspause	break
72.	Arbeitspflicht	duty to work
73.	Arbeitsplatz	job
74.	Arbeitsplatzschutz für Wehr- und Zivildienstleistende	job protection during compulsory military or community service
75.	Arbeitsrecht	labour law
76.	Arbeitsschutz	health and safety
77.	Arbeitsschutzausschuss	health and safety committee
78.	Arbeitsstätte	workplace
79.	Arbeitsteilung	division of labour
80.	Arbeitsunfähigkeitsbescheinigung	certificate of incapacity for work
81.	Arbeitsunfall	accident at work
82.	Arbeitsverhältnis	employment relationship
83.	Arbeitsverhinderung	prevention from working
84.	Arbeitsvermittlung	job placement
85.	Arbeitsvertrag	contract of employment
86.	arbeitsvertragliche Pflichten	obligations under the contract of employment
87.	Arbeitsvertragsschluss	conclusion of the contract of employment
88.	Arbeitsverweigerung	refusal to work
89.	Arbeitswissenschaft	"work science"
90.	Arbeitszeit	working time
91.	Arbeitszeitschutz	restrictions on working hours
92.	Arbeitszeitverkürzung	reduction of working hours
93.	Arbeitszeitvorschriften	regulations on working hours
94.	ArbG	ArbG
95.	Arrest	distraint order
96.	Aufenthaltsberechtigung	right of abode
97.	Aufenthaltserlaubnis	residence permit
98.	Aufenthaltsgenehmigung	permission to reside

154.	Berufsschule	vocational training school
155.	Berufsunfähigkeit	occupational incapacity
156.	Berufsverband	occupational union
157.	Berufsverbot	occupational ban
158.	Berufswahlfreiheit	freedom of occupational choice
159.	Berufung	appeal
160.	Beschäftigungsförderungsgesetz	Improvement of Employment Opportunities Act
161.	Beschäftigungsgesellschaft	job creation company
162.	Beschäftigungsverbot	employment ban
163.	Beschlussverfahren	"Beschluss" procedure
164.	Beschwerde	"Beschluss" procedure appeal
165.	Besetzungsregelungen	staffing rules
166.	Besitzstandsklausel	*status quo* clause
167.	Besoldung	pay (of career public servants)
168.	Bestandsgarantie	guarantee of existence
169.	Betätigungsgarantie	guarantee of activity
170.	Beteiligungsrechte des Betriebsrats	participation rights of the works council
171.	Betrieb	establishment
172.	betriebliche Altersversorgung	occupational pension scheme
173.	betriebliche Arbeitsschutzorganisation	workplace health and safety arrangements
174.	betriebliche Berufsausbildung	company vocational training
175.	betriebliche Übung	custom
176.	Betriebsabsprache	semi-formal works agreement
177.	Betriebsabteilung	department
178.	Betriebsänderung	substantial alteration to the establishment
179.	Betriebsarzt	works doctor
180.	Betriebsaufspaltung	company split-up at establishment level
181.	Betriebsausschuss	works council executive committee
182.	Betriebsbeauftragter	specialist officer at establishment level
183.	betriebsbedingte Kündigung	redundancy
184.	Betriebsbesetzung	occupation (of the workplace)
185.	Betriebsbusse	disciplinary sanction
186.	Betriebsdatenerfassung	capture of production data
187.	Betriebseinschränkung	reduction of operations
188.	Betriebsfeier und -ausflug	works holiday and outing
189.	Betriebsferien	fixed works holidays
190.	Betriebsfrieden	peaceful co-operation within the establishment
191.	Betriebsgeheimnis	trade secret
192.	Betriebsgruppe	work group
193.	Betriebsinhaberwechsel	change of ownership of an establishment
194.	Betriebsjustiz	company discipline
195.	Betriebsklima	general establishment culture
196.	Betriebskrankenkasse	company health insurance fund
197.	Betriebsnachfolge	successor establishment
198.	betriebsnahe Tarifpolitik	establishment-specific bargaining
199.	Betriebsobmann	works spokesperson
200.	Betriebsordnung	works rules
201.	Betriebsrat	works council
202.	Betriebsräteversammlung	General Meeting of Works Councils
203.	Betriebsratshaftung	works council liability
204.	Betreibsratsmitglied	works council member
205.	Betriebsratswahl	works council election
206.	Betriebsrisiko	"works risk"
207.	Betriebsschliessung	shutdown of an establishment
208.	Betriebssicherheit	safety at work

209.	Betriebsstillegung	closure of an establishment
210.	Betriebsstörung	interruption of operations
211.	Betriebsteil	part of an establishment
212.	Betriebsübergang	transfer of an establishment
213.	Betriebsübernahme	acquisition of an establishment
214.	Betriebsunfall	industrial accident
215.	Betriebsveräusserung	alienation of an establishment
216.	Betriebsvereinbarung	works agreement
217.	Betriebsverfassung	works constitution
218.	Betriebsversammlung	works meeting
219.	Betriebswegeunfall	accident *en route*
220.	Betriebszugehörigkeit	length of service
221.	Bewerberauswahl	personnel selection
222.	Bewerbung	job application
223.	Bewerbungsunterlagen	job application documents
224.	Bezirkspersonalrat	regional staff council
225.	Bezugsgrösse	reference wage
226.	BfA	BfA
227.	BFH	BFH
228.	BGH	BGH
229.	Bildungsurlaub	educational leave
230.	Binnenmarkt	internal market
231.	Bio- und Chemotechnologien	biotechnology and chemical technologies
232.	Bismarcksche Sozialgesetzgebung	Bismarck's social security legislation
233.	Bordpersonal	on-board personnel
234.	Bordvertretung	on-board representation
235.	Boykott	boycott
236.	BRG	BRG
237.	Bruttovergütung	gross pay
238.	Bummelstreik	go-slow
239.	Bundesanstalt für Arbeit	Federal Employment Service
240.	Bundesanstalt für Arbeitsschutz	Federal Institute for Occupational Health and Safety
241.	Bundesarbeitsgericht	Federal Labour Court
242.	Bundesangestelltentarifvertrag	National Agreement for Public Sector White-Collar Workers
243.	Bundesbeamte	federal career public servants
244.	Bundesländer	Länder (of the Federal Republic)
245.	Bundesministerium für Arbeit und Sozialordnung	Federal Ministry of Labour and Social Affairs
246.	Bundesrat	Federal Council
247.	Bundesregierung	Federal Government
248.	Bundessozialgericht	Federal Social Security Court
249.	Bundestag	Federal Parliament
250.	Bundesverband der Deutschen Industrie	Confederation of German Industry
251.	Bundesvereinigung der Deutschen Arbeitgeberverbände	Confederation of German Employers' Associations
252.	Bundesverfassungsgericht	Federal Constitutional Court
253.	Bundesverwaltungsgericht	Federal Administrative Court
254.	Bürokommunikationstechnik	office communications technology
255.	BVerfG	BVerfG
256.	BVerwG	BVerwG
257.	CGB	CGB
258.	Christlicher Gewerkschaftsbund Deutschlands	Christian Trade Union Federation of Germany
259.	DAG	DAG
260.	Datenschutz	data protection

261.	Datenschutzbeauftragter	data protection officer
262.	DBB	DBB
263.	demokratische Willensbildung	democratic decision-making
264.	Demonstrationsstreik	demonstration strike
265.	Deregulierung	deregulation
266.	Deutsche Angestelltengewerkschaft	German White-Collar Workers' Union
267.	Deutscher Beamtenbund	German Federation of Career Public Servants
268.	Deutscher Gewerkschaftsbund	German Federation of Trade Unions
269.	DGB	DGB
270.	Dienst nach Vorschrift	work-to-rule
271.	Diensterfindung	job-related invention
272.	Diensteid	oath of service
273.	Dienstherr	public sector employer
274.	Dienstleistungsabend	late-night opening
275.	dienstliche Angelegenheiten	service-related matters
276.	Dienstordnungsangestellte	white-collar workers bound by special service regulations
277.	Dienstreise	business travel
278.	Dienststelle	public sector establishment
279.	Dienststellenleiter	public-sector establishment head
280.	Dienstvereinbarung	establishment agreement (public sector)
281.	Dienstvergehen	breach of duty (by career public servant)
282.	Dienstverhältnis	service relationship
283.	Dienstvertrag	contract for services
284.	Dienstvorgesetzter	superior official
285.	Dienstwagen	company car
286.	Dienstwohnung	company housing
287.	Differenzierungsklausel	differential treatment clause
288.	DIN	DIN
289.	Direktionsrecht	employer's right to issue instructions
290.	Direktversicherung	direct insurance
291.	Direktzusage	direct guarantee
292.	Diskriminierungsverbote	anti-discrimination laws
293	dispositives Recht	discretionary law
294.	Disziplinarrecht	disciplinary law for career public servants
295.	Doppelarbeitsverhältnis	dual jobholding
296.	Doppelbesteuerungsabkommen	double taxation agreement
297.	Doppelverdiener	dual income couple
298.	Drittwirkung	third-party effect of constitutional rights
299.	Druckkündigung	dismissal under third-party pressure
300.	duales System	dual system (of vocational training)
301.	Durchschnittslohn	average wage
302.	Effektivklausel	actual-pay clause
303.	ehrenamtliche Richter	lay judges
304.	Eigengruppe	self-constituted employee group
305.	Eingruppierung	grading
306.	Einheitsgewerkschaft	unified trade union
307.	Einigungsstelle	establishment-level arbitration committee
308.	Einkommensteuer	income tax
309.	Einpersonenbetriebsrat	single-member works council
310.	Einspruchsgesetz	statute not requiring assent (of the Federal Council)
311.	Einstellungsfragebogen	application form
312.	einstweilige Verfügung	interlocutory injunction
313.	Einwirkungspflicht	duty to exert influence
314.	Elternurlaub	parental leave

315.	Erhaltungsarbeiten	maintenance of essential supplies and services
316.	Erholungsurlaub	annual holiday
317.	Ersatzkasse	white-collar workers' health insurance fund
318.	Ersatzzeit	period treated as a contribution period
319.	erwerbstätige Zivilbevölkerung	civilian working population
320.	Erwerbsunfähigkeit	total disability
321.	Erziehungsgeld	childcare payment
322.	Erziehungsurlaub	childcare leave
323.	Erziehungszeit	childcare period
324.	Europäische Aktiengesellschaft	European Company
325.	Europäische Sozialcharta	European Social Charter
326.	europäisches Gemeinschaftsrecht	European Community law
327.	Fachkräfte für Arbeitssicherheit	works safety experts
328.	Fachverbandsprinzip	principle of occupational organization
329.	Fairnessgebot	fairness principle
330.	faktisches Arbeitsverhältnis	*de facto* employment relationship
331.	FDGB	FDGB
332.	fehlgegangene Vergütungserwartung	unfulfilled expectation of consideration
333.	Feierschichten	unworked shifts
334.	FG	FG
335.	Finanzgerichtsbarkeit	system of finance courts
336.	Firmentarifvertrag	company agreement
337.	Flexibilisierung	flexibilization
338.	fliegendes Personal	flight personnel
339.	Fortsetzungskrankheit	recurring illness
340.	Frauenarbeitsschutz	protection of women at work
341.	Frauenbeauftragte	women's officers
342.	Frauenförderung	advancement of women
343.	freie Erfindung	independent invention
344.	freier Beruf	profession
345.	freier Mitarbeiter	freelance
346.	Friedenspflicht	peace obligation
347.	Fünf-Tage-Woche	five-day week
348.	Fürsorgepflicht	duty of care
349.	Fusion	merger
350.	Gastarbeiter	guest worker
351.	Gebietskörperschaften	territorial authorities
352.	gefahrengeneigte Arbeit	hazardous work
353.	gefährliche Stoffe	dangerous substances
354.	Gegnerfreiheit	independence from the opposing side
355.	Gehalt	salary
356.	geldwerte Leistung	payment in kind
357.	Geltungsbereich von Tarifnormen	scope of normative provisions
358.	Gemeinde	municipality
359.	Gemeinschaftswahl	joint election
360.	Generalstreik	general strike
361.	Gerätesicherheit	safety of equipment
362.	Gerichtsbarkeit	(system of) jurisdiction
363.	geringfügig Beschäftigte	"marginal" part-time workers
364.	Gesamtbetriebsrat	company works council
365.	Gesamtjugend- und Auszubildendenvertretung	company representative body for young workers and trainees
366.	Gesamtpersonalrat	general staff council
367.	Gesamtzusage	general undertaking by employer
368.	Geschäftsführer	managing director

426.	Informationsrechte des Betriebsrats	information rights of the works council
427.	informelle Regelungen	informal rules
428.	Inhaltsfreiheit	freedom of contractual content
429.	Inhaltskontrolle	control of contractual content
430.	innerbetriebliche Weiterbildung	in-service training
431.	Insolvenz	insolvency
432.	Insolvenzschutz	protection in the event of insolvency
433.	institutionalisierte Interessenvertretung	institutionalized representation of interests
434.	Interessenausgleich	reconcilement of interests
435.	Internationale Arbeitsorganisation	International Labour Organization
436.	internationales Arbeitsrecht	international labour law
437.	Investivlohn	invested pay
438.	Job Sharing	job sharing
439.	Jugendarbeitsschutz	youth employment protection
440.	Jugend- und Auszubildendenvertretung	representative body for young workers and trainees
441.	juristische Person	legal person
442.	kalte Aussperrung	"cold" lock-out
443.	Kampfbeteiligung von besonderen Arbeitnehmergruppen	participation in industrial action by particular employee groups
444.	Kampfparität	balance of bargaining power
445.	KAPOVAZ	"KAPOVAZ"
446.	Kernzeit	core time
447.	Kettenarbeitsverträge	consecutive short-term contracts
448.	Kinderarbeit	child employment
449.	Kinderbetreuung	childcare
450.	Kindergeld	child benefit
451.	Kirchen	Churches
452.	kirchliche Mitarbeitervertretung	ecclesiastical staff representation body
453.	kirchliches Arbeitsrecht	ecclesiastical labour law
454.	Knappschaft	mineworkers
455.	Koalition	collective industrial organization
456.	Koalitionsfreiheit	freedom of association (right to organize)
457.	Koalitionszweck	purpose of a collective industrial organization
458.	kollektives Arbeitsrecht	collective labour law
459.	Kommunalverband	association of municipalities
460.	Kommune	municipality
461.	konkurrierende Gesetzgebungskompetenz	concurrent legislative powers
462.	Konkurs	bankruptcy
463.	Konkursausfallgeld	bankruptcy non-payment benefit
464.	Konsultationspflicht	duty to consult (public sector)
465.	Konzern	group (of companies)
466.	Konzernbetriebsrat	group works council
467.	konzertierte Aktion	concerted action
468.	Krankengeld	sickness benefit
469.	Krankenkasse	health insurance fund
470.	Krankenpflegetag	day's leave for sick-nursing
471.	Krankenvergütung	sick pay
472.	Krankenversicherung	health insurance
473.	Krankheit	illness
474.	krankheitsbedingte Kündigung	dismissal on grounds of ill health
475.	Krankmeldung	notification of illness
476.	Kündigung	termination
477.	Kündigungsfrist	period of notice
478.	Kündigungsschutz	protection against dismissal
479.	Kündigungsschutzklage	application for protection against dismissal

480.	Kurzarbeit	short-time working
481.	Kurzarbeitergeld	short-time allowance
482.	Ladenschluss	shop closing hours
483.	LAG	LAG
484.	Landesarbeitsgericht	Land Labour Court
485.	Landesbeamte	career public servants at Land level
486.	Laufbahn	career branch
487.	Lehre	apprenticeship
488.	Leichtlohngruppen	light-work pay grades
489.	Leiharbeitgeber	temporary worker's employer
490.	Leistungslohn	payment by results
491.	Leistungsstörung	temporary non-performance
492.	Leitende Angestellte	executive staff
493.	Lohn	wage
494.	Lohn-Preis-Spirale	wage-price spiral
495.	Lohn- und Gehaltsabzüge	deductions from pay
496.	Lohn- und Gehaltstarifvertrag	pay agreement
497.	Lohnausfallprinzip	loss-of-pay principle
498.	Lohnfortzahlung	continued payment of remuneration
499.	Lohngleichheit	equal pay
500.	Lohngruppe	pay grade
501.	Lohnpfändung	attachment of earnings
502.	Lohnrückforderung	right to reclaim pay
503.	Lohnsteuer	earnings tax
504.	Lohnsteuerkarte	earnings tax card
505.	Lohnzahlung	payment of remuneration
506.	Lohnzuschlag	pay supplement
507.	magisches Viereck	"magic square"
508.	MAK-Werte	MAC values
509.	Management	management
510.	Mankohaftung	deficit liability
511.	Manteltarifvertrag	framework agreement on employment conditions
512.	Marktwirtschaft	market economy
513.	Massenentlassung	collective dismissal
514.	Massenproduktion	mass production
515.	Massregelungsverbot	ban on disciplinary treatment
516.	Mehrarbeit	overtime exceeding maximum working hours
517.	Mehrarbeitsvergütung	overtime premium pay
518.	Meinungsfreiheit	freedom of opinion
519.	Mikroelektronik	microelectronics
520.	Minderheitenschutz	protection of minorities
521.	Mindestarbeitsbedingungen	minimum conditions of employment
522.	Mitarbeiterbeteiligung	financial participation (by employees)
523.	MitbestErgG	MitbestErgG
524.	MitbestG	MitbestG
525.	Mitbestimmung	co-determination
526.	Mitbestimmungsrechte des Betriebsrats	co-determination rights of the works council
527.	MitbG	MitbG
528.	mittelbare Diskriminierung	indirect discrimination
529.	Mitwirkungsrechte des Betriebsrats	consultation rights of the works council
530.	Montan-Mitbestimmung	co-determination in the coal, iron and steel industry
531.	Montanindustrie	coal, iron and steel industry
532.	Mutterschaftsgeld	maternity allowance

533.	Mutterschutz	maternity protection
534.	Nachtarbeit	night work
535.	Nachteilsausgleich	reconcilement of disadvantage
536.	Naturalvergütung	payment in kind
537.	Nebentätigkeit	second job
538.	Nebentätigkeitsverbot	prohibition of second jobs
539.	negative Koalitionsfreiheit	"negative" freedom of association
540.	Nettolohnvereinbarung	net pay arrangement
541.	neue Beweglichkeit	"neue Beweglichkeit"
542.	neue Produktionskonzepte	new production concepts
543.	neue Produktionstechnologien	new production technologies
544.	neue Technologien	new technologies
545.	Neutralität des Staates	impartiality of the state
546.	Nichtzulassungsbeschwerde	non-admission petition
547.	Normalarbeitsverhältnis	typical employment relationship
548.	Notarbeiten	emergency work
549.	Öffentlicher Dienst	public service
550.	Öffnungszeiten	hours of opening
551.	ordentliche Gerichtsbarkeit	system of ordinary courts
552.	ordentliche Kündigung	termination with notice
553.	Ordnungsfunktion des Tarifvertrages	normative function of collective agreements
554.	Ordnungsprinzip	supersedence principle
555.	Organisationsklauseln	closed shop clauses
556.	OVG	OVG
557.	paritätische Mitbestimmung	parity co-determination
558.	Parlamentsvorbehalt	reservation of parliamentary powers
559.	Pause	break
560.	Pensions- und Unterstützungskassen	pension and benevolent funds
561.	Pensions-Sicherungs-Verein	Pension Security Association
562.	Personalakte	personal file
563.	Personaleinsatz	labour utilization
564.	Personalfragebogen	recruitment questionnaire
565.	Personalführung	personnel management
566.	Personalhoheit	authority to appoint and dismiss staff
567.	Personalinformationssystem	personnel information system
568.	Personalplanung	human resource planning
569.	Personalpolitik	personnel policy
570.	Personalrat	staff council
571.	Personalratswahl	staff council election
572.	Personalreserve	supernumerary staff
573.	Personalversammlung	general staff meeting
574.	Personalvertretung	staff representation (body)
575.	personenbedingte Kündigung	dismissal on grounds of personal capability
576.	Persönlichkeitsrecht	right to privacy of the individual
577.	politischer Streik	political strike
578.	Praktikum	work experience
579.	Prämie	bonus
580.	Prämiensystem	incentive bonus system
581.	Probearbeitsverhältnis	probationary employment relationship
582.	Produktionsweise	mode of production
583.	produktive Winterbauförderung	promotion of winter construction
584.	Produktivität	productivity
585.	Produktzyklus	product cycle
586.	Prokura	commercial power of attorney
587.	Provision	commission
588.	Prozessvertretung	representation in court

642.	Schwerbehindertenbeauftragter	disabled-employee officer
643.	Schwerbehindertenschutz	protection for disabled employees
644.	Schwerbehindertenvertretung	representative body for disabled employees
645.	Schwerpunktstreik	selective strike
646.	Sicherheitsbeauftragter	safety officer
647.	Solidaritätsbeitrag	non-union members' levy
648.	Sonn- und Feiertagsarbeit	work on Sundays and public holidays
649.	Sonn- und Feiertagsruhe	rest on Sundays and public holidays
650.	sozial- und umweltverträgliche Technikgestaltung	human- and environment-centred technology strategy
651.	Sozialadäquanz	"Sozialadäquanz"
652.	Sozialauswahl	social criteria for redundancy
653.	soziale Marktwirtschaft	social market economy
654.	Sozialgerichtsbarkeit	system of social security courts
655.	Sozialgesetzbuch	Social Security Code
656.	Sozialpartnerschaft	social partnership
657.	Sozialplan	"social plan"
658.	Sozialrecht	social security law
659.	Sozialstaatsprinzip	welfare state principle
660.	Sozialversicherung	social security
661.	Sozialversicherungsausweis	social security card
662.	Sozialversicherungsbeitrag	social security contribution
663.	Sozialversicherungspflicht	social security obligation
664.	Spesen	expenses
665.	Sprecherausschuss der Leitenden Angestellten	representative body for executive staff
666.	Sprungrechtsbeschwerde	direct judicial review application
667.	Sprungrevision	direct appeal on a point of law
668.	staatliche Berufsausbildung	statutory vocational training
669.	staatliche Schlichtung	statutory dispute resolution
670.	Staatsvertrag	treaty
671.	Stabilitätsgesetz	Stability Act
672.	Steuer	tax
673.	Streik	strike
674.	Streikarbeit	performance of work during a strike
675.	Streikbrecher	strikebreaker
676.	Streikleitung	strike leadership
677.	Streikposten	picket
678.	Streikunterstützung	strike pay
679.	Strukturwandel	structural change
680.	Stückakkord	money piecework
681.	Stufenvertretung	hierarchical representation body
682.	subjektives Recht	individual's right
683.	Subvention	subsidy
684.	systematischer Arbeitsplatzwechsel	job rotation
685.	Tantieme	share of profits
686.	Tarifautonomie	collective bargaining autonomy
687.	Tarifbindung	binding effect of collective agreements
688.	Tarifeinheit	exclusivity of collective agreements
689.	Tariffähigkeit	capacity to conclude collective agreements
690.	Tariffonds	employee investment fund
691.	Tarifgemeinschaft Deutscher Länder	Employers' Association of German Länder
692.	Tarifkonkurrenz	conflict between collective agreements
693.	Tarifnormen	normative provisions (of collective agreements)
694.	Tarifpartner	parties to a collective agreement
695.	Tarifregister	register of collective agreements

696.	Tarifverhandlungen	collective bargaining
697.	Tarifvertrag	collective agreement
698.	Tarifvertragsparteien	parties to a collective agreement
699.	Tarifzuständigkeit	collective bargaining jurisdiction
700.	Taylorismus	Taylorism
701.	Technikfolgenabschätzung und -bewertung	technology impact analysis and assessment
702.	technische Normen	technical standards
703.	technischer Arbeitsschutz	protection against technical hazards at work
704.	teilautonome Arbeitsgruppen	semi-autonomous work groups
705.	Teil- oder Schwerpunktstreik	partial or selective strike
706.	Teilzeitarbeit	part-time work
707.	Telearbeit	telework
708.	Tendenzbetrieb	"Tendenzbetrieb"
709.	Treuepflicht	duty of loyalty
710.	Treuhandanstalt	Treuhand Agency
711.	Truckverbot	ban on the truck system
712.	Überarbeit	overtime
713.	überbetriebliche Mitbestimmung	co-determination above establishment level
714.	Übergangsgeld	interim payment
715.	Übermassverbot	prohibition of disproportionate measures
716.	Überstunden	overtime
717.	Überstundenvergütung	overtime pay
718.	übliche Vergütung	rate for the job
719.	ultima-ratio-Prinzip	*ultima ratio* principle
720.	Unfallschutz	protection against accidents
721.	Unfallverhütungsvorschriften	accident prevention regulations
722.	Unfallversicherung	accident insurance
723.	Union Leitender Angestellter	Association of Executive Staff
724.	Unmöglichkeit der Arbeitsleistung	impossibility of performance
725.	Unternehmen	company
726.	Unternehmensaufspaltung	company split-up
727.	Unternehmensautonomie	company autonomy
728.	Unternehmensformen	forms of company
729.	Unternehmenskultur	corporate culture
730.	Unternehmensorgane	company organs
731.	Unternehmensorganisation	company organization
732.	Unternehmensübernahme	acquisition of a company
733.	Unternehmensverfassung	company constitution
734.	Unternehmer	entrepreneur
735.	Unternehmerfreiheit	free enterprise
736.	Urabstimmung	strike ballot
737.	Urlaub	leave (of absence)
738.	Urlaubsgeld	holiday bonus
739.	Urteilsverfahren	"Urteil" procedure
740.	Verbänderecht	law on associations
741.	Verbandstarifvertrag	association-level agreement
742.	Verbesserungsvorschläge	suggestions for improvements
743.	Verdachtskündigung	dismissal on grounds of suspicion
744.	Vereinigung der kommunalen Arbeitgeberverbände	Federation of Municipal Employers' Associations
745.	Verfahrensinnovation	process innovation
746.	Verfahrenskosten	legal costs
747.	Verfassung	Constitution
748.	Verfassungsbeschwerde	constitutional appeal
749.	Verfassungsgerichtsbarkeit	system of constitutional courts

750.	Vergleich	settlement
751.	verhaltensbedingte Kündigung	dismissal on grounds of conduct
752.	Verhältnismässigkeitsgrundsatz	proportionality principle
753.	Verleiher	lessor
754.	Verletztenrente	industrial injury pension
755.	vermögenswirksame Leistungen	capital-forming payments
756.	Verrechnungsklausel	offset clause
757.	Verrechtlichung	juridification
758.	Versetzung	transfer
759.	Versorgungsanwartschaft	occupational pension expectation
760.	Versorgungszusage	assurance of an occupational pension
761.	Vertragsfreiheit	freedom of contract
762.	Vertrauensleute	union workplace representatives
763.	Vertrauensmänner und -frauen der Schwerbehinderten	employee representatives for the disabled
764.	vertrauensvolle Zusammenarbeit	co-operation in good faith
765.	Verwaltungsakt	act of administration
766.	Verwaltungsgerichtsbarkeit	system of administrative courts
767.	Verwirkung	forfeiture
768.	Verzicht	waiver
769.	Vollstreik	all-out strike
770.	Volontär	unpaid trainee
771.	Vor- und Abschlussarbeiten	preparatory and shutting-down tasks
772.	Vorbehalt des Gesetzes	reservation of statutory powers
773.	Vorgesetzter	superior
774.	Vorruhestand	early retirement
775.	Vorstand	management board
776.	Vorstellungskosten	costs of attending for interview
777.	Wahlvorstand	electoral board
778.	Warnstreik	"Warnstreik"
779.	Wartezeit	qualifying period
780.	Wegezeit	travel-to-work time
781.	Wehrdienst- und Zivildienstpflichtige	people liable for compulsory military or community service
782.	Weihnachtsgeld	Christmas bonus
783.	Weiterbeschäftigung	continued employment (during dismissal proceedings)
784.	Werksbesetzung	occupation (of the workplace)
785.	Werkstarifvertrag	company agreement
786.	Werkstudent	casual student worker
787.	Werktage	working days
788.	Werkwohnung	company housing
789.	Wettbewerbsverbot	restraint on competition
790.	wilder Streik	unofficial strike
791.	Wintergeld	winter allowance
792.	Winterhilfen für die Bauwirtschaft	winter assistance for the construction industry
793.	Wirtschaftsausschuss	economic committee
794.	Wirtschaftsdemokratie	economic democracy
795.	Wirtschaftslenkung	"steering" of the economy
796.	Wirtschaftsrecht	commercial law
797.	Wirtschaftsrisiko	economic risk
798.	Wochenarbeitszeit	working week
799.	Wochenendarbeit	weekend work
800.	Zeit-Arbeitsvertrag	fixed-term employment contract
801.	Zeitakkord	time piecework
802.	Zeitarbeit	temporary work

NUMBERED ALPHABETICAL LIST OF ENTRIES IN ENGLISH

ENGLISH

GERMAN

xliv

1

INTRODUCTION

1. The labour market situation

1.1 Rules and institutions do not operate in a vacuum; they fulfil their respective functions in the context of particular facets of society, and it is impossible to comprehend their relative importance without having some knowledge of the context concerned. Since in the case of industrial relations this means the labour market, at least a brief outline of its characteristics is necessary.

1.2 For the purposes of the industrial relations structure to be described here, only the labour market trend in the original Federal Republic is of relevance: it is in this context that the rules and institutions have evolved which are now being transferred intact to the newly incorporated Länder. The most important stage in this development was the lengthy phase of full employment which lasted from the 1950s until the 1970s. The elements of the system that were created during that period have since proved to continue to hold good in the situation of unemployment with which the Federal Republic has been faced since the mid-1970s. Although the number of jobs rose steadily in the 1980s, unemployment did not decrease to the same extent. It has fluctuated around a level of about 7 per cent. The use of short-time working, which assumed dramatic proportions in the late 1970s and early 1980s in the original Federal Republic, has since subsided to a calmer level.

1.3 As far as real unemployment is concerned, the main reason for its relative persistence lies in the fact that in recent years the labour market has had to meet an increased demand for jobs stemming from new population groups ("Aussiedler", *i.e.* ethnic German immigrants from Eastern Europe, and "Übersiedler", *i.e.* internal migrants from eastern Germany). This trend will continue for some while.

1.4 The level of unemployment is unevenly distributed geographically. As a general rule it is lower in high-pay areas than in low-pay areas, which indicates that labour costs cannot be regarded as a major cause; other, structural reasons must be far more significant.

1.5 The structure of unemployment is essentially determined by four factors: level of vocational training, sex, age and state of health. Unskilled workers, women, older workers and workers with impaired health are over-represented among the unemployed. These are also the problem groups who have particular difficulty in reintegrating themselves into the labour market. Despite numerous special measures and schemes, there has been no real improvement in their situation. Quite the

1

opposite: the danger of their being fated to suffer long-term unemployment is obviously growing.

1.6 The only encouraging trend to be observed is in youth unemployment, which for several years has been exhibiting a marked and continuous decrease.

1.7 In the newly incorporated Länder, where market conditions are being created only gradually through privatization, the restructuring process is leading to high unemployment, at least temporarily. According to the official figures, at present the unemployment rate is running at around 10 per cent. Real unemployment is, however, much higher than this. Unemployment on such a dramatic scale has prompted the introduction of new expedients as a means of keeping it in check. One particularly interesting example of these job creation schemes can be found in the so-called "Beschäftigungsgesellschaften" (job creation companies).

1.8 Nor, of course, has the original Federal Republic remained immune to the negative phenomena associated with structural change. In some respects the effects of this change are the same as in other industrialized countries: unemployment as more than a merely temporary phenomenon, intensified international competition and a resultant increased pressure on costs, the introduction of new technologies, the growing importance of flexible mechanisms for adjustment to the market, the increasing necessity of shifting decision-making to autonomous decentralized levels, etc. These symptoms are all too familiar, and need no further explanation. It seems more useful to draw attention to those respects in which structural change in the Federal Republic differs appreciably from other comparable countries.

1.9 Industrial production continues to play a dominant role. As in other countries it is, of course, giving way to the service sector to some extent. But in the Federal Republic the shift is not so rapid or dramatic as it is in many other countries. The private service sector still employs significantly fewer people than manufacturing industry.

1.10 This quantitative aspect is not the only special feature that merits attention. It is equally important to stress the fact that, in terms of the labour market's regulatory mechanisms, people employed in the service sector enjoy exactly the same position as employees in manufacturing industry. The same "works constitution", *i.e.* the institutionalized system of employee representation, applies in both cases. There are strong trade unions in both sectors, so that the fact of not being employed in manufacturing industry does not entail any loss of collective protection. In many cases, indeed, union activity in the service sector operates more successfully and effectively than in some branches of industry. In short: as far as employee protection is concerned, it makes

2

relatively little difference whether workers are employed in manufacturing industry or in the service sector.

1.11 The comments made above concerning the proportional relevance of industrial production and services likewise apply to the ratio of manual workers to white-collar workers. Although the proportion of manual workers is declining continuously, matched by a corresponding increase in white-collar workers, here again the trend is emerging far more slowly than in many other countries. The shift over the past 20 years has amounted to only slightly more than 10 per cent.

1.12 A particularly important feature in the context under consideration here is the fact that in the Federal Republic, despite all gloomy statements to the contrary (mainly in the social sciences literature), full-time employment for an indefinite period of time still constitutes the typical case. Even so, it must not be overlooked that forms of peripheral employment are on the increase. The Improvement of Employment Opportunities Act of 1985 has, for instance, relaxed the restrictions on fixed-term employment and the hiring-out of temporary workers. However, these groups still represent a marginal phenomenon which is of little consequence in quantitative terms.

1.13 To sum up, it may be said that the effects of structural change on the composition of the working population are evidenced far less dramatically than in many other countries. Such effects as are discernible have had little impact on the industrial relations system. The resistance of this system is due in large measure to its high degree of juridification and institutionalization. It is, however, also important to note that, at least so far, the actors of industrial relations have shown themselves to be highly adept at adjusting the elements of the traditional system to new challenges. The power relationship between the employers' side and the trade unions has not changed, or at least not to any significant extent. The unions were able to achieve notable successes in the collective bargaining rounds of the 1980s. This picture is backed up by the fact that the unions have no cause to complain of any decline in membership; on the contrary, they can find satisfaction in a growth in their membership, albeit a slight one.

1.14 The spirit of social partnership between the employers' associations and the unions, one of the main features of industrial relations in the Federal Republic, has survived the challenges of structural change, at least up till now. Occasional indications of a deterioration in attitudes have proved to be misleading. Not only relations between the social partners themselves but also relations between them and the state (whether at Länder or at Federal level) have remained essentially intact. It is true that in the 1970s the unions withdrew from the structure of so-called "concerted action". This tripartite structure, which was

3

established for the purpose of harmonizing the interests of the state, the employers' associations and the unions, no longer exists as a formal institution. Nor is it likely ever to be revived. Despite this, a whole range of different forms of co-operation have taken shape since then. Regular meetings between representatives of the employers' associations or the unions and members of the Government are now the order of the day. When it came to the question of taking action to cope with the crisis in the steel industry, the Government, employers' associations and unions united in a corporatist arrangement and showed themselves perfectly able to co-operate. And at present it looks as if the debate on the social dimension will consolidate and institutionalize this tripartite dialogue still farther. For example, the "nationale Europakonferenz" (National Conference on Europe) is, essentially, nothing other than a form of concerted action for labour market problems arising from the internal market.

2. The structural elements of industrial relations

2.1   In the Federal Republic, almost all problem areas of working life are covered by statute law or executive orders based on statute law, providing a minimum level of protection. This minimum level of protection applies to all employees, whether they are trade union members or not. Consequently, collective agreements are able to build on a statutorily guaranteed foundation and so have the function purely of improving still farther the protection that exists in any case.

2.2   The principal feature of formalized industrial relations in the Federal Republic is the system of institutionalized employee participation. In the private sector, employee interests are protected at one level by works councils, company works councils and group works councils and at another level by employee representatives on the supervisory boards of large companies. In the public sector, the system of staff representation provides a corresponding representation of interests at all levels of the hierarchical structure of state administration. An important point to note in both cases is that these representative bodies safeguard the interests of all employees: here again, trade union membership makes no difference. Although separate statutes regulate employee participation in the private sector and the public sector respectively, establishing formally different structures, the position of employees is essentially the same in both sectors. Most of the protective legislation makes no distinction between the two. Collective bargaining policy in the two sectors is closely aligned. In some instances unions in the private sector (notably IG Metall, the Metal Industry Union) act as trendsetters for particular areas of regulation, and in other instances it is unions

4

in the public sector (notably ÖTV, the Public Services, Transport and Traffic Union) which perform this role. The very fact that the function of pacemaker is interchangeable points to the relatively high degree of homogeneity of collectively agreed conditions in the two sectors.

2.3. There is, however, one particular group in the labour force to whom none of this applies, *i.e.* career public servants ("Beamte"). Career public servants are not employed under a normal contractual employment relationship, but a public-law service relationship. They are not covered by the rules of labour law, but by career public service law. Their terms and conditions of employment are regulated solely by statute. Although career public servants have the right to form associations, these associations are not permitted to conclude collective agreements. According to prevailing legal opinion, career public servants are not only excluded from the freedom to engage in collective bargaining but also, in contrast to employees in general, do not possess the right to strike. In recent times, growing doubt is being voiced regarding the legally binding nature of this presumption of a prohibition on strike action. Such doubt is mainly founded in the fact that the special position of career public servants is becoming less and less justified by the function they perform. Nowadays, they are employed not only in posts in the traditional public administration but also, for example, in the education sector (schools, universities) as well as in the postal service, the railways and other service sectors. In these areas of activity, it appears increasingly difficult to understand why it is necessary to accord the individuals concerned the special status of career public servants. However, being equated in law with other employees would not just bring these career public servants advantages (such as the right to strike and collective bargaining autonomy). They would also acquire a whole series of disadvantages, since from many individual aspects they are in a far better position than other employees. Whatever the various considerations, the debate concerning career public service is a many-layered one and as yet unresolved. Quite possibly, only moves to achieve standardization in the context of the EC Common Market will eventually lead to fresh thinking on the legal status of this category.

2.4 To complete even a brief outline of the complex structure of formalized industrial relations, one further key element must be mentioned, namely, the system of Labour Courts.

2.5 The separation of the Labour Courts from the ordinary system of courts was prompted by recognition of the fact that labour law constitutes an independent field with extremely specific structures, rather than a mere subdivision of civil law. This special branch of jurisdiction, introduced in 1926, is a three-tier system with local Labour Courts of first instance, Land

5

Labour Courts as the appeal instance and the Federal Labour Court as the judicial review instance. At all three levels the courts include, in addition to professional judges specializing in labour law, unpaid lay judges who represent the employers and the unions. This formal integration of the two sides into the process lends these courts especial authority and heightens the perceived legitimacy of their decisions.

2.6 The Labour Courts system not only performs an essential role in the interpretation of existing law, but also in the making of law. The Labour Courts Act expressly empowers the Federal Labour Court to undertake the function of further development of the law. Since the legislature is obviously not in a position itself to make the normative adjustments necessitated by social change, and since it is obviously hesitant itself about regulating such contested areas of collective law as the right to strike, the Federal Labour Court has no alternative but to step into the breach and perform the role of "substitute lawmaker" which is thrust upon it. Alongside statute law, judge-made law has consequently become an important element of labour law.

3. The collective bargaining system

3.1 Freedom of association (in this context, the specific right to form collective industrial organizations) and hence collective bargaining autonomy are guaranteed by Article 9(3) of the Basic Law. The salient aspects of collective bargaining law are regulated in the Collective Agreements Act.

3.2 In theory, and according to the letter of the law, collective agreements may be concluded not only between trade unions and employers' associations but also between the unions and individual employers. Although such company agreements do exist, they are the exception. The normal pattern is the so-called association-level agreement, concluded between individual unions on the one side and individual employers' associations on the other. These association-level agreements cover either the entire territory of the Federal Republic for a given industry or a particular region within a given branch of industry. The reason why collective bargaining policy is so geographically extensive lies in the structure of the organizations on both sides. In the Federal Republic the unions are industry-based, in accordance with what is known as the principle of industrial organization. This means that in principle there is only one union for each branch of manufacturing industry or service industry. Bearing in mind that, of the 16 unions affiliated under the umbrella organization of the German Federation of Trade Unions (DGB), five fall within the public sector, leaving only 11 for the entire private sector, it becomes very apparent how wide-ranging their radius of operation must be in order to

6

provide the necessary coverage. For instance, the Metal Industry Union (IG Metall) encompasses such diverse branches as the automobile industry, the electrical and electronics industry, the engineering industry, the shipbuilding industry and the steel industry, to name but a few. Where there is doubt as to which union is responsible for which area of activity, the DGB itself issues a decision in order to avoid any overlap or competition.

3.3 All these unions are organized on a national basis. There are regional and local subdivisions, but the power centre is the central union body, with its Executive Committee. It is there that strategies are developed and major decisions are taken. Given this structural background, it is immediately evident that the unions pursue a predominantly macroeconomic perspective rather than a microeconomic one. Their concern must inevitably lie not with the situation of employees within a particular establishment or company but with the overall situation of employees in the branch of activity, industry or service sector concerned. To avoid jeopardizing solidarity within the organization, union leaders also have a manifest interest in achieving relatively uniform standards for the employment conditions of all their members.

3.4 On the employers' side the organizational structure is essentially the same. The employers' associations which are united in the Confederation of German Employers' Associations (BDA) are also industry-based in accordance with the principle of industrial organization, and likewise pursue a macroeconomic rather than a microeconomic perspective. For these associations, the interest in establishing relatively uniform employment conditions for all members rests on considerations relating to competition.

3.5 A geographically extensive bargaining policy is able to accommodate the particular circumstances within individual companies only to a very limited extent. In many cases, collectively agreed provisions which are therefore inevitably generalized and vague still need to be translated into a more specific form relevant to individual establishments and companies. However, it is possible for the collective bargaining parties to delegate regulatory powers to the works council and the individual employer and at the same time to define the limits within which these actors may operate at establishment level. Increasing use has been made of this possibility in recent years. During the 1980s such collective agreements combining geographically extensive bargaining policy with decentralized regulation were concluded, in particular, on the arrangement of working time.

3.6 Under collective bargaining law in the Federal Republic, there is neither an obligation to negotiate nor a compulsory arbitration procedure in the event of a breakdown of negotiations. The question of whether and in what manner dispute resolution bodies should be established, and which powers should be conferred on them, rests entirely in the hands of the collective bargaining parties themselves. On this basis, joint dispute resolution agreements exist for all collective bargaining regions, in which the joint dispute resolution procedure is regulated in specific detail. Under the vast majority of these agreements, the parties are free to choose whether to refer a dispute to the dispute resolution body and, in particular, whether to agree to abide by its settlement proposal. In these circumstances, industrial action is the sole remaining instrument for achieving the conclusion of a collective agreement. This key role of industrial action in the functioning of collective bargaining means that the law on industrial action, in giving dimension to the respective strength of the two sides, is of outstanding importance. In its capacity as a "substitute lawmaker", the Federal Labour Court not only developed the structures of this area of law more or less autonomously during the 1950s, but since then has made a number of significant adjustments. In doing so, the Court has sought on each occasion to base its reasoning on the practical experience of previous labour disputes and to develop rules which take the needs of both sides into account. Recently, however, this pragmatic and compromise-minded strategy as adopted by the Court has met with opposition from the employers and the unions. This lack of acceptance is most clearly indicated by the fact that almost all major rulings on industrial action during the 1980s led to appeals to the Federal Constitutional Court, whether by the employers or by the unions.

3.7 The relative peace obligation is understood in the Federal Republic to be an inherent element of collective agreements. It means that, for the duration of the agreement, neither of the parties is permitted to engage in any form of industrial action with the intention of altering the existing content of the agreement.

3.8 Regulations laid down in a collective agreement on the formalities of entering into or terminating an individual employment relationship, and on the conditions determining its content, have a normative effect. They are directly and compulsorily applicable to those members of the contracting union who are employed by an employer who is, in turn, a member of the contracting employers' association. Although these standards established by collective agreement may be improved on to the employee's benefit under an individual contract of employment, they may not be worsened. In cases of contravention, employees have the opportunity of taking the matter before the Labour Court. The Collective Agreements Act makes provision for an official procedure whereby, subject to certain conditions, the applicability of a collective agreement can be extended to include non-union members as well. In practice, however, this official extension of collective agreements plays only a marginal role. But it is important for all practical purposes to note that, even though only union members formally enjoy the benefit of the normative affect of collectively agreed terms, employers usually extend them voluntarily to non-union members.

3.9 Regulations laid down in a collective agreement which refer to matters beyond the scope of the individual employment relationship and are of collective relevance ("Betriebsnormen", *i.e.* normative provisions relating to the establishment), or which refer to the powers of employee representation at establishment level ("betriebsverfassungsrechtliche Normen", *i.e.* normative provisions relating to the law on the works constitution), likewise apply directly and compulsorily. In this case, however, there is no distinction between union members and non-union members; provided that the employer belongs to the contracting employers' association, such collectively normative provisions cover employees regardless of whether they are union members or not. A number of collective agreements from the 1980s broadened the participation rights of the works council on matters concerning working hours and training and in this way created structures in which non-union members are included *nolens volens.*

4.   Institutionalized employee participation

4.1   The works constitution
4.1.1 The representation of employee interests dates back originally to initiatives by employers in the 1870s. This explains why works councils in the private sector and staff councils in the public sector are, to this day, institutionally separate from the trade unions. The unions have, nevertheless, succeeded in the meantime in exerting considerable influence on the recruitment of members of these representative bodies. Some 85 per cent. of works council and staff council members are union members. In addition to achieving this tie-in with the actual composition of the councils, the unions have since been granted specific powers by statute. An important example is, in particular, the union's supportive function with respect to works council and staff council activities.
4.1.2 Since such differences as exist between the respective systems of employee representation in the public sector (staff representation) and in the private sector (the works constitution) are of no significance for the purposes of the context under discussion here, it will suffice to outline the principal features of the works constitution.

4.1.3   A works council should be formed in every establishment where there are at least five employees entitled to vote (*i.e.* aged 18 or over) of whom at least three have been employed there for six months or longer. In many small establishments, however, this statutory regulation is not followed. The question of whether or not a works council is formed depends on the employees of the particular establishment. If they refrain from forming such a body, they forgo the opportunities for participation which are provided for by statute. There are all kinds of reasons why employees in small establishments forgo these rights of their own accord, ranging from simple lack of information to varying degrees of gentle pressure from the employer.

4.1.4   In companies with several establishments that each have a works council, a company works council must be formed. However, the individual works councils are not subordinate to the company works council; the latter responsible only for matters which cannot be dealt with at individual establishment level. In the holding company of a group of companies a group works council also may be formed which is then responsible for matters that can only be dealt with at group level. Although provided for by statute, this opportunity is very rarely used in practice.

4.1.5   The term of office for the works council has recently been increased from three to four years. No limits are imposed on re-election, which is common practice. For works councils above a specified minimum size (governed by the number of employees in the establishment), the council may demand that a certain number of its members be given full-time release from work so that they are able to devote themselves exclusively to works council activities. All other works council members are also entitled to carry out their works council duties during working time and to be released from their work to the extent necessary for this purpose. Comprehensive guarantees regarding pay, employment and protection against dismissal enable council members to pursue a non-opportunistic and consistent policy in the representation of employee interests. The fact that members are entitled to attend training courses during working time and, furthermore, to be provided with the forms of information and reference material necessary for their activities fosters professionalism in works council policy. An important point to note in this connection is that all costs necessarily incurred for works council activities must be borne by the employer concerned.

4.1.6   The specific participation rights granted to the works council are defined in detail by statute. These rights cover personnel, social and economic matters, and are most extensive in the area of social matters and least extensive in that of economic matters. They range from mere information and consultation rights to rights of control and veto and, beyond this, to what is the most

10

important legal position of all: the true right of co-determination. In matters where the works council possesses such a right of co-determination, the employer may not take any action without its consent. What is more, the council itself can take the initiative and require that certain action be taken. In cases where no agreement can be reached, both sides are free to refer the issue to what is called an establishment-level arbitration committee (''Einigungsstelle''), whose decision takes effect as a substitute for agreement between the employer and the works council.

4.1.7 This establishment-level arbitration committee, which is almost always set up purely on an *ad hoc* basis, consists of equal numbers of assessors appointed by the employer and the works council respectively, and is presided over by an impartial chairperson. The choice of this impartial chairperson may either be agreed between the works council and the employer or, failing such agreement, may be left to the decision of the Labour Court under a special procedure. The committee's discretionary powers are delimited solely by consideration of the interests of the employees concerned on the one hand and those of the establishment on the other. Its decision requires only a simple majority of the votes recorded. Both the employer and the works council have the formal option of referring the committee's decision to the Labour Court for examination. However, the fact that the committee's discretionary powers are so wide makes it extremely unlikely that its decision would be overturned. In practice, therefore, in the vast majority of cases the committee's decision prevails.

4.1.8 The importance of the establishment-level arbitration committee cannot be emphasized strongly enough. Since there is no way of knowing in advance who will chair it and hence who will have the casting vote, it is impossible to predict the outcome of its deliberations. Furthermore, from the employer's point of view, the committee not only entails a loss of time but also incurs substantial expenditure on costs. It is therefore hardly surprising that the committee's function is mainly a preventive one: in many cases the mere possibility of its being called in leads to early compromises which would otherwise not come about.

4.1.9 The matters in which the works council possesses a right of co-determination are specified exhaustively by statute. They are of varying significance and in total are not all that numerous. However, the mere existence of such a right in particular matters has considerable implications as regards the works council's position in general. Since the employer has to take care to avoid unnecessary conflicts with the council in order to be able to count on its co-operation in matters that are subject to co-determination, this greatly strengthens the council's position even in areas where, under the statutory provisions, its position is in fact comparatively weak. The works council may conclude

11

works agreements with the employer which have a normative effect in the same way as collective agreements and concern the same matters that are also open to regulation by collective agreement. The question of conflict between collective agreements and works agreements is one of the most difficult problems of labour law.

4.1.10 The legislators have sought to prevent any element of competition between the works councils and the unions, since this could weaken the system as a whole in the representation of employee interests. In matters where the works council has no right of co-determination and is therefore able to achieve the conclusion of a works agreement only on a voluntary basis, it must not be able to act as a competitor of the unions, which in any case possess, as collective bargaining parties, the means of exerting pressure in the form of strike action. It is therefore laid down by statute that the conclusion of a works agreement on material terms and conditions of employment which in the branch of activity and geographical region concerned are regulated (or usually regulated) by collective agreement is prohibited even if the collective agreement does not apply to the employment relationships within the specific establishment concerned. The mere fact that the union has made the regulation of a particular matter its own business is enough to constitute an absolute ban on its regulation by the works council. In establishments where employment relationships are not covered by the collective agreement (*i.e.* where the employer and employees are not members of the contracting organizations), it means that there can be no form of collective regulation at all. However, this ban on regulation, which has perhaps proved to be too rigid, is one provision (among others) that is steadfastly ignored. Despite the statutory rule works councils and employers have, for example, persisted in fixing by works agreement outline pay scales which in many cases are higher than the rates set by collective agreement. Such contravention of the law has always been tolerated by the unions, for the simple reason that any protest on their part would annoy their own members, who benefit from these unlawful agreements.

4.1.11 It is, however, expressly laid down by statute that the parties to a collective agreement may include provisions in the actual agreement authorizing the works council and the employer to formulate, at their own level, supplementary and more specific regulations. For a long time the unions hesitated to agree to such provisions, known as ''Öffnungsklauseln'' (opening-up clauses). In their view, tolerating the practice of unlawful works agreements was one thing, but making the works council an actor in the collective bargaining system on an official basis, as it were, was quite another. But in the bargaining rounds of the 1980s it became apparent that integrating the parties at

12

establishment level into the bargaining structure was the only way in which the parties to collective agreements could accommodate the requirements of increased flexibility. Thus (as mentioned above in 3.5), in the collective agreements concerning, for example, weekly working hours in a number of industries, an average figure was fixed which was to be observed over a specified period by the workforce as a whole. Within clearly drawn limits, however, different working hours could then be fixed for individual employees, groups of employees or separate departments. Furthermore, the decision was left open as to whether working hours should be the same every week or shorter one week and longer another. All these matters were left to be regulated by the parties at establishment level in the form of a works agreement. However, in order not to leave the works council in the weak position accorded to it in this respect under the Works Constitution Act, the unions caused the council to be granted, by collective agreement, a right of co-determination extending beyond the provisions of the Act. This strengthening of the works council's position (which has not gone entirely uncontested) makes the council an increasingly influential competitor of the union. As yet, such a tendency for the central collective-agreement level and the decentralized works-agreement level to be combined in one homogeneous system has succeeded to only a limited extent, since the "microperspective" of the works council by no means always coincides with the "macroperspective" of the unions. This represents a major challenge for the unions, and one to which they will need to address themselves earnestly over the next few years.

4.1.12 In contrast to all this, the relationship between the collective agreement and the works agreement is regulated quite differently in matters where the works council possesses, from the start, a right of co-determination and hence a strong position. In this case, only a collective agreement which covers the employment relationships in the particular establishment concerned (*i.e.* where the employer and employees are members of the contracting organizations) can affect the right of co-determination and hence the possibility of concluding a works agreement. Even then, the right of co-determination is supplanted only where the collective agreement regulates the matter in question in such detail and so exhaustively that there is no margin left for more locally appropriate decisions in implementing it. Where some scope remains for such decisions, the works council retains its right of co-determination and hence the possibility of concluding a works agreement. The reason why the relationship between the collective agreement and the works agreement is differently defined in these matters which are subject to co-determination is perfectly simple. Where the works council's position is a strong one, it must not be reduced without any replacement, since this would create a decision-making vacuum leaving room for a revival of the employer's unilateral decision-making power, *i.e.* precisely what the right of co-determination was intended to remove.

4.2. **Employee representation on the supervisory board**

4.2.1 Under the traditional system of company law there was no provision for employee representation in company organs. In meeting the unions' demand for a voice in company policy, the approach adopted was not a complete reshaping of the company constitution. Instead, the traditional structure was retained and employee representation was simply fitted into the existing company organs. This has given rise to a whole range of problems and inconsistencies, by no means all of which have been satisfactorily resolved. For example, the duty of secrecy traditionally imposed on shareholders' representatives applies in exactly the same way to employee representatives, although in their case the interest in communicating information necessarily takes a quite different form. Secondly, the sole formal obligation on employee representatives, as on shareholders' representatives, is to be guided by the interests of the company, which means that the objectives seen as falling within this category have to redefined. Thirdly, employee representatives receive the same payment as shareholders' representatives, and this has prompted special arrangements to prevent too wide a gulf from opening up between them and the rank and file whom they represent. This catalogue of problems could be continued at will. All that matters in the present context is to point to the consequences of the fact that the company constitution was not fundamentally restructured but simply maintained as it was, with employee representation added on.

4.2.2 In a system where it is confined to the supervisory board, employee representation does not mean participation in management. Responsibility for the business management of the company lies solely with the management board. The powers of the supervisory board are restricted to supervising the activities of the management board, plus the task of appointing and removing its members. This latter function must not be overestimated, however, given the limited choice of personnel available. As far as the real scope for supervision is concerned, in at least most instances the management board, with its full-time members and constant access to staff experts, is so well-equipped to prepare and present decisions that it is difficult for the supervisory board, whose members are engaged full-time in other functions and which normally meets only at intervals of several months, to impose alternative positions or introduce modifications.

14

4.2.3. Only in the system operating in the coal, iron and steel industry does employee representation extend into the management board. Here, the member of the management board who is responsible for personnel and social matters, the so-called "employee director", cannot be appointed against the votes of the employee representatives. This extension of employee representation into the management board is not, however, without its problems; it confronts the management board member concerned with a conflict of loyalties which quite often resolves itself in the direction of streamlined integration with the board's group identity.

4.2.4 Employee influence is at its strongest in the system of employee representation in the coal, iron and steel industry, where there is statutory provision (initially under the 1951 Coal, Iron and Steel Industry Co-Determination Act) for true parity on the supervisory board and an "impartial" chairperson whose function is to tip the balance in the event of deadlock. In other industries, the system as established by the 1952 Works Constitution Act for companies of a specified legal form with at least 500 employees limits the proportion of employee representatives on the supervisory board to only one third. These two systems represent extremes in another respect as well: whereas the presence of external union representatives is a strongly developed element of the system in the coal, iron and steel industry, it plays almost no role in the 1952 system.

4.2.5. The Co-Determination Act of 1976 should be seen as a kind of compromise between the other two systems. It gives the shareholders' side a slight advantage and relegates the influence of the unions farther into the background than in the coal, iron and steel industry. The Act covers all companies of a specified legal form with at least 2,000 employees, and thus almost all large companies in the private sector. Whereas the practical importance of this system is, if anything, growing, that of the coal, iron and steel industry system is dwindling, for the simple reason that the industries which it covers are becoming less and less important. Although the legislators have attempted on a number of occasions (most recently in November 1988) to check its only too dramatic decline, this does not alter the fact that the system will be of only marginal importance in the long term.

4.2.6 Whereas the employers failed in their application to the Federal Constitutional Court to have the 1976 Co-Determination Act declared unconstitutional, on the other hand the unions have likewise remained unsuccessful in their efforts to raise the 1976 system to the level of co-determination in the coal, iron and steel industry system. So it looks as if there will be no change in the situation, at least within the foreseeable future.

4.2.7 The practical importance of employee representation on the supervisory board can be comprehended only if it is seen in

15

relation to the representation of employee interests by the works council. In almost all cases, those employee representatives on the supervisory board who belong to the workforce of the particular company concerned are also members of the works council, usually leading ones. This provides a channel whereby information obtained within the supervisory board can be utilized for the works council's activities, and vice versa. For the reasons outlined above, the management board obviously has an interest in maintaining good co-operation with the works council; in many cases, therefore, an informal structure has evolved in which the management board holds preliminary discussions with the internal employee representatives to clear up difficult matters. In this way, the supervisory board is never really confronted with particularly controversial issues. Any such plans are revised before they reach this stage, in order to avoid conflict with the works council members. Here too, the effect is therefore mainly a preventive one.

5.   The prominence of the law

5.1   Industrial relations in the Federal Republic are largely determined by legal rules covering almost every area, together with a multiplicity of institutions. In order to understand the structure of the industrial relations system, the first step must be to come to grips with the structure of its juridification. This is, of course, reflected in the selection of terms for the present Glossary. The weight given to the legal and institutional aspect is necessarily quite different from that in a Glossary relating, for example, to the United Kingdom. In compiling and defining the terms an attempt has been made to do justice to this aspect while at the same time, by including reference to the related sociological circumstances, to avoid overemphasizing the legal dimension.

6.   The perspective of the Glossary

6.1   The Glossary is being published at a time when industrial relations in the region of the former German Democratic Republic are still in a phase of transformation. However, the goal of this development is already fixed: the actors, institutions and rules are to be the same in the newly incorporated Länder as in the original Federal Republic. This process of harmonization is already well under way. The trade unions and employers' associations of the original Federal Republic have extended their field of action to the newly incorporated Länder and have created structures there which make it possible to conclude collective agreements for these Länder as well. Many such agreements are already in existence. In the meantime,

16

works councils have also already been formed, employee representatives have been elected to supervisory boards and the system of Labour Courts, like the employment administration, is in the process of being established. In other words, the industrial relations system as dealt with in the Glossary will continue unchanged in the original Federal Republic and will encompass the newly incorporated Länder in essentially the same form. It therefore makes sense to confine the definitions given in the Glossary to this particular system. No description is given of the quite differently circumstanced industrial relations of the former German Democratic Republic, nor of the transitional arrangements which were valid for only a relatively short time and in most cases have already expired. Mention is made only of prominent institutions which in the process of restructuring are playing a conspicuous role in terms of industrial relations ("Beschäftigungsgesellschaft", "Treuhand", etc.).

6.2   Although it is an established fact that the formal structure of industrial relations in the newly incorporated Länder will be identical with that in the original Federal Republic, it is still far from certain whether this means that it will also be identical in its functioning. This will primarily depend on how far it proves possible to create the same living conditions in the newly incorporated Länder as in the former Federal Republic. That is still a long way off. And it will also depend on whether the actors in the newly incorporated Länder put the system into practice in the same way as the actors in the original Federal Republic have done in the past and are still doing. In other words, whether the transfer of the formal structure to the newly incorporated Länder will be accompanied by an equally seamless transfer of attitudes is still very much an open question. It is possible that, despite being identical with the system in the original Federal Republic in terms of form, the reality of industrial relations in the newly incorporated Länder could differ in nature. Such speculation does not, however, fall within the purview of this Glossary.

A

1. **ABFINDUNG — COMPENSATION FOR JOB LOSS**:
   Payment made in settlement of an employee's legitimate claim,
   especially in the event of job loss. However, employees are entitled
   to compensation in the event of job loss only subject to certain
   basic conditions. This is the case, firstly, if in an **application for
   protection against dismissal** the Labour Court, having ruled that
   the **termination** of an employment relationship by the employer
   is invalid, then (on the employee's or employer's application)
   dissolves the employment relationship and orders the employer
   to pay appropriate compensation (Protection Against Dismissal
   Act §§ 9,10). The amount of such compensation is decided at
   the discretion of the court (a sum not exceeding 12 months' pay,
   or 18 months' pay in the case of employees aged over 50). The
   main criteria applied in fixing the amount are the employee's age
   and length of continuous service; other factors are the employee's
   social circumstances (marital status, dependants, state of health)
   and prospects in the labour market, the extent to which the
   dismissal is deemed to be unfair ("sozialwidrig"), and the
   employer's economic situation.

   Secondly, entitlement to compensation can also arise from a
   "social plan" (Works Constitution Act §§ 111,112) or **collective
   agreement**. Many rationalization agreements make provision for
   compensatory payments, graduated according to the employee's
   length of service and age, in the event of redundancy (in this
   context the German term means "redundancy payment").

2. **ABMAHNUNG — WARNING**: Reprimand issued by the
   employer against an employee's performance or other conduct
   as not conforming to the contract of employment. It has a dual
   function: it is intended to induce the employee to remedy such
   conduct and at the same time, should the employee fail to comply
   with this demand, prepares the way for **dismissal on grounds
   of conduct**. The **proportionality principle** that underpins the
   legal provisions governing dismissal requires that an employee
   be given a formal warning before any steps are taken to effect
   such a dismissal. The only circumstances in which a warning is
   not necessary are where it would be pointless because, for
   instance, it is quite clear that the employee would in any case
   not heed it or where the employee's misconduct has been
   especially serious. A warning is deemed to have been given when
   the employer informs the employee clearly of the nature of the
   offence and indicates the legal consequences of repeated offences.
   It can be given orally or in writing by any person designated to
   issue instructions to the employee. If, following a warning, an
   employee has continued to work for some considerable time

without incurring further reprimand, the warning in question loses its effect with respect to the legal procedure governing dismissal. Depending on the seriousness of the offence, this is generally the case after some two or three years have elapsed.

A formal warning is to be distinguished from **disciplinary sanctions**; these require collective authorization through, for instance, a works agreement.

3. **ABRUFARBEIT — VARIABLE WORKING HOURS**: See "**KAPOVAZ**".

4. **ABSCHLUSSFREIHEIT — FREEDOM TO CONCLUDE AN EMPLOYMENT CONTRACT**: The freedom to decide whether or not to enter into a **contract of employment** at all, and if so with whom. The **employer**, as a matter of principle, has freedom of choice in the matter. Compulsory employment quotas apply only in a few exceptional cases laid down by law or collective agreement. The only other constraints on the employer's freedom in hiring personnel are connected with the **co-determination rights of the works council** and the ban on discrimination arising from the principle of **equal treatment**.

Employees, for their part, are free to choose whether or not to accept a job vacancy offered to them, provided they are not expressly prohibited from entering into a particular type of employment relationship. This also applies to the unemployed, although if they refuse a suitable offer of employment they then lose their entitlement to all unemployment payments for a period of 12 weeks.

5. **ABWEHRAUSSPERRUNG — DEFENSIVE LOCK-OUT**: See **lock-out**.

6. **ACHT-STUNDEN-TAG — EIGHT-HOUR DAY**: See **maximum working hours**.

7. **AFG**: Arbeitsförderungsgesetz (Employment Promotion Act). See **Federal Employment Service**.

8. **AKKORD — PIECEWORK**: Payment system which comes ahead of the **incentive bonus system** as the most widely used form of **payment by results** in the Federal Republic. With piecework, earnings are directly dependent on the number of units of work performed. This means, on the one hand, that through industriousness and dexterity employees have the chance of earning a higher **wage** than would be possible with **time-based pay**. On the other hand, employees on piecework are exposed

20

to increased work pressure and a considerable degree of control, and any relaxation of their efforts is reflected in their pay. It is therefore particularly important that the rates fixed for piecework should be reasonable and fair.

In the case of **money piecework**, pay is determined by multiplying the number of units of output by a fixed price that is attached to each unit. Because of the difficulties involved in adjusting this whenever there was a pay increase, the money piecework system is no longer used today.

In the case of **time piecework**, pay is determined both by the time factor, *i.e.* a standard time allowed for each unit of output, and by the money factor, *i.e.* the amount to be earned per minute. This is at least one sixtieth of the hourly wage of the corresponding **pay grade**, but there is usually an additional piecework premium of about 15 per cent. Difficulties often arise in fixing the standard time allowed. The principle is that when working at standard performance employees should earn the hourly rate of the comparable time-based pay, and if they exceed standard performance they will earn extra. If they fail to reach standard performance, they earn less than the comparable time-based pay. Standard performance is the rate of output which a reasonably competent, trained and experienced employee can maintain under normal working conditions throughout normal working hours without harmful effects on health. Allowance is made for time for personal needs, minor disruptions in the work flow and short breaks. The time factor is fixed using ergonomic methods such as RefA (formerly the "Reichsausschuss für Arbeitszeitermittlung" (Reich Time and Motion Study Committee), now the "Verband für Arbeitsstudien und Betriebsorganisation e.V." (Work Study and Work Organization Association)) or MTM (Methods-Time Measurement). The time factor makes it simpler to adjust the money factor when pay increases are awarded.

9. **AKTIENGESELLSCHAFT — PUBLIC LIMITED COMPANY**: See **forms of company, shareholder**.

10. **AKTIONÄR — SHAREHOLDER**: A shareholder is a **company member** of the **form of company** known as a public limited company (AG) whose participation is attested and represented by the share. Any natural or legal person or association of persons possessing assets can become a shareholder by taking up shares when a public limited company is formed or purchasing them subsequently in the context of an increase in share capital or by transfer through a stock exchange. A shareholder's obligation consists in the payment of their contribution to the share capital,

21

and their rights consist in entitlement to a dividend and the right to vote and demand information at the **shareholders' meeting**. Non-voting shares confer no voting rights, but the memorandum of association can also provide special rights for certain shareholders. A shareholder's influence on the company and the way it is run depends on the size of their holding. In the case of companies whose share capital is widely spread through public subscription ("Publikums-AG"), the voting right of the individual smaller shareholders is exercised by the banks at which a share is deposited ("Depotstimmrecht", *i.e.* banks' right to vote customers' deposited shares) or by shareholders' associations.

11. **AKTIONSPROGRAMM "ARBEIT UND TECHNIK" — "WORK AND TECHNOLOGY" ACTION PROGRAMME**: The central aims of this action programme, funded and launched by the Federal Government in 1989 and known as the AuT Programme, are health protection through the reduction and prevention of harmful stresses, and the adaptation of work and technology to take account of human factors. In order to formulate comprehensive strategies for preventing possible hazards and stresses, the adaptation potential of work and technology needs to be studied and then properly exploited. To this end, the programme encompasses not only the technical aspects but also the health, organizational and skills aspects. Trends on similar lines to the AuT Programme are also to be found in the demands and efforts being made in connection with **technology impact analysis and assessment** and **human- and environment-centred technology strategy**, and certain features of **corporate cultures**.

12. **AKTIONSPROGRAMM "HUMANISIERUNG DES ARBEITSLEBENS" — "HUMANIZATION OF WORKING LIFE" ACTION PROGRAMME**: Funded and launched by the Federal Government in 1974 and concluded in 1989, this action programme (known as the HdA Programme) supported investigations into the possibilities of adjusting working conditions to human needs (**humanization of work**). Studies carried out under the programme covered, for example, the automation of dangerous work, variation of the machine-imposed pace of work, forms of self-regulation of the work sequence and its result, and the practical aspects of the **flexibilization** of **working time**. Since 1989 similar projects have been supported under the **"Work and Technology" Action Programme**.

13. **ALLGEMEINE ORTSKRANKENKASSE — PUBLIC HEALTH INSURANCE FUND**: See **company health insurance fund, health insurance, health insurance fund**.

22

14. **ALLGEMEINVERBINDLICHKEIT VON TARIF-VERTRÄGEN — EXTENSION OF COLLECTIVE AGREEMENTS**: By means of an official procedure called "Allgemeinverbindlichkeitserklärung" (Order Imposing Extension, issued by the Minister for Labour), the applicability of an existing **collective agreement** can be extended to include employees and employers not bound by the agreement (Collective Agreements Act § 5). Such a generally applicable agreement then has the same direct and mandatory force for these employees and employers as it has for the employment relationships bound by the agreement by virtue of membership of a contracting organization. Without this incorporation of **non-union members** into the **scope of normative provisions**, there would be a situation where many employees were not covered by any collective agreement, especially in sectors such as the building industry or retail distribution with a large number of small enterprises whose owners are not members of any association.

The precondition for an Order Imposing Extension is that the employers bound by the collective agreement in question should together employ at least 50 per cent. of all the employees working within the occupational and geographical area covered by the agreement (counting both those already bound by the agreement plus non-union members). In addition, the procedure must be deemed to be in the public interest, notably because terms and conditions of employment in the area concerned would otherwise fall below the generally prevailing level.

Of the 24,000 or so association-level agreements in force in 1989, only some 540 in various branches of the economy were made generally applicable by extension, mainly in the building industry, retail trade, textiles industry and metalworking trades. The majority of the agreements concerned were **framework agreements on employment conditions**, with only a small proportion of actual **pay agreements**. In all, in 1989 there were about 4 million employees working in industries covered by collective agreements made generally applicable by extension.

15. **ALLIIERTE STREITKRÄFTE — ALLIED FORCES**: Members of the armed forces stationed on the territory of the Federal Republic in accordance with the NATO Troops Statute, together with the civilians connected with them, enjoy extraterritoriality rights. Civilians employed by the Allied Forces are therefore not covered by the provisions of the **works constitution**; the regulations on staff representation (in the public sector) apply to them, but they have virtually no real co-determination rights. If such non-German enterprises are non-military, they are not covered by extraterritoriality on a collective

basis but by the Works Constitution Act, even if civilians there follow their own regulations.

16. **ALTERSGRENZE — RETIREMENT AGE**: See **statutory retirement pension**.

17. **ALTERSRUHEGELD — STATUTORY RETIREMENT PENSION**: Attainment of the retirement (or pensionable) age brings entitlement to a retirement pension under the **statutory pension scheme**. A different term ("Pension") is used in the case of **career public servants** ("Beamte"). At present, the retirement age is 60 for women and 63 for men; because of the changed population structure and increasing expenditure on pension insurance, from the years 2012 and 2006 respectively it is to be raised to 65.

18. **ALTERSTEILZEIT — PARTIAL RETIREMENT**: In order to reduce unemployment and create jobs for younger job-seekers, various legal regulations have been adopted in recent years which enable employees to enter retirement early.

Under the so-called 59 Rule, members of the **statutory pension scheme** who have reached the age of 60 and during at least eight of the previous ten years have been working in an occupation subject to compulsory pension insurance or have been treated as equivalent thereto in law, are granted, on application, an early retirement pension following a period of unemployment of at least 52 weeks within the last year and a half. Employers frequently took advantage of this procedure to reduce the average age of their workforce, terminating the employment relationships of older employees by mutual consent with them and compensating them for the loss of income resulting from unemployment. To prevent abuse of **unemployment insurance**, in such cases employers are now required to repay the unemployment benefit paid out to the employee.

As an alternative to the shorter working week for which the trade unions were pressing, in 1984 an Early Retirement Rule was introduced. Under this Rule, employees who had reached the age of 58 and in the preceding five years had been liable to contributions under the statutory pension scheme for at least three years were given the opportunity, by mutual consent with their employer or under the terms of a **collective agreement** or **works agreement**, to terminate their employment relationship and enter into a form of early retirement subsidized by the **Federal Employment Service** (BfA). The qualifying conditions for payment of the subsidy from the BfA were that the job vacancy thus released should be filled with a registered unemployed person or an accepted **vocational trainee** and that during this period of early retirement the employer should pay the employee at least 65 per cent. of the pay earned by a comparable employee. The subsidy amounted to 35 per cent. of the early retirement payments made by the employer.

In 1989 this Rule was replaced by the introduction of partial retirement. Under this procedure, employees who have reached the age of 58 and who, for the period between the ages of 58 and 65, wish only to reduce their **working time** to half of the collectively agreed hours (subject to a minimum of 18 hours per week), can claim partial retirement. During partial retirement, the employer has to pay such employees 20 per cent. over the collectively agreed part-time pay (*i.e.* approximately 70 per cent. of their former net pay) and pay in contributions ensuring them entitlements under the statutory pension scheme as if they were earning 90 per cent. of their former full-time pay. This extra expenditure by the employer is reimbursed by the Federal Employment Service provided that the part-time job released in each case is filled with an unemployed person. Use of the partial retirement procedure has to be regulated by collective agreement. By the beginning of 1990 partial retirement applications had been made by some 200 companies, but only half of them were approved.

19. **ALTERSVERSORGUNG — OLD-AGE PENSION PRO-VISION**: Apart from personal savings, financial provision for employees after they have reached retirement age is ensured via the **statutory pension scheme** and also **occupational pension schemes. Career public servants** ("Beamte"), after retirement or in the event of incapacity for work, receive what is called "Ruhegehalt" (retirement pay) from their former **public sector employer**.

20. **ANBAHNUNG DES ARBEITSVERHÄLTNISSES — PRE-CONTRACTUAL OBLIGATIONS IN THE EMPLOY-MENT RELATIONSHIP**: Even before a **contract of employment** is concluded, a legal relationship of obligation exists between applicant and **employer**, since already at this stage the two parties have to place trust in each other. This pre-contractual relationship gives rise to specific protective obligations between the parties, infringement of which can lead to liability for damages. For instance, the applicant is under an obligation to answer truthfully such questions on the **application form** as the employer may ask out of legitimate interest. Reciprocally, the employer must disclose all the facts which it may be important for potential employees to know in deciding whether or not they

wish to enter into the employment relationship. In addition to detailed information on the nature of the job, this also includes the prospects regarding its stability.

21. **ÄNDERUNGSKÜNDIGUNG — DISMISSAL FOR VARIATION OF CONTRACT**: The **protection against dismissal** provided by the law protects not only the stability but also the actual terms of the **contract of employment**. An employer who wishes to continue the employment relationship with an employee but to alter its terms and conditions has to pronounce a dismissal for variation of contract. Since it is a form of **termination** this is a declaration of intention to end the contract, but at the same time it incorporates an offer from the employer to the employee to continue the employment relationship under altered terms and conditions (Protection Against Dismissal Act § 2). As a rule, the circumstances are those of an ordinary **termination with notice**.

There are three possible ways in which employees can respond to a dismissal for variation of contract. First, they can accept the offer incorporating variation unreservedly, thereby attesting their agreement to the variation of contract. Alternatively, they can confine themselves to accepting the offer incorporating variation subject to the reservation (which they must then invoke within three weeks by making an **application for protection against dismissal**) that the variation of the terms and conditions of employment is unjustified. Lastly, they can reject the offer incorporating variation. In this last case, since no action complaining against dismissal is brought before a court, dismissal for variation of contract ends the employment relationship.

The same rules apply when an employer pronounces a dismissal for variation of contract without giving the correct period of notice, subject to the more stringent conditions governing the validity of **summary termination**.

22. **ANFECHTBARKEIT DES ARBEITSVERTRAGES — VOIDABILITY OF THE EMPLOYMENT CONTRACT**: Since the **employment relationship** is founded in a contract it must be possible for absence of intention or knowledge, for example through mistake (Civil Code § 119), menace or fraudulent misrepresentation (Civil Code § 123), to be also taken into account. Consequently a **contract of employment**, like other contracts, is voidable. Its voidability is not excluded even if the employment relationship is already being performed. However, since the contract cannot be set aside retrospectively, as a matter of principle it can only be voidable with effect for the future. The provisions governing **protection against dismissal** do not apply to the voidability of the employment contract.

A point to note is that mistake on the part of the employer regarding an employee's attributes does not always constitute a justified ground for voidability. For example, if an employer asks inadmissible questions in an **application form** for job applicants the employee can deliberately answer them falsely without incurring any consequences.

23. **ANGESTELLTER — WHITE-COLLAR WORKER**: Traditionally, a white-collar worker has been seen as an **employee** who performs work demanding predominantly mental effort. Pragmatically, differentiation of the white-collar worker from the **manual worker** is based on current thinking, which is essentially influenced by social security legislation. In this legislation the definition of white-collar status follows the classification of occupational groups given in the 1924 White-Collar Workers' Social Insurance Act (§ 3).

In practice, the distinction between manual and white-collar workers is rapidly becoming blurred. It is still of relevance today with respect to **periods of notice**, **sick pay**, representation on the **works council** and the **supervisory board**, and social security. In 1989 there were 11 million employees classed as white-collar workers in the Federal Republic, while the number of manual workers had fallen to 10.7 million.

24. **ANGRIFFSAUSSPERRUNG — OFFENSIVE LOCK-OUT**: See **lock-out**.

25. **ANNAHMEVERZUG DES ARBEITGEBERS — EMPLOYER'S NON-ACCEPTANCE OF THE WORK PERFORMANCE**: Circumstance in which the employee duly offers to perform work and the employer fails to accept it. It makes no difference whether the employer does not wish to provide the employee with work or is actually unable to do so; the situation is classed as non-acceptance without necessarily being through any fault of the employer.

The general rule is that employees are deemed to have duly offered the performance of work if they go in person to the workplace in order to work. However, their personal presence is unnecessary if in response to their oral offer to perform work they have been told by the employer that it will not be accepted. If the employer informs employees in the context of **termination** of the employment contract that, with immediate effect, they will no longer be provided with work, for the purposes of making an **application for protection against dismissal** they are deemed to have duly offered the performance of work. The consequence of the employer's non-acceptance of the performance of work is that employees retain their entitlement to remuneration, without having to make up the time during which work was not performed (Civil Code § 615).

26. **AOK**: See **Public Health Insurance Fund** (Allgemeine Ortskrankenkasse).

27. **ARBEITER — MANUAL WORKER**: Manual workers (also called "blue-collar" workers) are **employees** who perform work demanding predominantly physical effort. Drawing distinctions based on this criterion has now become difficult. More and more individual job profiles combine both mental and physical work, such as the complex jobs done by technicians. Classification as a manual worker is based on current thinking, which in practice is essentially influenced by social security legislation. This means that the concept of the manual worker is defined by negative differentiation from that of the **white-collar worker**: any employee who is not classed as a white-collar worker is a manual worker.

This differentiation still has practical consequences today with respect to **sick pay**, **periods of notice**, representation on the **works council** and the **supervisory** board, and social security legislation. By 1989 the number of manual workers in the Federal Republic had fallen to 10.7 million.

28. **ARBEITERKAMMER — CHAMBER OF LABOUR**: Term used in Bremen as synonym of **Arbeitnehmerkammer**.

29. **ARBEITGEBER — EMPLOYER**: An employer is any natural or **legal person** who employs an **employee** in the context of an **employment relationship**. The employer is the person entitled to another's services within the meaning of the contract of service as regulated by the Civil Code. In the case of a natural person the employer may be, but need not necessarily be, the employee's immediate **superior**: employers can also designate another natural person to be this superior for the purposes of interpreting and exercising their rights deriving from the employment relationship. In the special case of **career public servants** ("Beamte") a different term, *i.e.* "Dienstherr" (**public sector employer**), is used to indicate the employing party to the **career public service relationship**.

30. **ARBEITGEBER-ARBEITNEHMER-BEZIEHUNGEN — EMPLOYER-EMPLOYEE RELATIONS**: See **industrial relations, informal rules**.

31. **ARBEITGEBERHAFTUNG — EMPLOYER LIABILITY**: The **employer** is liable to the **employee** for material damage within the context of the employment relationship in accordance with the general principles of civil liability. The employee must also be compensated for typically work-related damage not recompensed as part of **remuneration**. However, for personal injury to the employee caused by **accidents at work** the employer is liable only in the case of deliberate intention or accidents that have occurred in the normal course of their work. In all other cases personal injury to the employee is covered by the **accident insurance** financed by employers. Under this system, the injured employee has no entitlement to compensation for pain and suffering ("Schmerzensgeld").

32. **ARBEITGEBERVERBAND — EMPLOYERS' ASSOCIA-TION**: Employers can organize in a local, district or Land employers' association. These regional trade associations, which are constituted separately by industry in accordance with the **principle of industrial organization**, are generally (unless already functioning at Land level) grouped into Land associations. These in their turn are normally members of two associations: both a central trade association, *i.e.* the national association of an industry at Federal level (*e.g.* Gesamtmetall (Federation of the Metal Trades Employers' Associations) or Bundesarbeitgeberverband Chemie (Federation of Employers' Associations in the Chemical Industry)); and also a multi-industry Land association grouping all trade associations together at Land level (*e.g.* Vereinigung der Hessischen Unternehmerverbände (Federation of Employers' Associations in Hesse)).

These central trade associations and multi-industry Land associations also belong to an umbrella organization, the **Confederation of German Employers' Associations** (BDA). Public sector employers are organized in the Tarifgemeinschaft Deutscher Länder (Employers' Association of German Länder) and the Vereinigung der kommunalen Arbeitgeberverbände (Federation of Municipal Employers' Associations); these bodies are not members of the BDA. In all, there are at present well over a thousand employers' associations.

The degree of organization among German employers is relatively high. In manufacturing industry, banking and insurance it reaches approximately 80 per cent.; organized employers employ over 90 per cent. of all employees. In other sectors the figures are somewhat lower, mainly because of the large number of non-organized small enterprises.

The subscriptions paid by employers to the employers' associations are generally calculated on the basis of the wage bill

29

they notify to the "Berufsgenossenschaften" (**Occupational Health and Safety Agencies**).

33. **ARBEITNEHMER — EMPLOYEE**: An employee is a person who, under a contract in private law, performs work in the service of another, in a relationship of personal subordination and subject to direction and control. The deciding factor in this definition is that the employee is in a position of subordination to another's authority. Where no relationship of subordination exists but the individual concerned is economically dependent on the enterprise, they may be a **person treated in law as similar to an employee**. Employees are subdivided into two groups: **manual workers** and **white-collar workers**.

    Career public servants ("Beamte") and judges, who are employed in a special service relationship under public law, are not classed as employees. Other categories not classed as employees include family members who assist without any contractual obligations, voluntary helpers who provide their services for religious or charitable reasons, individuals in the process of special rehabilitation, and convicts.

34. **ARBEITNEHMERÄHNLICHE PERSON — PERSON TREATED IN LAW AS SIMILAR TO AN EMPLOYEE**: A gainfully employed individual who, although not in a relationship of subordination to another's authority, is in a position of economic dependence. Examples include **homeworkers** and **commercial representatives** who work for more than one principal, and artistes, musicians and **freelances** who are not in a fixed employment relationship.

    Such individuals come under the **system of labour courts** and are treated as equivalent to **employees** as regards, for example, their entitlement to **leave**. **Collective agreements** can also be concluded for them. In general, the provisions of **labour law** apply to them as far as these concern protective provisions relevant to the fact of economic dependence, and not subordination to an employer's authority, in the performance of work. This is so even if for other reasons the interests involved are comparable to those of an employee.

35. **ARBEITNEHMERBETEILIGUNG — EMPLOYEE PARTICIPATION**: Also referred to as "workers' participation". See **capital-forming payments, co-determination, financial participation, institutionalized representation of interests, invested pay, share of profits, works constitution**.

36. **ARBEITNEHMERERFINDUNGEN — INVENTIONS BY EMPLOYEES**: As a matter of principle, the law gives the employer ownership of the result of the employee's work; employees are deemed to have received compensation in full in the form of their pay, regardless of the value of what they produce. An exception is made to this principle in the case of inventions by employees. It applies to inventions which are patentable or registrable as designs, and which are either based mainly on the enterprise's experience and work or have resulted from the employee's contractually stipulated work in the enterprise (known as a "Diensterfindung", *i.e.* job-related invention). By making a written declaration (within four months after being informed of the invention by the employee), the employer can assert an unlimited or limited claim to such an invention. In the case of an unlimited claim, all rights deriving from the job-related invention pass to the employer. At the same time, the employee is entitled to fair compensation. In the case of a limited claim, this entitlement exists only if the employer makes use of the job-related invention. With an invention which is not job-related (known as a "freie Erfindung", *i.e.* independent invention), the employee must offer the employer a pre-emptive, non-exclusive right to use the invention on reasonable terms, before exploiting it in any other way while the employment relationship remains in force; however, this applies only if the invention falls within the sphere of activity of the employer's enterprise.

37. **ARBEITNEHMERFREIZÜGIGKEIT — FREEDOM OF MOVEMENT FOR WORKERS**: Freedom of movement for workers implies, first and foremost, the abolition of any form of discrimination in the EC Member States on the grounds of the nationality of the individual employee. It excludes nationals of other countries and stateless persons. These can, however, engage in any form of paid employment in the Federal Republic as the spouses or children (up to the age of 21) of a beneficiary.

As a ban on discrimination, freedom of movement for workers encompasses differentiation on grounds of nationality with regard to employment, pay and other terms and conditions. It is law that is directly applicable in all EC Member States, which means that the individual can invoke it against any Member State. It follows from the ban on discrimination that an employee who is an EC national has rights covering: applying in response to actual job offers; mobility for the purposes of seeking work (freedom of movement); residence for the purposes of carrying on employment; and continuance of the right of abode after the employment has ended.

There are exceptions to the right of mobility inasmuch as it

31

does not apply to those employed in the public administration and freedom of movement may be restricted on grounds of threat to public security, order or health. Also, in the Federal Republic even nationals of EC Member States need a special **residence permit**. This is granted on production of valid identity papers together with a certificate of appointment from the employer or a certificate of employment. On the other hand, nationals of EC Member States do not need a **work permit**.

38. **ARBEITNEHMERHAFTUNG — EMPLOYEE LIABILITY**: Liability of the employee towards the employer or third parties can arise from deliberate or negligent infringement of **pre-contractual obligations in the employment relationship, obligations under the contract of employment** and a civil wrong. The Federal Labour Court has ruled that the employee has only limited liability for material damage caused to the employer in the context of **hazardous work**.

In the case of personal injury prejudicial to fellow-workers arising from **accidents at work** caused by the employee, the civil-law liability of the person causing the injury is replaced by the entitlement of the injured person to claim against the institution responsible for employer-financed **accident insurance**, as regulated by the Reich Social Insurance Code. This liability is not subject to proof of negligence, and there is no entitlement to compensation for pain and suffering ("Schmerzensgeld"). The institution concerned can claim damages from the employee who caused the injury if they caused the accident deliberately or through gross negligence.

For all damage and injury to third parties and for material damage to employees of the same enterprise, the employee causing the damage has unlimited liability in the first instance. If, however, the damage has occurred in the context of hazardous work, the employee has a claim against the employer for exemption from liability.

39. **ARBEITNEHMERKAMMER — CHAMBER OF LABOUR**: Chambers of Labour are legally constituted self-administering associations of employees whose purpose is to ensure that employees' interests receive adequate consideration in the context of legislation, administration and court decisions; nowadays they exist in the Federal Republic only in two Länder, namely Bremen and Saarland. In Saarland (where the term used is "Arbeitskammer") all employees are members of the Chamber of Labour, whereas in Bremen (where the term used is "Arbeiterkammer") only employees in industry are members. In both cases, a compulsory subscription of 0.1 per cent. of gross pay is levied. Although there is close co-operation between the

trade unions and the surviving Chambers of Labour, there is no intention to enlarge their sphere of activity or establish additional Chambers.

Chambers of Labour are to be distinguished from the professional representative bodies of industry and allied trades, *i.e.* the **Chambers of Industry and Commerce** and the **Chambers of Craft Trades**. Until now only the employers' side has been represented in Chamber of Industry and Commerce branches, while at least one third of the members in all Chamber of Craft Trades branches are qualified craftworkers.

40. **ARBEITNEHMERRECHTE — EMPLOYEE RIGHTS**: The general rights of **employees** include:
    a. **basic rights**, notably the **freedom of occupation** and **freedom of contract** and "positive" and **"negative" freedom of association**; and
    b. the provisions on employee protection, **protection against technical hazards at work** and **protection against dismissal**.
    In addition, employees are entitled to:
    a. be properly informed about their tasks and responsibilities, and about the nature of the work activity concerned and the way in which they fit into the overall workflow;
    b. be consulted in connection with establishment matters and management decisions that affect individuals;
    c. make their own suggestions regarding the organization of the workplace and the workflow;
    d. receive an explanation of the components of their **remuneration** and how it is calculated;
    e. be allowed access to their **personal files**;
    f. put forward complaints and have them replied to and remedied, in cases where this is within their rights.
    Employees can consult a member of the **works council** in connection with discussions of pay and access to personal files, and can also bring complaints before the works council.

41. **ARBEITNEHMERSCHUTZ — EMPLOYEE PROTECTION**: Employee protection comprises all the regulations on rights in employment which take account of the employee's particular position of vulnerability in the employment relationship. They include, notably, **health and safety, restrictions on working hours, youth employment protection, protection against dismissal** and **maternity protection**.

42. **ARBEITNEHMERSPARZULAGE — EMPLOYEE SAVINGS SUPPLEMENT**: To encourage the long-term investment of **capital-forming payments** by employees, the state grants an

33

employee savings supplement. Under the Fifth Capital Formation Act as amended on January 1, 1990, capital-forming payments in the form of savings with building societies and participation in productive assets (*e.g.* shares, investment fund certificates, holdings in private limited companies) up to a sum of 936 Deutschmarks per calendar year attract a supplement. The supplement is 10 per cent. for savings with building societies and 20 per cent. for investments. It is granted only to employees whose taxable income does not exceed 27,000 Deutschmarks (54,000 Deutschmarks for married couples with joint tax assessment). This income limit is raised by 1,800 Deutschmarks for each dependent child.

Formerly, the supplement was paid out together with employees' pay by the employer, who then offset it against the **earnings tax** to be paid over to the Tax Office; since January 1, 1990 employees apply for it themselves from the Tax Office.

43. **ARBEITNEHMERÜBERLASSUNG — HIRING-OUT OF LABOUR**: System in which a hiring-out employer (**lessor**) puts one of their **employees** at the disposal of a third party (lessee) to perform work for a fixed or open-ended period. Also referred to as "Leiharbeit". The relationship is characterized by the fact that, although there is a contract of employment between the lessor and the employee and a special contract between the lessor and the lessee, no contract exists between the employee and the lessee and the employee in fact only has representation by way of the **works council** of the lessor's establishment.

For the general protection of employees hired out in this way ("Leiharbeitnehmer"), and in order to prevent their being employed on a short-term basis when demand is high and then dismissed when demand falls, the habitual hiring-out of labour as a business is subject to a number of special regulations. It is deemed to be practised as a business if the lessor runs an establishment with the main purpose of making a profit from the hiring-out of labour. Firms that hire out employees are obliged to register with the authorities, which makes it possible to monitor the development of the lawful hiring-out of labour as a business.

In order to evade the statutory restrictions imposed on businesses that hire out labour, the scale of unlawful hiring out of labour has increased. In some sectors of the economy it greatly exceeds the scale of lawful activity.

There has also been an increase in the number of businesses that lawfully hire out labour (often also called "Zeitarbeit", *i.e.* temporary work). At present there are approximately 5,000 such firms, employing some 350,000 employees from almost all sectors of activity.

44. ARBEITSAMT — EMPLOYMENT OFFICE: The local Employment Offices are the lowest stage in the administrative structure of the **Federal Employment Service**.

45. ARBEITSBEREICHERUNG — JOB ENRICHMENT: Form of redesign of jobs as a response to the call for **humanization of work**. It involves changing the nature of the work content in such a way that greater demands are made on the **skills** of employees, who are also given more scope for using their own discretion.

46. ARBEITSBEREITSCHAFT — ON-CALL: Unlike British use of the term because implying presence at the workplace, this is defined as time during which an employee is alert and attentive but in a (physically) relaxed state. It is a part of **working time** during which the employee does not need to be physically active but is present at the **workplace** and has to be ready to engage in the work process at any time. The type of work involved is normally one in which the alternation between direct activity and on-call time is not fixed. As a matter of principle the employee must be paid for on-call time, but this may be in the form of a flat-rate payment. In cases where guarding and control tasks are a feature of the job in question such time does not constitute on-call time but the contractually stipulated work activity: these cases include doorkeepers, or the operators of modern machines in the monitoring of **new technologies**, where, in particular, the mental and intellectual stress is equivalent to heavy physical work.

47. ARBEITSBESCHAFFUNGSMASSNAHMEN — JOB CREATION SCHEMES: As a means of enabling unemployed people who are difficult to place to be more easily inserted into the employment system, the Employment Promotion Act (§§ 91 ff.) makes provision for the temporary employment of such individuals under job creation schemes with funding from the **Federal Employment Service** (BfA); however, to ensure that existing jobs will not be threatened the BfA sponsors only forms of work which are socially useful and which without job creation schemes either would not be done at all or could be given only low priority. The schemes are usually run by local authorities and charity organizations. The number of people employed under such schemes has increased enormously in the last few years, owing to the extremely large number of long-term unemployed and to economic restructuring in eastern Germany. In 1991 it reached about 350,000. The so-called **job creation companies** are an important form of job creation in eastern Germany.

48. **ARBEITSBESCHEINIGUNG — CERTIFICATE OF EMPLOYMENT**: To enable entitlements to be claimed from **unemployment insurance**, the employer has to furnish a certificate of employment. The employer is under an obligation with respect both to the **Federal Employment Service** and to the employee to make out the certificate. It contains particulars of the nature of the job performed, the dates on which the employment relationship began and ended and the reason for its termination, and the **remuneration** paid and other emoluments. This information is used for calculating unemployment benefit and unemployment assistance. If the certificate is incomplete or incorrect, the employer is obliged to remedy this.

49. **ARBEITSBEZIEHUNGEN — LABOUR RELATIONS**: See **industrial relations**.

50. **ARBEITSDIREKTOR — EMPLOYEE DIRECTOR**: In public limited companies and private limited companies which are subject to **co-determination**, an "employee director" must be appointed either as a full member of the **management board** (enjoying equal rights) or, in the absence of a management board, as one of the managers. The employee director (who has responsibility for staff and social matters) is appointed or removed by the **supervisory board**, and in companies in the **coal, iron and steel industry** this cannot be done against the wishes of the elected employee representatives in this **company organ**. In all other companies subject to co-determination the employee director frequently enjoys the confidence of the employee representatives. Failing appointment by normal procedure, an employee director can also be appointed by the court of registration at the proposal of one of the parties concerned.

51. **ARBEITSENTGELT — REMUNERATION**: Payment of the agreed remuneration is the employer's main obligation under the contract of employment; it is the counterpart of the employee's obligation to provide the agreed performance of work. The amount of remuneration may be set by **collective agreement** or **works agreement** as well as by the **contract of employment**. If there are no express terms of pay, the employer is liable for the payment of the rate for the job (Civil Code § 612). In addition to actual pay in the form of **wage** or **salary**, remuneration may include **bonuses, commission** and a **share of profits**.

The employer's basic liability is for the payment of **gross pay** unless, as an exception, the parties have agreed on a **net pay arrangement**. The **payment of remuneration** is in principle effected in cash, but cashless methods of payment may be agreed on and these are very common. There is a **ban on the truck system**; despite this, **payment in kind** is permissible.

The general principle is that the employer has to remunerate the employee only for the performance of work that the employee has, in turn, provided. The only cases in which this principle does not apply are **sick pay, employer's non-acceptance of the work performance, impossibility of performance** and "**works risk**", and **leave**.

52. **ARBEITSERLAUBNIS — WORK PERMIT**: In principle, all individuals who are not German within the meaning of the **Basic Law** need a work permit (Employment Promotion Act § 19). Permits are issued in the light of the labour market situation and the personal circumstances in each individual case. EC subjects and aliens with **right of abode** do not need a work permit.

A work permit may be issued with or without restriction to a specific form of work in a specific **establishment** ("Betrieb"). Spouses and children of an alien who have lived in the Federal Republic for a specified period can also obtain a work permit. However, a work permit cannot be obtained for taking up employment in the context of the **hiring-out of labour**. Permits are issued at the limited discretion of the **Federal Employment Service**, through the appropriate local Employment Office.

Certain individuals are able to obtain a special work permit irrespective of the above conditions. They include people who for the five years immediately preceding the period of validity of the work permit have been lawfully engaged in continuous employment in the Federal Republic, and aliens married to a German citizen whose habitual place of residence is in the Federal Republic. Children of foreign citizens who are lawfully resident in the Federal Republic are entitled to be granted a work permit if they have accompanied one or both parents to the Federal Republic before reaching the age of 18 and have there completed schooling or concluded a vocational training contract. The Federal Labour Court has ruled that a contract of employment is invalid if it was concluded in the knowledge that the employee did not possess a work permit. Nevertheless, in accordance with the principles of the *de facto* **employment relationship** there is still entitlement to pay; the employer can, however, refuse to provide work without the situation being deemed to be one of non-acceptance. If the employee does not yet possess a work permit but one is expected to be issued, the contract of employment is only provisionally invalid and becomes valid when the permit is issued. If the work permit lapses in the course of an existing employment relationship, this does not automatically nullify the contract of employment. A separate act of termination is needed.

Depending on the individual case this will be either ordinary **termination with notice** or **summary termination**, the deciding factor being whether the employer needs to refill the job immediately or can reasonably be expected to accept a delay. General and special **protection against dismissal** applies in all cases. Employment without a work permit is punishable by a fine imposed on both employer and employee.

53. **ARBEITSERWEITERUNG — JOB ENLARGEMENT**: Form of redesign of jobs as a response to demands for **humanization of work**. It involves increasing the scope of the work content in such a way that a number of similar tasks are added on to the employee's existing tasks, but are at the same skill level.

54. **ARBEITSFÖRDERUNG — PROMOTION OF EMPLOY-MENT**: See **Federal Employment Service, unemployment insurance**.

55. **ARBEITSGERICHT — LABOUR COURT**: See **system of labour courts**.

56. **ARBEITSGERICHTSBARKEIT — SYSTEM OF LABOUR COURTS**: One of the five **systems of jurisdiction** comprised by procedural law in the Federal Republic. It is a special and exclusive jurisdiction for hearing disputes under labour law. Whether a case is dealt with by the labour courts is determined by the Labour Courts Act (Arbeitsgerichtsgesetz).

It is a three-tier system, with first-instance Labour Courts (ArbG), Land Labour Courts (LAG) and the Federal Labour Court (BAG). Every case relating to labour law is heard by the appropriate local Labour Court in the first instance. The individual panels (or chambers) of these courts, as also the Land Labour Courts, have one career judge and two **lay judges** on the bench; the panels (or senates) of the Federal Labour Court have three career judges and two lay judges. A career judge always presides. If one of the Federal Labour Court senates wishes to deviate from the rulings of another, or if fundamentally important questions of law are to be decided, the Grand Senate meets, consisting of the President of the Federal Labour Court, the longest-serving senate president, four other career judges and four lay judges.

The Land Labour Courts hear **appeals** and **"Beschluss" procedure appeals** against decisions of the first-instance Labour Courts, and the Federal Labour Court hears **appeals on a point of law** and **judicial review applications** against decisions of the Land Labour Courts and also **direct appeals on a point of law** and **direct judicial review applications** against decisions of the first-instance Labour Courts. There are special rules on **representation in court** for the labour courts system.

In the absence of any Ministry for the administration of justice with responsibility for all branches of the judicial system, the first-instance Labour Courts and Land Labour Courts come under the supervisory authority of the individual **Ministries of Labour at Land level**; the supervisory authority for the Federal Labour Court is the **Federal Ministry of Labour and Social Affairs**.

57. **ARBEITSGERICHTSVERFAHREN — LABOUR COURT PROCEDURE**: Compared with procedure for conducting court proceedings in the other systems of jurisdiction, the labour court procedure exhibits a number of special features. For instance, depending on the nature of the dispute at hand the Labour Courts use either the **"Urteil" procedure** or the **"Beschluss" procedure**. In the case of the "Urteil" procedure, a preliminary **conciliation hearing** before the president of the chamber is obligatory. There are also special regulations on the amount of **legal costs** and liability for costs. In addition, the rules on **representation in court** are different, notably in allowing representation by representatives of the **trade unions** and **employers' associations**.

58. **ARBEITSKAMMER — CHAMBER OF LABOUR**: Term used in Saarland as synonym of **Arbeitnehmerkammer**.

59. **ARBEITSKAMPF — INDUSTRIAL ACTION**: Term used to refer to a situation where the employers' or employees' side takes collective action to exert economic pressure on the other **party to a collective agreement** in order to achieve a particular goal. (In some contexts the term may be better translated as referring to a particular "labour dispute".) Such action is the means of coercion necessary to the conclusion of a **collective agreement**; if it were not available, the **collective bargaining autonomy** provided under constitutional law would be meaningless. The right to bargain collectively presupposes that the social partners can establish and maintain a balance of bargaining power.

Statute law does not give a definition of industrial action. The concept features in several treaties under international law (European Social Charter, European Convention on Human Rights, ILO Convention No. 87) and Federal statutes. However, no systematic interpretation of industrial action emerges from these provisions. Its treatment under labour law is therefore based almost entirely on **judge-made law**. The **Federal Labour Court**, in particular, has laid down a number of criteria and rules. Forms of industrial action are **strikes** by employees, **lock-outs** by employers and **boycotts**, which may be used by both.

Under social security law, employees directly involved in such industrial action receive neither **unemployment benefit** nor **short-time allowance**; those indirectly involved are entitled to them only subject to modified conditions of eligibility. As regards **health insurance**, the fact that pay is discontinued means that insurance cover lapses after three weeks from the start of the industrial action. If industrial action goes on for some time employees can maintain their own insurance cover if they so wish.

In the Federal Republic of Germany industrial action is usually taken only by **trade unions** and **employers' associations**. Compared with other industrialized countries, the number of labour disputes and working days lost as a result is extremely low.

60. **ARBEITSKAMPFBEREITSCHAFT — WILLINGNESS TO TAKE INDUSTRIAL ACTION**: To be able to achieve its goal of improving the economic and social situation of its members, a **collective industrial organization** must be capable of exerting pressure on the opposing side with the threat of industrial action. Willingness to take this action is therefore generally a characteristic of such an organization, but is not an absolutely essential qualification. The only essential requirement is that the organization can represent its members' interests effectively.

61. **ARBEITSKAMPFRICHTLINIEN — UNION STRIKE GUIDELINES**: The **German Federation of Trade Unions** (DGB), like the **German White-Collar Workers' Union** (DAG), has drawn up guidelines on strike procedure which have been generally incorporated into the standing rules of the **trade unions** affiliated to the DGB. These guidelines define the following separate phases of a labour dispute:
1. decision by the union to initiate a **strike**;
2. decision by the union to conduct a **strike ballot** among union members;
3. invitation to union members to take part in the ballot;
4. ballot;
5. authorization by the appropriate union body of the actual decision to strike;
6. strike call to union members;
7. actual withdrawal of labour.

Measures leading up to a strike, which include the ballot, are not themselves classed as part of the dispute.

62. **ARBEITSLOSENGELD — UNEMPLOYMENT BENEFIT**:
Unemployment benefit is an insurance payment paid out under
unemployment insurance which functions as a substitute for pay.
It is intended, in the event of **unemployment**, to enable insured
employees to maintain, with certain limitations, their former
standard of living. The eligibility criteria for receiving
unemployment benefit (Employment Promotion Act §§ 100 ff.)
are firstly the completion of a qualifying period throughout which
the employees concerned must have been in an **employment
relationship** subject to compulsory insurance, and secondly that
they must register as unemployed at the appropriate local
Employment Office. The minimum qualifying period is currently
one full year of employment.

At present, unemployed workers with at least one dependent
child receive 68 per cent. (63 per cent. in other cases) of their
last net pay. The period of entitlement varies according to age
and ranges from 12 months for claimants aged up to 42 to 32
months for those aged 54 and over.

63. **ARBEITSLOSENHILFE — UNEMPLOYMENT ASSIST-
ANCE**: Unemployment assistance is a state benefit in the sense
of social assistance payable to the needy unemployed who have
no entitlement to **unemployment benefit** because they have not
fulfilled the qualifying period or who, although they meet the
other eligibility criteria (Promotion of Employment Act §§ 134
ff.), have already exhausted their entitlement.

In contrast to unemployment benefit, unemployment assistance
is financed not from contributions but by the Federal Government
from general tax revenues. Notably, unemployment assistance
is governed by the principle of subsidiarity when the unemployed
person has at their disposal other sources of income or other
subsistence entitlements in respect of their immediate family.
Thus, any monetary income and assets of unemployed individuals
are taken into account. Furthermore, the unemployed are obliged
to remedy their state of need by first asserting all other viable
subsistence entitlements.

Unemployment assistance currently amounts to 58 or 56 per
cent. of the last monthly net pay.

64. **ARBEITSLOSENVERSICHERUNG — UNEMPLOY-
MENT INSURANCE**: Unemployment insurance is the branch
of statutory **social security** that insures employees against the
risk of **unemployment**. The primary purpose of unemployment
insurance is the prevention of loss, and only secondarily does it
include protection against loss in the form of payments
(**unemployment benefit**). It therefore provides not only insurance

payments but also funding for job creation and protection and, in the context of employment promotion, funding for fostering vocational training, entry into active employment and occupational rehabilitation. The provision of **unemployment assistance** is not an unemployment insurance matter.

Despite its primarily preventive function, the main form of provision paid out from unemployment insurance constitutes payments to ensure the means of existence for employees during periods of unemployment. For this, people employed in jobs subject to statutory social security contributions are entitled (usually after a specified qualifying period has been completed) to claim payments which are neither dependent on the unemployed individual's degree of need nor liable to be reduced when other forms of income are taken into account. Unemployment insurance is administered by the **Federal Employment Service**.

65. **ARBEITSLOSIGKEIT — UNEMPLOYMENT**: The situation of workers who wish to work but who are (usually temporarily) without work. The causes of unemployment can be: structural weaknesses in the national economy as a whole (for example, obsolete technology or business management methods), regional and sectoral depressions, cyclical and seasonal fluctuations (for example, caused in the building industry by weather conditions at different times of the year) and a mismatch between skill requirements and workers' abilities.

The level of unemployment is indicated by the "Arbeitslosenquote" or unemployment rate (number of people registered as unemployed as a percentage of the total number of people in employment and seeking employment). This rate is calculated monthly by the **Federal Employment Service**. With the basis for calculation that is used at present, individuals who are medically unfit for work, who are taking part in re-training or **job creation schemes** or whose entitlement to **unemployment benefit** has run out are excluded from the unemployment statistics.

The level of unemployment in the Federal Republic has been subject to fluctuations. Whereas the situation on the **labour market** (after a relatively high level of unemployment up to the mid-1950s) was marked by a strong demand for labour between 1960 and 1966 and again from 1969 to 1971, in the mid-1970s unemployment rose steeply as a result of the economic crisis, **structural change** and the trend in the world economy (in 1976 the unemployment rate was 5.8 per cent.), followed by only a slight drop when the economic crisis eased over the next few years. At the beginning of the 1980s unemployment again rose abruptly, reaching its peak in 1983 at 2.5 million unemployed (unemployment rate 10.2 per cent.). Since then, although on a falling curve unemployment in western Germany has persisted at a high level. The unemployment rate is about 6.8 per cent. A major cause is the very broad range of people who fall into the category of the long-term unemployed and whose lack of appropriate skills makes them difficult to place in employment.

In eastern Germany unemployment is high, as a result of the radical restructuring process. The officially measured rate is around 10 per cent., but a great many of the workers who make up "real" unemployment are not included in the statistics because they are counted as short-time workers or are working under job creation schemes or in **job creation companies**.

66. **ARBEITSMARKT — LABOUR MARKET**: Viewed ideally, the labour market is the context in which **employees**, the sources of the supply of labour, and **employers**, the sources of the demand for labour, seek to match together their respective requirements and the prices of those requirements and to conclude an appropriate **contract of employment**. Consequently, it is one of the most conflict-prone areas of **industrial relations**. Because of the wide range of different reasons people have for taking a job, and the special position of the self-employed, the labour market is not identical with the **civilian working population** as it exists at any given time.

Historically, the free labour market came into being as a result of the widespread loosening of personal ties to the locality of employment, the deregulation of traditional minimum terms and conditions in favour of the poor and day-labourers, and the loss of significance of forms of organization based on occupational status groups (*e.g.* guilds) in the wake of industrialization in the first half of the nineteenth century. However, since their own labour is the workers' sole means of earning a living, they were usually forced to enter into an employment relationship on whatever terms were offered. The resultant injustices led to an increasingly intensive (and bitterly fought) struggle by the workers to assert their interests collectively on the labour market through the formation of **trade unions** and the conclusion of **collective agreements**. Nowadays, these mechanisms for regulating the labour market have gained recognition and in the Federal Republic are protected by the constitutionally guaranteed **freedom of association** and **collective bargaining autonomy**. Regulating the labour market with a bias in favour of employees proved difficult, particularly in periods of high **unemployment**, not least because at such times employers were able to threaten them plausibly with the use of the so-called "reserve army" of the unemployed. To equip themselves to overcome this weakness of their position in the labour market at least to some extent, the trade unions, which originally included only skilled workers, very soon began to organize unskilled workers and other categories as well. In the Federal Republic the unions, which are mostly industry-based according to the **principle of industrial organization**, include all employees working in a given industry or branch of the economy. However, it should by no means be assumed that there is an identity of interests among employees; trade union policy, particularly in manufacturing industry, is still geared just as before to skilled workers employed under the terms and conditions of a **typical employment relationship**, and influenced by the heterogeneity of the labour market. This heterogeneity takes the form of rigid segmentation of the market according to skills, age, sex, etc., as well as regional differences. And within individual **establishments** there is further differentiation again, between the so-called core workforce and peripheral workforce.

Regulation of the labour market is advantageous for the employers as well, since within the scope of application of a collective agreement the basic conditions for concluding contracts of employment are the same for all employers bound by the agreement, which prevents individual employers from having competitive advantages because of differences in wage costs. Further restriction of the labour market flows from the **Federal Employment Service's** monopoly of **job placement** and the institution of an **unemployment insurance** scheme and other benefits deriving from the **welfare state principle**.

67. **ARBEITSMINISTERIEN DER LÄNDER — MINISTRIES OF LABOUR AT LAND LEVEL**: The Ministries of Labour of the individual Länder are the highest labour authorities at Land level. In contrast to the **Federal Ministry of Labour and Social Affairs** they have only a very limited area of responsibility: because of the **concurrent legislative powers** of the Federation, there is very little labour legislation at individual Land level and the Länder are authorized to issue Orders only in a few specialized fields. In addition to safeguarding the state's policy interests in matters relating to working life, their chief responsibility is to act as the supreme authority for health and safety at work. This involves numerous administrative functions connected with the implementation of labour legislation and the control of state inspection authorities.

68. **ARBEITSMOTIVATION — MOTIVATION TO WORK**: Concept encompassing the driving forces and stimuli to do work,

in both the occupational and the non-occupational context, which underlie work behaviour. They relate, for example, to the necessity of securing an income, social status, a position of power within the enterprise and the need for self-fulfilment. In the developed Western societies there is a discernible tendency, particularly among highly skilled employees, for intrinsic motivation to become predominant and material motivation to become less important (changing values). Individual motivation also contains shared values absorbed from the surrounding culture and society and from the work environment, in the latter case partly stimulated by specific **corporate cultures**. Depending on whether they are adopted outwardly or recognized inwardly, these norms are perceived either as personally accepted values or as an imposed constraint.

69. **ARBEITSORGANISATION — WORK ORGANIZATION**: Manner of allocating tasks and labour in line with a company's objectives and the **skills** of its employees, and the corresponding design of workplaces. Workshop manufacture and so-called production "islands" are both examples of a decentralized form of work organization, whereas in **mass production** work organization is highly centralized. In the latter case, the need for such control arises because the work is broken down into standardized, elementary and rigidly specified steps and skill requirements are consequently low. Demands that press for **humanization of work** are a reaction against the principle of organizing production known as **Taylorism**, with its alienating and monotonous working conditions. The work and job structures that result from a given form of work organization directly affect flexibility of production, **motivation to work** and **productivity**. In the context of what are nowadays dubbed **new production concepts**, forms of work organization in which individual jobs cover a complete segment of work activity are gaining increasing importance as a means of utilizing the opportunities offered by **new production technologies**.

70. **ARBEITSPAPIERE — EMPLOYMENT DOCUMENTS**: Term used to indicate documents that include the statutory insurance card and **earnings tax card**, the health insurance fund certificate, leave certificate, certificate of employment issued on termination and, where applicable, a **reference**. The pay record card used in the construction industry and the seafarer's papers also fall under this heading, but **job application documents** do not. The employer is under an obligation to keep employment documents carefully and to return them to the employee when the

employment relationship comes to an end; a **quittance acknowledging settlement** (of all outstanding claims) is often signed to certify their receipt.

Failure to produce employment documents does not make the employment relationship invalid, but it may lead to the imposition of an **employment ban**.

Employment documents which must be given to the employee by the employer on entering into the contract of employment include pay record books for homeworkers, a copy of the agreed terms and conditions in the context of a **vocational training relationship**, documentation on the basic content of the employment relationship in cases of **hiring-out of labour**, and documentation on agreement to a covenant for a **restraint on competition**. Lastly, the Federal Minister for Labour and Social Affairs may stipulate that in certain industries employees must be given pay packets and work payslips.

The employer does not have a **right to withold performance** in respect of employment documents on the grounds of a counter-claim on the employee.

71. **ARBEITSPAUSE — BREAK**: Synonym of **Pause**.

72. **ARBEITSPFLICHT — DUTY TO WORK**: The **contract of employment** implies the fundamental obligation for the **employee** to provide the performance of work as agreed under the contract. The nature and location of this duty to work stem from the content of the contract, which has to comply with provisions laid down by law and collective agreement. Within this contractual framework, the **employer's right to issue instructions** then enables employers to give concrete form to the employee's duty to work, *i.e.* to specify in detail what the work consists of and where it must be performed.

The obligation on employees to put their labour at the employer's disposal is confined to the **working time** laid down by law, collective agreement or the individual contract of employment. They therefore have the right to take on a **second job**, provided that this is not effectively excluded by contractual provisions or is not prejudicial to the contractual duty to work.

73. **ARBEITSPLATZ — JOB**: An employment position or post, whether occupied or not, in a company's work organization.

The term is also used in the sense of the ''workplace'' where work is done, *e.g.* factory or office premises.

74. **ARBEITSPLATZSCHUTZ FÜR WEHR- UND ZIVILDIENSTLEISTENDE — JOB PROTECTION DURING COMPULSORY MILITARY OR COMMUNITY SERVICE**: Special job protection is provided for manual workers,

white-collar workers and vocational trainees, and essentially also for career public servants, homeworkers and commercial representatives, while they are doing their compulsory military service (or community service as conscientious objectors), are recalled for military exercises, have to serve on the reserve list for the armed forces, or are called up for an indefinite period for purposes of national defence.

The statutory provisions on job protection in the event of call-up for military service stipulate that during military service the **employment relationship** is merely quiescent, not interrupted, but that the fundamental obligations of employer and employee are suspended. Apart from a few exceptions, the period of such service is credited as employment experience or continuous **length of service**, but does not count towards length of training. This is particularly important with respect to pay increases based on length of service and to the calculation of entitlements to retirement and survivors' pensions (**occupational pension scheme, social security**). In addition to the general principle that no disadvantages must be suffered as a result of doing military service, there are also special protective provisions, the most important being an absolute ban on dismissal via **termination with notice** of the employment relationship by the employer during the period between employees receiving their call-up papers and finishing their compulsory military service, during military exercises and service on the reserve list, and in the event of defensive combat. Other forms of dismissal are still permissible, but must be for reasons unconnected with the performance of military service.

In the public service, candidates who are applying for a job directly after completing compulsory military service have to be given preference over other job-seekers with the same qualifications.

The regulations relating to individuals doing military service apply by analogy to conscientious objectors performing community service.

The Federal Labour Court has ruled that this form of job protection also applies to other EC nationals. Turkish employees have a **right to withold performance** as regards their performance of work during the shortened period of military service that they are required to do.

75. **ARBEITSRECHT — LABOUR LAW**: The entire body of legal rules that have bearing on work performed under another's authority, involving overlap between private and public law. **Individual labour law** covers the relations between employer and employee, including the appropriate special regulations.

47

Collective labour law establishes the norms governing the legal relationships of the employees within an establishment (a) with each other and (b) *vis-à-vis* their employer (in the form of the **works constitution** and **co-determination**) and, beyond this, the legal relationships of the trade unions and employers' associations with each other and *vis-à-vis* the state. Labour law falls within the field of **concurrent legislative powers** of the Federation. Its **sources of law** also include **judge-made law**, notably that developed by the labour courts.

76. **ARBEITSSCHUTZ — HEALTH AND SAFETY**: See **protection against technical hazards at work, safety at work, safety of equipment, workplace health and safety arrangements**.

77. **ARBEITSSCHUTZAUSSCHUSS — HEALTH AND SAFETY COMMITTEE**: In establishments where **works doctors** and **works safety experts** are appointed, the employer is required to set up a health and safety committee grouping together all the institutions of the **workplace health and safety arrangements**. The committee is composed of the employer (or the employer's appointed representative), two members of the **works council** designated by the council itself, and the works doctor, safety expert and safety officer representatives. The committee meets at least quarterly, to confer on matters of **protection against technical hazards at work** and **protection against accidents** and to co-ordinate the work of the individual institutions.

78. **ARBEITSSTÄTTE — WORKPLACE**: The main objective of **protection against technical hazards at work** is the safe and humane design of workplaces for employees. This is the purpose of the Arbeitsstättenverordnung (Workplaces Decree), which lays down that all workplaces in industry, small-scale crafts and trades ("Handwerk") and the insurance and commercial sector must comply with the 30 or so **Federal Ministry of Labour and Social Affairs** Directives implementing the Decree, with the provisions currently in force on health and safety at work and accident prevention, with generally accepted rules on safety techniques, industrial medicine and occupational hygiene, and with other established ergonomic findings. These provisions include standards on the size, lighting, ventilation and temperature of workplaces, protection against noise, dust and gases, and the provision of sanitation facilities.

79. **ARBEITSTEILUNG — DIVISION OF LABOUR**: See **mass production, Taylorism**.

**80. ARBEITSUNFÄHIGKEITSBESCHEINIGUNG —
CERTIFICATE OF INCAPACITY FOR WORK**: If employees
fail to provide their contractually agreed performance of work
because of **illness**, they must ensure that their employer receives
an immediate **notification of illness**. **Manual workers** are then
required to present to their employer, no later than by the third
calendar day of the illness causing their incapacity for work, a
medical certificate from a doctor of their own choice attesting
their incapacity for work (Continued Payment of Wages Act § 3).
Although no such statutory requirement exists for other
employees such as white-collar workers, the Federal Labour Court
invariably holds that, unless the parties have agreed otherwise,
this obligation applies to all employees.

A certificate of incapacity for work does not amount to
conclusive proof of the existence of an employee's incapacity for
work through illness, but constitutes prima facie evidence of it.
If employers wish to challenge it, they have to disprove it in legal
proceedings. Entitlement to **sick pay** is not dependent on
presentation of a certificate of incapacity for work, but the
employer has a **right to withold performance** in respect of
payment of sick pay until a certificate is presented.

The obligation to present such a certificate ranks as a subsidiary
obligation under the contract of employment. Failure to comply
can therefore lead in individual cases to a formal warning or
dismissal.

81. ARBEITSUNFALL — ACCIDENT AT WORK: An accident
is any unexpected event that leads to injury. If this happens to
an individual covered by statutory **accident insurance** as arising
out of and in the course of their employment, it is classed as an
accident at work. The concept relates only to bodily injury, *i.e.*
any physical or mental impairment.

There are two preconditions for compensation: an act
demonstrably in the service of the employer and a causal
relationship between the accident, the event leading to the injury,
and the work activity covered by insurance. Hazards of everyday
life are also covered, but not hazards that have universal effect
(*e.g.* natural disasters).

In terms of location, as a general principle insurance protection
starts on arrival at the place where, by reason of the **employer's
right to issue instructions**, the work is to be done. Within this
context protection continues during **breaks** or **stand-by** duty but
not during mealtimes. Outside the context of this location, the
so-called "accident *en route*" (*i.e.* an accident sustained while the
employee concerned is travelling between home and workplace)
also counts as an accident at work.

49

Classification as an accident at work also applies if the accident occurs during the keeping, conveyance, maintenance or repair of equipment. "Equipment" is understood to mean all technical articles that are used in the course of production to achieve a company's objective, with the exception of work clothing. "Keeping" means accommodating equipment at the workplace or some other place, while "conveyance" means any transportation that is primarily for the purpose of changing the location of equipment and not for the movement of a person. Lastly, an **occupational illness** is treated as an accident at work.

The official statistics for 1989 showed a total of 1.6 million accidents *en route* and accidents at work. Compared with the figures for 1985, there had been a general decrease in the number of accidents, including a drop in the number of fatal accidents by 16 per cent. to 1,515.

82. **ARBEITSVERHÄLTNIS — EMPLOYMENT RELATION-SHIP**: An employment relationship comes into being by virtue of a valid **contract of employment**. Whereas the contract of employment consists only of the specific arrangements relating to work that are agreed between **employer** and **employee**, the employment relationship encompasses the entire legal relationship between the contracting parties. The rights and obligations concerned may be laid down either by the individual contract or by collective agreement or law. This difference between the employment relationship and the contract of employment is particularly evident in the situation where the contract of employment is invalid and the employee has already entered into employment. In these circumstances, there still exists a legally valid employment relationship with retrospective effect including all rights and obligations between employer and employee, in the form of the *de facto* **employment relationship**.

83. **ARBEITSVERHINDERUNG — PREVENTION FROM WORKING**: If employees are prevented from performing their work, the effects on their entitlement to remuneration vary according to circumstance. In cases where no special entitlement to **continued payment of remuneration** is stipulated by law, their entitlement is governed by the rules on **impossibility of performance**, supplemented by the concept of **"works risk"**.

The general principle is that, in cases where employees are prevented from performing their work, they lose their entitlement to remuneration only if this prevention has been caused through their own fault or if another person's fault causing the prevention is imputable to them. They are also still entitled to remuneration in cases of the **employer's non-acceptance of the work performance**.

84. **ARBEITSVERMITTLUNG — JOB PLACEMENT**: The function of job placement is to bring job-seekers into contact with employers for the purpose of forming **employment relationships**. The **Federal Employment Service** (BfA) has sole responsibility for this function, which is carried out mainly through local **Employment Offices** (Employment Promotion Act §§ 13 ff.), free of charge and impartially.

An employer can notify the Employment Office of a request for a new employee in person, by telephone or in writing, providing a suitable description of the requirements of the job concerned. The Employment Office recommends an employee by issuing a placement card, or forwards the job application documents presented by the potential employee. The choice of which applicant to hire is left to the employer's own discretion.

In carrying out placement, the BfA has to take account of the particular features of job vacancies, the suitability of job-seekers and their personal circumstances. To this end, it can arrange for job-seekers to undergo medical and, with their consent, psychological examination and assessment. It may not assist in the formation of employment relationships for which the terms and conditions are less favourable than those laid down by the relevant collective agreement.

85. **ARBEITSVERTRAG — CONTRACT OF EMPLOYMENT**: The contract of employment is a contract of service by which the **employee** undertakes to perform work in accordance with instructions (Civil Code § 611). This contract establishes an **employment relationship**. Since the terms and conditions of employment and the rights and obligations of the parties to a contract of employment are fixed mainly by statute, **collective agreement** and **works agreement**, the actual contract need only contain the time and nature of the activity concerned. Any benefits agreed on that exceed these fixed minimum terms and conditions to the employee's advantage also form part of the contract. The contract may not, however, deviate from the provisions of statute law, collective agreements or works agreements to the employee's disadvantage; to this extent, **freedom of contract** is restricted in labour law. In principle, the **conclusion of the contract of employment** need not be in any particular specified form.

86. **ARBEITSVERTRAGLICHE PFLICHTEN — OBLIGATIONS UNDER THE CONTRACT OF EMPLOYMENT**: For the employee, the fundamental obligation arising from the contract of employment is to perform the contractually agreed work, and for the employer it is to pay the appropriate

remuneration. In addition to this, the parties to the contract have numerous subsidiary obligations, the most important being the employee's **duty of loyalty** and the employer's **duty of care**. These already apply when negotiations on the contract of employment start, since even at this stage there is a relationship of mutual trust that can lead to liability for compensation.

87. **ARBEITSVERTRAGSSCHLUSS — CONCLUSION OF THE CONTRACT OF EMPLOYMENT**: A **contract of employment** between employer and employee comes into being as a result of offer and acceptance, in accordance with the regulations of the Civil Code. In principle, the contract need not be in any particular form; it may be concluded orally or in writing, expressly or impliedly. By way of exception, however, a requirement that it should be in written form may be imposed by the contract itself or by the relevant **collective agreement**. Contracts of employment with public-law bodies are required by collective agreement to be in writing in all cases.

For a contract of employment to come into being, the precondition is always that the parties must have agreed that work is to be performed in return for remuneration. The precise (or more detailed) definition of the work to be done by the employee falls within the province of the **employer's right to issue instructions**. If the amount of remuneration is not specified, the employee is entitled to the **rate for the job**.

88. **ARBEITSVERWEIGERUNG — REFUSAL TO WORK**: Term used to indicate the situation where an employee unlawfully refuses to carry out a task permissibly assigned to him or her on the basis of the **employer's right to issue instructions**. If the refusal to work has caused damage to the employer, the latter can institute legal proceedings against the employee claimimg **entitlement to damages**. In cases of refusal to work the employer is not bound by the obligation of **continued payment of remuneration**. Furthermore, refusal to work constitutes a justifiable ground, following a formal **warning**, for dismissal via ordinary **termination with notice** with notice and even, in serious cases, **summary termination**.

89. **ARBEITSWISSENSCHAFT — "WORK SCIENCE"**: Can be defined as the study of the factors associated with human work, in order to use it as efficiently as possible by adapting working conditions to human physical, intellectual and psychological characteristics. (Etymologically it is allied to the term "ergonomics", but is used with a broader range of meaning.) Both the **employer** and the **works council** are responsible for

compliance with the established findings of "work science" regarding the arrangement of work to suit human needs. If employees become subjected to particular stress as a result of changes in **work organization** that contradict such findings, the works council can demand that appropriate action be taken to prevent, alleviate and offset it. In conjunction with industrial medicine, "work science" has a direct influence on **health and safety** requirements. It is also relevant to the efforts being directed towards **humanization of work, technology impact analysis and assessment**, and **human- and environment-centred technology strategy**.

90. **ARBEITSZEIT — WORKING TIME**: Working time signifies the span of time from the start to the finish of work (excluding **breaks**) during which employees must at least put their labour at the employer's disposal at the **workplace**. It may, however, be established by **collective agreement, works agreement, custom** or the **contract of employment** that periods of time for changing clothes, for instance, count as part of working time. The time limits within which work is permitted are specified by restrictions on working hours. In addition, numerous subsidiary concepts are of relevance to the more precise definition of working time; **business travel, flexitime, maximum working hours, on-call, overtime** and **overtime exceeding maximum working hours, part-time work, rest on Sundays and public holidays, rest periods, shiftwork, short-time working, stand-by, travel-to-work time**.

Since what is due under the contract of employment is not the actual product of work but the effort to perform, working time is one of the most important criteria for quantifying what employees provide in return for the remuneration paid to them. It also governs the level of output and labour productivity within the establishment. In addition, it is important as an instrument in distributing the total employment available in the national economy as a whole amongst a given number of individuals. Calls for shorter working hours are connected with this aspect of working time. In the associated **flexibilization** of working hours, an attempt is being made to accommodate both the need on the part of companies to achieve the most efficient possible utilization of their plant and the wish of employees for less rigid working hours.

The actual scheduling of working hours, and hence also in practice their length, is subject to a **co-determination right of the works council**. It is in any case possible for the length of working hours to be fixed via a works agreement provided that the right to do so has been reserved by collective agreement.

Special regulations apply for **career public servants** ("Beamte"); in principle, however, they too have a **working week** of 40 hours. Ergonomic methods used in studies on working time are of decisive importance in setting rates of pay for **piecework**.

91. **ARBEITSZEITSCHUTZ — RESTRICTIONS ON WORKING HOURS**: Restrictions which fix **maximum working hours**, regulate the **scheduling of working time** and stipulate **breaks, rest periods** and **rest on Sundays and public holidays** are imposed in the form of **regulations on working hours**.

Restrictions on working hours are an important element of general **employee protection**. Contracts of employment whose terms violate these restrictions are null and void, and in cases of infringement of the restrictions the employee has a **right to withhold performance** and is entitled to claim damages. Enforcement of the restrictions is also supported by the obligation on the employer to display a copy of the Working Time Statute (Arbeitszeitordnung) at a suitable place in the establishment, to post up a notice showing the starting and finishing times of normal daily working hours and breaks, and to keep documentary records of departures from normal daily working hours that must be made accessible both to the works council and to the **Labour Inspectorate** for the purposes of monitoring the observance of working hours.

92. **ARBEITSZEITVERKÜRZUNG — REDUCTION OF WORKING HOURS**: Setting working time at less than the normal working hours as fixed on the basis of the **eight-hour day** and the **five-day week**. Such a reduction is permissible in law and is usually regulated by collective agreement. There are numerous possible ways of effecting it while observing the **regulations on working hours**:
   a. shortening the actual length of the working day or **working week**;
   b. enabling employees to have more days off by accumulating time credits, while maintaining normal working hours;
   c. increasing **leave** entitlement;
   d. reducing total annual working hours, by varying the length of the working day or working week according to the time of year or by lengthy periods of leave of absence (**sabbatical leave**);
   e. shortening the length of working life (**partial retirement**);
   f. various forms of **part-time work**.

The reasons behind the reduction of working hours are increased **productivity** and the concern of the **trade unions** to distribute between the same number (or a growing number) of employees the declining amount of labour required. The goal of most member organizations of the **German Federation of Trade Unions** is the 35-hour week. In the printing and metal industries this goal will be reached by the year 1995.

In 1989, 5 per cent. of all full-time employees worked fewer than 35 hours per week, 62 per cent. worked 36-40 hours, 11 per cent. worked 41-45 hours and 21 per cent. worked 45 hours or more, showing that there is also a wish among employees themselves for shorter working hours. The trend is further encouraged by levels of income which enable the working population to forgo the pay corresponding to a 40-hour week without lowering their standard of living. Companies, on the other hand, are anxious to utilize their full plant capacity and to maintain or extend operating time. In addition, in many branches of the economy there is a shortage of employees possessing the necessary skills. Consequently, companies are directing their efforts at adapting the shorter working hours won by the unions to their own needs by means of a **flexibilization** of working hours, in some cases involving differentiation between certain employee groups. In addition to **rationalization**, this has resulted in stronger demands for more extensive use of **shiftwork** and **weekend work**.

Reduction of working hours is a commonly used method of relieving the stress on employees whose work is particularly arduous. It means more leisure, but also the opportunity to enhance existing skills or acquire new ones.

Part-time work represents a special form of reduced working hours. As distinct from the reduction of general working hours by collective agreement, in the case of part-time work normal working hours shorter than those of full-time employees are agreed under the contract of employment. **Short-time working** is not classed under the heading of reduction of working hours.

93. **ARBEITSZEITVORSCHRIFTEN — REGULATIONS ON WORKING HOURS**: Laws and decrees imposing restrictions on working time. In quantitative terms, the most important are the following: the Working Time Statute (Arbeitszeitordnung) with amending law and implementing regulations, the Shop Closing Hours Act (Ladenschlussgesetz) with supplementary regulations, the Maternity Protection Act (Mutterschutzgesetz), the Youth Employment Protection Act (Jugend-arbeitsschutzgesetz), the Federal Career Public Servants Act (Bundesbeamtengesetz), and the Industrial Code (Gewerbeordnung) with special provisions on exceptions to **rest on Sundays and public holidays**. In addition, there are special regulations for other particular groups of employees (*e.g.* bakers, drivers), for dangerous establishments and forms of work (*e.g.*

the steel industry) and for the hotel and catering industry, and separate provisions under the laws of individual Länder. Within the limits fixed by all these regulations, **working time** is also regulated by collective agreement.

94. **ArbG**: Labour Court (Arbeitsgericht) of first instance. See **system of labour courts**.

95. **ARREST — DISTRAINT ORDER**: See **interlocutory injunction**.

96. **AUFENTHALTSBERECHTIGUNG—RIGHT OF ABODE**:
Right of abode (Aliens Act § 27) is granted to **aliens** who:
   1. have possessed a **residence permit** for eight years or, after being granted authorization to stay (**permission to reside**), have possessed an indefinite residence permit for three years;
   2. lawfully provide their own means of living;
   3. have paid minimum contributions to the statutory pension scheme or some other form of old-age pension insurance;
   4. have not been convicted of any offence during the last three years; and
   5. in whose case the other grounds for the grant of a residence permit apply.

   In special cases the minimum period for the possession of a residence permit is shortened to five years. For couples who live together as husband and wife, it suffices if the economic requirements are satisfied by one of the spouses.

   The right of abode is not subject to any geographical restrictions or time limit and also may not carry any conditions or obligations. Its holders do not need a **work permit**.

97. **AUFENTHALTSERLAUBNIS — RESIDENCE PERMIT**:
Permission to reside is granted in the form of a residence permit if an **alien** is permitted to live in the Federal Republic without restriction to any particular purpose (Aliens Act §§ 15-26). Special requirements apply for the subsequent admittance of spouses, family members, children and aliens who as minors were formerly habitually resident in the Federal Republic. There are other separate regulations for employees who are EC nationals.

98. **AUFENTHALTSGENEHMIGUNG — PERMISSION TO RESIDE**: All **aliens** living in the Federal Republic must have permission to reside (Aliens Act § 3). It is granted in the form of a **residence permit** and the **right of abode**, and in the form of leave to stay for a limited period and for a specific purpose and authorization to stay for reasons under international law or

urgent humanitarian reasons and also by reason of the political interests of the Federal Republic.

The grant of permission to reside is normally subject to the conditions that there should be no grounds for deportation or other reason for refusal and that the alien concerned should be able lawfully to provide their own means of living. Permission to reside may be subject to a time limit and geographical restrictions.

99. **AUFLÖSUNGSANTRAG — APPLICATION FOR DISSOLUTION**: See **application for protection against dismissal, compensation for job loss.**

100. **AUFSICHTSRAT — SUPERVISORY BOARD**: Under company law, the supervisory board is a **company organ** which is required in the case of registered co-operative societies (eG) and public limited companies (AG); is obligatory in the case of private limited companies (GmbH) only if certain preconditions apply; and is optional in all other cases. Its essential function is to supervise the way in which the business is managed. It represents the company in dealings with the **management board** and possesses the authority to appoint and remove the members of that board. The size of the supervisory board varies according to the size of the company and, if the company is subject to **co-determination**, to the form this has to take. The board appoints a chairperson and vice-chairperson from among its members and meets at least once a year. Only natural persons who do not form part of the company management may be members of the supervisory board. They are appointed from among the society members, **shareholders** or company members at the general meeting, **shareholders' meeting** or **company general meeting** and, in companies subject to co-determination, from among the employees (using various methods of election). Of all the employee representatives on the supervisory boards of companies subject to co-determination, some 80 per cent. are members of trade unions affiliated to the **German Federation of Trade Unions** .

101. **AUFWENDUNGSERSATZ — REIMBURSEMENT OF EXPENSES**: See **employer liability, expenses.**

102. **AUSBILDENDER — VOCATIONAL TRAINING EMPLOYER**: The other partner, with the **vocational trainee**, in the formation of a **vocational training relationship**. As the person who selects another for vocational training, the "Ausbildender" is usually the employer. Although employers who are parties to vocational training relationships must

personally fulfil certain qualifying requirements, they need not necessarily carry out the training themselves but can appoint a **vocational training instructor** for the purpose.

103. **AUSBILDER — VOCATIONAL TRAINING INSTRUCTOR**: An employer who is a party to a vocational training relationship can appoint a training instructor to be responsible for providing the actual training for a **vocational trainee**. This training instructor must possess the necessary professional qualifications; there are differing regulations on the relevant requirements for industry and for the small-scale crafts and trades sector.

104. **AUSBILDUNGSVERBUND — JOINT TRAINING SYSTEM**: Term used to indicate a form of co-operation between establishments and public authorities for the joint provision of training in listed occupations recognized as requiring formal training. The very nature of such a system means that more of the training may be given in other establishments than within the establishment where the trainee has entered into a vocational training relationship with the **vocational training employer**. There is no objection to this, provided that the latter is still able to exert a significant influence on the manner in which the training is carried out. If this is not the case, the other establishments concerned are classed as external training centres, in which **vocational training** may be carried out only if this is both necessitated by the training itself and permitted under the training regulations.

105. **AUSBILDUNGSVERGÜTUNG — VOCATIONAL TRAINING PAY**: An employer who has entered into a **vocational training relationship** with a vocational trainee must pay the trainee an appropriate level of training pay (Vocational Training Act § 10). The pay must increase at least annually with the trainee's age and as the training progresses. Any **non-pay benefits** counted as part of it, such as board and lodging, may not amount in value to more than 75 per cent. of the pay. If trainees work for more than the regular daily working hours they are entitled to adequate extra pay. If, as an exception, trainees have worked on Sundays or public holidays as permitted by law, within certain limits they can also demand time off in lieu. Trainees are also entitled to receive their pay for the time during which they have to be released from work to attend **vocational training school**.

Vocational training pay is frequently regulated by collective agreement. The amount varies widely in different occupations.

In 1990, for example, it ranged from approximately 210 Deutschmarks in the first year of training in dressmaking (280 Deutschmarks in the third year) up to approximately 1,100 Deutschmarks in the third year of training in the construction industry. It must be paid no later than on the last working day of each month. In the event of **illness**, vocational trainees continue to receive their pay for up to six weeks.

It is important to distinguish vocational training pay from the training grant as provided for under the Work Promotion Act, which is not a form of remuneration.

106. **AUSGLEICHSABGABE — COMPENSATORY TAX**: See **Central Agency for the Disabled, protection for disabled employees**.

107. **AUSGLEICHSQUITTUNG — QUITTANCE ACKNOWLEDGING SETTLEMENT**: Document in which employees who are leaving their jobs both acknowledge receipt of their **employment documents** and attest that they have no outstanding claims against the employer. In the interests of the employee, such a waiver, particularly of the assertion of any entitlement to **remuneration** that may arise, is valid only within narrow limits. The question of which claims are covered by the quittance depends on the mutual intention of employer and employee or on the true meaning of the quittance, which is determined by how the employee could have construed it. This, in turn, is established by **interpretation**. Unless further claims are expressly listed in the document, the general rule is that only **wage** and **salary** entitlements are covered by the quittance. As a matter of principle, the employee's right to make an **application for protection against dismissal** and to assert retrospective entitlements to retirement pay or **continued payment of remuneration** remains unaffected.

108. **AUSHILFSARBEITSVERHÄLTNIS — CASUAL EMPLOYMENT RELATIONSHIP**: An employment relationship that is entered into in order to meet a temporary increase in staffing requirements. If the employer's need for "casual" labour is continuous, a casual employment contract is not permissible and a normal employment relationship must be entered into. A casual employment relationship may be for a limited period only. If so, its effect in law is governed by the rules on **fixed-term employment relationships**.

Frequently, the purpose of a casual employment relationship is merely to accommodate either temporary or **"marginal" part-time workers**. The conditions for exemption from social security in these cases are regulated in the **Social Security Code IV**.

59

109. AUSLÄNDER — ALIEN: Any person who is not a German within the meaning of the **Basic Law**. In addition to German citizens, people not classed as aliens also include ethnic German refugees or exiles, together with their spouses and children, who have been admitted to the territory of the German Reich within the borders as at December 31, 1937.

Under the statutory provisions on aliens, a distinction is made between privileged and non-privileged aliens. Privileged aliens occupy a preferential position in terms of substantive or procedural law. This category includes stateless aliens or foreign refugees and nationals of EC Member States. A non-privileged alien is any alien who is subject to the general statutory provisions on aliens, and hence has to make an individual application for **permission to reside** and for a **work permit**.

110. AUSLÄNDERBEHÖRDE — PUBLIC AUTHORITY RESPONSIBLE FOR ALIENS: Normally the authorities of the internal administration at district or city borough level. Their powers include material jurisdiction over the allocation of **residence permits** and the **right of abode**. In addition, they decide on all measures concerning aliens. The legal process for appeal against their decisions is via the **system of administrative courts**.

They do not, however, have jurisdiction over the allocation of **work permits**, which lies with the local **Employment Office** and, in the event of legal dispute, the **system of social security courts**.

111. AUSLÄNDISCHE ARBEITNEHMER — FOREIGN WORKERS: The general principle is that, in order to take up employment in the Federal Republic, foreign workers must possess, in addition to a valid passport or alternative authentication, a **residence permit** or the **right of abode** and a **work permit**. The rules do not apply in this form to employees who are EC nationals, who in this respect are able to avail themselves of the **freedom of movement for workers**.

At one time, mainly in the 1960s, foreign workers were recruited by the Federal Employment Service, on the basis of recruitment agreements with a number of countries (**guest worker**). Agreements of this kind still exist today with Italy, Spain, Greece, Portugal, Morocco, Yugoslavia, Tunisia and Turkey. Official recruitment has since been discontinued. The fact that numbers still continued to increase slightly until 1980 was essentially due to the freedom of movement for workers between EC Member States. In the mid-1980s the Federal Government set about reducing the number of foreign workers

(Turkish workers in particular) by means of repatriation schemes. As a result of these measures, some 100,000 foreign workers returned to their native countries. In 1989 there were approximately 1.7 million foreign workers living in the Federal Republic, and in all about 4.9 million aliens.

112. **AUSLEGUNG — INTERPRETATION**: Legal rules often contain blanket clauses with undefined legal concepts. Rules and agreements are also sometimes ambiguous. It is the function of **case law,** through the process of interpretation by the courts, to give a precise definition of the content of blanket clauses or ambiguous rules or agreements. In interpreting a rule the court starts by seeking to draw inferences from the wording and tenor of the statute or agreement. After a historical interpretation of the rule, an attempt is finally made to translate into practice what was the original intention when it was drafted. If by following this process the court hearing a case arrives at a decision that is a precedent not covered by the wording of the rule, it constitutes **further development of the law**.

113. **AUSSCHLIESSLICHE GESETZGEBUNGSKOMPETENZ — EXCLUSIVE LEGISLATIVE POWERS**: The exclusive legislative powers of the Federation are definitively regulated in Article 73 of the **Basic Law**. On the basis of interpretation of the Constitution these exclusive powers can be extended, under restrictive conditions, by powers accruing to the Federation from the nature of the subject-matter or by virtue of connection with the subject-matter, both of these being the so-called "Annexkompetenz" (powers of accrual). In the areas of regulation that are assigned specifically to the Federation, the legislative bodies of the individual **Länder** have no right to legislate; should a Land law nevertheless be enacted, it is null and void. Although the **Federal Parliament** can empower the Länder by Federal statute to regulate for themselves a matter that is assigned exclusively to the Federation, this has no significance in practice. Rather, the constitutional reality is marked by growing dominance on the part of the Federal legislature.

114. **AUSSCHLUSSFRIST — TIME LIMIT**: Term referring to a strict time limit (specified in a **collective agreement** or **contract of employment**) which has the effect of making the enforcement of a claim dependent on its being asserted by a contracting party within a set period. Once this period has expired, the claim lapses irrevocably.

To ensure that claims arising from the contract of employment are settled speedily, almost all **framework agreements on employment conditions** specify a strict time limit regulated in what are called expiry clauses ("Verfallklauseln"). If under the collectively agreed rules all reciprocal claims arising from the employment relationship are subject to the set period, the time limit applies not only to claims arising from a collective agreement but also to statutory claims and claims arising from the individual contract of employment. However, the basic circumstances of the employee that determine contractual status, such as entitlement to a grading appropriate to the job or entitlement to the provision of a retirement pension (pension expectation), remain exempt. The expiry clause usually specifies the point at which the set period starts, *e.g.* when a claim first comes into being, is assessed or reaches maturity, or when the employment relationship is terminated. If this is not expressly specified, the date of maturity of the claim is the deciding factor in cases of doubt.

Time limits, which apply even if the parties to a contract of employment are unaware of them, must be automatically observed by the Labour Courts.

115. **AUSSCHLUSSKLAUSEL — EXCLUSION CLAUSE**: Exclusion clauses in collective agreements prohibit the employer from granting certain collectively agreed privileges to **non-union members**.

The exclusion clause is a form of **differential treatment clause** and is therefore, like the latter, held by the **Federal Labour Court** to be unlawful. The question of whether a provision in a collective agreement is to be deemed an exclusion clause is determined by **interpretation**.

116. **AUSSCHREIBUNG — JOB ADVERTISEMENT**: A written invitation from an employer to people at large, or to a particular group of people, to apply for a job. It usually indicates the post to be filled, the date when employment is to start and the skills required. An advertisement is not necessarily mandatory, except in the case of **career public servants** ("Beamte"), but the **works council** may require that all job vacancies in an **establishment**, or those for particular jobs, must be advertised. A **works agreement** on the internal advertisement of job vacancies is the usual form of participation by the works council in **human resource planning**.

Job advertisements must not be worded in a gender-specific manner and may be restricted to men or to women only in cases where membership of that particular sex is a genuine occupational qualification for the nature of the work. The works council has the duty of monitoring the employer's observance of this ban on discrimination, but infringements do not give the council the right to refuse its consent to an appointment. Only applicants who have themselves suffered prejudice as a result can effect a penalty, in the form of a claim for compensation. The amount of compensation is based on the wasted expenditure incurred or on a month's pay, in so far as the applicant's individual rights are affected. If a job is advertised publicly through advertisements in the press, these are deemed to be merely an invitation to submit applications to the employer, and there is no entitlement to reimbursement of the **costs of attending for interview**.

117. **AUSSENDIENSTMITARBEITER — FIELD WORK-FORCE**: Employees who do not perform their work at a fixed workplace but (as in the case, for example, of a **commercial representative**) are engaged in visiting customers are classed as members of the field workforce. Their employment relationships are often characterized by the fact that the **scheduling of working time** differs from that for jobs tied to a fixed location and that they are paid **expenses** to cover their expenditure.

118. **AUSSENSEITER — NON-UNION MEMBER**: Term (with the literal meaning of "outsider") used in the industrial relations field to refer to employees who are not union members and hence not covered by **collective agreements**. In principle, they cannot claim entitlements arising from a collective agreement, since its **normative provisions** do not apply to non-union members. However, the **parties to a collective agreement** can agree that non-organized employees are to receive equal treatment ("Aussenseiterklausel", *i.e.* non-member clause, in a collective agreement). Also, an equal treatment arrangement can be made expressly or impliedly between employer and employee which grants the employee entitlement under the contract of employment to the collectively agreed rates of pay. Lastly, non-organized employees can be included in the scope of application of a collective agreement through the procedure of **extension of collective agreements**.

In 1989 just on 8 million employees were directly covered by collective agreements; but approximately 18.5 million were covered indirectly, because of arrangements under individual contracts of employment, actual practice, or the extension procedure.

The **trade unions** cannot exert pressure on non-organized employees to become union members, since this would be an infringement of their **"negative" freedom of association**. However, since they have an interest in giving preference to their members (whose contributions finance union activities) and so giving non-organized employees more incentive to join, the unions seek to persuade them to do so by means of **closed shop clauses**, **exclusion clauses** and **differential treatment clauses**.

119. **AUSSERBETRIEBLICHE AUSBILDUNGSSTÄTTE — EXTERNAL TRAINING CENTRE**: See **joint training system**.

120. **AUSSERDIENSTLICHES VERHALTEN — CONDUCT IN PRIVATE LIFE**: As a general principle, conduct in private life is the employee's personal concern and has no effect on the **employment relationship**. From the point of view of possible repercussions of private conduct on an individual's employment, a distinction is made according to the category and function of the employee concerned. For instance, the criteria normally applied to **career public servants** ("Beamte"), to **white-collar workers** occupying senior posts and positions of trust and to employees in a **"Tendenzbetrieb"** are different from those applied to other employees. Otherwise, however, conduct outside working hours is relevant only if it seriously disrupts peaceful relations within the establishment or has a direct bearing on the employment relationship (*e.g.* drunken driving in the case of a professional driver, or a finance-related offence in the case of a bank cashier).

121. **AUSSERORDENTLICHE KÜNDIGUNG — SUMMARY TERMINATION**: "Extraordinary" termination of a contractual relationship without (in contrast to "ordinary" termination with notice) observing the due **period of notice**, and usually without any notice. In the cases where it is permissible, summary termination enables the contracting parties to extricate themselves immediately from particularly severe hardships arising from the contract. Since in the case of an **employment relationship** an abrupt termination can result in severe difficulties for the other party to the contract, in this context unilateral summary termination is permitted only if there is just cause. The circumstances must be such that the party terminating the contract cannot reasonably be expected to continue the employment relationship until the period of notice has expired (Civil Code § 626). Whether this is in fact the case is decided by careful balancing of the respective interests of the parties concerned. In this procedure the **proportionality principle** applies, *i.e.* unilateral summary termination is permissible only if no more moderate remedy is available (such as a formal **warning, disciplinary sanction, dismissal for variation of**

contract or ordinary **termination with notice**) that can adequately safeguard the legitimate interests of the party terminating the contract.

For summary dismissal by the employer, most instances of just cause are where the employee is in fundamental breach of the contract of employment. These include, for example, refusal to perform the work due under the contract, persistent violations of the works rules, and criminal offences that have a bearing on the employment relationship. In some circumstances it can suffice if the employee is merely suspected of having committed a serious misdemeanour (**dismissal on grounds of suspicion**). The employee need not necessarily have been proved to be at fault, although this increases the gravity of the offence. Matters of this nature which justify summary dismissal by the employer are usually connected with the employee's person or conduct. Operational reasons connected with the establishment itself, such as a **substantial alteration to the establishment, closure** or **bankruptcy**, are part of the "**works risk**" that has to be borne by the employer and do not justify summary dismissal. **Dismissal under third-party pressure can**, however, also be held to be justified summary dismissal.

For the employee to terminate the employment relationship without due notice, instances of just cause include frequent or substantial default on the part of the employer in paying remuneration, and serious violations of the employer's **duty of care** such as endangering the employee's life or health. Wanting to leave immediately so as to be able to conclude a more favourable contract of employment elsewhere does not, however, constitute just cause for resignation without notice.

Unilateral summary termination of the employment relationship must be declared within a period of two weeks from the date when the party having just cause for terminating it first had reliable knowledge of such cause. In legal proceedings for an **application for protection against dismissal**, the employer summarily terminating the relationship must prove that the just cause exists and that this time limit has been observed.

122. **AUSSERTARIFLICHE ANGESTELLTE — WHITE-COLLAR WORKERS EXEMPT FROM COLLECTIVELY AGREED TERMS**: Concept comprising those white-collar workers (usually occupying senior posts) who are either explicitly excluded by the contracting parties from the **scope of normative provisions** (in which case they are "geborene", *i.e.* automatically exempt) or accorded this special status under their contract of employment (in which case they are "gekorene", *i.e.* chosen to be exempt). In the case of those who are automatically exempt,

the definition often refers to the particular position of **executive staff** in terms of participation law. Those who are chosen to be exempt by this being stipulated in their contract of employment cannot actually be excluded from the body of employees covered by a collective agreement, but their status usually brings them special privileges, for example with respect to **occupational pension schemes** or in the form of attractive **non-pay benefits**.

123. **AUSSPERRUNG — LOCK-OUT**: A tactical decision by one or more **employers**, in the context of a **labour dispute**, to deny the possibility of work and payment of remuneration to a group of employees without prior termination of their contracts of employment.

A lock-out may occur in various forms. If a number of employers impose a lock-out on the initiative of the **employers' association** responsible for collective bargaining, this constitutes an association-level lock-out. Depending on its extent, a distinction is made between a total lock-out and a partial or selective lock-out. In the former case, all the employees in a given establishment or collective bargaining region are denied the possibility of work. In the second case, the lock-out is confined to certain employees in the establishment or to certain establishments within the region affected by the dispute.

The **Federal Constitutional Court**, in its decision of June 6, 1991 confirming the position adopted by the Federal Labour Court, has ruled that a lock-out is a lawful defensive weapon for employers against **strikes** but is permissible only to the extent that it is necessary to ensure workable collective bargaining autonomy, that is, keeps within the bounds of the **proportionality principle**. Hence, constitutional protection is given only to appropriate defensive lock-outs; an offensive lock-out which initiates a labour dispute without prior industrial action on the part of employees is, on the contrary, unlawful.

According to the Federal Labour Court, the only situation in which a defensive lock-out is lawful is where it is imposed in retaliation against **partial or selective strikes** in order to avert the danger of such strikes seriously undermining the solidarity on the employers' side which is necessary for **association-level agreements**. The Court has ruled that the allowable extent of lock-out in such cases is governed by the extent of the strike action taken. If the strike is restricted to fewer than 25 per cent. of employees in the collective bargaining region concerned, a further 25 per cent. of employees may be locked out. If more than 25 per cent. of employees in the collective bargaining region concerned are on strike, the employers' need to extend the coverage of the dispute is correspondingly less. Consequently, in all no more than 50 per cent. of employees may be on strike or locked out. A lock-out which is directed only against the members of a striking union and exempts **non-union members** is unlawful, since it constitutes an infringement of the "positive" **freedom of association**.

At the level of the individual **contract of employment**, the general rule is that the lock-out has a suspensive effect: the main obligations stemming from the employment relationship, namely, the obligation on one party to perform work and the obligation on the other to pay remuneration, are suspended.

If a lock-out is unlawful, the employees affected retain their entitlement to remuneration in accordance with the Civil Code § 615. In addition, it gives rise (as in the case of strikes) to claims for default and compensation. It also constitutes just cause for employees who are affected to terminate the employment relationship without notice.

124. **AUSWAHLRICHTLINIEN — GUIDELINES FOR PER-SONNEL SELECTION**: See **personnel selection**.

125. **AUSZUBILDENDER — VOCATIONAL TRAINEE**: The vocational trainee and the **vocational training employer** are the parties to the formation of a **vocational training relationship**. The trainee is the party who receives training. If trainees are minors, it is necessary to obtain the consent of their legal representative to the conclusion of the contract. The trainee's rights and obligations are regulated by the vocational training relationship. Individuals receiving **work experience**, **unpaid trainees** and **casual student workers** are not vocational trainees within the meaning of the law.

126. **AuT**: See **"Work and Technology" Action Programme** (Aktionsprogramm "Arbeit und Technik").

127. **AZO**: Arbeitszeitordnung (Working Time Statute). See **maximum working hours**.

B

128. **BAG**: Bundesarbeitsgericht (Federal Labour Court). See **system of labour courts**.

129. **BAT**: Bundesangestelltentarifvertrag (National Agreement for Public Sector White-Collar Workers). See **public service**.

130. **BDA**: See **Confederation of German Employers' Associations** (Bundesvereinigung Deutscher Arbeitgeberverbände).

131. **BDI**: See **Confederation of German Industry** (Bundesverband der Deutschen Industrie).

132. **BEAMTE — CAREER PUBLIC SERVANTS**: According to constitutional law, the special category of employees known as "Beamte", *i.e.* career public servants, are individuals who are appointed (**appointment of career public servants**) by the state (the Federal Government or the authorities of the individual Länder), a **municipality** or other **legal persons** under public law, by being given a letter of appointment containing the words "appointed to the **career public service relationship**". They have the benefit of a special, state-administered **duty of care** on the part of their **public sector employer**, in respect of whom they, in turn, are subject to a special **duty of loyalty**. Appointment to the career public service relationship is permissible only in order to take on **sovereign functions** of public administration or functions which, for reasons of national security or particular importance for public life, cannot be entrusted exclusively to individuals who are employed in an employment relationship under private law.

133. **BEAMTENERNENNUNG — APPOINTMENT OF CAREER PUBLIC SERVANTS**: In contrast to other employees, whose employment relationship is founded in a synallagmatic contract under private law, **career public servants** ("Beamte") are appointed by sovereign act. Such appointment establishes the nature and substance of their legal status. This applies both to the initial formation of a **career public service relationship** and to the conversion of an existing one into one of a different type. Appointment is manifested outwardly in the presentation of a letter of appointment, the form of which must comply with the Career Public Service Framework Act (Beamtenrechtsrahmengesetz). In the Career Regulations (**career branch**) the formation of the career public service relationship is referred to as "engagement". Appointment is based on an assessment of qualifications, aptitude and technical proficiency.

Gender, lineage, race, beliefs, religious or political convictions and background or connections may not, as such, be taken into account. In the recent past the question of political convictions was handled differently, via the practice of **occupational bans**.

As a form of positive action for the **advancement of women**, the question of whether women should be given preferential consideration for appointment is the subject of growing debate.

134. **BEAMTENPENSION — CAREER PUBLIC SERVICE RETIREMENT PENSION**: See **statutory retirement pension**.

135. **BEAMTENSTREIK — STRIKE BY CAREER PUBLIC SERVANTS**: Although **career public servants** ("Beamte") have the right to form a **collective industrial organization**, the Administrative Courts have ruled that they do not have the right to **strike**. The **Federal Constitutional Court** denies them both the right to strike and the right of refusal (in a form similar to a strike) to perform their duties, on the grounds of the basic principles of **career public service**. This prohibition safeguards the proper functioning of the state and its administrative authorities (**reservation of career public service functions**). It means that any form of refusal to perform their duties that has the nature of industrial action, such as a **work-to-rule**, is also prohibited. The courts also recognize that, in the event of strikes by manual and white-collar workers in the public service, career public servants may be used as **strikebreakers** and must obey instructions to that effect. Nevertheless, this ban on strikes by career public servants is the target of growing criticism. Apart from the fact that the career public service in its traditional mould is itself being widely called into question, a ban on striking is in any case not felt to be its inevitable corollary. For instance, in 1989 large numbers of unionized career public servants (teachers) in several Länder withdrew their labour in order to press home their demands for shorter working hours.

136. **BEAMTENVERHÄLTNIS — CAREER PUBLIC SERVICE RELATIONSHIP**: The legal relationship that exists between **career public servants** ("Beamte") and their **public sector employer**. To that extent it is the equivalent in public law to an **employment relationship** under private law, and it enshrines the rights and obligations applicable to the parties concerned. Its legal basis is career public service law in the sense of the entire body of statutory provisions that regulate the legal relationships of career public servants. These are, essentially, the Federal Career Public Servants Act (Bundesbeamtengesetz), the Career Public Servants' Pensions Act (Beamtenversorgungsgesetz)

(employer's **duty of care**), the Federal Career Public Service Pay Act (Bundesbesoldungsgesetz) (**pay**), the Federal Disciplinary Code (Bundesdisziplinarordnung) (**disciplinary law**), and the Federal Decree on Career Branches (Bundeslaufbahnverordnung) (**career branch**). These laws relate to **federal career public servants**. Corresponding legislation at Land level, plus the Career Public Service Framework Act (Beamtenrechtsrahmengesetz), applies to **career public servants at Land level.**

137. **BEAMTENVORBEHALT — RESERVATION OF CAREER PUBLIC SERVICE FUNCTIONS**: Under the **Basic Law**, the permanent performance of **sovereign functions** of public administration may be entrusted only to members of the **public service** who are bound by a public-law relationship of service and loyalty. This qualifying condition is met by **career public servants** and also, according to the overwhelming weight of opinion, by **white-collar workers bound by special service regulations** employed in social security institutions. It is not, however, met by other public-sector manual workers and white-collar workers, who are essentially restricted to the railways, postal services, energy sector and public services and utilities. This reservation of functions is seen as an institutional guarantee of the **career public service.**

138. **BEDINGTES ARBEITSVERHÄLTNIS — CONDITIONAL EMPLOYMENT RELATIONSHIP**: The Federal Labour Court has ruled that, owing to the uncertainty it creates for the employee, a condition of avoidance in the contract of employment (*i.e.* a condition which operates to bring the **employment relationship** to an end if specified circumstances occur) is in principle unlawful and therefore invalid. The employee cannot be made to shoulder the entrepreneurial risk in this way.

The following example may serve as an illustration. If an employer concludes an arrangement with **guest workers** whereby the employment relationship is automatically terminated if they fail to report back for work on the first day after annual holidays spent visiting their native country, this is deemed to be invalid, since it does not allow control by the courts as provided for under protection against dismissal.

139. **BEFÖRDERUNG — PROMOTION**: In general, any improvement in employment position. Technically, promotion in the case of **career public servants** (''Beamte'') denotes appointment to a different post with a higher final basic salary. As a rule, this involves a change of official title. Promotion is

usually carried out subject to evidence of satisfactory performance by the candidate; the regulations on the **appointment of career public servants** apply by analogy. Promotion to certain posts is not possible until a minimum length of service has been completed.

140. **BEFRISTETES ARBEITSVERHÄLTNIS — FIXED-TERM EMPLOYMENT RELATIONSHIP**: As a general principle, setting a fixed term to an employment relationship is lawful. However, in order to curb evasion of regulations on employee protection, judicial decisions by the labour courts have imposed severe restrictions on the circumstances in which it is permitted to enter into a fixed-term employment relationship. For such a relationship to be valid, it must not be designed to evade the provisions on protection against dismissal and there must be a justifying reason for its limitation in time. Such a reason is, for example, recognized in the case of **probationary, seasonal** and **casual employment relationships** and of contracts with theatrical performers, musicians and junior academics. The duration of a fixed-term employment relationship must be in keeping with the reason that underlies it. Reasons which do not stem from the actual employment relationship itself but are connected with economic and labour market policy are generally not recognized as constituting justification. The fact that the future allocation of budget funds (*e.g.* in local government) is uncertain is therefore not sufficient reason. In the case of **consecutive short-term contracts**, there is a presumption against substantive justification for setting a fixed term.

Under the **Improvement of Employment Opportunities Act** that was passed in 1985 and extended in 1989, for the period up to December 31, 1995 the necessity of a substantive reason has been removed and a fixed term of up to 18 months has been pronounced permissible if an employee is a new recruit or if, on completion of vocational training, an employee can only continue to be employed on a temporary basis because there is no vacancy available for a permanent employee. In addition, an employer who has been in business for no more than six months and who employs no more than 20 employees is permitted to specify a fixed term of 24 months for contracts of employment. In making these provisions the legislators were motivated by a policy of assisting the labour market.

The burden of proof as regards the presence of a justifying reason or the preconditions imposed by the Improvement of Employment Opportunities Act rests upon the employer. If a fixed term has been set unlawfully, the legal consequence is not that the contract of employment becomes invalid, but that the employment relationship is treated as if an open-ended contract had been concluded. The fixed term that was specified then becomes a minimum duration for the employment relationship, and during this minimum duration the only form of termination possible is **summary termination** for just cause.

141. **BEITRAGSBEMESSUNGSGRENZE — INCOME LIMIT FOR CHARGEABLE CONTRIBUTIONS**: See **social security contribution**.

142. **BELEGSCHAFT — WORKFORCE**: The entire body of manual workers and white-collar workers employed in an **establishment** or **company**.

143. **BEREITSCHAFTSDIENST — STAND-BY**: Outside working hours, an employee who is on stand-by remains at a place specified by the employer, in order to undertake work if the need should arise. It differs from **on-call** duty in that an employee who is on stand-by does not need to be in a state of alertness. The payment due from the employer in return for stand-by duty is usually regulated in collective agreements; these generally stipulate that stand-by duty should attract remuneration, which may be in the form of a flat-rate payment. Extra time off is also provided for in many instances. When employees have had to work while on stand-by and are then prevented by the **regulations on working hours** from also working their normal **shift**, the question of whether or not they lose their pay entitlement for the latter is also regulated by collective agreement.

144. **BERGMANNSVERSORGUNGSSCHEIN — MINER'S PROTECTION CERTIFICATE**: Owing to the particular dangers associated with the occupation of miner, special protection is provided in Lower Saxony, North Rhine-Westphalia and Saarland for miners who, after having been employed in the mining industry for some considerable time, are unable to continue working underground or would incur the risk of total premature disability if they were to do so. This protection is provided for in the legislation of the individual Länder via a miner's protection certificate. In Lower Saxony holders of such certificates are treated as **disabled persons**; in North Rhine-Westphalia and Saarland the legislation provides a separate form of social protection, but this too is modelled on **protection for disabled employees**: for instance, these certificate holders likewise enjoy special protection against dismissal.

145. BERUFSAUSBILDUNG — VOCATIONAL TRAINING: Vocational training is organized as a **dual system,** *i.e.* **company vocational training** is combined with **statutory vocational training** in a **vocational training school**.

146. BERUFSAUSBILDUNGSVERHÄLTNIS — VOCATIONAL TRAINING RELATIONSHIP: A vocational training relationship comes into being between the **vocational training employer** and the **vocational trainee** when they conclude a vocational training contract. Training employers are under an obligation to provide trainees with a comprehensive, predominantly practical training in the recognized occupation that the trainees have chosen. They are also responsible for seeing that trainees attend the **vocational training school** and for releasing them from work for this purpose, while continuing to pay them their **vocational training pay**. Employers must also make the necessary equipment and materials available to trainees. Trainees, for their part, must endeavour to acquire the knowledge and skills needed in order to practise the recognized occupation they have chosen. They must fill in a record book supplied by their employer on the progress of their training. They are under an obligation to keep trade and business secrets, *i.e.* to observe a **restraint on competition**. A special feature of the training period, which is up to three years in duration, is the statutorily regulated probationary period: the **probationary employment relationship** lasts for no less than one month and no more than three months. The vocational training relationship automatically comes to an end on completion of the training period or when the final examination has been successfully passed. During the probationary period, the vocational training relationship can be terminated by either party at any time without observing a period of notice. Once the probationary period has been completed, however, the training employer may dismiss the trainee only for just cause. Apart from this **summary termination**, a trainee who does not wish to continue receiving training in the occupation concerned can terminate the vocational training relationship by giving a four-week **period of notice**. In addition, the legal assumption is that the provisions of labour law also apply to the vocational training relationship.

147. BERUFSAUSÜBUNGSFREIHEIT — FREEDOM OF OCCUPATIONAL PRACTICE: Freedom in arranging the content, extent, form and means of practising an occupation constitutes part of the **freedom of occupation** enshrined in Article 12 of the **Basic Law**. It can be regulated by statute or by government provisions based on a statute. A great many government rules have a regulatory effect on the way in which an occupation may be practised; these include, notably, the whole of **commercial law** and **labour law**. The Basic Law allows the legislators extensive freedom here for shaping economic policy.

The rules must, however, conform with the **proportionality principle**, *i.e.* any such regulations must be imposed by the legislators for material reasons that are in the public interest, they must be appropriate and necessary to the achievement of the aim in view and their negative consequences for the individuals who are subject to them must be justified by the aims at which they are directed.

148. BERUFSBEAMTENTUM — CAREER PUBLIC SERVICE: The career public service is guaranteed as an institution in the **Constitution** (Basic Law, Article 33 (5)). Its historical development dates back to the 17th century, when the sovereign rulers of the time, in the process of establishing a higher administration, created a service relationship fashioned unilaterally by the sovereign and founded on a special notion of performance of duty. After the end of the First World War, in the Weimar Republic the duty to serve the common good came to the forefront as a special characteristic of **career public servants** (''Beamte''): the Weimar Constitution guaranteed the status of the career public servant as a servant of the state. Since then, this duty to serve the common good has been an important factor in shaping both the attitudes of career public servants themselves and the expectations of the general public.

The institutional guarantee of career public service simultaneously ensures its underlying structural principles, such as the fact that it is governed by public law and is entered into for life and hence constitutes a main or lifelong occupation, the principle of the **career branch**, the **duty of care** on the part of the **public sector employer**, and the entitlement to the appropriate pay for the post concerned.

Career public service imposes on ''Beamte'' a special **duty of loyalty** towards their public employer. Their eligibility requirements also include allegiance to the Constitution, and hence the will to obey all the provisions of the Constitution and a positive attitude towards its fundamental principles, which they must affirm by swearing an **oath of service**. To that extent, every applicant and career public servant is expected to be prepared at all times to demonstrate active support for the free and democratic constitutional order (**occupational bans**). Lastly, career public servants are under an obligation to exhibit obedience to their public employer and **superior official**, political discretion, official secrecy, and impartiality (politically and otherwise) in performing the duties of their office. The basic principles of career public service axiomatically prohibit **strikes by career public servants**.

149. **BERUFSBILDUNGSWERK — VOCATIONAL TRAINING UNIT**: Vocational training units are rehabilitation centres at supra-company and supra-regional level which provide initial training for disabled young people who, owing to the nature and severity of their handicap or disability, cannot be trained in general training establishments. The purpose is to give then a skilled qualification. As well as the necessary training resources, vocational training units are equipped with complementary social, medical and psychological services and leisure and sports facilities in order to provide the best possible training for the particular group being catered for. Residential accommodation is available for the disabled trainees, and each unit incorporates a **vocational training school**. There are at present 38 such units in the Federal Republic, providing some 10,000 training places.

150. **BERUFSFREIHEIT — FREEDOM OF OCCUPATION**: The **basic right** of freedom of occupation gives all Germans the right to choose freely their occupation, place of employment and place of training (**freedom of occupational choice**) and the right to practise their occupation freely within the provisions of the current legislation (**freedom of occupational practice**) and prohibits, with certain exceptions, enlistment by government bodies to perform **forced labour** (Basic Law, Article 12).

Freedom of occupation does not in itself predetermine any particular economic system (any more than the other provisions of the Basic Law do); however, by guaranteeing relatively extensive personal protection against forms of state intervention (**occupational bans, "steering" of the economy**) it does allow quite broad scope for individual independence in choosing and practising an occupation.

The legal effect of freedom of occupation is essentially limited to a defensive one. Only in a few instances has the **Federal Constitutional Court** ruled that it implies a personal claim against the state for material benefits; access to higher education is a notable example. It does not imply a right to work in the sense of an entitlement to employment or a claim for the institution of job creation schemes.

Freedom of occupation applies to all lawful activities that are carried on regularly in order to acquire the material means of living, irrespective of whether the work in question is done as an employee or on a self-employed basis. It is a right possessed not only by natural persons but also by companies with registered offices on German territory, provided that their activities are carried on for gainful purposes and that they serve to implement the freedom of the individuals who operate them. The greater the degree of personal participation on the part of such company members (as opposed to purely financial participation), the greater is the protective effect afforded here by freedom of occupation. Aliens are not able to invoke freedom of occupation as such, although they can invoke general freedom of action. Citizens of EC Member States, however, are provided by Community law with protection for freedom of occupation equivalent to that of German citizens.

151. **BERUFSGENOSSENSCHAFT — OCCUPATIONAL HEALTH AND SAFETY AGENCY**: The "Berufsgenossenschaften" are social **accident insurance** institutions which are organized by public-law agencies. They fall into three major groups: industrial, agricultural and maritime. Only employers are members of the Agencies.

152. **BERUFSHILFE — STATE OCCUPATIONAL ASSISTANCE**: Term used to refer to all forms of social **accident insurance** provision by which, following an **accident at work** or an **occupational illness**, insured individuals are given appropriate assistance to enable them to resume their former occupation or take up a different one, and to keep or obtain a job. Such assistance may take the form of **interim payments**, an **industrial injury pension**, reimbursement of travel costs, transport for the disabled, or domestic help in the home.

153. **BERUFSKRANKHEIT — OCCUPATIONAL ILLNESS**: To be classed as an occupational illness, an illness must be either one contracted by an individual covered by statutory **accident insurance** in the course of one of the activities named in the Reich Insurance Code (Reichsversicherungsordnung), or one of the illnesses listed in the Occupational Illnesses Decree (Berufskrankheitenverordnung) as amended up to December 8, 1976. For accident insurance purposes, an occupational illness is treated as an **accident at work**. In addition, for the purposes of paying compensation the **Occupational Health and Safety Agencies** are required to treat as an accident at work any case of illness which, although not named in the Decree, according to current medical knowledge is attributable to an employee's work.

Statistics from the Central Association of Industrial Occupational Health and Safety Agencies show that, of 39,706 cases of illness notified in 1986, only 3,317 were recognized as occupational illnesses. Also, in 1987 there were some 193,000 cases of premature retirement due to illness, over 50 per cent. of which (for men and women combined) involved conditions affecting the circulatory system, skeleton, muscles and connective tissue.

154. **BERUFSSCHULE — VOCATIONAL TRAINING SCHOOL**: **Statutory vocational training** takes place in vocational training schools. Compulsory attendance at these schools starts at the end of general compulsory schooling, and its duration differs in individual Länder. The schools give **vocational trainees** instruction in the predominantly theoretical aspects of particular occupations and also extend their general education. The employer is required to release trainees from work for the time during which they receive instruction at the vocational training school and also for a period of time specified in the Vocational Training Act for both preparing and finishing course work.

The employer is also responsible for a trainee's regular attendance at the vocational training school. In cases where instruction takes place on Saturdays the employer may require the trainee to work on all other working days in the week, but the trainee is then entitled to receive **overtime premium pay** from the employer.

155. **BERUFSUNFÄHIGKEIT — OCCUPATIONAL INCAPAC-ITY**: Occupational incapacity is deemed to exist when, as a result of **illness** or other impairment or diminution of their physical or mental faculties, an individual is left with less than 50 per cent. of the earning capacity, in suitable employment, of a comparable insured person with similar training and equivalent knowledge and skills. Suitable employment is taken to mean all types of work which are commensurate with the duration and nature of the individual's training and with the requirements of their former occupation and employment and which are actually possible for the individual to perform. Work for which they were re-trained is classed as suitable, but types of work that represent a loss of occupational status are not. The interpretation also depends on the existence of suitable jobs.

Formal assessment of occupational incapacity is made by the insurance institution (**statutory pension scheme**), on the basis of medical opinion. If it is confirmed the insured individual, subject to fulfilling the 60-month qualifying period, is entitled to an occupational incapacity pension.

156. **BERUFSVERBAND — OCCUPATIONAL UNION**: See **principle of industrial organization, principle of occupational organization**.

77

157. BERUFSVERBOT — OCCUPATIONAL BAN: Occupational bans are official edicts which prohibit individuals, or groups of people identified by certain characteristics, from practising a particular occupation. Such bans deprive those affected of the right to **freedom of occupational choice** and are therefore compatible with the **freedom of occupation** only within narrow limits.

Up till now, the Federal Constitutional Court has held that bans which debar all applicants or a certain group of applicants from practising an occupation are permissible only if their purpose is to provide protection that is demonstrably necessary for the group concerned, such as the ban on the employment of women as miners and the ban on **child employment**, or if they help to protect an existing public administration monopoly such as the monopoly in the provision of postal services and the monopoly of the Federal Employment Service in providing job placement services.

Bans affecting particular individuals are more common. The penalty for criminal offences connected with the practice of an occupation may include banning the offender from continuing to practise that occupation, either for a specified period or for life. For certain occupational groups, in the event of serious misdemeanour such a ban may also be imposed by the public authorities or (as in the case of the legal profession, for example) by a profession's own disciplinary body. The concept of the "Berufsverbot" or occupational ban became widely known not in connection with its legal meaning but in the context of the political debate on the debarring of so-called radicals, *i.e.* followers of extremist right-wing or (more usually) left-wing parties, from employment in the **public service**. The so-called Radicals Decree (Radikalenerlass) issued in 1972 by the Ministers-President of the **Länder** required all members of the public service to guarantee to demonstrate active support at all times for the free and democratic constitutional order within the meaning of the Basic Law. Membership or support of a political party seeking to change the existing constitutional order by lawful means was deemed to be incompatible with this, even in the case of individuals occupying minor posts in the public service unconnected with security who had been employed in them for some considerable time without occasioning complaints. The implementation of the Radicals Decree gave rise to heated controversy from the very outset. Particular criticism was levelled at the so-called routine investigation which was conducted by the Federal and Länder Offices for the Defence of the Constitution (Verfassungsschutz) as part of the procedure before the appointment of an applicant. Nowadays the Radicals Decree is rarely used.

158. **BERUFSWAHLFREIHEIT — FREEDOM OF OCCUPA-TIONAL CHOICE**: The right to choose an occupation freely without pressure from external influences forms part of **freedom of occupation** (Basic Law, Article 12). The existence of government regulations on **freedom of occupational practice** means that any form of government restriction on choice of occupation constitutes a particularly intrusive invasion of the freedom of the individual and is admissible only within narrow limits. A distinction is made between three basic instances:

1. Restrictions on access to particular occupations on the basis of subjective criteria relating to an individual's characteristics, such as examination results or personal attributes and qualities, are admissible only in so far as they are necessary to the proper performance of the occupation and are therefore deemed to be in the general interest. The legislators have broad discretionary scope as regards the definition of occupational profiles and hence the personal characteristics that applicants must possess in order to practise given occupations. Unjustifiably restrictive requirements may not, however, be imposed.

2. There are far stricter conditions governing the admissibility of restrictions based on objective criteria. These are restrictions relating to external realities over which the individual applicant has no control, such as imposing an upper limit on the number of people practising a given occupation (after the manner of the feudal "system of estates"). Such restrictions on access to an occupation are admissible only if they are necessary in order to protect particularly important assets of general interest, such as the nation's health, against serious dangers. One major area in which objective restrictions are applied is access to higher education. They may be imposed only if all available teaching capacity is being fully utilized. The decision as to whether this is actually so is subject to the authority of the **system of administrative courts**. In some fields of study a large proportion of students regularly avail themselves of administrative law channels to gain access to public higher education institutions that are refusing such access. These rules do not apply to private educational institutions.

3. **Occupational bans** ("Berufsverbote") that apply automatically to particular groups of people are required to satisfy very specific conditions.

159. **BERUFUNG — APPEAL**: Appeal is the **remedy at law** against decisions delivered by a Labour Court of first instance in the **"Urteil" procedure**. Appeals go before a Land Labour Court for decision, thus enabling a rehearing by the higher court in which a fresh statement of the facts is generally admissible. Appeal

79

is always allowable in disputes not relating to pecuniary rights, *i.e.* where the claim being pursued by legal action is not directed at money or objects of monetary value; in disputes relating to pecuniary rights it is allowable where the value of the cause of appeal exceeds 800 Deutschmarks and if the lower court gives leave to appeal, and in the event of a second judgment in default. For disputes heard by the **"Beschluss" procedure**, there is a corresponding **"Beschluss" procedure** appeal.

Appeal is also available in proceedings before the ordinary, social security and administrative courts in accordance with the relevant rules of procedure.

160. **BESCHÄFTIGUNGSFÖRDERUNGSGESETZ — IMPROVEMENT OF EMPLOYMENT OPPORTUNITIES ACT**: The Improvement of Employment Opportunities Act, which came into force on May 1, 1985, is an important regulatory instrument for the **flexibilization** and deregulation of labour relations. It tightened the conditions under which a works council is able to enforce a **"social plan"**, created outline regulations for the first time on **part-time work**, **job sharing**, and **"KAPOVAZ"**, extended from three to six consecutive months the permitted period for which agencies can hire out a temporary worker to the same third party in the context of the **hiring-out of labour**, and greatly extended the opportunities for employers to use **fixed-term employment relationships**. The relaxed provisions on fixed-term contracts and the period for hiring out temporary workers, which were originally intended to last only until 1990, have since been extended to December 31, 1995.

Another expression of the wish to create greater flexibility is the fact that the Act (§ 6) allows the minimum conditions stipulated in the statutory regulations on part-time work to be worsened by collective agreement. The decisions of the Federal Labour Court are not consistent on this matter. Whereas the Court's various divisions (also known as "senates") all concur in holding that § 6 does not allow part-time employees to be actually excluded from the group covered by the **scope of normative provisions**, collectively agreed unequal treatment of part-time employees as compared with full-time employees is held by one division (without further substantiation) to be lawful and by another (invoking the principle of **equal treatment**) to be unlawful.

161. **BESCHÄFTIGUNGSGESELLSCHAFT — JOB CREATION COMPANY**: An institution which offers skill training programmes and organizes **job creation schemes** for employees who are on **short-time working** or faced with **unemployment**.

The concept of the job creation company was developed and

pressed for by the **trade unions** as a transitional solution for companies affected by **structural change**. In eastern Germany job creation companies are being extensively subsidized; in most instances there they are established jointly by establishments faced with closure, the **municipalities** and educational institutions, and to some extent the unions. The **Treuhand Agency** also invests in holding companies for operating a job creation company. The purpose of job creation companies is to safeguard the income and upgrade the skills of the employees concerned. The high costs involved in establishing and operating them are felt to be justified, since the individuals concerned would otherwise be drawing **unemployment benefit** but without the opportunity of development training.

162. **BESCHÄFTIGUNGSVERBOT — EMPLOYMENT BAN**: Employment bans apply to potential employers of people who are subject to **occupational bans** ("Berufsverbote"), prohibiting such employers, reciprocally, from employing individuals or groups who are banned from performing that particular type of work.

This meaning of the term should not be confused with its other meaning of a restriction on **working time**, for instance on public holidays or at weekends.

163. **BESCHLUSSVERFAHREN — "BESCHLUSS" PROCEDURE**: In addition to cases where the Labour Courts rule on disputes in labour law by the **"Urteil" procedure**, for certain disputes they use the "Beschluss" procedure. These are disputes arising from the 1972 Works Constitution Act, the 1976 Co-Determination Act and the 1952 Works Constitution Act relating to the election of employee representatives to the supervisory board, and decisions on the **capacity to conclude collective agreements** and **collective bargaining jurisdiction** of employees' and employers' organizations.

This "Beschluss" procedure differs from the "Urteil" procedure in that there are no adversary parties, only interested parties. The employer, the employers' association, the works council and the trade union can be an interested party. Furthermore, it is up to the court itself to ascertain the underlying facts from the petitions of interested parties and to take evidence. No preliminary **conciliation hearing** (compulsory in the case of the "Urteil" procedure) is held, but in some instances a **compromise** is possible under the "Beschluss" procedure also. There are special rules on **legal costs**: with the "Beschluss" procedure there are no court fees, and in the case of a dispute between the employer and the works council the employer bears all other costs.

The **remedies at law** available in this procedure are the "**Beschluss**" **procedure appeal** and **judicial review application** or **direct judicial review application**.

"Beschluss" procedures are also used, in correspondingly different forms, in the ordinary, finance, social security and administrative courts.

164. **BESCHWERDE — "BESCHLUSS" PROCEDURE APPEAL**: Term used to refer, primarily, to the remedy at law against orders made by a Labour Court of first instance in the "**Beschluss**" **procedure**. Such appeals are heard by the relevant Land Labour Court. As with the remedy of **appeal** in the "**Urteil**" **procedure**, the interested parties can lay a new statement of the case before the higher court; in addition, it is up to the Land Labour Court itself to ascertain the facts afresh.

The same term is also used for the remedy at law against (subsidiary) decisions of the Labour Courts which, in particular, extend beyond the hearing of the main issue, such as orders to take evidence. Here too, the relevant Land Labour Court is the appellate court.

A number of procedural regulations provide for an immediate appeal subject to a time limit. It must be lodged within two weeks.

The remedy of "Beschluss" procedure appeal is also available under the rules of procedure for the ordinary, finance, social security and administrative courts.

165. **BESETZUNGSREGELUNGEN — STAFFING RULES**: Rules on staffing levels, which without exception are agreed in **collective agreements**, oblige the employer to employ a certain number of employees on certain machines (quantitative staffing rules) or to use for certain types of work only employees possessing a particular level of training (qualitative staffing rules). There is a long tradition of such rules in German collective bargaining practice: their use, initially in the printing industry and subsequently in other industries as well, dates back to the turn of the century. They are still widespread in the printing sector, where they are a way of stipulating the use of a specified number of employees on printing machines and their level of training. Since provisions of this kind are an encroachment on the employer's personal freedom to make such decisions, the employer's **freedom of occupational practice** as protected by the Basic Law and protection of the right of ownership are cited as grounds for doubting that excessively extensive application of such provisions would be constitutional. No such doubts are caused by the existing rules, which usually restrict the employer's scope for decision-making only in certain areas. (Sometimes also called "manning rules".)

166. BESITZSTANDSKLAUSEL — *STATUS QUO* CLAUSE:
Status quo clauses in collective agreements have a purpose similar to that of **actual-pay clauses**. They safeguard the employee's entitlements as already acquired under the contract of employment, stipulating that existing more favourable conditions of employment may not be changed for the worse by the entry into force of the **collective agreement** concerned. The result is that, although possible ways remain for employers to release themselves from obligations exceeding the collectively agreed provisions (*e.g.* by resorting to **dismissal for variation of contract** or exercising a reserved right of cancellation of contract), the entry into force of the collective agreement will not itself constitute a motive for exercising these rights.

167. BESOLDUNG — PAY (OF CAREER PUBLIC SERVANTS):
Career public servants ("Beamte") employed by the Federal Government, the Länder and the local authorities, and also judges, are entitled to the pay specified for their particular post. Its amount is not (as in an ordinary **employment relationship**) fixed by contract, but regulated by statute (Federal Career Public Service Pay Act, *i.e.* Bundesbesoldungsgesetz). This entitlement comes into being immediately on the **appointment of career public servants**.

Under the Act, their pay contains the following components. First there is a basic salary, which is rated according to post occupied, pay grade and continuous length of service. The decisive factor governing this element of pay is the **career branch** in which a career public servant is employed. On top of this a local supplement is paid which takes account of factors such as travel to work, marital status and number of children. In addition there are allowances, for example, for overtime necessitated by the post occupied. Unless these have been granted irrevocably they are not, however, taken into account for the purposes of calculating the retirement pension (which is referred to as "Ruhegehalt" or retirement pay in the case of career public servants).

168. BESTANDSGARANTIE — GUARANTEE OF EXISTENCE: The **Basic Law** not only guarantees the right of the individual to join with others in forming an association, *i.e.* in this context a **collective industrial organization**, but also guarantees the existence of associations themselves. The **trade unions** and **employers' associations** are protected in law as regards their existence, their organizational independence and their activities as associations.

83

This constitutional guarantee signifies, first and foremost, that the state cannot encroach on their existence or impede it beyond the extent necessary to protect other rights recognized by law. It also prohibits third parties from taking any action that encroaches on the existence of the organization. Lastly, these organizations are also protected in relation to their members. They are able, especially through their own **standing rules**, to stipulate the payment of membership contributions, reasons for expelling members and rules on maintaining internal discipline and to specify periods of notice for withdrawal from membership. The expulsion of a member can be examined in the **system of ordinary courts**.

169. **BETÄTIGUNGSGARANTIE — GUARANTEE OF ACTIVITY**: The constitutionally protected right of associations, *i.e.* in this context **collective industrial organizations**, to pursue their activities relates, first and foremost, to the improvement of ecohomic and working conditions by concluding **collective agreements** on their own authority. However, this constitutional protection extends beyond **collective bargaining autonomy** as such and encompasses every form of activity in which they engage in their capacity as associations in order to perform the functions specified in Article 9(3) of the Basic Law. These functions include safeguarding their interests by having a voice in the legislative process, participating in employee representation bodies in both the private and public sectors, and representing their members in matters heard by the Labour Courts.

The collective organizations also have a constitutionally protected right to engage in forms of **industrial action** in the event of disputes over matters that can be regulated by collective agreement, because the courts have ruled that the organizations must be guaranteed competence in the "core area" of a collective bargaining system and hence also the right to strike when this is absolutely necessary in order to attain their goals as associations.

The constitutionally protected right to pursue their activities also implies the **trade unions'** right to engage in publicity and canvassing.

170. **BETEILIGUNGSRECHTE DES BETRIEBSRATS — PARTICIPATION RIGHTS OF THE WORKS COUNCIL**: Generic concept encompassing collective rights in the context of the **works constitution**. They cover the **information rights**, **consultation rights** and **co-determination rights of the works council**.

171. **BETRIEB — ESTABLISHMENT**: In **labour law**, the establishment is an organizational unit within which the entrepreneur, either alone or in conjunction with a **workforce** and utilizing technical resources and non-technical resources such as know-how, regularly pursues certain objectives which involve work processes and are not directed purely at satisfying personal requirements. Production plants and service facilities, administrative departments, theatres, ships, hospitals and the offices of solicitors, architects, engineers, etc., are all examples of an establishment. Thus, an establishment in this sense is characterized by the organization of the physical and human factors involved in work (whereas an enterprise or **company** is characterized in terms of the economic or notional objective lying behind this) and implies a unitary organization with decision-making powers in matters relating to employees and labour relations. Provided that this is the case, it is actually possible for several enterprises together to form one establishment. The establishment itself may be subdivided into a number of parts or **departments**. The provisions of the **works constitution** relate to the establishment, and a **works council** can be elected only for an establishment. The circumstances that exist within an establishment, the location of an establishment and continuous **length of service** in the same establishment are important as regards, for example, **protection against dismissal, leave**, membership of **trade unions**, and the scope of **collective agreements** and legislation. An establishment ceases to exist if its organizational unit is split up as a result of a **substantial alteration** in the form of **closure of an establishment** or incorporation in or amalgamation with another establishment; it does not, however, cease to exist as a result of the **transfer of an establishment**, *i.e.* the **acquisition** or **change of ownership of an establishment**.

172. **BETRIEBLICHE ALTERSVERSORGUNG — OCCUPATIONAL PENSION SCHEME**: To supplement the benefits from the **statutory pension scheme** for retirement and disability pensions for employees, many companies operate an occupational pension scheme. Under such schemes the employer voluntarily arranges **assurance of an occupational pension** for the benefit of the employees within the company; this can take various legal forms, with differing implications as regards company profits and taxation. The most important are **direct guarantee, direct insurance**, and **pension and benevolent funds**. A considerable degree of freedom is allowed in arranging such schemes, including combinations of different systems. However, the Improvement of Occupational Pension Schemes Act (Gesetz zur Verbesserung

der betrieblichen Altersversorgung) lays down binding regulations on a number of important points, particularly on the non-forfeiture of **occupational pension expectation** and **protection in the event of insolvency**.

In 1989, 63 per cent. of all industrial firms in the Federal Republic (accounting for 72 per cent. of all employees in industry) were operating occupational pension schemes. Large companies are over-represented in these figures. Smaller firms are far more reluctant to take on the long-term financial commitments entailed by such a scheme.

173. **BETRIEBLICHE ARBEITSSCHUTZORGANISATION — WORKPLACE HEALTH AND SAFETY ARRANGE-MENTS**: For the protection of employees' health, every employer is required to set up workplace health and safety arrangements, the scale of which depends on the size of the establishment and the hazards involved in the production process. In all cases, employers must fulfil (either personally or by delegation to third parties) the obligations imposed on them under the regulations on **protection against technical hazards at work**. In certain cases they also have to appoint **works doctors, safety officers** and **works safety experts**, a **data protection officer**, pollution control and radiation protection officers and a **disabled-employee officer**, and set up a **health and safety committee**. The **works council** performs an important function within the workplace health and safety arrangements. It has **co-determination rights** as regards arrangements for the prevention of accidents at work and occupational illnesses and for health protection, particularly in connection with changes to jobs, work methods and the work environment. The works council's tasks also include monitoring compliance with health and safety legislation and regulations, advising the employer on health protection matters and co-operating with the **Labour Inspectorate** and the institutions responsible for statutory **accident insurance**. To enable the works council to perform these functions, the employer must provide it with prompt and comprehensive information. The basic elements of these workplace health and safety arrangements are regulated by the Works Constitution Act and the 1973 Occupational Health and Safety Act (Gesetz über Betriebsärzte, Sicherheitsingenieure und andere Fachkräfte für Arbeitssicherheit). This Act is not directly applicable to the public sector. Since, however, the public sector is required to provide equivalent protection in terms of industrial medicine and work safety for employees, health and safety arrangements there are basically the same as those in the private sector.

174. BETRIEBLICHE BERUFSAUSBILDUNG — COMPANY VOCATIONAL TRAINING: Vocational training is organized as a **dual system**, *i.e.* **statutory vocational training** in a **vocational training school** is accompanied by vocational training within the **vocational training employer's** establishment. In the latter, the emphasis is on teaching **vocational trainees** the practical skills they will need in their future occupations. This company vocational training constitutes the private-law side of vocational training; the trainee enters into a vocational training contract with the training employer. The training employer is responsible for seeing that the trainee attends the vocational training school.

175. BETRIEBLICHE ÜBUNG — CUSTOM: A custom comes into being as a result of a consistent practice followed by the employer over a lengthy period of time which gives employees the impression that the employer intends to continue with it in the future. As in the case of a **general undertaking by employer**, it is interpreted as an implied and binding declaration of intent on the part of the employer. In cases where the practice is to their benefit, acceptance of this declaration of intent by the employees generally ensues by their tacit consent; where it affects them adversely, their acceptance is deemed to exist if they are or ought to be aware of it and continue working without further comment.

Custom constitutes one of the **sources of law** in **labour law**. Hence, matters such as the granting of **bonuses, occupational pension** entitlements and other special payments, the introduction of practices falling within the scope of the **employer's right to issue instructions** (*e.g.* in relation to **working time**) and the adoption of criteria for interpreting **contracts of employment** may all be based on custom. A common way of preventing regular entitlements from becoming established on the basis of custom is to stipulate in the contract of employment that any additional arrangements must be agreed in writing. Alternatively, the benefit in question can be granted with the proviso that it may be discontinued at any time or with a disclaimer of any commitment for the future.

In the **public service** the principle is that in cases of doubt the employer fulfils only statutory and collectively agreed obligations, and employees are consequently unable to rely on the future continuance of a given practice. Employers can abolish a custom for the future by making a unilateral declaration to that effect. When introducing new arrangements they have to observe the principle of **equal treatment,** and any decisions on **pay** policy involve a **co-determination right of the works council**. A custom also ends when the actual circumstances underlying it cease to exist or it is replaced by a new custom. If, however, entitlements or expectations have already acquired individual contractual status, the validity of a custom with respect to the employees concerned can be withdrawn only by **termination** of the contract of employment or **dismissal for variation of contract**, subject to the provisions of **protection against dismissal**. A custom can be changed by a **works agreement** that provides more favourable conditions; works agreements that change conditions for the worse can replace a custom only under special circumstances. And if the required circumstances apply, the implied declaration of intent that is inherent in a custom can also be contested and revoked.

176. **BETRIEBSABSPRACHE — SEMI-FORMAL WORKS AGREEMENT**: An informal agreement between the **employer** and the **works council** for which no specific regulations are laid down by the statutory provisions of the **works constitution**. It is to be distinguished from informal rules on the one hand and the **works agreement** on the other. Like the latter, however, it signifies a contractual understanding and presupposes a due and proper decision on the part of the works council. Semi-formal works agreements have no normative force directly affecting individual **employment relationships**, and are therefore often used to regulate purely individual cases. Such agreements are lawful and can contain subject-matter relating to all reciprocal obligations between the employer and the works council and to the exercise of the **co-determination rights of the works council**, provided the law does not stipulate that the matters in question must be covered by a works agreement and provided there is no question of evading the restrictions applying to works agreements.

177. **BETRIEBSABTEILUNG — DEPARTMENT**: See **part of an establishment**.

178. **BETRIEBSÄNDERUNG — SUBSTANTIAL ALTERATION TO THE ESTABLISHMENT**: Concept which relates to an instance of co-determination within the **works constitution** (Works Constitution Act §§ 111 ff.). It covers major decisions on the **closure**, reduction of operations or relocation of the **establishment** or of important **parts** of it, amalgamation with other establishments, fundamental changes in the establishment's organization, objectives or equipment, and the introduction of radically different work methods and production processes. **Rationalization** programmes and the introduction of new technologies are examples falling under this heading. The assumption is, for the cases listed, that the changes may result

in serious disadvantages for the **workforce** or for large sections of it. Consequently, in establishments regularly employing more than 20 employees eligible to take part in works council elections the **works council** must be given prompt and full information on any such proposed changes. In practice, substantial alterations to the establishment constitute the main area of use of the **participation, information** and **co-determination rights of the works council** in economic matters, and entitle the works council to a **reconcilement of interests** and a **"social plan"**.

Special aspects arise in the case of eastern Germany under the Law for the Regulation of Unresolved Questions of Property and the Law concerning the Split-up of Companies Administered by the **Treuhand Agency**. In instances of company split-up and company split-up at establishment level and of establishment split-off, the regulations provide special information rights and a three-month interim mandate for the works council.

179. **BETRIEBSARZT — WORKS DOCTOR**: In 1989 there were over 20,000 works doctors in employment in the Federal Republic. Their legal status and appointment procedures conform with the regulations applicable to **works safety experts**. Works doctors must, however, be qualified to practise medicine and possess specialist knowledge of industrial medicine. They are bound by the obligation to observe professional medical secrecy, even towards the employer. As part of the **workplace health and safety arrangements** they are required to perform functions similar to those of the works safety experts, but from the medical viewpoint. For instance, in addition to **protection against technical hazards at work** they are responsible for examining and advising the establishment's employees in matters connected with industrial medicine, evaluating the findings from such examinations and making recommendations to the employer on measures to prevent **accidents at work** and **occupational illnesses**, organizing first aid within the establishment and training medical auxiliaries. They work in close co-operation with the works safety experts and, like the latter, are represented on the establishment's **health and safety committee** (1973 Occupational Health and Safety Act §§ 1 ff., 8 ff.).

180. **BETRIEBSAUFSPALTUNG — COMPANY SPLIT-UP AT ESTABLISHMENT LEVEL**: Term used to refer to the division of what was formerly a single company into two separate legal entities, generally in the form of what are called holding companies and operating companies. From the point of view of labour law, such a split-up can involve the **transfer of an establishment** and a **substantial alteration to the establishment**.

If such a step is being contemplated, the **economic committee** must be informed. A company split-up at establishment level is of considerable significance as regards the preconditions for the formation of a **works council** and the scope of the **participation rights of the works council**.

Special aspects arise in the case of eastern Germany under the Law for the Regulation of Unresolved Questions of Property and the Law concerning the Split-up of Companies Administered by the **Treuhand Agency**. In instances of company split-up and company split-up at establishment level and of establishment split-off, the regulations provide special information rights and a three-month interim mandate for the works council.

181. **BETRIEBSAUSSCHUSS — WORKS COUNCIL EXECUTIVE COMMITTEE**: If a **works council** has nine or more members, it must form an executive committee consisting of its chairperson, vice-chairperson and a number of additional members scaled according to the size of the works council. The composition of the committee must comply with the principle of **protection of minorities**. The committee deals with routine matters. If such a committee is formed, the works council can then set up other committees and delegate specific functions to them. The appointment of an **economic committee** is not, however, dependent on the existence of a works council executive committee.

182. **BETRIEBSBEAUFTRAGTER — SPECIALIST OFFICER AT ESTABLISHMENT LEVEL**: A specialist officer is an individual entrusted with safeguarding particular interests and performing particular functions within an establishment, who is specially qualified for the purpose and given special powers. Typical examples are **safety officers** and **disabled-employee officers**, and officers responsible for waste management, control of water and air pollution, radiation protection and **data protection**. In many cases the appointment of specialist officers by the employer, which is generally a requirement under the relevant legislation on **employee protection**, must be done in consultation with the works council and notified to the competent authorities.

183. **BETRIEBSBEDINGTE KÜNDIGUNG — REDUNDANCY**: **Termination with notice** or (in exceptional cases) **summary termination** of an **employment relationship** by the **employer** is classed as redundancy if it is for a reason which, in contrast to **dismissal on grounds of personal capability** or **on grounds of conduct**, falls exclusively within the employer's sphere of

influence in running the company (Protection Against Dismissal Act § 1, Civil Code § 626). For employment relationships covered by **protection against dismissal**, redundancy is lawful only if justified by urgent operational requirements. This is so if the employer proves that a job has actually ceased to exist in the establishment and that the employee concerned can therefore no longer be employed. The reasons for the job loss may be internal or external. They mainly relate to economic, technical or organizational changes such as rearrangement of the work process, for example as the result of rationalization programmes or plant and departmental closures, a shortage of orders, a decline in sales, and a lack of raw materials or capital. The **transfer of an establishment** is not, however, an admissible reason.

The decision on what measures are necessary in such situations lies with the employer. If an employee makes an **application for protection against dismissal**, the employer's decision can be examined by the courts only from the point of view of whether it is obviously unfair, unreasonable or arbitrary. This is purely a procedure for controlling abuses and applies only to extreme cases. A far more important feature is the fact that, as a matter of principle, the employer's and employee's interests have to be weighed against each other and the **proportionality principle** must be observed. This means that a redundancy is generally unlawful if the employee (possibly following re-training or further training that the employer can reasonably be expected to provide, or an amicable amendment of contract) can continue to be employed in another available job within the establishment or company; preserving the job in question by cutting down **overtime** or, where there is a temporary shortage of work, introducing **short-time working** is considered to be another reasonable solution. A lawful redundancy is valid if, in selecting from among the employees concerned the one who is to be dismissed, the employer has followed the correct procedure, *i.e.* the principle of **social criteria for redundancy**.

184. **BETRIEBSBESETZUNG — OCCUPATION (OF THE WORKPLACE)**: Term used to refer to the unlawful occupation of the premises of an **establishment** or **part of an establishment** by the **workforce** or a third party, against the will of the person entitled (the employer, or a receiver during bankruptcy proceedings) and without any justificatory reason. Also known in English as a "sit-in". Justification is deemed to exist if the person entitled has obstructed the execution of a court order to continue the business of the establishment by closing it down, or is required to refrain from closing it down. A court order to this effect may be founded, for example, on the infringement

of **works constitution** provisions regarding a **reconcilement of interests**.

185. **BETRIEBSBUSSE — DISCIPLINARY SANCTION**: A disciplinary sanction is a punishment that is imposed for the purpose of maintaining order and safety within the **establishment**. It is not a penalty fixed by contract, and must also be clearly distinguished from a formal **warning** issued under the terms of the individual contract of employment. Nor does it have the nature of a penalty in law. Hence, as in the case of **disciplinary law for career public servants**, if an employee's act also infringes criminal legislation a disciplinary sanction can be imposed in addition to a court sentence. Such sanctions may be introduced only by **collective agreement** or **works agreement**. The conditions under which they are imposed must be specifically defined and made generally known within the establishment. Common examples of conduct subject to disciplinary sanctions are theft, smoking in the workplace in establishments where there is a fire hazard, carrying out collections of money, political agitation, and engaging in trade while at work. Sanctions may take the form of a caution, a reprimand or a fine, but not dismissal. So-called humiliating punishments ("Ehrenstrafen"), which are made publicly known throughout the establishment, are also unlawful. Before a disciplinary sanction is imposed, the employee concerned must be given an opportunity to be heard and the **co-determination right of the works council** must be duly observed. Where a caution or reprimand has been recorded in their **personal file**, an employee can protest against this and demand that it be deleted if the circumstances justifying the sanction did not exist or the legislation on co-determination has been infringed.

186. **BETRIEBSDATENERFASSUNG — CAPTURE OF PRODUCTION DATA**: See **new production technologies**.

187. **BETRIEBSEINSCHRÄNKUNG — REDUCTION OF OPERATIONS**: See **substantial alteration to the establishment**.

188. **BETRIEBSFEIER UND -AUSFLUG — WORKS HOLIDAY AND OUTING**: Works holidays and outings are forms of event that are widely used to seek to foster the employees' sense of identification with the company, the **general establishment culture** and the **corporate culture**. Participation cannot be made compulsory, nor can **overtime pay** or **overtime premium pay**

be claimed for such days. Accidents that occur on works holidays and outings are classed as **accidents at work**.

189. **BETRIEBSFERIEN — FIXED WORKS HOLIDAYS**: Term used to refer to the practice of arranging for the entire **workforce**, or a section of it, to take their **annual holidays** at the same time. Since the scheduling of fixed holidays by the employer is required to be fair and reasonable, the advance allocation of holiday entitlements for the coming year so that they are always out of season or at inconvenient times of year is unlawful. The **co-determination right of the works council** must in any case be observed. Employees who do not yet have a full holiday entitlement when the fixed holidays begin must nevertheless be granted it prematurely or, alternatively, it must be made possible for them to work (otherwise the situation would be deemed to be **employer's non-acceptance of the work performance**). In such cases, however, provided that the employees' interests are adequately upheld it can be agreed to exclude pay entitlements. Employees who are ill, or those who cannot be granted holidays for other reasons, must be allowed to take their holiday at a different time.

190. **BETRIEBSFRIEDEN — PEACEFUL CO-OPERATION WITHIN THE ESTABLISHMENT**: A state of peaceful co-operation within the establishment signifies that the **employer** and the **workforce** work together without any serious disruptions. The employer and the **works council** are under obligation to uphold this peaceful co-operation. However, this does not mean that, in following the principle of **co-operation in good faith**, each side has to accept the ideas of the other without objection. Thus, in the event of **industrial conflicts** it is only forms of **industrial action** within the establishment that are excluded, not the general assertion of rights. Referral to an **establishment-level arbitration committee** is widely invoked as a procedure for resolving conflicts.

In addition, the works council can refuse its consent to the appointment of a prospective employee if there are grounds indicating that the candidate will disrupt peaceful co-operation within the establishment by engaging in unlawful conduct, and can also demand the dismissal of an existing employee if the employee in question has already repeatedly caused serious disruption to it. Not every form of disruptive behaviour (such as objecting to the ideas pursued by the employer or works council) is necessarily enough to justify sanctions imposed by them, particularly **dismissal on grounds of conduct**, to preserve peaceful co-operation within the establishment. However, the requirements imposed by **case law** for the justification of such measures are not very stringent.

191. **BETRIEBSGDBBEHEIMNIS — TRADE SECRET**: A trade secret is a piece of information which is actually secret, is of significance for the employer and can be seen by the employee to be confidential. The duty not to divulge such secrets is one of the general **obligations under the contract of employment** whose infringement justifies **dismissal on grounds of personal capability** or on **grounds of conduct**. Separate protection for confidential information is also provided by rights to refuse to give evidence in legal proceedings and by provisions on secrecy in the context of the **works constitution** and for members of **management boards** and **supervisory boards**. The duty of professional secrecy that serves to protect trade secrets starts when the **employment relationship** begins and (at least if there is a contractual covenant to that effect) continues even after it has ended. In cases where the duty of secrecy restricts the employee's freedom for self-fulfilment and development, particularly as regards utilizing their occupational knowledge and experience, it constitutes a **restraint on competition** for which they have a right to compensation.

192. **BETRIEBSGRUPPE — WORK GROUP**: A number of employees who have been formed into a team by the employer for the purpose of achieving a certain work result are referred to as a work group. In contrast to a **self-constituted employee group**, in this case the individual employees each have their own **contract of employment** with the employer. By virtue of the **employer's right to issue instructions**, the formation and disbandment of such organizational groups lie solely in the employer's hands. This means that the individual members of a group have no say in deciding its composition. But it is the employer's duty, when occasion arises, to assign extra staff to the group and, in the event of **leave** or **illness**, replacements. If the employer fails to co-operate in this way, the members of the group are entitled to the level of **remuneration** which they would have achieved at full working capacity. This legal consequence is important where, for example, a **piecework** rate has been fixed for the group as a whole. On the other hand, the group's earnings decrease if output drops and (where this is contractually agreed) if performance is poor. In such cases the group is jointly liable on a per capita basis.

The work group leader is chosen by the employer, and the group spokesperson by the members of the group. For good reasons, they are often one and the same person. The leader supervises work performance and attendance, monitors the time taken to perform tasks and decides when short periods of time off and leave are to be granted. If duly authorized, the work group leader is also entitled to receive pay on behalf of the group.

The fixing of collective remuneration for a work group is subject to the **co-determination right of the works council**, which, in particular circumstances, can also cover the process of forming such a group.

193. **BETRIEBSINHABERWECHSEL — CHANGE OF OWNERSHIP OF AN ESTABLISHMENT**: See **transfer of an establishment**.

194. **BETRIEBSJUSTIZ — COMPANY DISCIPLINE**: See **disciplinary sanctions**.

195. **BETRIEBSKLIMA — GENERAL ESTABLISHMENT CULTURE**: A concept which sums up the entire range of social, psychological and organizational factors that influence working conditions within an establishment. In addition to general matters such as pay and fringe benefits and welfare facilities, management style and measures directed at the **humanization of work**, these factors include schemes explicitly connected with personal relations between employees, the **corporate culture** and the social atmosphere, such as **works holidays and outings** or the encouragement of company sporting activities.

196. **BETRIEBSKRANKENKASSE — COMPANY HEALTH INSURANCE FUND**: **Companies** are permitted to set up their own **health insurance funds** if they employ at least 450 employees who are subject to compulsory insurance, and if they have obtained the consent of the competent authority.

The number of company health insurance funds has been increasing steadily since 1987 and there are at present some 720 in existence. This trend is emerging against a background of rising costs in the health sector and a relatively broad base of unemployed workers and other individuals who are not economically active. Setting up a company health insurance fund enables both the company and its employees to reduce their expenditure on statutory **health insurance**, since a company fund has to bear only the risks of the employees concerned and their families, and the majority of those insured also actually pay contributions. In 1991 the average contribution rate in the case of company health insurance funds was 11 per cent. of **gross pay** in western Germany and 12.2 per cent. in eastern Germany, as against 12.3 and 12.8 per cent. respectively in the case of Public

95

Health Insurance Funds (AOK). Since the continued proliferation of company funds threatens the Public Funds with the exodus of regular contributors, the **Federal Social Security Court** has ruled that the establishment of a company health insurance fund can be prohibited if, as a result, the contribution rate of the Public Fund concerned would rise to at least 10 per cent. above the average rate of neighbouring Public Funds.

197. **BETRIEBSNACHFOLGE — SUCCESSOR ESTABLISH-MENT**: See **transfer of an establishment**.

198. **BETRIEBSNAHE TARIFPOLITIK — ESTABLISHMENT-SPECIFIC BARGAINING**: The structure of the collective bargaining system in the Federal Republic, with the large scale and wide coverage of the respective **parties to a collective agreement**, means that the **collective agreements** concluded are necessarily couched in very general terms. Consequently, the policy known as establishment-specific bargaining refers to clauses in collective agreements which delegate the regulatory powers of the **collective industrial organisations** (within specified limits) to the actors of the **works constitution**, *i.e.* the **employer** and **works council** concerned. An important area for which this approach is adopted is the implementation of collectively agreed regulations on the **reduction of working hours** and elements of **qualitative bargaining policy**. This form of establishment bargaining, in which managers and works council members give effect to collectively agreed terms negotiated by employers' associations and unions at regional or national level in the light of circumstances in individual establishments, must be distinguished from so-called **company agreements**, which particular companies conclude for themselves with trade unions.

199. **BETRIEBSOBMANN — WORKS SPOKESPERSON**: See **single-member works council**.

200. **BETRIEBSORDNUNG — WORKS RULES**: The rules laid down by **works agreements** on **working time** and **breaks**, **workplace health and safety arrangements**, **disciplinary sanctions** and other matters relating to work within the establishment, are generally collected together in a set of works rules.

201. **BETRIEBSRAT — WORKS COUNCIL**: As the form of **institutionalized representation of interests** for employees within an **establishment**, the works council is an organ of the **works constitution**. It serves the establishment and the

workforce. The means it has at its disposal for fulfilling this function are its rights of participation, *i.e.* the **information**, **consultation** and **co-determination rights of the works council**. It is empowered to conclude **works agreements** for the establishment, and is authorized to institute legal actions under the **"Beschluss" procedure** if its rights are disregarded. Its relationship to the workforce is governed by the duty to conduct its business impartially, without regard to race, religion and creed, nationality, origin, political or union activity, sex, or age. Consequently, **manual workers** and **white-collar workers** and (in principle) both sexes, as well as the individual **departments** of the establishment, must have representation on the council proportional to their presence among the workforce. The council is elected in accordance with the provisions on **works council elections**. It is not bound by the decisions of **works meetings** and cannot be voted out of office. It can, however, be removed from office by the Labour Court for gross violation of its duties. It must observe the principles of the **peace obligation** and **co-operation in good faith** towards the employer, and is also required to co-operate with those **trade unions** which have a presence in the establishment and with the relevant **employers' association**.

The requirement for setting up a works council is that the establishment in question should regularly employ at least five employees who are eligible to vote. The term of office is four years. The size of the council depends on the number of employees in the establishment who are eligible to vote; provided that it has several members, the council elects two of them as its chairperson and vice-chairperson. Council members enjoy special **protection against dismissal**. Membership ends after expiry of the term of office, resignation, termination of the **employment relationship**, loss of eligibility, expulsion, or dissolution of the council by court decision. The works council is not capable of possessing assets and cannot be held liable under the law. The employer bears the costs of the council's activities and in this respect is also liable for the council's actions. In companies where there are several works councils, a **company works council** must also be formed. In a **group (of companies)**, a **group works council** is formed in addition to this, if the company works councils of the member companies so decide. The interests of **executive staff** are protected not by the works council but by a separate **representative body for executive staff**.

In a number of companies which operate branch establishments or subsidiaries in various EC Member States, special "works councils" have been set up for the purpose of voicing the interests of employees in all their establishments throughout the

Community. These bodies do not, however, have institutional backing comparable to that of the German-style works council, nor corresponding rights.

202. **BETRIEBSRÄTEVERSAMMLUNG — GENERAL MEETING OF WORKS COUNCILS**: In **companies** where there is a **company works council**, the General Meeting of Works Councils is a prescribed institution of the **works constitution**. Its function is the equivalent, in this context, of the **works meeting**. The General Meeting is convened at least once a year by the company works council, and consists of the chairpersons and vice-chairpersons of the company's individual establishment **works councils** plus the other members of their **works council executive committees**. Each of the works councils can also send other members to the General Meeting. The General Meeting is not a public session; however, it may also be attended by members of the **representative body for disabled employees** and the **company representative body for young workers and trainees**, and external full-time officials of the **trade unions** represented in an establishment and of the relevant **employers' association**. The company works council is required to report to the General Meeting on its activities, and the employer reports on personnel and labour relations matters and, as far as the protection of confidential business information and **trade secrets** allows, on the company's economic position. The General Meeting is not able to take decisions that are binding on the company works council or individual works councils.

203. **BETRIEBSRATSHAFTUNG — WORKS COUNCIL LIABILITY**: See **works council, works council member**.

204. **BETREIBSRATSMITGLIED — WORKS COUNCIL MEMBER**: The office of works council member is honorary and carries no extra remuneration. Any expenses necessarily incurred are, however, reimbursed. Works council members may neither enjoy privileges nor suffer disadvantages as a consequence of holding office. They are guaranteed retention of their level of pay and job grading after their term of office has expired, to ensure the smooth and unrestricted continuation of their working life. They also enjoy special **protection against dismissal**. Their duties connected with the **works constitution** are generally carried out during **working time**, and they are entitled to be released from work for this purpose. This also applies to attendance at training courses, in so far as these are of a nature and scope necessary to the proper performance of their duties as members of a works council. In addition to this, in **establishments** with

more than 300 employees a certain number of works council members, depending on the size of the establishment, must be given full-time release from work. Individual members are also entitled to up to four weeks' educational leave during their term of office. Works council members are under an obligation not to divulge confidential business information or **trade secrets** (Works Constitution Act §§ 37 f., 79). Personal liability on their part for actions of the works council can arise only if in conducting its lawful business they exceed the council's powers or commit unlawful acts.

205. **BETRIEBSRATSWAHL — WORKS COUNCIL ELECTION**: The works council election is the institution under the **works constitution** for establishing a **works council** and appointing **works council members** (Works Constitution Act §§ 13 ff., Electoral Code §§ 1 ff.). Regular elections are held every four years, during the period between March 1 and May 31. Voting is by direct secret ballot and the electoral procedure follows the principles of **group-based election** and **protection of minorities**. An extraordinary election has to be held if, for example, the works council resigns, the number of its members drops below the required minimum, the election is challenged, or the number of employees regularly employed in the establishment decreases or increases by half (subject to this being by at least 50 employees). Responsibility for conducting the election lies with an electoral board. An election may be challenged if important rules of procedure have been infringed. The costs of works council elections are borne by the employer. All employees in the establishment who on the day of the election are aged 18 or over are eligible to vote, with the exception of **executive staff**. All those employees eligible to vote who on the day of the election have been employed in the establishment for at least six months are eligible for election.

In some two thirds of all establishments the manual workers and white-collar workers opt for a joint election ("Gemeinschaftswahl") rather than separate group-based elections. The percentage of the electorate actually voting is generally around 80 per cent.

206. **BETRIEBSRISIKO — "WORKS RISK"**: As a general principle, if in a synallagmatic contract it becomes impossible through no fault of either party for an obligor to render their performance, the latter also loses entitlement to the counter-performance. Since the **contract of employment** is a synallagmatic contract, according to this principle the employee loses entitlement to **remuneration**. This would be so in all cases where

employees cannot work because of a technical impossibility beyond the control of the **employer**. However, in order that employees should retain their entitlement to remuneration if, for example, lack of energy, raw materials, machinery or labour makes it impossible to work, in a decision dating back to 1923 the courts developed the doctrine of "works risk" ("Betriebsrisiko"). Since that time it has been accepted by the courts that in principle the employer must normally bear this risk. But the obligation to continue paying remuneration does not apply in the event of **partial or selective strikes** in the particular establishment concerned. In the case of indirect effects from **industrial action** elsewhere, in principle the employer again has to bear the risk. There are two exceptions to this rule, as follows. First, if on economic grounds the employer cannot reasonably be expected to continue the establishment's operation, appropriate pay reductions are permissible. Second, if the indirect effect of industrial action influences the balance of bargaining power between the collective bargaining parties in dispute, both the employer and the employees must bear the risk resulting from industrial action. Such influence is assumed to exist if, for example, the collective industrial organizations covering the establishment concerned are closely connected, either in identity or organizationally, with the parties in dispute. It makes no difference here whether the adverse effects on the establishment result from a strike or from a **lock-out**. If it becomes necessary to introduce **short-time working** as a result of the indirect effects of industrial action, the apportionment of working time falls under the **co-determination rights of the works council.**

In contrast to this concept of "works risk", the scope of the doctrine of **economic risk** covers cases where the work to be performed would not be viable economically.

207. **BETRIEBSSCHLIESSUNG — SHUTDOWN OF AN ESTABLISHMENT**: Shutdown is a measure taken by the authorities to prevent the continued operation of an **establishment** for which a permit, licence, concession or authorization is required but is not presented.

208. **BETRIEBSSICHERHEIT — SAFETY AT WORK**: A concept covering both matters relating to the person of the employee, *i.e.* **workplace health and safety arrangements and protection against technical hazards at work**, and matters relating to material or physical objects, *i.e.* **safety of equipment**.

209. **BETRIEBSSTILLEGUNG — CLOSURE OF AN ESTABLISHMENT**: The closure of an establishment means

that the community formed by **employer** and **workforce** ("Betriebsgemeinschaft") comes to an end, because the **entrepreneur** abandons the pursuit of the establishment's objective, either permanently or for a period of time which is both of unspecified duration and of economic significance. Closure constitutes a **substantial alteration to the establishment** and a cause for **redundancy**.

210. **BETRIEBSSTÖRUNG — INTERRUPTION OF OPERATIONS**: See "works risk".

211. **BETRIEBSTEIL — PART OF AN ESTABLISHMENT**: Term used for a geographical or organizational sub-unit of an **establishment**. Within the context of the **works constitution**, it is classed as an establishment in its own right only if the minimum number of employees required for the formation of a **works council** are employed in it and they are geographically distant from the main establishment or independent in terms of type of work and organization. The criterion that determines independence is the degree of freedom exercised by the management of the part or department concerned in taking decisions on matters which in the context of labour relations policy are subject to the **co-determination rights of the works council** (Works Constitution Act § 4). A part or department of an establishment in this sense can change hands and be closed down through **transfer of an establishment**. In the event of this form of **closure of an establishment**, employees who enjoy special **protection against dismissal** must in principle be transferred to another part or department.

212. **BETRIEBSÜBERGANG — TRANSFER OF AN ESTABLISHMENT**: Term indicating a change in the ownership of an establishment. It can give rise to particular problems for the employees working in it; the new owner often wishes to reduce the workforce, change its composition or avoid being bound by **collective agreements** and **works agreements** that were formerly applicable or by individual clauses in existing contracts of employment. Under provisions which were introduced in 1980 (Civil Code § 613a), partly to bring the law into line with current EC Directives, in the event of the transfer of an establishment or an organizationally separable **part of an establishment** from one **employer** to another by legal transaction, such as sale or leasing, a procedure is laid down (as complex as it is difficult to define) for a reconcilement of interests between the new owner and the employees concerned. The basic idea of this regulation is that the employees should neither suffer

101

disadvantages nor gain advantages from the change of ownership. The new employer is therefore automatically and fully bound by the existing employment relationships from the date of actually assuming the status of employer.

This also includes the collective agreements and works agreements binding on these employment relationships, provided that their regulatory scope is not covered by collective agreements or works agreements already existing in an establishment belonging to the new owner. The employment relationship with the former employer ends on this same date, provided that the employee makes no objection to the transfer to a new owner.

Continuity in the event of a change of ownership is also guaranteed in collective labour law. The **works council** remains in office, provided that the organization of the establishment has not been changed in such a way (by a **merger**, for instance) as to make this impossible. A co-determination right exists in the event of a transfer of ownership, but only if it is connected with a **substantial alteration to the establishment**.

Special aspects arise in the case of eastern Germany under the Law for the Regulation of Unresolved Questions of Property and the Law concerning the Split-up of Companies Administered by the **Treuhand Agency**. The regulations are intended to assist the privatization of formerly state-owned enterprises. To safeguard employee rights during the transition they provide, for instances of **company split-up** and **company split-up at establishment level** and of establishment split-off, special information rights and a three-month interim mandate for the works council.

213. **BETRIEBSÜBERNAHME — ACQUISITION OF AN ESTABLISHMENT**: See **transfer of an establishment**.

214. **BETRIEBSUNFALL — INDUSTRIAL ACCIDENT**: See **accident at work**.

215. **BETRIEBSVERÄUSSERUNG — ALIENATION OF AN ESTABLISHMENT**: See **transfer of an establishment**.

216. **BETRIEBSVEREINBARUNG — WORKS AGREEMENT**: A works agreement is a written agreement between the **employer** and the **works council** which has a direct and compulsory effect on individual **employment relationships** and labour relations within the establishment (Works Constitution Act § 77(4)). In terms of personnel, its scope refers only to those employees in an establishment who are covered by the **works constitution**; executive staff are therefore excluded.

Works agreements may regulate all matters relating to the establishment, provided that there are no statutory or collectively agreed provisions to the contrary. In addition to the fundamental regulation of formal and standard conditions of employment, they can also include agreed arrangements on practical matters concerning the content of the employment relationship, in so far as they are matters where there is a **co-determination right of the works council**. In these cases, precedence as between the works agreement and the **collective agreement** is not governed by the usual system of hierarchical ranking, but by the **favourability principle**. For these matters covered by co-determination a works agreement is in fact mandatory: failing voluntary agreement, a decision is reached by the establishment-level arbitration committee.

In order to protect **collective bargaining autonomy**, however, it is unlawful for works agreements to contain provisions on remuneration and other employment conditions which are regulated, or usually regulated, by collective agreement (Works Constitution Act § 77(3)). A collective agreement can, nevertheless, expressly permit the conclusion of works agreements to supplement it.

Precedence as between the works agreement and the contract of employment is governed by the favourability principle. A works agreement cannot, therefore, "spoil" rights that employees have acquired by virtue of a contract of employment. If entitlements exist which are based on rules applying to the entire establishment, particularly a **custom** or **general undertaking by employer**, the courts have ruled that employees' entitlements may be reduced only if, in the event of restructuring, the agreement is in the form of a collective arrangement which is no less favourable overall, or if the commercial basis for the entitlements no longer exists.

Works agreements concluded by **company works councils** and **group works councils** on matters falling within their areas of responsibility apply respectively to the company and to the company group according to these same principles.

217. **BETRIEBSVERFASSUNG — WORKS CONSTITUTION**: The works constitution forms the basis for the institution of employee representation bodies within **establishments**, and their rights and obligations. Together with the **co-determination** enshrined in the **company constitution**, it is the core of the system of **institutionalized representation of interests**. It is governed by the Works Constitution Act (Betriebsverfassungsgesetz) of 1972 (which is sometimes also referred to in English as the Labour/Management Relations Act). The principal active organ

of the works constitution is the **works council**. Regulations on collective employee representation bodies are also laid down in the relevant statutes for **disabled persons** or on **representative bodies for executive staff**. The works constitution also contains individual rights relating to consultation and grievances which the **employee** can assert even in establishments where there is no works council. Otherwise, the various **participation rights of the works council** provided for in the works constitution are vested in the council alone.

The works constitution applies to all establishments located in the Federal Republic which are organized under private law. In the **public service**, these matters are governed by provisions on **staff representation**. Participation rights as provided for in the **works constitution** are not applicable to Church institutions and **Religious Communities** (Works Constitution Act § 118), which have their own **ecclesiastical staff representation** bodies. In the category of establishment known as a **"Tendenzbetrieb"** the **co-determination rights of the works council** are restricted; special regulations also apply to garrisons maintained by the Allied Forces.

In terms of personnel, the scope of the works constitution covers only those within an establishment who are employees within the meaning of the Act (§ 5); **executive staff**, for example, are excluded. The Act requires the works council and the **employer** to work together on a basis of **co-operation in good faith** and with due regard to rules contained in statutes and **collective agreements**. This does not, however, place the works council in a position of direct subordination to the **trade unions** as representative bodies. Rather, within individual establishments the unions perform a supportive and monitoring role. Union officials possess a right of access to establishments in which they have union members. With the exception of provisions on penalties and administrative fines, all disputes on matters concerning the works constitution fall within the jurisdiction of the **Labour Courts**, which decide them according to the **"Beschluss"** procedure. Under the Act (§§ 40 f.), all costs connected with the works constitution are borne by the employer.

The historical precursors of an institutionalized system of employee representation were the workers' committees instituted in the mining industry from 1905, the manual and white-collar workers' committees instituted in all establishments with more than 50 employees from 1916, and the legal guarantee of employee representation provided by the Works Councils Act (Betriebsrätegesetz) of 1920. Forms of employee representation as provided for in the works constitution have existed since the Works Constitution Act of 1952. The Act of 1972 then broadened the scope of the works council's co-determination rights and completely re-codified the works constitution. This Act can therefore be viewed as an industrial equivalent of the democratization of the state. The Federal Parliament's Standing Committee on Co-Determination (Mitbestimmungskommission) has also expressed the opinion that, with due regard to the protection of human dignity and the right of individuals to develop their personality freely as enshrined in the Basic Law, the subordination of the employee to other people's managerial and organizational authority is acceptable only if the guarantees of freedom afforded by the **Constitution** are reflected in the opportunity to have a voice in the shaping of the work process. The Act of 1972 consequently contains minimum participation rights which can in principle be extended.

In a number of companies which operate branch establishments or subsidiaries in various EC Member States, special "works councils" have been set up for the purpose of voicing the interests of employees in all their establishments throughout the Community. These bodies do not, however, have institutional backing comparable to that of the German-style works council, nor corresponding rights.

218. **BETRIEBSVERSAMMLUNG — WORKS MEETING**: The works meeting is an organ of the works constitution consisting of all the **employees** of an **establishment**, with the exception of **executive staff** (Works Constitution Act §§ 42 ff.). It serves as a means of direct communication between the **workforce** and the **works council**. The topics discussed can include all matters relating to the establishment connected with collective-bargaining and labour-relations policy and economic matters. The works meeting is not a public session; however, members of the **company works council**, the **employer**, officials of those **trade unions** which have a presence in the establishment and of the **employers' association** concerned and, if pertinent, other individuals may also be invited by the works council to attend. The meeting is not able to take decisions that are binding on the works council or the employees. The works council arranges regular works meetings at least once every calendar quarter. If reasons of time or organizational difficulties make it impossible to convene a full meeting, works meetings for parts or departments of the establishment must be held. The works council can convene an extraordinary works meeting; it is required to do this if so requested by the employer or by at least one quarter of all the employees eligible to vote in works council elections. The employer must be informed of the agenda. Regular meetings, or extraordinary meetings held at the behest of the employer,

take place in principle during **working time** without loss of pay. The particular nature of an establishment may, however, necessitate holding it at some other time. This may entitle employees to additional **remuneration**, pay for **travel-to-work time** and reimbursement of travel expenses. No supplements for **work on Sundays and public holidays**, **overtime** or **overtime exceeding maximum working hours** are, however, payable on these occasions.

219. **BETRIEBSWEGEUNFALL — ACCIDENT *EN ROUTE*:** Term indicating an accident sustained by an employee on a journey undertaken in the establishment's interest, including travelling between home and the workplace. It is classed as an **accident at work**.

220. **BETRIEBSZUGEHÖRIGKEIT — LENGTH OF SERVICE:** Term used to denote the state of legal relationship with an **establishment** as an **employee** or **vocational trainee** and its continuous duration. A given length of continuous service is specified as a precondition in the case of numerous statutory and contractual provisions, particularly regarding **protection against dismissal**, **leave**, the **works constitution** and **occupational pension schemes**. If a company has several establishments, time spent employed in any of them counts towards the total length of continuous service. Continuity of service is not interrupted either by the **transfer of an establishment** or by maternity leave or compulsory military and community service. Generally speaking, continuity of service is not affected by actual periods of interruption, but only by legal termination of the contract of employment. Length of service in a previous **employment relationship** is credited as service in the new one if it is closely and substantively connected with it and the interruption has not been for longer than four months (**consecutive short-term contracts**).

221. **BEWERBERAUSWAHL — PERSONNEL SELECTION:** Personnel selection is carried out in accordance with the aims of **human resource planning**. As part of the procedure the **employer** may check the **job application documents** submitted with a **job application**, ask for references and make inquiries. Employees can, however, forbid a prospective employer to make inquiries of their current employer. If their wishes are disregarded and they suffer damage as a result, applicants must be paid compensation by the individual who made the inquiries. The employer is permitted to enlist the services of handwriting experts and to use psychological aptitude testing, but in such cases the

consent of applicants is required. Their consent is also needed for examinations by a works doctor or an outside medical adviser. The cost of these procedures is borne by the employer. Personnel selection is strongly influenced by guidelines on the hiring of new employees, transfers, re-grading and dismissals. In establishments regularly employing up to 1,000 employees, such selection guidelines may be introduced only with the agreement of the **works council**; in establishments with more than 1,000 employees, the works council can insist on their introduction.

222. **BEWERBUNG — JOB APPLICATION**: A job application is the means by which prospective employees demonstrate their interest in concluding a contract of employment with an employer. In many cases it is submitted in response to a **job advertisement**, and with **job application documents** enclosed.

223. **BEWERBUNGSUNTERLAGEN — JOB APPLICATION DOCUMENTS**: When a prospective employee submits a job application in writing, the job application documents usually include a covering letter, a curriculum vitae, a photograph and copies of references. The job advertisement itself often states what documents are required. The employer is under an obligation to ensure their safekeeping and to treat them as confidential. As a general principle, applicants have no entitlement to reimbursement of the **costs of attending for interview**. In establishments regularly employing more than 20 employees entitled to vote in works council elections, the documents of all job applicants must be shown to the works council.

224. **BEZIRKSPERSONALRAT — REGIONAL STAFF COUNCIL**: A regional staff council is formed at the intermediate level of public administration in the Federal Government and the Länder (**hierarchical representation body**). In conjunction with the relevant **public-sector establishment head** of an intermediate-level public authority, it is empowered to decide on those matters subject to co-determination on which a **staff council** and establishment head of an authority at the lower level of public administration have been unable to reach agreement, and which they have referred (within six days and through the official channels) to the intermediate-level authority for a decision. The members of the regional staff council are elected by all the employees of the **public sector establishments** belonging to the sphere of activity of the intermediate-level public authority, in accordance with the standard procedure for **staff council elections**. If elections for a staff council and for the higher-level representation bodies are held at the same time, they are

107

conducted by an electoral board at the lower level on behalf of the regional or main electoral board. The composition of the regional staff council follows the same principles as those for a staff council.

225. **BEZUGSGRÖSSE — REFERENCE WAGE**: The reference wage is important for the purposes of certain social benefits and earnings limits, and is calculated annually for the coming year on the basis of the figures for the preceding year. It serves as the basis, for example, for fixing maximum and minimum amounts below which employees may be classed as **"marginal" part-time workers** or above which membership of the statutory **health insurance** scheme or other branches of **social security** ceases to be compulsory.

226. **BfA**: See **Federal Employment Service** (Bundesanstalt für Arbeit).

227. **BFH**: Bundesfinanzhof (Federal Finance Court). See **system of finance courts**.

228. **BGH**: Bundesgerichtshof (Federal Court of Justice). See **system of ordinary courts**.

229. **BILDUNGSURLAUB — EDUCATIONAL LEAVE**: Under legislative provisions of individual **Länder** employees are entitled, subject to certain conditions, to four or five days' educational leave per year. During this time they are given release from work to attend a course of instruction furthering their vocational or political education, for example in order to increase their knowledge of foreign languages, learn about computers or improve their political education. The cost of such further education must be borne by the participants themselves. Statutory entitlements to paid educational leave are provided for in the following Länder: Berlin, Bremen, Hamburg, Hesse, Lower Saxony, North Rhine-Westphalia, Saarland and Schleswig-Holstein.

230. **BINNENMARKT — INTERNAL MARKET**: By signing the Single European Act in 1986, the EC Member States committed themselves to the establishment of a single European internal market. The conditions required for the internal market are to be created by December 31, 1992. Necessary measures include the abolition of controls on persons and goods at the Community's internal frontiers, and the harmonization of national tax systems,

technical standards, business and company law (**forms of company**), and all other provisions which form an obstacle to the free movement of goods and services within the internal market. In the process of progressively establishing the internal market the regulations on **freedom of movement for workers** are also to be extended to students, pensioners and the unemployed and mutual recognition is to be accorded to the various professional and educational qualifications of Member States. One criticism levelled at the harmonization measures is that their implementation could lead to disadvantages for employees as regards **protection against technical hazards at work** and **safety of equipment,** and as regards the future development of the structures of **institutionalized representation of interests.**

The Agreement with the European Free Trade Area countries (EFTA) on the creation of a European Economic Space seeks to extend the internal market beyond EC Member States. The subject of the Agreement is the free exchange of persons, goods, capital and services.

231. **BIO- UND CHEMOTECHNOLOGIEN — BIOTECH-NOLOGY AND CHEMICAL TECHNOLOGIES:** Terms covering the application of biological and chemical means and methods in industrial processes to assist the production process and the manufacture and transformation of materials. In the case of biotechnology, this frequently relates to the use of algae, bacteria and yeasts produced or modified by way of genetic engineering. Chemical technologies are used extensively and their potential applications are continually expanding in the form of numerous substitution processes, particularly in the metal processing industry, and via the growth of **microelectronics**. Both types of technology are characterized by an increased degree of integration and automatic control of machines, and the resultant changes in the flow of materials have considerable impact on delivery and supply systems and the overall workflow. Hence, the structure of suppliers alters, and assembly work gives way to control and monitoring activities. This may raise the level of **skills** demanded of employees. Also, these technologies necessitate new regulations on **workplace health and safety arrangements**. The **works council** must be informed of their proposed introduction.

232. **BISMARCKSCHE SOZIALGESETZGEBUNG — BISMARCK'S SOCIAL SECURITY LEGISLATION:** What is known as Bismarck's social security legislation dates back to the Imperial Message of November 17, 1881 to the Reichstag

(National Parliament), in which the conviction was expressed "that the healing of social wrongs must be sought not solely through the repression of social democratic excesses but just as much by positively advancing the well-being of the workers". In the era that followed, regulations were passed on the three most common areas of risk:

1. The Law concerning Health Insurance for Workers (Gesetz betreffend die Krankenversicherung der Arbeiter) of June 15, 1883 provided for the introduction of national compulsory insurance for most manual and white-collar workers in industry up to an annual earnings level of 2,000 Reichsmarks. This insurance was subsequently extended to the transport sector and to workers in agriculture and forestry. On April 10, 1892 the entire set of provisions was promulgated afresh in the form of the Health Insurance Act (Krankenversicherungsgesetz).

2. On July 6, 1884 there followed the Accident Insurance Act (Unfallsversicherungsgesetz) for workers in particularly dangerous establishments. Later, the construction industry and agriculture and forestry were included. On July 13, 1887 accident insurance was decreed for the shipping sector.

3. The provisions were completed on June 22, 1889 by the Law on Invalidity and Old Age Insurance for Workers, Journeymen and Apprentices (Gesetz über Invaliditäts- und Alterssicherung für Arbeiter, Gehilfen und Lehrlinge), irrespective of wage level.

In introducing a social security policy Bismarck's laws anticipated, in its main features, the present system of **social security**.

233. **BORDPERSONAL — ON-BOARD PERSONNEL**: See **flight personnel**.

234. **BORDVERTRETUNG — ON-BOARD REPRESENTA-TION**: Term used to refer to the representative body which is an organ of the **works constitution** for individual seagoing vessels of shipping companies on which the crew normally includes at least five members entitled to vote under the works constitution (Works Constitution Act § 115). It has the same rights and obligations, appropriately modified, as a **works council**.

For the on-board personnel of airline companies there is, in principle, no representative body. In some cases, however, bodies similar to that for seagoing vessels are provided for under **collective agreements** for the **flight personnel** of individual aircraft.

235. **BOYKOTT — BOYCOTT**: A boycott is a particular form of **industrial action**, signifying a systematic campaign waged by the employers' side or the employees' side to prevent the opposing

collective-bargaining party from pursuing their gainful activity. This can be effected both by the disputing parties themselves and through the agency of third parties. The latter case involves a triangular relationship between the party declaring the boycott ("Boykottierer"), the party putting the boycott into practice ("Boykottant") and the party against whom the boycott is directed ("Boykottierter"). A boycott can take numerous forms. It can apply to contracts of employment, to the effect that employers refuse to hire certain employees ("Einstellungssperre", *i.e.* employment blacklist) or, conversely, that employees refuse to enter into employment with certain employers. It can, however, also apply to other aspects of gainful activity, for example when a trade union calls on sympathetic organizations or the general public not to purchase ("Absatzsperre", *i.e.* sale of goods blacklist) or deliver ("Liefersperre", *i.e.* delivery blacklist) the goods of certain employers. In terms of the law on industrial action, by far the most important form is a boycott imposed in support of a strike. Boycotts are rarely used as a form of industrial action in the Federal Republic, except in the shipping sector: they occur there, for example, when the members of a ship's crew are on strike and dockworkers who are not involved in the strike refuse to load or unload the ship.

236. **BRG**. Betriebsrätegesetz (Works Councils Act). See **works constitution**.

237. **BRUTTOVERGÜTUNG — GROSS PAY**: In principle, the **remuneration** which is due from the employer to the employee in return for the work performance rendered by the latter is a gross sum. The employer is obliged under public law to hold back, from this gross sum, earnings tax, church tax (where applicable) and social security contributions and to pass these **deductions from pay** to the authorities concerned. Generally speaking, legal actions concerning remuneration are directed at the payment of gross pay. The situation is different if the employer and employee have agreed on a **net pay arrangement**.

238. **BUMMELSTREIK — GO-SLOW**: Industrial **action** by employees which takes the form of a collective non-performance or poor performance of the contractual obligation to work, *i.e.* in which they slow down their pace of work or deliberately work badly, is known as a go-slow. Meticulous observance of work regulations and safety provisions to the point of seriously disrupting the establishment's normal practice or bringing it to a standstill is also classed as a go-slow. This latter form, which is called a **work-to-rule**, occurs almost exclusively in the public

service, not least because **strikes by career public servants** ("Beamte") are prohibited. The go-slow is deemed to be an unlawful form of industrial action, even in circumstances where a total withdrawal of labour in the form of a strike would be lawful.

239. **BUNDESANSTALT FÜR ARBEIT — FEDERAL EMPLOYMENT SERVICE**: The Federal Employment Service (BfA) is the agency which performs the functions specified in the Employment Promotion Act (Arbeitsförderungsgesetz), particularly **job placement** and the planned promotion of employment (§§ 33 ff.), the implementation of **job creation schemes** and the administration of **unemployment insurance**. It is a self-governing body headed by a tripartite Administrative Council made up of equal numbers of employee, employer and government representatives. Its outside agencies are the local Employment Offices and, as intermediate authorities, Land Employment Offices in the individual Länder. The central functions of placement are undertaken by its Central Job Placement Service (Zentralstelle für Arbeitsvermittlung) in Frankfurt am Main, and research on **labour market** trends is carried out by the Institute for Labour Market and Occupational Research (Institut für Arbeitsmarkt- und Berufsforschung) at the Federal Employment Service's headquarters in Nuremberg. In 1989 some 70,000 people were employed in the system of employment administration.

240. **BUNDESANSTALT FÜR ARBEITSSCHUTZ — FEDERAL INSTITUTE FOR OCCUPATIONAL HEALTH AND SAFETY**: This Institute, which comes under the **Federal Ministry of Labour and Social Affairs** and has its headquarters in Dortmund, is responsible for promoting and co-ordinating all measures for the protection of employees against operational and occupational hazards. To this end, it regularly develops programmes directed primarily at providing information on the analysis of accidents at work, dangerous materials, occupational illnesses and the **humanization of work**. Its administration is in the hands of an Executive Board, on which the employers' associations and trade unions, employment authorities of the individual Länder, accident insurance institutions, works safety experts and works doctors and the scientific community are all represented. The Executive Board advises the Institute on the preparation of research programmes and other basic policy programmes.

112

241. **BUNDESARBEITSGERICHT — FEDERAL LABOUR COURT**: See **system of labour courts**.

242. **BUNDESANGESTELLTENTARIFVERTRAG — NATIONAL AGREEMENT FOR PUBLIC SECTOR WHITE-COLLAR WORKERS**: Widely referred to by the initials BAT. See **public service**.

243. **BUNDESBEAMTE — FEDERAL CAREER PUBLIC SERVANTS**: Term referring specifically to those **career public servants** ("Beamte") whose **public sector employer** is the Federal Government; they are directly employed in the federal administration. Career public servants in the federally owned institutions, corporations and foundations under federal law also fall within this category: for example, those employed in the Federal Railways (Bundesbahn) and Federal Postal Administration (Bundespost), the **Federal Employment Service**, the Federal Air Safety Authorities and the Federal Bank (Bundesbank). Federal career public servants are covered by the provisions of the **career public service relationship**.

244. **BUNDESLÄNDER — LÄNDER (OF THE FEDERAL REPUBLIC)**: The Federal Republic of Germany is a federal state. It consists of a central state, the Federation, and its member states, the Länder; together, they form the state as a whole. Within the meaning of the Federal German Constitution, the fact of this association means that both the state as a whole and the member states possess the status of a state in their own right. Hence they all have, within the limits of their **legislative powers**, the right of **legislation**. The constitutional order in each Land must conform to the principles of a republican, democratic and social state under the rule of law as laid down in the **Basic Law**.

   With some exceptions, administrative execution of federal statutes lies with the Länder as their own concern. In addition, they participate via the **Federal Council** in the legislation and administration of the Federation. And the exercise of government powers and performance of government functions normally fall to them.

245. **BUNDESMINISTERIUM FÜR ARBEIT UND SOZIAL-ORDNUNG — FEDERAL MINISTRY OF LABOUR AND SOCIAL AFFAIRS**: This Ministry is the supreme (federal) authority in the field of industrial relations. However, its responsibilities extend beyond this: they also include the social security system, the war victims' welfare service and other areas of social policy, and in some instances provision for members

of the liberal professions. It prepares **statutes** in the field of labour law, has wide-ranging powers for issuing **executive orders**, is responsible for the **extension of collective agreements** and maintains the register in which collective agreements are listed. In addition, it is a supervisory authority: the departmental supervisory authority for the **Federal Labour Court** and the **Federal Social Security Court**, the lawful supervisory authority for the **Federal Employment Service** and, lastly, the specialist supervisory authority for the Federal Insurance Office (Bundesversicherungsamt).

246. **BUNDESRAT — FEDERAL COUNCIL**: As the Länder Chamber, the Federal Council or Bundesrat is a federal body in which the individual **Länder** participate in the **legislation** and administration of the Federation. In contrast to the **Federal Parliament**, however, the members of the Federal Council are not appointed by the electorate but by the Land governments. They are subject to the instructions of their respective governments and are therefore not deputies within the meaning of the **Constitution**. Each Land has a certain quota of representatives in the Federal Council, depending on the number of inhabitants in that particular Land. Each Land may send as many members and additional substitutes as it has votes. Representatives of each Land must vote unanimously.

The Federal Council elects half of the judges of the **Federal Constitutional Court**. It has the right to initiate **statutes**. Furthermore, in some cases the actual enactment of federal statutes is dependent on its express assent (**statute requiring assent**). It can also make objection to many statutes that are passed by the Federal Parliament (**statute not requiring assent**). It is when the political majority in the Federal Council differs from that in the Federal Parliament that the weight of its influence is particularly evident; in these circumstances the Federal Council actually constitutes a counterweight to the **Federal Government** and can block certain policies.

247. **BUNDESREGIERUNG — FEDERAL GOVERNMENT**: The Federal Government, consisting of the Federal Chancellor (Bundeskanzler) and the Federal Ministers, is a federal body which acts collectively. It is not, however, an elected body as such. The **Federal Parliament** elects only the Chancellor. The latter, in turn, proposes individual Ministers to the Federal President (Bundespräsident) for appointment or, where applicable, for removal. Only limited powers are actually vested in the Government as a collectively acting body. It is the Chancellor who determines general policy (so-called

114

"Richtlinienkompetenz", *i.e.* responsibility for policy guidelines), and within these guidelines the individual Ministers then direct their respective spheres of action on their own responsibility. To that extent, the principle prevailing in the Government is a mixture of Chancellor's powers and departmental (ministerial) powers. As a collectively acting body, the Government has real decision-making powers only in cases of dissent between individual Ministers.

The Federal Government has the right to initiate **statutes** by tabling **Government Bills**. In addition, it may be given special statutory powers to issue **executive orders**, and hence can also act as a legislative body in the broader sense. Its term of office ends when a newly elected Federal Parliament assembles or when the office of Chancellor falls vacant for any other reason (death, resignation, or successful vote of no confidence naming an elected successor).

248. **BUNDESSOZIALGERICHT — FEDERAL SOCIAL SECURITY COURT**: See **system of social security courts**.

249. **BUNDESTAG — FEDERAL PARLIAMENT**: The Bundestag is the Parliament of the Federal Republic of Germany. It is the most significant expression of the principle of popular sovereignty. Its members are deputies who are elected by the people in universal, direct, free, equal and secret elections. Any person who is German within the meaning of the **Constitution**, is 18 years old and has been resident or had their permanent place of residence on Federal territory for at least three years is eligible to vote. Any person eligible to vote who has possessed German citizenship for at least one year is eligible for election.

The Federal Parliament's primary function is **legislation**. It can introduce Bills from among its members ("Initiativrecht", *i.e.* the right to table Bills), and passes **statutes**. In addition, it elects half of the judges of the **Federal Constitutional Court**. It also plays a direct part in appointments to all the Federal Courts via the Judges Electoral Committee, and in the election of the Federal President via the body called the Federal Assembly (Bundesversammlung). The Federal Parliament exercises a control function with respect to the **Federal Government** by way of members' questions, petitions and, in important cases, the appointment of parliamentary committees of inquiry with powers comparable to the public prosecutor's offices. Quite separately from this, the Federal Parliament may set up committees on any matter of interest, in any number it wishes. The Foreign Affairs Committee and the Defence Committee are, for example, standing committees.

250. **BUNDESVERBAND DER DEUTSCHEN INDUSTRIE — CONFEDERATION OF GERMAN INDUSTRY**: Body (known as the BDI) which promotes the general interests of German industry via research, information and lobbying activities, etc. (as distinct from the representation of interests in the labour relations field by the **BDA**).

251. **BUNDESVEREINIGUNG DER DEUTSCHEN ARBEITGEBERVERBÄNDE — CONFEDERATION OF GERMAN EMPLOYERS' ASSOCIATIONS**: The Confederation (known as the BDA) is the umbrella organization of private sector employers in manufacturing industry, commerce, banking, insurance, small-scale crafts and trades, agriculture, transport and the newspaper industry. It affiliates the central trade associations and the multi-industry Land associations of the **employers' associations**, and has its headquarters in Cologne.

The central trade associations and multi-industry Land associations belong to the Confederation as direct members. Via these, as their member associations, several hundred trade associations and approximately the same number of regional associations belong to it indirectly. The Confederation does not represent all groups of employers. The employers' association for the iron and steel industry is not a member, since in this sector the **employee directors**, who under the special system of **co-determination in the coal, iron and steel industry** are appointed by the **trade unions**, are represented on the collective bargaining committees of the employers' association. In the Confederation's view, this means that the association does not meet the qualifying criterion of having **independence from the opposing side**. Nor do the public sector employers belong to the Confederation; they have formed associations of their own, namely, at Land level the Employers' Association of German Länder (Tarifgemeinschaft deutscher Länder), and at local authority level the Federation of Municipal Employers' Associations (Vereinigung der kommunalen Arbeitgeberverbände).

252. **BUNDESVERFASSUNGSGERICHT — FEDERAL CONSTITUTIONAL COURT**: See **system of constitutional courts**.

253. **BUNDESVERWALTUNGSGERICHT — FEDERAL ADMINISTRATIVE COURT**: See **system of administrative courts**.

254. **BÜROKOMMUNIKATIONSTECHNIK — OFFICE COMMUNICATIONS TECHNOLOGY**: Term referring to systems which, by using **microelectronics**, enable the integration

of a variety of office functions previously performed by individual machines. In addition to conventional electronic data processing (EDP) it includes, in particular, the transfer of data. This is effected either nationally and internationally by using public telephone lines or more advanced telecommunications facilities (for example, ISDNs: integrated services digital networks), or within an establishment or company by means of local networks (for example, LANs: local area networks). A local area network, for instance, has links to public telecommunications channels and integrates the company's EDP system, telex and telephone equipment, text handling and word processing, and fax machines. Enormous increases in **productivity** can be achieved with this technology provided that, for example, every workstation is equipped with a terminal and that **work organization** and employees' **skills** have been properly adapted.

Experience to date indicates that the integration of a range of office tasks by means of such systems has so far not resulted in an erosion of gender-specific occupational segregation or opened up enhanced career opportunities for women. The most extensive application of these office systems is in the banking and insurance sector, where some 90 per cent. of all staff use such equipment.

255. **BVerfG**: Federal Constitutional Court (Bundesverfassungsgericht). See **system of constitutional courts**.

256. **BVerwG**: Federal Administrative Court (Bundesverwaltungsgericht). See **system of administrative courts**.

C

257. CGB: See **Christian Trade Union Federation of Germany** (Christlicher Gewerkschaftsbund Deutschlands).

258. CHRISTLICHER GEWERKSCHAFTSBUND DEUTSCHLANDS — CHRISTIAN TRADE UNION FEDERATION OF GERMANY: In 1957 this federation of Christian unions (referred to as the CGB) was formed as an exception to the principle of the **unified trade unions** that are organized in the **German Federation of Trade Unions** . As yet it has achieved only minor importance as a **party to collective agreements**. It has some 307,000 members. It is an umbrella organization for occupational unions, which combine together in three general associations for manual workers, white-collar workers and career public servants ("Beamte") respectively.

D

259. **DAG**: See **German White-Collar Workers' Union** (Deutsche Angestelltengewerkschaft).

260. **DATENSCHUTZ — DATA PROTECTION**: The purpose of data protection is to protect individuals from the consequences of any form of processing of personal data, but particularly computer processing, and thereby to safeguard the **right of self-determination over personal data**. Data protection is codified in the relevant statutes enacted in the Länder since 1970, the Federal Data Protection Act (Bundesdatenschutzgesetz) passed in 1978 and amended in 1990, and special rules applying to particular areas of the law. Such rules may also be laid down by **collective agreement** and **works agreement**.

Data protection incorporates the conditions for the processing of personal data, *i.e.* data containing information about an individual or facts relating to their person. Data processing comprises four stages: storage, amendment, transmission and erasure. The identity of the data user processing the data makes no difference: it may be a government institution, a private association or a private individual.

For data processing to be permissible, the data user must have a legitimate purpose. Justification may exist by virtue of detailed special rules or (most commonly the case to date) general clauses in the data protection statutes. These normally stipulate that, for data processing by public bodies to be permissible, it must be necessary for the proper performance of the functions assigned to these bodies. In the case of processing by private parties, the criterion is that when their respective interests are weighed against each other the interests of the user processing the data override those of the individual who wishes to protect their personal data.

The rights of the individual concerned are, most importantly, entitlements to be provided with information on the data being stored, to have inaccurate data corrected, to have the use of data prohibited if its accuracy cannot be established, and to have data erased if its processing was or has become unlawful. These rights do not, however, exist in cases where there are overriding considerations of secrecy. Individuals who have suffered damage are entitled to compensation irrespective of any fault on the part of a public authority and, in the case of a private party, if the latter fails to prove the absence of fault on their part. However, it is often the case that individuals who are the subject of data processing are actually prevented from exercising their rights because they know nothing about the storage of data relating to them. Even the work done by **data protection officers** can only partly offset this deficiency in the protection of legal rights.

119

In **labour law**, the **employer** may lawfully store personal data about employees provided that it is necessary in order to achieve the purpose of the employment relationship. This is generally the case as regards data on the employee's age, training and performance. **Co-determination rights of the works council** exist as regards the content of staff application forms and the introduction and use of technical devices designed to monitor behaviour and performance. A survey carried out by the Saarland **Chamber of Labour** in 1990 indicated that data protection within companies is inadequate.

261. **DATENSCHUTZBEAUFTRAGTER — DATA PROTEC-TION OFFICER**: Data protection officers have the task of overseeing observance of the regulations on data protection and advising on its implementation. Such officers have to be appointed by the Federal Government, by the Länder authorities and, supplementing the function of the Labour Inspectorate at individual establishment level, by private individuals who process personal data and regularly employ at least five employees. Officers carry out their duties independently and without having to follow instructions, and are subject only to the law. They are sworn to secrecy regarding the information that becomes known to them in the course of their work.

The Federal Data Protection Officer is elected by the **Federal Parliament**, and the Länder Data Protection Officers are appointed either by the Land Parliaments or by the Land Governments concerned. They are responsible for all the public administration institutions of the Federation or of their particular Land. The Federal Government and Land Government concerned provide them with staff and non-monetary resources.

262. **DBB**: See **German Federation of Career Public Servants** (Deutscher Beamtenbund).

263. **DEMOKRATISCHE WILLENSBILDUNG — DEMOCRA-TIC DECISION-MAKING**: Democratic decision-making is one of the characteristic features of a **collective industrial organization**. Although no **law on associations** exists in the Federal Republic, it is generally recognized that the definition of the organization's policy must be in accordance with the principles of democratic decision-making. This requirement is to ensure, as its corollary, that the interests of individual members of the organization are given adequate consideration. The principles of democratic decision-making are deemed to be fulfilled if a collective industrial organization has drawn up a formal set of standing rules regulating its internal structure and

if these rules guarantee a form of decision-making deriving from the general body of members (possibly via regularly elected representatives). The actual election of delegates and of the organization's principal governing body, and ballots concerning the organization's policy objectives, must themselves be democratic. Consequently, all enfranchised members of the collective industrial organization or of the corresponding representative body must be able to participate in elections and ballots, and it must be possible for all votes to be cast freely and without coercion. Lastly, all votes must count as equal.

264. **DEMONSTRATIONSSTREIK — DEMONSTRATION STRIKE**: See strike.

265. **DEREGULIERUNG — DEREGULATION**: See **employee protection, employment relationship, flexibilization, institutionalized representation of interests, juridification**.

266. **DEUTSCHE ANGESTELLTENGEWERKSCHAFT — GERMAN WHITE-COLLAR WORKERS' UNION**: This union, known as the DAG, organizes predominantly white-collar workers, but is open to such workers employed in all types of industry and establishment. Its members are divided into occupational groups as follows: commercial sector, banking, insurance, public sector, technical staff, career public servants ("Beamte"), skilled craftworkers, shipping and mining. This subdivision enables the interests specific to the members' particular occupations to be promoted. In addition, the Union is structured into Land associations, regional branches and local branches. It has its headquarters in Hamburg. For Germany as a whole, it cites a membership of approximately 575,000. In its role as a trade union, not an umbrella organization, the DAG concludes well over a thousand **collective agreements** annually.

267. **DEUTSCHER BEAMTENBUND — GERMAN FEDERATION OF CAREER PUBLIC SERVANTS**: This Federation, the DBB, mainly organizes career public servants ("Beamte"). Like the German White-Collar Workers' Union, it is organized on an occupational basis. At the end of 1989 it had just on a million members.

268. **DEUTSCHER GEWERKSCHAFTSBUND — GERMAN FEDERATION OF TRADE UNIONS**: This Federation, the DGB, is an umbrella association consisting of the following 16 individual unions organized by industry:

121

IG Bau, Steine, Erden (Union of Construction and Quarrying Industries)

IG Bergbau und Energie (Union of Mining and Energy Industries)

IG Chemie, Papier, Keramik (Union of Chemical, Paper and Ceramics Industries)

Gewerkschaft der Eisenbahner Deutschlands (German Railways Union)

Gewerkschaft Erziehung und Wissenschaft (Education and Science Union)

Gewerkschaft Gartenbau, Land- und Forstwirtschaft (Horticulture, Agriculture and Forestry Union)

Gewerkschaft Handel, Banken und Versicherungen (Commerce, Banking and Insurance Union)

Gewerkschaft Holz und Kunststoff (Timber and Plastics Union)

Gewerkschaft Leder (Leather Union)

IG Medien - Druck und Papier, Publizistik und Kunst (Union of the Media Industries - Printing and Paper, Publishing and Design), formerly two separate unions

IG Metall (Metal Industry Union)

Gewerkschaft Nahrung, Genuss, Gaststätten (Food, Drink and Tobacco and Catering Union)

Gewerkschaft Öffentliche Dienste, Transport und Verkehr (Public Services, Transport and Traffic Union

Gewerkschaft der Polizei (Police Union)

Deutsche Postgewerkschaft (German Post and Telecommunications Union)

Gewerkschaft Textil, Bekleidung (Textiles and Clothing Union)

Their combined membership is at present around 12 million, constituting a good third of the total employed labour force and about 80 per cent. of all unionized employees. More than a quarter of all members are women. The membership strength of the individual unions in their respective industries varies widely. The Metal Industry Union (IG Metall) is by far the strongest, with around 3.6 million members. The Federation is structured into Land associations, which in turn have district and local branches. The Federal Executive Board has its headquarters in Düsseldorf.

In 1989, in the German Democratic Republic the member associations of the "Freier Deutscher Gewerkschaftsbund" (FDGB, the Confederation of Free German Trade Unions) had a total of 9.6 million members. With the accession of the German Democratic Republic to the area of application of the Basic Law of the Federal Republic of Germany, during the year 1990 the FDGB itself and also its member organizations were disbanded.

269. **DGB**: See **German Federation of Trade Unions** (Deutscher Gewerkschaftsbund).

270. **DIENST NACH VORSCHRIFT — WORK-TO-RULE**: As well as taking the form of a total stoppage of work, a **strike** can also be conducted in a manner whereby the performance of work is only partly withheld, for instance by simply slowing down (**go-slow**) or by insisting on an exaggerated observance of work regulations and safety provisions. This latter case is referred to as a work-to-rule, and occurs mainly in the **public service**. It is used, in particular, as a means of side-stepping the strike ban which according to case law applies to **career public servants** ("Beamte"). As a declared form of industrial action the work-to-rule, like the go-slow, is deemed to be unlawful.

271. **DIENSTERFINDUNG — JOB-RELATED INVENTION**: See **inventions by employees**.

272. **DIENSTEID — OATH OF SERVICE**: One of the features of the **duty of loyalty** applying to **career public service** is that **career public servants** ("Beamte") are required to swear an oath of allegiance to the **Constitution**. For **career public servants at Land level**, Land legislation on career public service specifies forms of oath which normally relate to the Constitution and statutes of each particular Land.

273. **DIENSTHERR — PUBLIC SECTOR EMPLOYER**: A public sector employer is a **legal person** under public law or a public authority empowered to employ **career public servants** ("Beamte") in a **career public service relationship** (so-called "Personalhoheit", *i.e.* sovereign authority to employ and dismiss staff). The definition includes the Federation, **Länder** and **municipalities**, associations of municipalities and other public-law corporations, institutions and foundations which possess this right at the time of entry into force of the Career Public Service Framework Act (Beamtenrechtsrahmengesetz) or upon which the right is duly conferred by **statute, executive order** or **byelaws**. The public sector employer is to be distinguished from the **superior official** or direct **superior**, who serves as the means of giving practical shape and effect to the public sector employer's rights arising from the career public service relationship.

274. **DIENSTLEISTUNGSABEND — LATE-NIGHT OPENING**: See **shop closing hours**.

123

275. **DIENSTLICHE ANGELEGENHEITEN — SERVICE-RELATED MATTERS**: Within the ambit of staff representation law, service-related matters are all matters which concern the service relationship or employment relationship in the public sector and have reference to the **public sector establishment** as the employment unit. It is only on such matters that the **staff council** of the public sector establishment in question has co-determination rights and the option of referral to the next-higher **hierarchical representation body**. The substance and scope of the right to consultation and co-determination are regulated in detail in the Federal Staff Representation Act (Bundespersonalvertretungsgesetz).

276. **DIENSTORDNUNGSANGESTELLTE — WHITE-COLLAR WORKERS BOUND BY SPECIAL SERVICE REGULATIONS**: Term used to denote **white-collar workers** who are employed in **social security** institutions and who are covered by officially approved service regulations which lay down rights and obligations of the employment relationship. These white-collar workers are not employed under the appointment procedure for ''Beamte'', *i.e.* **career public servants** (**appointment of career public servants**), but under a private-law contract of employment. Also, disputes of rights arising from their employment relationship are dealt with under the **system of labour courts**. In other respects, however, their special service regulations are largely derived from the law on the career public service relationship, especially as regards **pay of career public servants**. They are to all intents and purposes ''Beamte'' on a private-law basis.

277. **DIENSTREISE — BUSINESS TRAVEL**: Term indicating any journeying between the place where an employee lives or where their employing establishment is located and a place beyond the boundaries of the municipality concerned which is designated by the employer as a place where work is to be performed. Failing any special agreements, remuneration is payable for time spent travelling or being away if business travel forms part of the main work performance due under the contract of employment or falls within normal **working time**. If it is accomplished outside normal working hours and the journey represents a particular burden on the employee (*e.g.* car driving), business travel attracts payment in the form of a contractually agreed supplementary payment. The same rule applies if in the course of lengthy business trips employees also spend free days away from the place where they live.

278. **DIENSTSTELLE — PUBLIC SECTOR ESTABLISH-MENT**: Like the concept of the **establishment** for the purposes of the **works constitution** in the private sector, the "Dienststelle" or public sector establishment is the employment unit taken as the basis for the public-sector staff representation laws of the Federation and the Länder. All the public authorities, entities and agencies of the Federation and the public-law corporations, institutions and foundations (**legal person**) directly controlled by the Federation are classed as public sector establishments. In the case of the Länder this applies *mutatis mutandis* to their own institutions. Administrative authorities at the lower level form a public sector establishment together with the offices attached to them if the latter are not organizationally independent. Branch offices and parts of a public sector establishment which are geographically distant from each other are classed as establishments in their own right if the majority of those employed in them so choose. In this case, a **general staff council** must be formed. The staff representation laws of the Länder contain corresponding regulations for **staff representation** in the Land administration.

279. **DIENSTSTELLENLEITER — PUBLIC-SECTOR ESTABLISHMENT HEAD**: The highest ranking **superior official** at a level of public administration, representing the peak of its hierarchy. Such office-holders possess the authority to act for the establishment as an employment unit and to conclude agreements with the **staff council**. When they are unable to do so, they can delegate a permanent representative to act on their behalf.

280. **DIENSTVEREINBARUNG — ESTABLISHMENT AGREEMENT (PUBLIC SECTOR)**: A public-law agreement, permitted by statute, between a **public-sector establishment head** (acting for the establishment as an employment unit) and the **staff council** on matters concerning employee relations (Staff Representation Act § 73). It is the equivalent of the **works agreement** in the private sector, and hence gives rise to contractual commitments between the parties to the agreement and has a normative effect on the **employment relationships** and **service relationships** of those employed in the public sector establishment. Agreements covering a smaller area are overridden by agreements covering a greater area. These regulations apply *mutatis mutandis* in the Länder.

281. **DIENSTVERGEHEN — BREACH OF DUTY (BY CAREER PUBLIC SERVANT)**: See **disciplinary law for career public servants**.

125

282. **DIENSTVERHÄLTNIS — SERVICE RELATIONSHIP**:
Term used to describe either a public-sector relationship contract
of service (see **public service**), or a contract entered into on a
self-employed or freelance basis (see **contract for services**).

283. **DIENSTVERTRAG — CONTRACT FOR SERVICES**: By
concluding a contract for services, the party supplying services
undertakes to perform the agreed services and the party
commissioning services undertakes to pay the agreed
consideration (Civil Code § 611); a service relationship thereby
exists. The contract for services is the basic form of contract for
the "sale" of services. It is characterized by the fact that what
is due from the supplier of services is not a specified result, but
effort directed towards it. It was out of the contract for services
that the **contract of employment** was developed. Members of
the **professions, freelances** and **persons treated in law as similar
to an employee** conclude with the party commissioning their
services not a contract of employment but an agency contract
(Civil Code § 675) or contract for services.

284. **DIENSTVORGESETZTER — SUPERIOR OFFICIAL**: The
office-holder possessing the authority to take decisions under
career public service law on personal matters concerning the
career public servants ("Beamte") subordinate to him or her.
This authority covers matters such as imposing disciplinary
measures, authorizing **business travel** and granting **leave**. It does
not, however, include the right to issue instructions to individuals
in the context of their work activities (authority for which lies
with their "Amtsvorgesetzter" or direct **superior**).

285. **DIENSTWAGEN — COMPANY CAR**: See **payment in kind**.

286. **DIENSTWOHNUNG — COMPANY HOUSING**: Synonym
of **Werkwohnung**.

287. **DIFFERENZIERUNGSKLAUSEL — DIFFERENTIAL
TREATMENT CLAUSE**: Differential treatment clauses are
provisions in collective agreements which are intended to ensure
that union members covered by the agreement enjoy more
favourable conditions of employment than **non-union members**.
As distinct from collectively agreed **exclusion clauses**, differential
treatment clauses make **union membership** the substance of the
collectively agreed rule of entitlement.

   The **Federal Labour Court** holds such clauses to be unlawful,
since they violate the fundamental right of positive and
"negative" freedom of association. The question of whether

a provision in a collective agreement is to be deemed a differential treatment clause is determined by **interpretation**.

288. **DIN**: German Standards Institute (Deutsches Institut für Normung). See **rationalization association, safety of equipment**.

289. **DIREKTIONSRECHT — EMPLOYER'S RIGHT TO ISSUE INSTRUCTIONS**: In the **contract of employment** the work due from the **employee** to the **employer** is indicated only in general terms. The employer therefore has the right to put this contractual obligation into definite terms and assign particular work tasks to the employee. The employee is under an obligation to obey orders given by the employer which keep within the limits of the employment contract and comply with the principles of natural justice, provided they do not infringe a **statute, collective agreement** or **works agreement**. Only in emergency situations may the employer require the employee to effect a performance not contractually due.

290. **DIREKTVERSICHERUNG — DIRECT INSURANCE**: Because it involves comparatively little bureaucratic effort, direct insurance is a particularly popular way of providing an **occupational pension scheme** in small and medium-sized companies. With this system, the employer takes out insurance policies with insurance companies for the benefit of individual employees or groups of employees. The beneficiary employees may be required to contribute towards the insurance premiums payable. The system enables the employer to avoid obligations to adjust **occupational pensions** and to relieve the company of the economic risks inherent in the **direct guarantee** system. Various forms of tax concession are available.

Another form of direct insurance through the employer is the upgraded insurance of employees under the **statutory pension scheme** by paying higher contributions. This form is, however, less effective in many cases. Also, it is not included in the protection provided under the Improvement of Occupational Pension Schemes Act (Gesetz zur Verbesserung der betrieblichen Altersversorgung).

291. **DIREKTZUSAGE — DIRECT GUARANTEE**: Direct guarantee is the most widely used form of providing **assurance of an occupational pension** under **occupational pension schemes**. With this system, the insured employees acquire direct claims against their employer, whose entire assets are pledged to cover liability for such claims. Special-purpose reserves are usually set

127

up: via the "capital cover" procedure for cases where employees with accumulated entitlements leave the company, and via the "expectation cover" procedure for regular adjustment to increasing **occupational pension expectations**.

The advantage of the system is that the special-purpose reserves are set against profit and therefore save tax, but remain within the company and available for its financial use until a pension actually becomes payable. Employers can take out reinsurance policies with insurance companies to safeguard capital cover for the direct guarantee in the event of financial difficulties.

292. **DISKRIMINIERUNGSVERBOTE — ANTI-DISCRIMINA-TION LAWS**: Term used for provisions prohibiting the prejudicial treatment of individuals because of certain characteristics or acts. Such bans on discrimination supplement the general principle of **equality before the law** and the labour-law principle of **equal treatment** by ensuring that differential treatment for reasons that infringe a given ban is automatically unlawful.

The primary source of anti-discrimination law is Article 3 of the **Basic Law**, which prohibits prejudice on grounds of sex, descent, race, language, homeland and origin, creed, religious and political beliefs, birth out of wedlock, or membership of a particular **collective industrial organization**. Other important provisions are the prohibition under Article 48 of the EEC Treaty of any discrimination against nationals of other EC Member States as compared with citizens of the Federal Republic, and in **labour law** the precept of **equal rights** (Civil Code §§ 611a, 612(3)) and the **ban on disciplinary treatment** (Civil Code § 612a).

Anti-discrimination laws are not intended to impose a blanket ban on differentiation between members of different sexes, religions, parties, etc. Their purpose is to prevent only differential treatment whose sole or predominant determining consideration is the characteristic in question. This means that such discrimination is difficult to establish, with a considerable risk that other grounds will be advanced as justification. Consequently, the standard of proof is relaxed in some respects for the individuals affected.

293. **DISPOSITIVES RECHT — DISCRETIONARY LAW**: Term used to refer to statutory regulations whose content may be changed by agreement between parties participating in the operation of the law. This is the case, for example, with contract law as under the Civil Code, characterized by the **freedom of contract**; it is also the case with numerous labour law statutes, although here subject to the proviso that the change constitutes

a divergence to the benefit of the employee (**favourability principle, labour law**). The opposite of discretionary law is **peremptory law**.

294. **DISZIPLINARRECHT — DISCLIPLINARY LAW FOR CAREER PUBLIC SERVANTS**: A part of career public service law (**career public service relationship**). For **federal career public servants** ("Bundesbeamte") it is regulated in the Federal Disciplinary Code, while **career public servants at Land level** ("Landesbeamte") are covered by the relevant Land Disciplinary Code. These various provisions are almost identical.

Substantive disciplinary law regulates penalties for breaches of duty by career public servants and hence any culpable violation of their obligations. It is aimed at upholding the public trust placed in the **career public service** by maintaining discipline and even, where appropriate, removing unfit persons from their post. Hence, even conduct unconnected with a career public servant's actual job may, within certain limits, be penalized if it has jeopardized people's trust in the public service. Also, the formal definition of a disciplinary procedure is intended to strengthen the legal status of career public servants.

The disciplinary procedure (formal disciplinary law) is largely modelled on criminal court procedure, and proceedings are conducted before special administrative courts which are disciplinary courts: for federal career public servants the Federal Disciplinary Court (Bundesdisziplinargericht) in Frankfurt am Main, and for career public servants at Land level the relevant disciplinary tribunal (Disziplinarkammer) or disciplinary board (Dienststrafkammer). If the breach of duty concerned is also a criminal offence within the meaning of the Penal Code, criminal proceedings may take place in parallel. The findings of the criminal courts (**system of ordinary courts**) are, however, binding on the disciplinary courts (so-called "findings of fact effect").

The disciplinary procedure ends in dismissal of the proceedings, an acquittal, or imposition of a disciplinary penalty. The penalties provided for in the various Disciplinary Codes are basically the following:
a. a reprimand, *i.e.* simply censure of certain conduct;
b. a fine representing up to one month's salary (**pay of career public servants**);
c. a cut in salary by up to one fifth for a period of up to five years;
d. transfer to a different post in the same **career branch** with a lower salary, which also means the loss of the grade formerly held;
e. dismissal from the public service, with the loss of all acquired entitlements and rights.

295. **DOPPELARBEITSVERHÄLTNIS — DUAL JOBHOLD-ING**: If an **employee** enters into more than one **employment relationship** at the same time, this is termed dual or multiple jobholding ("Mehrfacharbeitsverhältnis"). Such dual jobholding is valid in law only if the employee's total **working time** does not exceed the statutory **maximum working hours** limit (at present 48 hours per week). Although for the purposes of legal validity it is irrelevant whether the employee can actually perform both employment relationships properly, **entitlement to damages** against the employee may arise on the part of one or more employers if this is not so. However, the contract of employment often stipulates that the employee must not enter into another employment relationship in addition to the existing one.

296. **DOPPELBESTEUERUNGSABKOMMEN — DOUBLE TAXATION AGREEMENT**: See **tax**.

297. **DOPPELVERDIENER — DUAL INCOME COUPLE**: Term used to refer to a couple where both spouses are economically active. In the context of **social criteria for redundancy** the fact is often counted against such a couple; legal opinion is divided as to whether this procedure is lawful or unlawful.

298. **DRITTWIRKUNG — THIRD-PARTY EFFECT OF CONSTITUTIONAL RIGHTS**: As elements of an objective system of values, **basic rights** as enshrined in the Constitution not only have validity for the individual in relation to the state (*i.e.* in public and administrative law) but are also of importance in relation to other private individuals. The extent of this third-party effect differs from one area of law to another. In **labour law**, for example, whose function is to resolve conflicts between people possessing very unequal economic and social power (namely, between employers and employees), protection of the constitutional rights of the party who is economically and socially the weaker of the two plays an important part. Conversely, in areas where the contracting parties are on a relatively equal footing, such as company law and much of general civil law, the effect of constitutional rights is largely obscured by the overarching concept of the freedom of the individual.

The **Federal Labour Court** has taken the view that constitutional rights have direct effect within the context of the employment relationship. More recently, however, this view is given a somewhat more restrictive interpretation in the Court's decisions, according to which constitutional rights apply only indirectly via the general provisions of civil law.

299. **DRUCKKÜNDIGUNG — DISMISSAL UNDER THIRD-PARTY PRESSURE**: Term used to refer to the case where an **employer** terminates an **employment** relationship not on the basis of a decision arrived at personally but because business associates, trade unions, sections of the workforce or the works council compel the employer to do so by threatening such action as a breaking-off of business relations or a refusal to work. Dismissal in such cases is deemed to be a **redundancy**, which may be in the form of a **summary termination** or a **termination with notice**. For it to be deemed such, the precondition is that the employer must have demonstrated support for the employee in question and attempted to dissuade the third party or parties from applying pressure. If these efforts fail, such a dismissal is justified if the employer cannot reasonably be expected to accept the threatened prejudicial effects because of their serious economic consequences. This instance of dismissal must be distinguished from cases where pressure is exerted because of forms of conduct or personal attributes on the part of an employee which are in themselves adequate grounds for dismissal. Such cases do not constitute dismissal under third-party pressure, but **dismissal on grounds of personal capability** or **on grounds of conduct**.

300. **DUALES SYSTEM — DUAL SYSTEM (OF VOCATIONAL TRAINING)**: Name given to the system whereby vocational training is organized as a combination of **company vocational training** in the **vocational training employer**'s establishment and **statutory vocational training** in a **vocational training school**. Under this system, over a period of two to three years the **vocational trainee** receives training in parallel at two places, the establishment and the training school, which differ in their structure and in the type of instruction given. A vocational trainee is therefore simultaneously a vocational student.

301. **DURCHSCHNITTSLOHN — AVERAGE WAGE**: See **reference wage**.

131

E

302. EFFEKTIVKLAUSEL — ACTUAL-PAY CLAUSE: Clause in a collective agreement whereby the unions attempt to establish an entitlement to actual rates of pay exceeding the collectively agreed pay scale. There are two types of such clause: actual-pay guarantee clauses and limited actual-pay clauses.

Actual-pay guarantee clauses, which are intended to ensure that an existing enhanced rate of pay is treated as a collectively agreed pay level, have no legal validity. The **Federal Labour Court** holds that they violate the principle of **equality before the law**, since they result in differing minimum pay levels whereas the purpose of **collective agreements** is to establish uniform standards, and hence they contradict the principle that conditions of employment more favourable than those laid down in collective agreements are rightfully a matter to be agreed (and amended) freely in the individual contract of employment and do not fall within the province of collective regulation (**favourability principle**). Furthermore, with such clauses the requirement that collective agreements must be in written form is not properly fulfilled, since the individual levels of pay are not evident from the agreement.

Limited actual-pay clauses are frequently used by the parties to a collective agreement as a means of agreeing that an existing arrangement between employer and employee for a rate of pay exceeding the collectively agreed scale will continue to apply to the employee in relation to the new scale. These clauses too are invalid, for the same reasons as in the case of actual-pay guarantee clauses. The question of whether a provision in a collective agreement is to be classed as an actual-pay clause is decided by **interpretation** in the courts.

303. EHRENAMTLICHE RICHTER — LAY JUDGES: In many **systems of jurisdiction**, particularly in the **systems of labour courts** and **social security courts**, the courts have lay judges on the bench as well as career judges. The main purpose of appointing lay judges is to ensure that court decisions will incorporate due consideration of their specialized knowledge, based as it is on practical experience, and to foster public confidence in the courts. In the labour and social security courts, lay judges possessing the same powers as the career judges are on the bench at all levels. In the labour courts, the individual panels (chambers or senates) have an equal number of lay judges to represent the employers' and employees' sides respectively, appointed on the basis of nomination lists put forward by the trade unions and the employers' associations. In the social security courts, the lay judges are nominated by the relevant organizations and associations.

304. **EIGENGRUPPE — SELF-CONSTITUTED EMPLOYEE GROUP**: Term referring to a number of **employees** who have formed themselves into a team independently for the purpose of achieving a certain work result. In contrast to a **work group** formed by the employer, in this case the individual members do not necessarily each have their own contract of employment with the employer. Also, the employer has no say in deciding the composition of the group; if a member leaves the group and this so minimizes, impairs or otherwise substantially alters its work performance that it ceases to suit the employer's requirements, depending on the circumstances the employer may be entitled to dismiss the other members of the group by way of **summary termination**. Typical examples of self-constituted employee groups are gangs of plasterers or bricklayers, bands of musicians, etc., usually organized in a non-incorporated private association ("Gesellschaft bürgerlichen Rechts").

Legal relations with the employer may be established by the group as such, together with its members, or by the individual members alone. Depending on which is the case, the employer can assert claims against the group and possibly also against individual employees, and the group members can assert claims only against the group or against the employer, with the provisions of **labour law** always applying.

The group is represented by its leader or spokesperson, whose powers depend on the legal form chosen for it.

305. **EINGRUPPIERUNG — GRADING**: See **co-determination rights of the works council, general agreement on pay grades, pay agreement, remuneration**.

306. **EINHEITSGEWERKSCHAFT — UNIFIED TRADE UNION**: The trade union system in the Federal Republic is essentially concentrated in the member unions of the **German Federation of Trade Unions** (the DGB, formed in 1949), the **German White-Collar Workers' Union** (the DAG, founded in 1947) and the **German Federation of Career Public Servants** (the DBB, founded in 1950). In contrast to the unions during the period of the Weimar Republic, these organizations are not unions with particular ideological or party political links ("Richtungsgewerkschaften"). They style themselves unified trade unions, stressing as their chief characteristic the fact that they are ideologically and politically neutral. In 1957 the **Christian Trade Union Federation of Germany** (the CGB) was formed as a separate organization from the DGB.

133

307. EINIGUNGSSTELLE — ESTABLISHMENT-LEVEL ARBITRATION COMMITTEE: A private-law arbitration body within the establishment, as an element of the **works constitution** (Works Constitution Act § 76). It is the conflict resolution mechanism of **institutionalized representation of interests** provided for by law. An arbitration committee can be set up and perform its function on an *ad hoc* basis whenever disputes of interest arise between the employer and the works council, company works council or group works council (whichever is competent for the issue in question).

In circumstances where **co-determination rights of the works council** are enforceable, an arbitration committee may be formed even if only one of the parties so requests. Such a committee can also be established, by way of a **works agreement**, as a permanent body.

The decision reached by the arbitration committee (award) takes effect as a substitute for agreement between the employer and the works council. Normally, the formation of the committee must be at the request of both sides and its award has this validity as a substitute for agreement only if the parties within the establishment undertake beforehand to abide by it or accept it subsequently. In terms of legal effect, the award corresponds to a works agreement.

The competence of the committee and any possible infringements of the law or errors of judgment in its award may be examined by the courts under the **"Beschluss" procedure**.

As provided for by the law, the arbitration committee consists of equal numbers of assessors appointed by the employer and works council respectively, and an impartial chairperson. If agreement cannot be reached on the number of assessors and/or the choice of chairperson, the matter is decided by the Labour Court. In many cases arbitration committees are chaired by professional judges from the **system of labour courts**.

The costs of the arbitration committee are borne by the employer (Works Constitution Act § 76a). The chairperson and any external assessors are automatically entitled to be paid a fee by the employer; the amount of this fee depends on the time spent serving on the committee, the difficulty of the dispute under consideration and loss of income incurred, and is less for the assessors than for the chairperson. A corresponding rule on remuneration may also be laid down by the Federal Minister for Labour and Social Affairs by executive order.

In the context of **staff representation** in the public sector, the arbitration committee is a permanent body (Federal Staff Representation Act § 71). It constitutes the mechanism for settling disputes of interest between the **public-sector establishment head** on the one hand and the **staff council** or **general staff council** on the other. As provided for by the law, the arbitration committee is formed at the relevant top-level administrative authority and consists of six assessors, three of them appointed by the administrative authority and three by the relevant staff council, and an impartial chairperson. If agreement cannot be reached on the choice of chairperson, the matter is decided by the President of the **Federal Administrative Court**. The three committee members appointed by the staff council must be one **manual worker**, one **white-collar worker** and one **career public servant**, unless the issue under consideration concerns only career public servants or only manual and white-collar workers.

308. **EINKOMMENSTEUER — INCOME TAX**: See **deductions from pay, earnings tax, tax**.

309. **EINPERSONENBETRIEBSRAT — SINGLE-MEMBER WORKS COUNCIL**: In establishments normally employing 5-20 employees eligible to vote in **works council** elections, the works council consists of one person (Works Constitution Act § 9). In principle this person (also referred to as a "Betriebsobmann" or works spokesperson) has the same rights and obligations as a works council and **works council members**, with the exception of provisions which presuppose a larger number of employees. If more employees join the establishment subsequent to the election, the single-member works council may be invested with these **participation rights of the works council** as well.

310. **EINSPRUCHSGESETZ — STATUTE NOT REQUIRING ASSENT (OF THE FEDERAL COUNCIL)**: Term used to categorize any statute presented by the **Federal Parliament** which, according to the **Constitution**, does not require the assent of the **Federal Council** (*cf.* a **statute requiring assent**). In such cases an objection by the Federal Council, if overruled by the Federal Parliament, cannot prevent enactment of the statute. See **legislative powers**.

311. **EINSTELLUNGSFRAGEBOGEN — APPLICATION FORM**: Applicants for a job are frequently asked to fill in an application form. Where the employer uses such written application forms, their content is subject to the **co-determination rights of the works council**.

The application form may contain only questions which are

of legitimate interest to the employer for the purposes of the particular job vacancy. This is accepted as being the case, for example, with questions about pregnancy, the nature of disabilities, any relevant court convictions in the past, current and chronic illnesses (as far as these are relevant to the performance of the employment relationship) and debts and court orders for **attachment of earnings** (because of the administrative expense entailed). It has, however, been held as a general principle that the employer has no legitimate interest in asking questions about judicial investigations and pending criminal proceedings, the applicant's level of earnings with a former employer, or membership of trade unions, political parties and Religious Communities.

If an applicant deliberately gives false answers to questions on the application form which are deemed to be of legitimate interest to the employer and therefore admissible, this generally leads to **voidability of the employment contract**. Questions that are not admissible may, however, be deliberately answered falsely without incurring any consequences.

312. **EINSTWEILIGE VERFÜGUNG — INTERLOCUTORY INJUNCTION**: The interlocutory injunction is a legal remedy that can be used for the provisional protection of a claim not involving money. The procedure basically corresponds to that of a distraint order in the case of a money claim (seizure of goods as security for the future **enforcement of judgment**), and to that of a temporary decree in public law. The preconditions for the grant of an injunction are laid down in the Code of Civil Procedure.

There are three different forms of injunction, namely, a protective injunction ("Sicherungsverfügung") for protecting claims not involving money and a regulatory injunction ("Regelungsverfügung") for the temporary regulation of a legal relationship that is the subject of dispute. And lastly, within narrow bounds a settlement injunction ("Befriedigungs-verfügung") is also possible for the settlement, by way of exception, of a money claim as well. This is permissible only if effective protection of a legal right cannot be provided by any other means.

The interlocutory injunction is also of considerable practical importance in **labour court procedure**, since during the period of time that elapses between the institution of legal proceedings and final judgment developments can occur which may render the court's verdict *de facto* meaningless.

313. EINWIRKUNGSPFLICHT — DUTY TO EXERT INFLUENCE: In addition to the **peace obligation**, the **parties to a collective agreement** are bound by another contractual obligation arising from the **collective agreement**, namely, the duty to exert their influence. This means that they must use the means available to them under the law on associations to ensure that their respective members duly abide by the provisions of the agreement. Their duty to exert influence does not, however, make it compulsory for them to take steps against every individual breach of the agreement, for instance where an individual employer is temporarily failing to pay the collective agreed rates of pay because of financial difficulties. Its intention is, rather, to ensure that the provisions of the agreement are upheld as the general rule among their members and to prevent any deliberate moves to undermine these provisions, *e.g.* by means of industrial action contravening the peace obligation. In the case of **company agreements** the duty to exert influence falls directly on the individual employer who has concluded the agreement.

314. ELTERNURLAUB — PARENTAL LEAVE: Under some **collective agreements**, an employee who has completed a specified minimum continuous **length of service** in an establishment of a specified minimum size is allowed a period of parental leave following on directly from **childcare leave**. During this parental leave the **employment relationship** is suspended and no gainful employment may be undertaken with another employer. At the end of the period of parental leave the employee concerned is entitled to be reinstated in a job as nearly equivalent as possible to their former job. An employee who intends to resume the employment relationship in this way must notify the employer of the fact within a due period of notice before parental leave expires.

315. ERHALTUNGSARBEITEN — MAINTENANCE OF ESSENTIAL SUPPLIES AND SERVICES: In a **strike** situation, striking employees, whether union members or not, are under an obligation to carry out the work necessary to keep essential supplies and services going. Such work is also referred to as emergency work ("Notarbeiten" or "Notdienstarbeiten"); the purpose is to ensure that when the labour dispute comes to an end normal production can be resumed as soon as possible.

This covers, first and foremost, essential work ("Notstandsarbeiten"), *i.e.* work necessary to ensure that during the dispute the general population continues to be supplied with essential goods and services (food, electricity, gas, water and medical care), and maintenance work in the strict sense. It

137

includes work to maintain production facilities in the condition they were in at the start of the dispute, ongoing work to maintain production (possibly at a reduced level) that is necessary for technical reasons in order to prevent damage to industrial plant (blast furnaces, chemical plants), and processing work to prevent damage to products and production plants during the stoppage. It does not include work activities aimed at safeguarding the market share or customer base of the company affected by strike action, nor the further processing or transportation of products generated by essential work.

Employees are under an obligation to carry out such essential work by virtue of their duty of loyalty under the contract of employment, which is not suspended during a lawful strike. In addition the **union strike guidelines** drawn up by the German Federation of Trade Unions contain corresponding instructions for union members who are called upon to carry out essential work. Hence, an obligation also exists on this basis, although only in terms of the relationship between individual union members and their union.

No legal provisions exist which clarify whether the right to arrange essential work lies with the employer or with the striking union. In practice, both the actual nature and the extent of such work are usually decided by agreement between the employer and the strike leadership in the establishment affected.

316. **ERHOLUNGSURLAUB — ANNUAL HOLIDAY**: The most important form of entitlement to **leave** for **employees** and **persons treated in law as similar to an employee** is the entitlement to annual holiday. It constitutes a legal right to be released from work for a specified period, as provided for by the Federal Minimum Annual Holiday Act of 1963: the statutory annual holiday entitlement is 18 **working days** (§ 3). This entitlement is usually increased under the terms of the contract of employment and, in particular, via collective agreements. As a result the majority of employees nowadays have an annual holiday entitlement of 5-6 weeks.

Annual holiday must be granted as one consecutive period during the current calendar year. It can also be carried over into the first three months of the following year, provided this is justified by urgent reasons connected with the company or personal reasons. Employees themselves decide how they spend their annual holiday. They are, however, prohibited by law from undertaking during this period any gainful employment which contradicts the purpose of granting annual holiday, *i.e.* any gainful employment which is as arduous for them as their normal job. Before the start of their annual holiday, employees are entitled to be paid, for the whole of their holiday period, holiday pay at a rate corresponding to their level of earnings averaged over the immediately preceding 13 weeks. Over and above this, many **collective agreements** provide for the payment of an additional holiday bonus. If employees produce a medical certificate showing that they were ill during their annual holiday, the period away from work covered by the certificate does not count as part of their holiday entitlement. Employees must not dispose of their annual holiday entitlement for gain, nor may the employer purchase it from them. Disabled employees and young employees are entitled to longer annual holidays than other employees (see **protection for disabled employees** and **youth employment protection**).

The employer must take account of individual employees' wishes in deciding when their annual holidays are to be taken. A **co-determination right of the works council** exists for cases where there are differences of opinion between employer and employee and also for drawing up a holiday roster for the entire workforce. **Fixed works holidays** may also be arranged in this way.

317. **ERSATZKASSE — WHITE-COLLAR WORKERS' HEALTH INSURANCE FUND**: An approved alternative fund. See **health insurance, health insurance fund**.

318. **ERSATZZEIT — PERIOD TREATED AS A CONTRIBU-TION PERIOD**: Under special circumstances, certain periods during which an employee subject to compulsory insurance does not pay contributions into the **statutory pension scheme** are credited to the employee as periods equivalent to contribution periods. This means that they count towards the **qualifying period** necessary for benefits. Particular examples of periods treated in this way are periods of **unemployment** and compulsory military or community service and the **childcare period**.

319. **ERWERBSTÄTIGE ZIVILBEVÖLKERUNG — CIVILIAN WORKING POPULATION**: In 1989 the civilian working population in the Federal Republic totalled 26.9 million persons. Of these, 11 million (41 per cent.) were **white-collar workers**, 10.7 million (39.6 per cent.) were **manual workers**, 2.4 million (9.1 per cent.) were **career public servants**, 2.3 million (8.5 per cent.) were self-employed (*i.e.* **professions, entrepreneurs**) and 500,000 (1.8 per cent.) were assisting family members. The civilian working population as it exists at any given time is not identical with the number of people actually available to the **labour market**.

139

320. ERWERBSUNFÄHIGKEIT — TOTAL DISABILITY: Condition which is judged to exist if, as a result of **illness**, other infirmity or impairment of their physical and mental faculties, an individual insured under the **statutory pension scheme** has no foreseeable prospect of being able to continue undertaking regular gainful employment or of earning more than a marginal income from regular gainful employment. Total disability must apply to any form of employment whatever, irrespective of the individual's former occupational status and walk of life. The classification of total disability is established by the insurance institution, on the basis of medical opinion.

Individuals classed as suffering total disability are entitled to a total disability pension subject to an insurance period of 60 months prior to the materialization of total disability or an insurance period of 240 months prior to the claim.

Entitlements to pensions for **occupational incapacity** and for total disability are mutually exclusive.

321. ERZIEHUNGSGELD — CHILDCARE PAYMENT: Individuals who satisfy the criteria for entitlement to **childcare leave**, or fail to satisfy them only because they are not classed as **employees**, are entitled to childcare payment starting from the date of their child's birth, regardless of whether or not they actually take childcare leave. This childcare payment is a state benefit amounting to 600 Deutschmarks per month for the first 18 months of the child's life. From the seventh month onwards, the monthly payment decreases starting from certain income thresholds. During the period for which the child's mother receives the maternity allowance (**maternity protection**), this sum is counted towards the childcare payment (Federal Childcare Payment and Childcare Leave Act §§ 1 ff.).

Many individual Länder have their own arrangements for a family allowance or childcare payment.

322. ERZIEHUNGSURLAUB — CHILDCARE LEAVE: A special statutory leave entitlement for parents, for the purpose of caring for their child. The right to claim such leave is possessed by **employees** who live in a household with a child for whom they are entitled to have custody and who care for the child themselves, if during the period of childcare leave they do not engage in gainful employment. The same applies in the case of employment for up to 19 hours per week. No entitlement exists in the case of a married couple where one of the spouses is not economically active. If a child is cared for by more than one person fulfilling the conditions for entitlement, only one of these persons may claim childcare leave. They may, however, share the leave between them.

Childcare leave can be claimed starting from the end of the period of maternity protection, *i.e.* from 8 or 12 weeks after the birth (**maternity protection**), up to the end of the month in which the child becomes 18 months old (this is to be extended to two years as from 1993). During this period there is an entitlement to **childcare payment**. The main obligations arising from the **employment relationship** are suspended during childcare leave, which means that the employee does not have to perform work and the **employer** does not have to pay remuneration, unless they have reached an agreement on part-time work. Entitlement to payments from the employer which are in consideration not of actual work performance but of loyal service, for example, continues unchanged.

There is an absolute ban on dismissal during childcare leave, with the same conditions applying as during the period of maternity protection. For the purposes of **health insurance**, **unemployment insurance**, the **statutory pension scheme** and **occupational pension schemes**, the period of childcare leave is basically treated as a period of employment counting towards entitlements (Federal Childcare Payment and Childcare Leave Act §§ 15 ff.).

Childcare leave is claimed by approximately 97 per cent. of parents (the father being the one who takes leave in fewer than 1 per cent. of cases).

323. **ERZIEHUNGSZEIT — CHILDCARE PERIOD**: For the purposes of pension calculation (**statutory pension scheme**), the first 12 months after the birth of a child are referred to as the childcare period and credited as a compulsory insurance period to whichever parent devotes themselves to care of the child and does not engage in gainful employment. For children born from 1992 onwards, the childcare period is increased to three years.

In the case of eastern Germany, special interim regulations which also permit gainful employment apply until 1997.

324. **EUROPÄISCHE AKTIENGESELLSCHAFT — EUROPEAN COMPANY**: Concept also referred to as Societas Europea (SE). See **forms of company**.

325. **EUROPÄISCHE SOZIALCHARTA — EUROPEAN SOCIAL CHARTER**: The European Social Charter (ESC) was signed by the Federal Republic of Germany on October 18, 1961 and ratified by the Federal Parliament and has been in force since February 26, 1965. In terms of labour law, its significance in

principle extends far beyond that of the European Convention on Human Rights. Article 5 of the ESC grants **freedom of association** for the employers' side as well. Furthermore, Article 6 guarantees both for **employers' associations** and for **trade unions** the right to take **industrial action**. According to Article 31, these rights may be restricted only in exceptional circumstances. Contrary to the provisions of Federal German law, according to the ESC a **strike by career public servants** also is lawful. For the rest, the ESC contains a series of detailed regulations on social security and conditions of employment which were basically already the standard in German law.

According to the main body of legal opinion the ESC does not constitute national law, but purely an obligation on the Federal Republic in terms of international law. From this, the **Federal Labour Court** infers that direct application by Germany's courts is prohibited. However, since by the act of ratification the Federal Republic has undertaken to implement the ESC, its regulations are significant for the courts as regards the **interpretation** of **statutes** and still more as regards **further development of the law**

The Charter on fundamental social rights for employees that was adopted by the EC Member States in 1989 is also known as the European Social Charter. The purpose of this agreement is to fix certain minimum standards in order to prevent the advent of the single **internal market** from occasioning competition disadvantageous to employees.

326. EUROPÄISCHES GEMEINSCHAFTSRECHT — EUROPEAN COMMUNITY LAW: In the Federal Republic of Germany, a distinction is commonly made between primary and secondary Community law.

Primary Community law consists of the three Treaties establishing the European Coal and Steel Community, the European Economic Community (the Treaty of Rome) and the European Atomic Energy Community. Despite the fact that it has its source in treaties, this Community law is not international law, but constitutional law *sui generis* for EC Member States. Accordingly, the EC Treaties (especially the Treaty of Rome) have created a legal system binding on the Member States which is valid at national level and must be applied by national courts. Whenever a legal question touches on the scope of one of the EC Treaties, the latter's treaty law takes direct effect. Consequently, these provisions have the rank of a **statute** as far as **labour law** is concerned.

Secondary Community law comprises the legislation enacted by virtue of these three Treaties, *e.g.* **Directives**.

F

327. **FACHKRÄFTE FÜR ARBEITSSICHERHEIT — WORKS SAFETY EXPERTS**: Works safety experts are qualified safety engineers, technicians and specialists who assist the employer with **protection against accidents** and **protection against technical hazards at work**. They occupy a largely autonomous position within the **workplace health and safety arrangements**: they do not have to follow anyone's instructions in applying their expertise, within the staff hierarchy they are answerable directly to the head of the establishment, and they are not necessarily employees of the establishment in question. In practice, however, this legal independence is limited by the fact that, like **works doctors**, to a varying degree they are economically dependent on the employer and have only an advisory and monitoring function, without any decision-making powers.

   The employer is required to appoint works safety experts in cases where this is necessary because of the nature of the establishment and its associated accident risks and health hazards, the size and composition of the workforce and the organization of the work (Occupational Health and Safety Act § 5). Their appointment is subject to a **co-determination right of the works council**.

   The functions performed by works safety experts comprise advising the employer, and any other bodies responsible for health and safety at work (including the works council), on the organization of the establishment, working methods and accident prevention; carrying out safety checks on plant and equipment and work processes; monitoring compliance with health and safety regulations; educating the workforce about hazards and protective measures; and training **safety officers**. They work in close co-operation with the works doctors and, like the latter, are represented on the establishment's **health and safety committee** (Occupational Health and Safety Act §§ 6 ff.).

328. **FACHVERBANDSPRINZIP — PRINCIPLE OF OCCUPATIONAL ORGANIZATION**: A feature of trade union structure whereby, in contrast to the **principle of industrial organization**, employees are grouped according to their particular occupation. The DAG (**German White-Collar Workers' Union**) and the DBB (**German Federation of Career Public Servants**) are two such occupational unions.

329. **FAIRNESSGEBOT — FAIRNESS PRINCIPLE**: A requirement derived from the **proportionality principle**, constituting a legal limit which must be observed when engaging in **industrial action**. It means that a **strike** must be conducted in accordance

143

with the rules of fair play and must not be aimed at destroying the other side's means of existence. When the dispute is over, both sides must co-operate in restoring industrial peace.

330. **FAKTISCHES ARBEITSVERHÄLTNIS — *DE FACTO* EMPLOYMENT RELATIONSHIP**: Concept developed to cover the case where a **contract of employment** was invalid from the start or has been validly declared void but the employee has already performed work. In order to prevent the work performance already provided under these circumstances from being nullified in accordance with the principles of the law on unjust enrichment (which would entitle the employee to remuneration only for that part of the work performance from which the employer has actually gained pecuniary benefit), the courts treat this *de facto* employment relationship as valid retrospectively. This means that, in respect of the past period before the contract of employment became known to be void or was declared void, the same entitlements accrue to the employee as he or she would have acquired if a valid contract had existed. The advantageous implications of this legal institution are evident as regards **sick pay, overtime pay** or **employer's non-acceptance of the work performance**. These favourable consequences for the employee of recognizing a *de facto* employment relationship do not ensue if the legal system has to disallow it on the grounds of more serious considerations, *e.g.* because of an infringement of criminal law or contravention of public policy. Cancelling the *de facto* employment relationship with respect to the future presents no problems.

331. **FDGB**: Freier Deutscher Gewerkschaftsbund (Confederation of Free German Trade Unions). See **trade union**.

332. **FEHLGEGANGENE VERGÜTUNGSERWARTUNG — UNFULFILLED EXPECTATION OF CONSIDERATION**: Individuals who, because of their personal relationship to another (*e.g.* relatives, affianced), perform work without any **remuneration** being agreed for it may nevertheless be entitled to remuneration or deferred payment of remuneration. Although there are no statutory provisions on the matter, by the process of judicial **further development of the law** the Federal Labour Court has established such an entitlement, subject to the following conditions. Firstly, either no remuneration must have been paid for the work performed or only modest remuneration that is in obvious disproportion to the performance provided. Secondly, there must be or have been an expectation that the work performance provided would be recompensed in the future by

the handover of property or assets. Lastly, there must be a factual connection between these conditions. If the expected handover of assets then fails to materialize, the entitlement to remuneration or entitlement to deferred payment corresponds to the usual level of pay for the type of work concerned.

333. **FEIERSCHICHTEN — UNWORKED SHIFTS**: Alternative term used for **short-time working**.

334. **FG**: Finanzgericht (Finance Court). See **system of finance courts**.

335. **FINANZGERICHTSBARKEIT — SYSTEM OF FINANCE COURTS**: The courts in this system rule on public-law matters relating to taxes and levies, for example disputes between the state and the **employer** regarding the proper collection and paying over of **deductions from pay**. It is a two-tier system; the Finance Courts (FG) are the courts of first instance, and appeals are heard by the Federal Finance Court (BFH). The individual panels (or chambers) of the Finance Courts have three career judges and two **lay judges** on the bench, while the Federal Finance Court has only career judges. Legal costs are payable for actions before these courts, but the parties are permitted to represent themselves.

336. **FIRMENTARIFVERTRAG — COMPANY AGREEMENT**: On the employers' side, the capacity to conclude **collective agreements** is not confined to **employers' associations**, trade associations or an umbrella organization. A collective agreement may also be concluded by an individual employer (Collective Agreements Act § 2(1)). Alternative terms used for such company agreements are "Haustarifvertrag" and "Werkstarifvertrag".

Despite being a member of an employers' association, an employer is technically entitled to conclude such an agreement. The question of whether or not employers are permitted to do so under the terms of their membership of an association and its internal rules has no bearing on the validity of the agreement. Provided there is no **peace obligation** arising from an **association-level agreement**, the unions may use industrial action to compel such employers to conclude a company agreement.

The conclusion of separate company agreements with individual employers is particularly desirable in cases where the general conditions agreed collectively with an association are not appropriate for them (**establishment-specific bargaining**). In 1989 there were approximately 8,000 company agreements in force, covering some 500,000 employees.

337. **FLEXIBILISIERUNG — FLEXIBILIZATION**: In the German debate on the structure and organization of **industrial relations,** flexibility is a term used to stand for everything "new" and the quest for deregulation in all its various forms.

In the process of adjusting to changed contextual conditions and maintaining and improving competitiveness, it is especially in the traditional areas of **mass production** that efforts are being made to respond flexibly to differentiated and fluctuating demand and to shape the production structure accordingly. The **new production concepts** (which are not confined to manufacturing industry alone) have a bearing on the use of employees' social and mental abilities as a factor of production. This is because replacement of the old machines by complex and sophisticated **new production technologies** is bound up with a growing demand for increased skills, versatility and efficiency on the part of workers. Without the appropriate labour, the enormous potential of this capital-intensive equipment cannot be properly exploited.

Against this background, flexibility is becoming a key concept that may be used to justify each and every change introduced in working conditions and structures. Focal points in the flexibility debate are **working time, protection against dismissal** and, to a lesser extent, **maternity protection, youth employment protection** and **protection for disabled employees**. Efforts to achieve flexibility seek to get away from the so-called **typical employment relationship**, although the latter in fact offers, from the point of view of working time, multifarious ways of satisfying the requirements of both companies and society, by means of **night work, shiftwork, weekend work, short-time working** or **overtime**. Obstacles to flexibility exist within **establishments** themselves, which in many instances are dependent on a constant availability of labour. This means that implementing a **reduction of working hours,** for example, results in increased control and administrative costs, a fact which has deterred some companies in the Federal Republic from actually making use of the possibility of a flexible working week of between 37 and 40 hours for all employees already created by the metal industry **collective agreement** of 1984.

338. **FLIEGENDES PERSONAL — FLIGHT PERSONNEL**: Term used to refer to airline employees. Although they are in principle not covered by the **works constitution**, corresponding provisions may be agreed under **collective agreements**. For example, a collective agreement exists for all the flight personnel of the Deutsche Lufthansa airline which, modelled on the Works Constitution Act, provides for a group, company and crew

146

representative body (for the respective types of employment) with corresponding powers.

339. **FORTSETZUNGSKRANKHEIT — RECURRING ILLNESS**: If separate bouts of illness are due to the same underlying medical condition, they are classed together as a recurring illness. The burden of proof for this lies with the employer. In cases of a recurring illness, as a general rule the employee is entitled to only one period of **sick pay**, *i.e.* for a total of six weeks. This does not apply if the employee has worked for at least six months between separate bouts of illness or if the employment relationship has been interrupted during the interval between them.

340. **FRAUENARBEITSSCHUTZ — PROTECTION OF WOMEN AT WORK**: The body of legal provisions intended to safeguard women (who, on the grounds of real or presumed differences between men and women, are deemed to require protection in certain respects) from particular stresses and disadvantages in working life. Under this heading a distinction is made between:
   a. provisions intended to prevent discrimination against women in the male-dominated world of work (**equal rights**), *i.e.* above all the principle of equal pay and the prohibition of gender-specific job advertisements;
   b. provisions connected with biological differences, such as **maternity protection** and certain **employment bans** for women;
   c. provisions on facilities in the **workplace** stipulating, for example, that there should be separate lavatories, washrooms and changing rooms.
   However, the **regulations on working hours** for women, which at present lay down special rules including a maximum working day of 10 hours and longer **breaks**, and whose compatibility with the principle of **equality before the law** is open to question, are to be made the same as the provisions applying to men under a proposed new Working Time Act. The former ban on **night work** for female employees has now been declared by the Federal Constitutional Court to be unconstitutional.

341. **FRAUENBEAUFTRAGTE — WOMEN'S OFFICERS**: Officially appointed individuals who represent women's interests within particular units of public administration (municipalities, for example). Their tasks include keeping a check within the context of the unit concerned on the observance and implementation of the provisions on **protection of women at work** and **advancement of women** in administration activities both internally and externally. Their powers are generally

restricted to monitoring and advisory functions, with little scope for actual decision-making.

342. **FRAUENFÖRDERUNG — ADVANCEMENT OF WOMEN**: In order to make **equal rights** for men and women in working life a reality, various positive measures for the advancement of women have been taken in the last few years. These include the so-called **quota system**, the appointment of **women's officers** and attempts to make it easier for women to combine family and career. This can be achieved by making available (to men as well) adequate **part-time work** opportunities, **parental leave**, etc., and by guaranteeing that such shorter working hours and absences from the establishment do not impair an employee's promotion prospects.

343. **FREIE ERFINDUNG — INDEPENDENT INVENTION**: See **inventions by employees**.

344. **FREIER BERUF — PROFESSION**: In its present-day meaning, the somewhat traditional concept of "the professions" (sometimes also called "liberal professions") encompasses occupations in the service sector which call for advanced learning or training. They are not **businesses** or trades ("Gewerbe"). They include, notably, lawyers, accountants, doctors and consultant psychologists, architects, artistes and writers. An activity is classed as a business or trade, however, if the gain acquired depends on the skilled labour of others. As a general rule, individuals pursuing a profession are not covered by the statutory system of **accident insurance** and so have to take out such insurance privately.

345. **FREIER MITARBEITER — FREELANCE**: Term used to refer to individuals who are not in a fixed and permanent **employment relationship** but carry out individual commissions (usually not in immediate succession) on the basis of **contracts for services**. In this situation, the freelance is free to choose whether or not to accept a particular commission, but he or she has no automatic legal entitlement to be granted such commissions. Freelances are not in a position of personal subordination to the person commissioning their services and are therefore not **employees**, but in certain circumstances they may be classed as **persons treated in law as similar to an employee**.

346. **FRIEDENSPFLICHT — PEACE OBLIGATION**: The peace obligation places the **parties to a collective agreement** under an obligation to maintain industrial peace for the duration of the agreement in question. Specifically, neither of the parties may

seek to push through demands to alter the existing content of the agreement by taking any form of **industrial action**. If they violate this, they make themselves liable for damages both with respect to the association that has not violated the agreement and with respect to an individual member of that association.

The peace obligation does not, however, preclude industrial action aimed at achieving the collective agreement of terms and conditions not already laid down in the content of the agreement in question. Consequently, if it is wished to prohibit any industrial action whatever for the duration of the collective agreement (absolute peace obligation), a specially agreed arrangement is necessary. In practice, extension of the peace obligation beyond the date of expiry of a **collective agreement** has particular significance. It enables full use to be made of all opportunities for negotiation for the purposes of reaching a new agreement, thereby preventing premature labour disputes.

347. **FÜNF-TAGE-WOCHE — FIVE-DAY WEEK**: The five-day week is the definition normally used to denote a weekly **working time** of up to 40 hours that excludes Saturday as a **working day**. In some sectors there is a five-day week by collective agreement. This usually means that any work done on Saturdays attracts corresponding **pay supplements**.

348. **FÜRSORGEPFLICHT — DUTY OF CARE**: As a subsidiary obligation under the contract of employment, the **employer** must ensure that employees do not suffer any damage in connection with the provision of their work performance. Among other things, the duty of care requires the employer to provide and maintain a safe workplace, to provide employees with adequate means and information to prevent accidents at work, to ensure fair working relationships within the establishment and to take account of the personal concerns of individual employees in making all decisions. In legal terms, the duty of care derives from the obligation on employees to conform to the conventions of the employer's establishment and from their economic dependence; its counterpart is the **duty of loyalty** for **employees**.

A special duty of care exists in the context of the **career public service relationship**. Here, the **public sector employer** is under an obligation to ensure the well-being of **career public servants** ("Beamte") and their families. This obligation implies an actionable legal right on the part of career public servants to benevolent and just treatment, legal protection and protection against danger and assault, and material assistance in cases of birth, illness and death. The duty of care also has a part to play as regards **promotion**; although there is no automatic legal right to promotion, career public servants can make an application to the **system of administrative courts** to obtain a declaratory judgment on whether their public employer's current practice as regards promotion constitutes a violation of the duty of care in their own case. Thus, the duty of care implies in general an obligation on the part of the public employer to ensure for the career public servant a standard of living (not viewed in terms of remuneration) which is accommodated to the degree of responsibility of the post occupied, the importance of the career public service, and general economic and social conditions (the so-called "Alimentationsprinzip", *i.e.* maintenance principle). The duty of care also includes an obligation to ensure adequate pension provision after retirement, which is reflected in all the legislation regulating career public service (**pay (of career public servants), career branch**).

349. **FUSION — MERGER**: As permitted strictly in accordance with the statutory regulations, a merger is the amalgamation of joint-stock companies (**forms of company**) without liquidation or legally transacted transfer by way of universal succession: one of the original companies continues to exist or a new company is formed, and the other companies are absorbed.

In **labour law**, mergers are of relevance in terms of the **transfer of an establishment**, but only in appropriate exceptional cases do they constitute a **substantial alteration to the establishment**. They are, however, of considerable significance as regards the binding effect of **contracts of employment** on the **employer** in cases where the newly formed company is not a member of an **employers' association** or belongs to a different one.

G

350. **GASTARBEITER — GUEST WORKER**: Colloquial term for foreign **manual workers** used predominantly to describe **foreign workers** in low-paid manufacturing jobs.

351. **GEBIETSKÖRPERSCHAFTEN — TERRITORIAL AUTHORITIES**: Public-law entities whose jurisdiction is defined in terms of a geographically demarcated portion of national territory. They are also **legal persons** under public law, although constituted not on a membership basis but on a territorial basis. Their members are the people living in the area in question. The most important territorial authorities are the **municipalities** (*i.e.* local administration areas) and **associations of municipalities**; by extension, they also include the government authorities, *i.e.* the Federal Government and the **Länder**.

352. **GEFAHRENGENEIGTE ARBEIT — HAZARDOUS WORK**: Category distinguished by the Federal Labour Court to cover cases where the inherent nature of the work to be performed involves a high probability that even the most careful employee will make occasional mistakes which, although when considered separately were avoidable on each occasion and have therefore been caused through negligence, are shown by experience, given human fallibility, to be likely to occur. Since it would be unreasonable to burden employees with general liability to pay compensation for damage that may arise from work assigned to them by the employer, for this category of work the distribution of risk in the employment relationship does not follow the normal contractual principles.

In distributing the risk of loss in the context of such work, case law allocates liability on the basis of the following three instances. If employees cause damage intentionally or through gross negligence, they bear sole liability. In cases of normal negligence, liability is divided between employer and employee. Lastly, where there has been only minor negligence the employee is exempt from liability; the employer alone bears the risk of loss. The burden of proof for the existence of gross negligence or intention lies with the employer.

353. **GEFÄHRLICHE STOFFE — DANGEROUS SUBSTANCES**: Some of the chemicals used in production harbour considerable risks for the environment and for the people employed. Protection against the hazards originating from such substances is therefore an important element of **protection against technical hazards at work**. Of the numerous legal provisions regulating the matter, the most important are: the Law Con-

cerning Protection Against Dangerous Substances (short title Chemikaliengesetz, *i.e.* Chemicals Act); the Order Concerning Dangerous Substances (Gefahrstoffverordnung, *i.e.* Dangerous Substances Order); the Twelfth Order Implementing the Federal Pollution Control Act (Störfallverordnung, *i.e.* Major Accidents Order); and the Order Concerning Protection Against Ionizing Radiation (Strahlenschutzverordnung, *i.e.* Radiation Protection Order).

The Chemicals Act regulates declaration, manufacture and permitted and prohibited uses for certain dangerous substances and preparations. The Dangerous Substances Order, enacted pursuant to EC Directives, defines the provisions of the Chemicals Act in more specific terms and, among other things, stipulates requirements on identification, controls and due care in connection with the keeping, processing and delivery of dangerous substances and preparations.

The Major Accidents Order, conceived as a reaction to the Seveso disaster at a chemical plant near Milan in July 1976, stipulates requirements on safeguards for the prevention of major accidents and on notification of their occurrence to the authorities by operators of production plants which would endanger the surrounding area in the event of an accident. The Radiation Protection Order regulates, for establishments in which radioactive substances are used, the licensing procedure, handling of radioactive substances and radiation protection for employees and the environment.

354. **GEGNERFREIHEIT — INDEPENDENCE FROM THE OPPOSING SIDE**: One of the criteria for being recognized as possessing the **capacity to conclude collective agreements** is that a **collective industrial organization** should be "gegnerfrei", *i.e.* not subject to influence from the opposite side. This criterion reflects the conviction that the organization can properly represent its members' interests only if it is independent of its direct counterpart and also of third parties (*e.g.* the state, Religious Communities and political parties). The requirement for it to be independent of political parties is interpreted here as meaning that there must be neither automatic dual membership of the political party and collective industrial organization nor unilateral financial dependence.

The principle of the **unified trade union** in no way prevents union members from having an individual commitment to political parties.

355. **GEHALT — SALARY**: Term denoting the regular **remuneration**, payable monthly, of a **white-collar worker**. It differs from

the wage of a **manual worker** in that the dependence of the amount of remuneration on the work performance is looser. Although white-collar workers may suffer cuts in salary for making mistakes without excuse, for instance, or may be entitled to **overtime premium pay** for work done in excess of the statutory maximum working hours, the agreed monthly salary is not directly determined by the amount of time actually worked. Hence, the amount of a white-collar worker's remuneration is unaffected by days such as holidays on which no work is done or (in contrast to a manual worker employed under a **payment by results** system) by minor interruptions to work. On the other hand, white-collar workers are often required to work longer hours than the agreed normal working hours for the establishment concerned, without being entitled to the corresponding ordinary **overtime pay**.

356. **GELDWERTE LEISTUNG — PAYMENT IN KIND**: Term used synonymously with **Naturalvergütung**.

357. **GELTUNGSBEREICH VON TARIFNORMEN — SCOPE OF NORMATIVE PROVISIONS**: The provisions laid down in the normative part of a **collective agreement** apply only to those employment relationships which fall within the scope of the agreement in terms of time, geographical area and the establishments, occupations and personnel concerned. These normative provisions take effect from the date laid down in the agreement. In principle, the collective agreement covers all **contracts of employment** which are concluded or have been in existence between the date on which it comes into force and the date on which it ends. Furthermore, its normative provisions remain in effect even after it ends, unless they are replaced by different arrangements under a contract of employment or works agreement but in particular until a new collective agreement is concluded (so-called "Nachwirkung", *i.e.* continuing effect). As a rule, a collective agreement states the collective bargaining area to which it applies. There are Federal, Länder and regional agreements as well as agreements that apply only in particular localities.

Given the **principle of industrial organization**, a collective agreement is usually concluded for a particular industry. An establishment is bound by whichever **collective agreement** corresponds to its main activity. The **parties to a collective agreement** can specify in each case the employee groups to whom it applies. The definition of pay grades for work of differing degrees of difficulty also forms part of an agreement's occupational scope. Lastly, a collective agreement applies to all personnel who fall within its scope in terms of time, geographical area and the establishments and occupations concerned and whom it does not expressly exclude. For example, white-collar workers occupying senior posts whose work is difficult to categorize and whose remuneration does not fit into the collectively agreed pay structure are frequently excluded from the scope of normative provisions (**white-collar workers exempt from collectively agreed terms**).

358. **GEMEINDE — MUNICIPALITY**: Term used synonymously with **Kommune**.

359. **GEMEINSCHAFTSWAHL — JOINT ELECTION**: See **works council election**.

360. **GENERALSTREIK — GENERAL STRIKE**: In a general strike, employees throughout all branches of the economy withdraw their labour and the whole of public life is thereby brought to a standstill. General strikes are deemed unlawful in the Federal Republic. An exception to this principle is the case where, exercising the right of resistance enshrined in the **Basic Law**, a general strike is used as a means of upholding or restoring the law.

361. **GERÄTESICHERHEIT — SAFETY OF EQUIPMENT**: Area covered by those particular provisions falling under the general heading of **protection against technical hazards at work** which are intended to ensure that tools, devices, machines, technical plant and vehicles employed in the production process are safe to use. The most important relevant provisions are the Equipment Safety Act (Gerätesicherheitsgesetz), Orders issued pursuant to the Industrial Code (Gewerbeordnung) for certain particularly dangerous types of plant, and the accident prevention regulations (**protection against accidents**) issued by the **Occupational Health and Safety Agencies**, together with numerous general codes of practice drawn up by bodies such as the German Standards Institute (DIN) and the German Association of Electrical Engineers (VDE) which apply these often abstract provisions to specific cases.

Under the Equipment Safety Act, all users and manufacturers of technical equipment are required to ensure that it complies with the general codes of practice and regulations on health and safety and accident prevention with the effect that, when it is used correctly, users and third parties are protected from risks of accident. General codes of practice are the standards adopted by the **Federal Ministry of Labour and Social Affairs** in certain lists of national and international health and safety regulations. Equipment subject to inspection is covered by special Orders (eight at present) issued by the Federal Government and numerous technical regulations whose requirements correspond to the current state of technical developments. These regulate, among other things, requirements on safety procedures and the licensing, use and testing of such equipment. Observance of the regulations on equipment safety is monitored by the **Labour Inspectorates**.

Important changes in the field of equipment safety will result from the need to adjust to EC provisions, particularly the so-called Equipment Directive of 1989. This standing item on the agenda lays down that, as normal practice, all manufacturers and importers will themselves carry out tests, and issue certificates accordingly, to ensure compliance with the Equipment Directive's safety criteria (which are worded in general terms), and that the products concerned may then be used within the Community without any further restriction. The safety criteria in the Directive are to be defined in more specific terms in uniform European standards.

362. **GERICHTSBARKEIT — (SYSTEM OF) JURISDICTION**: Term indicating, firstly, the activity of the state that is directed at putting the existing legal system into effect; this subdivides into the administration of justice and the systems of jurisdiction in the narrower sense. Here, jurisdiction is the activity of the courts in applying the law in particular cases, *i.e.* the power to deliver judgment. Organizationally, in the context of contentious jurisdiction it is divided into several branches, each of which has its own system of courts for dealing with that particular sphere: the **system of ordinary courts** (for civil and criminal cases) and the **systems of constitutional, administrative, finance, social security** and **labour courts**. Depending on their nature, disputes arising in the field of labour relations may fall under any one of these systems of jurisdiction.

363. **GERINGFÜGIG BESCHÄFTIGTE — "MARGINAL" PART-TIME WORKERS**: Individuals classed in this category, *i.e.* who work fewer than 15 hours per week and whose income does not exceed one seventh of the monthly reference wage or, where pay is higher, one sixth of the total income, are not subject to **unemployment insurance**, **health insurance** or the **statutory pension scheme**. In addition, they pay only a flat-rate earnings tax of 15 per cent. This also applies to individuals whose earnings remain within these limits and whose occasional employment within a given year totals no more than two months or 50 days.

There are more than 6 million employees in this category, mostly employed in nursing, messenger services, education and tutoring, retailing, and as relief drivers. So-called housewives constitute around two thirds of "marginal" part-time employees, and schoolchildren and students represent approximately one fifth.

The **social security card** serves as a means of preventing abuse of the special regulations applying to this category.

364. GESAMTBETRIEBSRAT — COMPANY WORKS COUNCIL: The company works council is an organ of the **works constitution** that must be formed in companies where there are several establishment **works councils** (Works Constitution Act § 47). The individual works councils are not subordinate to it. It is responsible for dealing with matters which concern the company as a whole or more than one establishment and so cannot be regulated at establishment level. Its functions also include appointing the members of the **economic committee**, matters connected with the employee representatives on the **supervisory board**, and the formation of a **group works council**. Lastly, individual works councils can delegate to the company works council those of their co-determination rights which otherwise, owing to the insufficient number of employees in individual establishments of a company, would not be exercised by the works councils concerned. Individual works councils that are composed exclusively of either white-collar or manual worker representatives appoint a single delegate to the company works council; otherwise, they appoint two. Single delegates are chosen by the works council as a whole, and where there are two they are chosen by the white-collar and the manual worker representatives respectively (**group-based election**). The same election procedure is followed for the substitute delegates. In principle the size of the company works council depends on how many individual works councils the company has, but different rules may be adopted by **collective agreement** or **works agreement**.

The company works council elects from among its members a chairperson and vice-chairperson, one of whom must be a white-collar delegate and the other a manual worker delegate. These represent the council in dealings with third parties. The council takes its decisions by majority vote; in this procedure single delegates from the works councils have as many votes as there are employees entered on the list of electors in the establishment concerned, and the same principle applies to the separate white-collar and manual worker delegates respectively. If the respective employee groups send several delegates to the company works council, they each have a proportional share of that group's votes. The council forms a **works council executive committee** consisting of its chairperson, vice-chairperson and a number of additional members. In accordance with the principle of **protection of minorities** each group must be represented on this company works council executive committee. The company works council is not capable of possessing assets, and the employer bears the costs of its activities.

365. GESAMTJUGEND- UND AUSZUBILDENDEN-VERTRETUNG — COMPANY REPRESENTATIVE BODY FOR YOUNG WORKERS AND TRAINEES: This body is an organ of the **works constitution** that must be formed in companies where there are several individual **representative bodies for young workers and trainees** at establishment level (Works Constitution Act §§ 72 f.). The latter are not subordinate to it. It is responsible for dealing with matters which concern the company as a whole or more than one establishment and so cannot be regulated at establishment level. Each of the establishment-level representative bodies sends one delegate, but the number of members may be increased by **collective agreement** or **works agreement**.

Corresponding provisions apply in the context of **staff representation** in the public sector (Federal Staff Representation Act § 64(2)).

366. GESAMTPERSONALRAT — GENERAL STAFF COUNCIL: An organ of public sector **staff representation** which must be formed if branch offices of a **public sector establishment** are classed as establishments in their own right (Federal Staff Representation Act § 55). It is elected by the employees of the main establishment and those of the branch offices, in accordance with the general procedure for **staff council election**. Structurally, the distribution of powers between the **staff council** and the general staff council corresponds to that between the **works council** and the **company works council** in the private sector. The general staff council is responsible for dealing with matters which can only be regulated uniformly for the main establishment and branch office establishments together. Before taking a decision, it must give their individual staff councils the opportunity to comment. The staff representation laws of the Länder contain corresponding provisions.

367. GESAMTZUSAGE — GENERAL UNDERTAKING BY EMPLOYER: A unilateral declaration by the **employer** to the workforce of the intention to provide a certain benefit. It is held by the Labour Courts to be a binding contractual offer to each individual employee, although it does not necessarily have to be made to each individual. The employee can accept this general undertaking either expressly or by implication through claiming the benefit. It then becomes part of the individual **contract of employment** and cannot be withdrawn unilaterally by the employer. However, because its general validity makes it part of collective law a general undertaking by the employer has equal ranking with a **works agreement**, and in accordance with the supersedence principle (the **favourability principle** is not involved) it can therefore be cancelled at a later date by a works agreement. In practice, a general undertaking by the employer frequently takes the form of the **assurance of an occupational pension**.

368. **GESCHÄFTSFÜHRER — MANAGING DIRECTOR**: In general, natural persons who, in the capacity of a **company organ** or member of one, undertake the senior management function in the **form of company** known as a "Gesellschaft" (incorporated company), for example the managing **company member** of a partnership or the management board of a **public limited company** (AG). Often, the managing director and the entrepreneur or **employer** are one and the same person.

In the narrower sense, the term denotes the managing director(s) of a private limited company (GmbH). The managing director is the statutory agent of the company. If other managing directors are also appointed, in principle they all manage and act for the company jointly. Inasmuch as the company is not subject to co-determination, their appointment and removal are effected through the company's general meeting. Their service relationship must be agreed and terminated separately. Managing directors are subject to a **restraint on competition** and as a general principle are not classed as **employees**, but legal proceedings concerning them may be heard in the **system of labour courts**.

369. **GESELLSCHAFT — INCORPORATED COMPANY**: See **forms of company**.

370. **GESELLSCHAFTER — COMPANY MEMBER**: A subscriber to and member of the **form of company** known as a "Gesellschaft" (incorporated company). Their share as agreed in the company's memorandum of association or deed of partnership may be effected in the form of a cash or non-cash contribution or a service. Their involvement in management depends on the type of company concerned, and ranges from day-to-day direct participation in the case of partnerships to no more than a share-based voting right at the **company general meeting** or **shareholders' meeting** in the case of joint-stock companies. Correspondingly, company members are either personally subject

to joint and several liability or are liable only to the value of their share (inasmuch as this is not yet fully paid), normally to the exclusion of all further liability.

371. **GESELLSCHAFTERVERSAMMLUNG — COMPANY GENERAL MEETING**: The decision-making body of the **company members** in various forms of company. In partnerships it is already implied by the fact that as a general principle the members, *i.e.* partners, manage the company jointly, while in joint-stock companies it is a statutory requirement as a **company organ**. Decisions are taken on a per capita basis and by agreement in the case of partnerships (unless the deed of partnership provides otherwise), but according to shares and by majority vote in the case of joint-stock companies. In a private limited company (GmbH) the powers of the general meeting range from appointing the management, and committing it on business policy, to declaring dividends. In fact, the way in which the general meeting is able to influence the activities of the management board depends on the extent to which the structure of the particular company allows for such independence. The **shareholders' meeting** of a public limited company (AG) normally has the least scope for influence.

372. **GESETZ — LAW**: Term embodying a distinction between a law in the strictly formal sense (more correctly rendered in English as "statute") and law in the substantive sense. Thus, a law in the formal sense (statute) is any edict of a body invested with **legislative powers**, whether the Federal legislature or one of the Länder legislatures. Observance of the formal legislative procedure laid down in the Constitution is a prerequisite. In most cases, a law in the formal sense (statute) is at the same time law in the substantive sense. Law in the substantive sense is any legal rule, *i.e.* any order founded in sovereign powers and directed at a large number of addressees, which contains a generally binding abstract precept and is applicable to a large number of individual cases. It follows from this that law in the substantive sense (with the exception of prescriptive (customary) law) always comprises laws in the formal sense (statutes). The **Constitution**, **executive orders** and local authority **byelaws** also fall within this definition. On the other hand, not every law in the formal sense (statute) is also law in the substantive sense. One such instance is where a statute enacted in the ordinary legislative procedure does not operate with general effect but (as with the Budget, for example) is binding only on the organs of central government.

373. **GESETZESVORBEHALT — RESERVATION OF STATU-TORY POWERS**: According to this principle, an administrative authority may function only by virtue of powers conferred by statute. In this sense, it is more restrictive than the principle of the **precedence of statutes**. Although **statute** in this context means a formal parliamentary statute, the traditional view is that an **executive order** is also sufficient, if and in so far as it is based on a formal statute. This stipulation for statutory powers derives directly from the **Constitution**: the principle of democracy requires that decisions which are important for the community at large be taken only by the Parliament duly elected for this purpose (**reservation of parliamentary powers**); and the principle of the constitutional state requires that legal relationships between the state and the individual citizen be regulated by general statutes which determine the actions of the authorities and enable the individual citizen to evaluate and be aware of those actions. A closely allied principle is the stipulation for statutory powers where **basic rights** are to be affected, which derives from the provision in the Constitution of the possibility of restricting basic rights by statute or in virtue of a statute. A key example in the labour relations field would be the limiting of **freedom of occupation**.

374. **GESETZESVORRANG — PRECEDENCE OF STATUTES**: Principle which expresses the binding effect of existing **statutes** on the administrative authorities. It means that the authorities may not take measures (*e.g.* in the employment field) that are contrary to a statute. This precedence has unrestricted and mandatory effect, and includes statutes in terms of both form and substance. A measure taken by the authorities which is unlawful in this sense may be contested by any aggrieved party in the **system of administrative courts**.

375. **GESETZGEBUNG — LEGISLATION**: There is a distinction between legislation in the substantive sense and legislation in the formal or verbal sense. In the substantive sense it describes legislation (interpreted broadly) as enactments of written rules of law, including **executive orders** and **byelaws**. Legislation in the formal or verbal sense signifies the process whereby statutes come into being through the prescribed correct legislative procedure, and paraphrases from the functional point of view the area of action rightfully ascribed to legislative authority.

Under the **Constitution**, legislative powers are in principle assigned to the **Länder** in so far as the Basic Law does not assign powers to the Federation in a particular matter. In reality, however, the main emphasis in legislation lies with the Federation, which has **exclusive legislative powers** *vis-à-vis* the Länder in

160

some areas of regulation and **concurrent legislative powers** in others, and in addition can enact a **framework statute** in some cases.

In **labour law** the legislators must have regard to the fact that beyond a certain point it has to be left to the **collective industrial organizations** to regulate terms and conditions of employment by **collective agreement**. Hence, some areas of labour law are not regulated by any statutes whatever, but are determined by the collective bargaining parties or **further development of the law** in court decisions.

376. **GESETZGEBUNGSKOMPETENZ — LEGISLATIVE POWERS**: Term used to denote the authorization, as codified in the **Constitution**, granted to an organ of the state to enact **statutes** in the context of a formal legislative procedure. A statute has legal effect only if the organ that has acted legislatively was competent under the Constitution in the matter to be regulated. See **concurrent legislative powers**.

377. **GEWERBE — BUSINESS**: Any permitted gainful activity of a certain duration that is pursued on a self-employed basis, excluding the **professions** and primary agricultural production. (The meaning also covers the English terms "trade" in its occupational sense and "industry" in the broad sense of any particular branch of activity.) The term "Gewerbebetrieb" therefore refers to any firm in commerce, small-scale crafts and trades, manufacturing industry and transport. The conduct of a business is regulated specifically in the Industrial Code (Gewerbeordnung) and by numerous supplementary statutes such as the Crafts Code (Handwerksordnung), the Retail Trade Act (Einzelhandelsgesetz) and the Hotels and Catering Act (Gaststättengesetz) and regulations for banks and credit institutions, insurance companies and the like. Any business carried on by a resident natural or **legal person** is an occupation and falls within the protection of the **freedom of occupation** guaranteed in the **Constitution**, which includes the freedom to engage in a trade or industry ("Gewerbefreiheit").

378. **GEWERBEARZT — INDUSTRIAL MEDICAL OFFICER**: These state medical officers advise **companies, works councils** and the **Labour Inspectorates** on matters relating to occupational medicine in connection with **protection against technical hazards at work,** the design of **workplaces, maternity protection** and **youth employment protection.** They are employed in the Länder administrative authorities and the **Federal Ministry of Labour and Social Affairs.**

379. **GEWERBEAUFSICHT(SAMT) — LABOUR INSPEC-
TORATE**: Labour inspection is the most important institution
of the state occupational health and safety system. It is carried
out by **Länder** authorities; responsibility lies with the **Ministries
of Labour at Land level,** each of which has their own network
of district offices, in some Länder with an intermediate authority
as well. The Labour Inspectorates are responsible for the
implementation of **protection against technical hazards at work,**
the enforcement of regulations on **workplaces, restrictions on
working hours, maternity protection** and **youth employment
protection,** and in some Länder also for certain aspects of
environmental protection. Labour inspectors have powers to enter
workplaces, carry out technical tests, require employers to answer
questions or produce documents, and remove samples of
substances to have them examined. They advise the relevant
company departments and **works councils** and offer help to
ensure that deficiencies and breaches of the law are rectified. In
many cases they can authorize exemptions from statutory
regulations. They can issue Notices binding on the employer and
enforce them by imposing penalties, and by Order can have the
whole or part of an establishment shut down and prohibit the
use of certain materials and equipment. In 1989 there were some
3,400 career public servants ("Beamte") employed in the Labour
Inspectorates, with responsibility for the inspection of 1.6 million
establishments. About a quarter of these establishments are visited
per year, resulting in approximately 1.6 million recorded
deficiencies.

380. **GEWERKSCIIAFT — TRADE UNION**: An employees'
association which has recognized status as a **collective industrial
organization**. Trade unions do not have status as **legal persons,**
for historical reasons, but in reality according to case law they
are essentially treated as if they were.

The trade union system in the Federal Republic of Germany
is not a completely unitary one; however, it is mainly concentrated
in the individual member unions of the **German Federation of
Trade Unions** (DGB), the **German White-Collar Workers'
Union** (DAG) and the **German Federation of Career Public
Servants** (DBB). These organizations do not see themselves as
unions with particular ideological or party political links
("Richtungsgewerkschaften"); on the contrary, they stress their
ideological and political neutrality. In addition to these three
unified trade unions, since 1957 the **Christian Trade Union
Federation of Germany** (CGB) has been in existence. There are
also a number of special associations for **executive staff** which
have joined forces to form an umbrella organization, the
Association of Executive Staff (ULA).

In all, almost 14 million employees in employment are union members. The average union density is a good 42 per cent.; it varies for different categories of employee and different industries. Career public servants ("Beamte") are the most highly unionized, followed by manual workers and, some way behind, white-collar workers. The strongest union by far is the Metal Industry Union (IG Metall), with approximately 3.6 million members, followed by the Public Services, Transport and Traffic Union (ÖTV) with about 2 million.

In 1989, in the German Democratic Republic 9.6 million members belonged to the "Confederation of Free German Trade Unions" (Freier Deutscher Gewerkschaftsbund, or FDGB). In the course of the German Democratic Republic's accession to the area of application of the Basic Law of the Federal Republic of Germany, the FDGB and its individual member unions were disbanded during 1990.

Unlike the **employers' associations**, the unions are organized centrally from the top down, with subdivisions at district and local levels. Individual employees are direct members of the national association. For the most part, the unions are industry-based, in accordance with the **principle of industrial organization**. The administrative apparatus and the benefits provided by the unions (**strike pay**) are financed from membership dues, normally levied at a rate of 1 per cent. of gross pay.

381. GEWERKSCHAFTLICHE UNABHÄNGIGKEIT — UNION INDEPENDENCE: See **independence from the opposing side**.

382. GEWERKSCHAFTLICHER STREIK — OFFICIAL STRIKE: The **Federal Labour Court** holds that a **strike** is lawful only if it is conducted by a trade union. Such official strikes are usually initiated with a preliminary **strike ballot** held among the union members of the establishments involved in the dispute. In many cases the **standing rules** of a union stipulate that a decision to take strike action must be backed by a qualified majority vote (*e.g.* in many cases 75 per cent. of the people voting). Generally, the approval of the union's executive committee is also necessary. Only then does the union issue the strike call to its members and invite non-union members to join in the strike. This procedure is based on the **union strike guidelines** drawn up by the German Federation of Trade Unions (DGB).

383. GEWERKSCHAFTLICHE WERBUNG — UNION PUBLICITY: It follows from the constitutionally protected **guarantee of activity** for **collective industrial organizations** that the **trade unions** have the right to engage in canvassing activities prior to elections for **works councils** and **staff councils**, to arrange for publicity and information material containing subject matter relating specifically to union affairs to be distributed within the establishment outside working hours by union members employed there, and to use noticeboards provided for displaying company information for union recruitment purposes.

384. GEWERKSCHAFTLICHES ZUGANGSRECHT — UNION RIGHT OF ACCESS: The (external) full-time officials of the **trade unions** that have a presence in an establishment must, after notifying the employer, be granted access to the establishment in order that the functions and powers of the unions as laid down in the **works constitution** and the Federal Staff Representation Act may be duly exercised. These include the right to influence the election and composition of the works council and the conduct of its business. Access to the establishment also gives the unions added opportunities to acquire information on company matters through personal contact with the workforce.

385. GEWERKSCHAFTSMITGLIEDSCHAFT — UNION MEMBERSHIP: Membership of a **trade union** presupposes that the **employee** has joined the union voluntarily. If employees satisfy the conditions for admittance, particularly the requirement that they are employed in the industry for which the union in question is responsible geographically and occupationally, as a rule they have a legal right to be admitted. Applicants whose views on key aspects of union policy are at variance with those of the union do not necessarily have to be admitted. In many cases the union's **standing rules** provide that a member may be expelled in the event of conduct detrimental to the organization. The main obligations of union members consist in promoting the organization's interests and also paying membership dues, which are graduated according to gross pay.

Members are able to have a voice in the important decisions of the union (**democratic decision-making**) as laid down in its standing rules. They are also entitled to the benefits provided by the union under its standing rules, particularly **strike pay** and legal advice in disputes relating to labour and social security law.

386. GLEICHBEHANDLUNG — EQUAL TREATMENT: A particular form of the general principle of **equality before the law** in the context of **labour law**. For this sphere of law it is one of the fundamental principles, to the effect that an **employer** may not, without material grounds, exclude individual **employees** or groups of employees in his or her establishment from preferential provisions or in any other way discriminate against them in respect of comparable employees. Violations lead in most cases to the disadvantaged employees being granted the right to be placed on an equal footing.

Enforcement of the principle of equal treatment presupposes, firstly, that the disadvantaged employees and the employees receiving preferential treatment are in a comparable position. This comparability is established on the basis of an investigation into conditions in the particular establishment to ascertain the true purpose of the preferential treatment. The finding is usually that employees who perform different work or are at different levels in the company hierarchy are not comparable; if the preferential treatment bears no relation to the nature of the work performed, this changes matters totally.

Secondly, the differential treatment at issue must be arbitrary, *i.e.* not based on objective reasons. This compels the employer to demonstrate material grounds for unequal treatment, provides a form of control and so has the effect of influencing employers to adopt a reasonable policy. However, the obligation to demonstrate material grounds does not provide a means of preventing any other than arbitrary forms of differential treatment.

Material grounds are deemed to exist, in particular, where the work performance of employees is different. Since within a given establishment numerous activities are performed that are almost impossible to compare with each other, and since evaluation of performance is subjective and numerous starting-points are consequently available to the employer for justifying differential treatment, the application of the principle of equal treatment centres on forms of preferential treatment that are unconnected, or only distantly connected, with the actual nature of the employee's work. In the field of remuneration this is the case, for example, with company benefits such as **occupational pension schemes**. Particular restrictions on the scope for differential treatment result from **anti-discrimination laws**, especially the principle of **equal rights** for men and women.

387. **GLEICHBERECHTIGUNG — EQUAL RIGHTS**: Principle which forms part of **anti-discrimination law** as laid down in the **Basic Law**. It prohibits any legal regulation under which men and women are treated differently solely on the grounds of gender, in so far as actual biological and functional differences do not make differentiation absolutely necessary. It is, for example,

assumed in the provisions on the **protection of women at work**. Over the past few decades numerous regulations have been adopted, particularly in the fields of family law and **labour law**, to end forms of legal discrimination against women and give them effectively equal opportunities with men. Deficiencies in the law have to a large extent been remedied by such regulations. However, significant real disadvantages and forms of **indirect discrimination** against women remain, particularly in economic life and politics. The question of whether and to what extent the principle of equal rights necessitates government measures to remedy this lack of equality and even justifies legal forms of discrimination against men, for example ''positive action'' such as applying **quota systems**, is still a subject of controversy. Such special measures for the **advancement of women** are held by the Administrative Courts to be lawful, provided they are adopted by virtue of a **statute**.

In the field of labour law, the principle of equal rights was incorporated into statutory law in 1980 in implementation of several EC Directives. However, this was in a form that was not consistent with EC law in every respect. In particular, there are still considerable deficiencies in the provisions on penalties for discriminatory practices on the part of employers as regards recruitment and promotion. As a matter of principle, all forms of sex discrimination which arise from acts done by the employer, **collective agreements** or **works agreements** are unlawful. Only in a few exceptional cases, however, is there an entitlement to have a particular act done, a particular benefit granted or damages paid in favour of the individual who has suffered discrimination (**job advertisement**).

388. GLEICHHEITSSATZ — EQUALITY BEFORE THE LAW: The idea that all individuals should possess equal rights is one of the central concepts of constitutional development in civil law. Hence, the **Basic Law** guarantees that all individuals shall be equal before the law (general principle of equality), that men and women shall have equal rights, and that no one may suffer prejudice or enjoy preference because of their sex, descent and race, language, homeland and origin, faith or religious or political beliefs (**anti-discrimination laws**).

The principle of equality guarantees equality under the law in the sense that a statute may not be applied differently in identical situations, and constitutes a prohibition of arbitrary action by the state to the effect that no one may suffer prejudice in the exercise of the authority of the state unless there are material grounds adequately justifying differential treatment. Despite all attempts to make the corresponding criteria objective, the

166

assessment of what represents differential treatment in particular circumstances involves subjective elements. Even the **Federal Constitutional Court** therefore allows the legislators extensive freedom in formulating the provisions of the law.

The principle of equality not only applies to the relationship between the individual citizen and the state but also has significance in private law (**third-party effect of constitutional rights**), although in this sphere it is largely obscured by the overarching principle of the freedom of the individual and contractual freedom. In **labour law**, however, the principle of **equal treatment** is of central importance.

389. **GLEITZEITARBEIT — FLEXITIME**: Arrangements under which there is no fixed time at which the day's work must commence and end. In the commonest pattern, within the flexible periods at either end of the working day employees choose their own times for starting and finishing work; during the so-called "core time" sandwiched between these two periods they are required to be present. In such arrangements the number of working hours due under the contract of employment is normally specified on a monthly basis, so that employees have a longer period over which to make up the hours due, subject to observance of the **restrictions on working hours**.

With the exception of actual production-line systems and cases where it is essential for workstations to be permanently staffed, from the organizational point of view flexible working hours are in principle possible in all workplaces. They usually entail the provision of monitoring mechanisms, *e.g.* special time clocks, to keep a check on the **working time** to be completed. Rules also need to be established on **breaks**, arrangements regarding **overtime** and procedures for balancing time credits and debits.

The introduction of flexitime is subject to a **co-determination right of the works council**.

390. **GLOBALSTEUERUNG — "GLOBAL STEERING"**: See **Stability Act**.

391. **GRATIFIKATION — SPECIAL BONUS**: Part of **remuneration** in the broader sense. Special bonuses are not (or not wholly) payments in return for work performed; they are granted by the employer to mark particular occasions (anniversaries, holidays, Christmas) and may also be intended as an incentive for the employee's future work. The payment of such bonuses may be stipulated by a **collective agreement**, **works agreement** or **contract of employment**. Entitlement may also be based on **custom**.

167

Special bonuses are often linked to repayment clauses ("Rückzahlungsklauseln"). These clauses are only valid to a limited extent if a special bonus, for example a Christmas bonus, is also intended as an incentive for the future. The Federal Labour Court holds that, provided an employee does not use the first due date in the following year for giving notice of termination, he or she can refuse to pay back a Christmas bonus exceeding 200 Deutschmarks. If the Christmas bonus amounts to more than one month's pay a longer period of commitment is permissible, but this may not extend so far that it would make a change of job impossible in practice for the employee.

392. GRENZEN DER TARIFMACHT — LIMITS OF BARGAINING POWERS: The **collective bargaining autonomy** conferred on the **collective industrial organizations** empowers them to establish legal rules to safeguard and improve working and economic conditions (Basic Law, Article 9(3)). The scope of these regulatory powers encompasses, for example, everything concerning the **contract of employment** or connected with its subject-matter. According to the predominant body of legal opinion, in establishing these provisions the parties to a collective agreement, like the legislators, have to observe **basic rights**. **Collective agreements** may therefore not encroach on the private life of employees. Statute law also takes precedence over collectively agreed provisions, unless it is not peremptory law, *i.e.* is either discretionary or discretionary in respect of collective agreements. The question of whether the collective bargaining parties must have regard to the public interest is a matter of controversy. It is universally agreed that collective agreements may change neither the organization of the courts or public authorities nor the **company constitution**.

393. GRUNDGESETZ — BASIC LAW: See **Constitution**.

394. GRUNDRECHTE — BASIC RIGHTS: Fundamental freedoms enshrined in a **Constitution** (in the Basic Law of the Federal Republic of Germany, for example) for the benefit of the individuals who are subject to the authority of the state. The Basic Law thereby continues the tradition of constitutional development in civil law of the past few centuries, in which the guarantee of civil and human rights has been a central concern. The protection of such rights afforded by the Basic Law is far more extensive than in earlier Constitutions in Germany and is frequently invoked. Basic rights are binding on **legislation**, the Executive and **case law** with the force of directly applicable law. Flowing from the leading legal principle of the guarantee of human dignity, the most important of the fundamental rights enshrined in the Basic Law include the right to personal liberty, life and inviolability of the person, the general **right to privacy of the individual, equality before the law**, freedom of faith and conscience, freedom of opinion in art and science, freedom of assembly, general **freedom of association** and the right to form collective industrial organizations, the right of ownership of private property and **freedom of occupation**, and the right of asylum for the politically persecuted. The Basic Law also guarantees the right to be heard in court before a lawful judge and a right of resistance against anyone who seeks to abolish the constitutional order. Some basic rights apply to everyone, and others only to individuals of German nationality. The partially disadvantaged treatment of aliens is in some respects offset by guarantees under international treaties which are also binding within Germany, particularly the European Convention on Human Rights and (for the benefit of nationals of EC Member States) the rights to freedom of movement and **anti-discrimination law** provided by the Treaty of Rome.

In addition to their traditional purpose of defending citizens against state intervention in the sphere of the freedom of the individual, basic rights as interpreted nowadays by the **Federal Constitutional Court** also have the function of safeguarding rights of participation in political, intellectual, economic and social life and may also (although with restricted scope) justify claims to certain state benefits (**welfare state principle**). Taken together, they form an objective system of values which strongly shapes the activity of the organs of the state and also acquires importance beyond public and administrative law by virtue of the so-called **third-party effect of constitutional rights**.

The Constitutions of the individual **Länder** also enumerate basic rights, differing in some cases from the Basic Law; since Federal law ranks higher, their provisions have valid effect only in so far as they guarantee more extensive rights.

Individual citizens who feel that their basic rights have been prejudiced by institutions of public authority can bring a **constitutional appeal** invoking these rights before the Constitutional Courts at Federal or Land level.

As a holder of basic rights, the citizen (and possibly legal persons too) is involved in all kinds of mutual connections, and as a result the rights and interests of third parties and the general community have to be considered, whilst as far as possible the guaranteed autonomy must be preserved. To enable this conflict to be resolved in a differentiated manner, the Basic Law contains a system of so-called limits to basic rights. These are as follows:

a. restrictions in the basic right itself, *e.g.* in the case of freedom of association;

169

    b. qualified and absolute stipulation of statutory powers, *e.g.* the inviolability of home and property;

    c. exercise of the basic right depends on formal permission with precise statutory regulation of the reasons for refusal, *e.g.* in the case of **freedom of occupational practice**;

    d. so-called constitutionally inherent limits, *e.g.* in the case of scientific and religious freedom;

    e. rules on the conflict of laws as applied to the basic rights of different holders.

With each of these restrictions, the prohibition in the Constitution of laws for individual cases must be observed and the essential substance of the basic right concerned must not be affected. The **proportionality principle** must also be taken into account. The extent to which restriction is permitted therefore depends on the importance of the interests being pursued, which are also legitimate under the Constitution. The Federal Constitutional Court leaves the legislators very considerable discretionary scope in balancing the importance of contrary interests. Where the decisions made are predictive, *i.e.* if at the time when legislation is being passed or government action is being examined from the constitutional point of view it is not clear whether the effects of restrictions will remain within proportional limits, the legislators must monitor their application in practice and rectify the regulations if necessary.

    Individuals who make use of certain basic rights with direct political impact (such as freedom of opinion and freedom of assembly) for the purpose of attacking the constitutional order may, by a ruling of the Federal Constitutional Court on application from the **Federal Government**, the **Federal Parliament** or a Land Government, be temporarily or permanently deprived of the right to exercise the basic right concerned. The practical significance of such constitutional regulation is very small.

395. **GRUPPENFÜHRER — WORK GROUP LEADER**: See **self-constituted employee group, work group**.

396. **GRUPPENWAHL — GROUP-BASED ELECTION**: Principle whereby, in **works council elections, manual workers** and **white-collar workers** elect their respective **works council members** separately. The two groups may in fact opt by secret ballot to hold a joint election instead. Group-based elections follow the system of proportional representation. If only one nomination is available or if only a **single-member works council** is to be chosen, election is by majority vote. The principles of group-based election also serve the purposes of the **protection of minorities**.

397. **GÜNSTIGKEITSPRINZIP — FAVOURABILITY PRINCIPLE**: Principle which offers the possibility of departing from the regulations laid down in higher-ranking **sources of law** in the field of **labour law** by improving on them in the employee's favour under the terms of the **contract of employment** and hence also in the form of **a general undertaking by employer** or on the basis of **custom**. The principle is guaranteed by the Constitution. In practice its importance is mainly evident in departures from **collective agreements** and **works agreements**, but also from **statutes**. It applies in the same way for the **public service**.

The question of whether a condition in an individual employment contract is more favourable than a higher-ranking norm is determined by means of a procedure of comparison which must include all the provisions on the two sides (group comparison). Little clarification has yet emerged from **case law** as to how the individual groups of provisions should be demarcated.

The comparison must be based on objective criteria. It must be certain from the outset that the favourability of the condition in the contract of employment is long-term. In general, terms and conditions which fall short of the collectively agreed standard cannot be offset by a level of pay in excess of the collectively agreed scale. If ultimately there is a preponderance of unfavourable elements or favourability cannot be established, the departure in question is not lawful and the higher-ranking norm prevails.

398. **GÜTETERMIN — CONCILIATION HEARING**: A compulsory first step of the **"Urteil" procedure** in the Labour Courts is a preliminary conciliation hearing to seek to bring about a **compromise** (Labour Courts Act § 54). During this session the president of the chamber has to discuss the whole dispute with the parties as regards the facts of the matter and the legal position and in the light of an assessment of the evidence presented. Approximately 50 per cent. of the disputes brought before the Labour Courts are settled by compromise at a conciliation hearing.

H

399. HAFTUNGSEINSCHRÄNKUNGEN — LIMITATIONS ON EMPLOYEE LIABILITY: In addition to the limitations which under the conditions stated elsewhere (see **employee liability**) already exempt an employee from liability in general circumstances, liability is also excluded or reduced if the work in question is classed as **hazardous work**. Contributory negligence on the part of the employer or the employer's representatives or agents can also result in a limitation.

400. HANDELSVERTRETER — COMMERCIAL REPRESENTATIVE: As a rule, a self-employed agent who arranges or concludes transactions for one or more **entrepreneurs**; a commercial representative is not an **employee**. Whether an individual is classed as a commercial representative or as an employee is judged not on the basis of their title but on the basis of the general circumstances of the situation. The main features identifying commercial representatives as such are that they arrange their working time as they please and assume their own business risk. On the other hand, if they have to follow instructions issued by the principal this indicates that the individual concerned is an employee, in the capacity of a member of the **field workforce**. Those commercial representatives who only undertake work on behalf of a single entrepreneur (called "Einfirmenhandelsvertreter") need special protection. They are classed as **persons treated in law as similar to an employee**, but cannot be covered by **collective agreements**. The rights and obligations of commercial representatives are regulated in the Commercial Code (Handelsgesetzbuch).

401. HANDWERKSKAMMER — CHAMBER OF CRAFT TRADES: Trade association to protect the interests of craft trades within a broad geographical region. Its members include both master and qualified craftworkers. It is organized as a public-law corporation and regulates **company vocational training**, issues rules for the conduct of examinations and maintains the Roll of Craftworkers, in which all craftworkers wishing to practise their trade on a self-employed basis are required to be registered. The central organization is the German Craft Trades Congress (Deutsche Handwerkstag).

402. HARMONIEVERBAND — "NON-CONFLICT" ASSOCIATION: An association in which both employer and employees are united. It does not qualify as a **collective industrial organization** and does not possess the **capacity to conclude**

172

collective agreements, for which **independence from the opposing side** is a precondition.

The definition of such an association, which inherently assumes the denial of any conflict of interests, is not deemed to apply to the situation where it is merely that members of an association at the same time perform functions of their social counterpart, *i.e.* if union representatives hold senior posts in public enterprises and social security institutions or are **employee directors** or **senior executives** performing management functions on the employer's behalf.

403. **HAUPTFÜRSORGESTELLE — CENTRAL AGENCY FOR THE DISABLED**: Administrative agencies which, under the Disabled Persons Act (Schwerbehindertengesetz), must be established at Land level to ensure the welfare of disabled persons and their protection under labour and social security law. They work in close co-operation with the **Federal Employment Service** (BfA). Specifically, they are responsible for the levy and expenditure of the **compensatory tax**, application of the law on **protection against dismissal** for disabled employees, provision of support after placement in a job ("nachgehende Hilfe", *i.e.* follow-up assistance) and the temporary withdrawal of **protection for disabled employees**. Whereas these agencies are responsible for all measures and benefits connected with safeguarding a disabled person's job, benefits that foster their actual integration into working life in the context of rehabilitation fall within the competence of the BfA.

404. **HAUPTPERSONALRAT — MAIN STAFF COUNCIL**: A main staff council is formed at the central level of public administration in the Federal Government and the **Länder** (Federal Staff Representation Act § 53(1)). In conjunction with the relevant **public-sector establishment head** of a top-level public authority, it is empowered to decide on those matters subject to co-determination on which it has proved impossible for agreement to be reached between the **hierarchical representation body** and establishment head, or **staff council** and establishment head, at the intermediate level of public administration and which the latter have referred (within six days and through the official channels) to the top-level authority for a decision. If the referral is effected by the establishment head, he or she must inform the staff council of the fact, stating the reasons. The main staff council also acts in certain cases where, although the matter to be regulated concerns a **public sector establishment** at the intermediate level of public administration, decision-making powers in the matter lie exclusively with the

173

corresponding authority at central level. Before reaching its decision, the main staff council must in all cases give the staff councils concerned the opportunity to comment. The members of the main staff council are elected by all the employees of the public sector establishments belonging to the sphere of activity of the top-level public authority, in accordance with the standard procedure for **staff council elections**. If elections for a staff council and for the higher-level representation bodies are held at the same time, they are conducted by an electoral board at the lower level on behalf of the regional or main electoral board. The composition of the main staff council follows the same principles as those for a staff council.

405. HAUPTVERSAMMLUNG — SHAREHOLDERS' MEETING: An organ of the **form of company** known as a public limited company (AG), within which the **shareholders** exercise their powers under the law and the company's articles of association by voting on resolutions. These powers include election and removal of their **supervisory board** members and the auditors and fundamental decisions on company policy (*e.g.* procurement and reduction of capital, winding-up of the company, change in the form of company, **merger**). It has no right to a say in matters of management, sole responsibility for which lies with the **management board**. The shareholders' meeting is held once a year as an ordinary annual general meeting in order to consider the annual accounts, to take decisions on approval of the acts of the management board and on the use of the profit available for dividend, and to fill seats that have fallen vacant on the supervisory board. An extraordinary shareholders' meeting must be convened if a minority of the shareholders representing 5 per cent. of the capital so require. Resolutions adopted at the shareholders' meeting must comply with the formalities laid down by law and may be challenged in the courts.

406. HAUSGEWERBETREIBENDE — PERSON CARRYING ON A BUSINESS FROM HOME: Individuals who, in a workplace of their own, *e.g.* in their home, employ no more than two non-family helpers or **homeworkers** and fabricate, prepare, process or pack goods for traders or **homework subcontractors**, while themselves contributing substantially to the actual work. Gainful utilization of the result of their work is, however, left to the trader who directly or indirectly commissions it from them, regardless of whether the materials used have been supplied by themselves or by the trader.

The special features of the **homework employment relationship** apply to individuals carrying on a business from home: they are not **employees** and are not subordinate to an **employer's right to issue instructions**, but are usually classed as **persons treated in law as similar to an employee**.

407. **HAUSTARIFVERTRAG — COMPANY AGREEMENT**: Term used synonymously with **Firmentarifvertrag**.

408. **HdA**: See **"Humanization of Working Life" Action Programme** (Aktionsprogramm "Humanisierung des Arbeitslebens").

409. **HEIMARBEITER — HOMEWORKER**: Individuals who, in a workplace of their own choosing, *e.g.* in their own home, undertake paid work, either alone or with the help of family members, for traders or **homework subcontractors**, but leave the gainful utilization of the finished result of their work to the trader who directly or indirectly commissions it from them, whether the materials required are procured by themselves or by the trader. It is a characteristic of homeworkers that they do not run a business, they undertake work in return for payment, but not necessarily with the intention of doing so over the long term. They therefore do not have to declare the practice of a business. They are, however, subject to earnings tax and social security contributions. The special provisions of the **homework employment relationship** apply to homeworkers: they are not **employees** and are not subordinate to an **employer's right to issue instructions**, but are classed as **persons treated in law as similar to an employee**.

410. **HEIMARBEITSAUSSCHUSS — HOMEWORKING COMMITTEE**: The competent Homeworking Committee of the labour authorities concerned decides, after hearing the representations of the parties involved, whether particular individuals or groups of individuals are equated with **homeworkers** or **persons running a business from home** because of their legitimate need for protection under labour law. This equal need for protection is assumed if the individuals or groups of individuals concerned are in a situation comparable to that of homeworkers or persons running a business from home in terms of their legal interests, the work performance they actually provide and their position in working life. This is particularly likely in the case of **homework subcontractors** or persons running a business from home who employ more than two non-family helpers or homeworkers.

411. **HEIMARBEITSVERHÄLTNIS — HOMEWORK EMPLOY-MENT RELATIONSHIP**: If a principal employs one or

175

more **homeworkers** or **persons running a business from home**, or individuals equated with such, homework employment relationships come into being. These are in principle covered by labour law, in so far as the provisions of the Homeworking Act (Heimarbeitergesetz) or the actual circumstances do not dictate otherwise.

A homeworker's **remuneration** is, similarly to **payment by results**, calculated on a piecework basis, and in some cases fixed times are allowed for particular tasks. The worker usually receives a **pay supplement** which represents an all-inclusive payment in lieu of entitlements to leave and sick pay. Apart from this, the contractual obligations correspond to those of other **employment relationships**, although the homeworker is not subordinate to any right on the part of the employing principal to issue instructions.

To prevent abuse of the employment of homeworkers, employing principals have to notify one of the Länder Employment Offices when they have entered into a homework employment relationship and submit six-monthly reports. They are required to distribute available work equally between individual homeworkers.

Special rules apply for ordinary **termination with notice** in the homework employment relationship. Initially, either party can terminate it with effect from the following day; after four weeks' employment the period of notice is two weeks, and with increasing duration of employment this gradually extends to a period of notice of three months at the end of the calendar quarter. Homeworkers are not covered by the provisions of general **protection against dismissal**. However, they enjoy special protection against dismissal as members of a **works council**, as **disabled persons** or in the context of **maternity protection**. If a homework employment relationship is terminated, it must be ensured that the employing principal does not evade the period of notice by allocating an increasingly smaller volume of work to the homeworker concerned so that the latter is paid less. If the volume of work allocated to the homeworker declines by 25 per cent., he or she is entitled to continue to receive the average level of pay earned over the 24 weeks preceding the **termination**.

A current trend is giving rise to an expansion of homeworking in the form of **telework**.

412. **HEUER — SEAFARER'S PAY**: The all-inclusive **remuneration** received by the crew members of merchant ships. Entitlement to such pay, as provided under the Seafarers Act (Seemannsgesetz), comes into being on entry into employment and falls due after an interval of one month or at the end of the

seafarer's employment relationship. However, entitlement to receive its actual payment exists only when in port. The seafarers's employment relationship carries an entitlement to meals and proper accommodation on board.

413. **HINTERBLIEBENENRENTE — SURVIVOR'S PENSION**: Term used to refer to the pension benefits payable to the survivors of a claimant under statutory **accident insurance** or the **statutory pension scheme**. Spouses and children of claimants, and also former spouses entitled to maintenance, are deemed to be survivors. If a survivor's pension is paid under statutory accident insurance, parents, step-parents and foster-parents also have a legitimate entitlement if they were being maintained by the claimant. The event insured against materializes on the death or official presumption of death of the claimant. The survivor's pension is paid under accident insurance if the claimant's death is the result of an **accident at work** or **occupational illness**. In all other cases it is paid under the statutory pension scheme.

General statutory pension provision is regulated for **manual workers** in Book 4 of the Reich Insurance Code (Reichsversicherungsordnung) and for **white-collar workers** in the White-Collar Workers' Social Insurance Act (Angestelltenversicherungsgesetz).

414. **HÖCHSTARBEITSZEIT — MAXIMUM WORKING HOURS**: The maximum duration of **working time** as laid down by regulations on working hours for the protection of employees. In practice, actual working hours are usually fixed by **collective agreements**. There is a difference between the limit on working hours imposed by law and the hours which an employee is required to work under a collective agreement or contract of employment. The most important provision on maximum working hours is the Working Time Statute (Arbeitszeitordnung, or AZO). In terms of personnel, the AZO in principle covers all employees aged over 18 in employment in the Federal Republic (AZO § 1); it specifically excludes the statutory agents of a company or co-operative society, authorized representatives and **executive staff** who have management responsibility for at least 20 employees. Similarly, it does not cover individuals to whom other **restrictions on working hours** apply, **homeworkers**, assisting family members and pharmaceutically trained staff working in dispensaries. Substantively, the AZO applies to all establishments and administrative entities under private and public law, but with exemptions for agriculture (including horticulture, viticulture and apiculture), forestry, livestock rearing, and secondary agricultural and forestry businesses (where

177

these supply purely personal requirements). Also, the AZO does not cover fisheries, seagoing shipping or aviation, including their associated land installations.

Under its provisions, normal working time on any one **working day** must not exceed eight hours (AZO § 3). This eight-hour day may, however, be exceeded in order to allow a different distribution of the total **working week**, to make up for time not worked and to perform **preparatory and shutting-down tasks**, subject to a daily maximum of 10 hours (AZO §§ 4 f.). In addition, for the purposes of alternating shift rotation in the context of fully continuous **shiftwork** it is permissible for male employees to work a shift of up to 16 hours once within any given period of three weeks, provided that twice within these three weeks they are granted an uninterrupted **rest period** of at least 24 hours (AZO § 10). Lastly, the statutory maximum working hours can be extended by the arrangement of permitted **overtime**, by collective agreement and, where there are special needs, by the **Labour Inspectorate** (AZO §§ 6 ff.). There is no limit on working hours for **emergency work**.

Where employees work together with **career public servants** ("Beamte"), the latter's working hours may be transferred to the employees or, in so far as the employees concerned are white-collar workers, apply to them directly. Other special regulations on maximum working hours are laid down for forms of work that are particularly arduous and hazardous to health, for women and for civilian employees in the armed forces.

415. HOHEITSAUFGABEN — SOVEREIGN FUNCTIONS: The public administration functions which are to be fulfilled on the basis of public law by the state (Federal Government, **Länder**), a **municipality** or other public-law institutions and authorities (**legal person**). As such they ensue from the **Constitution** or an individual **statute**. In fulfilling these functions the public authorities may effect lawful encroachments on the rights of the individual citizen ("Eingriffsverwaltung", *i.e.* freedom-restricting administration) or provide services for citizens ("Leistungsverwaltung", *i.e.* service-providing administration covering hospitals, schools, utilities, transport, etc.). The exercise of sovereign functions usually manifests itself in the form of an **act of administration**; an exception to this is the purely fiscal activity of the state in the sphere of private law.

Under the Constitution the state is directed to have sovereign functions performed by **career public servants** ("Beamte").

416. HUMAN RELATIONS: See **industrial relations, informal rules**.

417. HUMANISIERUNG — HUMANIZATION (OF WORK):
The adjustment of working conditions to human needs. It was
the focus of the Federal Government's **"Humanization of
Working Life" Action Programme** (HdA), which has since been
succeeded by the **"Work and Technology" Action Programme**
(AuT). There is also an obligation on employers and **works
councils** to comply with the established findings of **"work
science"** on the arrangement of work to take account of human
factors. In addition, the humanization of work is the subject of
qualitative bargaining policy. The demands being made in this
direction are a reaction against working conditions that are
hazardous to health, arduous and monotonous, *e.g.* in industrial
mass production. These demands can be satisfied by measures
such as automating dangerous work, varying the machine-
imposed pace of work and altering the ways in which work is
structured (*e.g.* **job rotation, job enlargement** and **job
enrichment**, and the formation of **semi-autonomous work
groups**).

In a broader and more value-oriented sense, the word
"humanization" is used to convey the idea that since it is people
who form the very core of the establishment it is no longer viable
to work on the assumption of an unbridgeable clash of interests
between employer and employee. Such divergences as there are
should consequently, it is felt, be resolved informally and as
between colleagues.

I

418. **IAO — ILO**: See **International Labour Organization** (Internationale Arbeitsorganisation).

419. **IHK**: See **Chamber of Industry and Commerce** (Industrie- und Handelskammer).

420. **INDEXLOHN — INDEXED PAY**: Term used where, under an agreement, the actual **pay** that must be paid by the **employer** is determined by reference to certain formulae with which the work performance due under the employment contract has no direct connection. In such cases actual pay may, for instance, be linked to changes in the gross national product (GNP) or the company's productivity.

   The indexing of pay is opposed in the Federal Republic, because of the effects on monetary policy. In practice, it is found only in pay arrangements with **white-collar workers exempt from collectively agreed terms** or **executive staff** under individual contracts of employment.

421. **INDIVIDUALARBEITSRECHT — INDIVIDUAL LABOUR LAW**: The area of **labour law** which regulates the relations between an individual **employee** and an **employer**. In particular, it covers the content and obligation aspects of the **contract of employment** and **employment relationship**, **employee rights** and **employee protection**.

422. **INDUSTRIE- UND HANDELSKAMMER — CHAMBER OF INDUSTRY AND COMMERCE**: These Chambers (initiated and endorsed by the state) are trade associations representing the interests of the business community; membership is compulsory and they are organized as self-administrating bodies under public law. All companies (single proprietorships, partnerships or legal persons under private or public law) must be declared to a Chamber of Industry and Commerce (IHK) when they are first formed. The Chambers advise the affiliated companies on economic matters, administer examinations in business studies and arbitrate in disputes relating to competition. The central body is the Association of German Chambers of Industry and Commerce (Deutsche Industrie- und Handelstag).

423. **INDUSTRIELLE BEZIEHUNGEN — INDUSTRIAL RELATIONS**: A subsystem of society in which the actors, *i.e.* the **employees** and **employers** with their organizations and the state authorities, interact to allocate the distribution of resources, status and conditions of reproduction. This gives rise to the

fundamental **industrial conflict** between capital and labour. Since the beginning of industrialization, of course, the respective interests and attitudes have become more differentiated and control and management techniques have become more refined. Also, increasing complexity has made administrative and production procedures more vulnerable to interruption and the integrating effects of modern welfare state systems have fostered consensus across society. It was as a result of this trend, for example, that in Germany there was very extensive agreement among employers and employees on the need to introduce successive **new technologies** and that their introduction has even been achieved with relatively little friction. The likelihood of conflict and corresponding resistance to innovation depend on the industrial relations structure and influence the flexibility of companies and of a country's entire economy.

The intricate network of industrial relations takes place at partly interconnected (hierarchical) levels:

a. direct labour relations (shop floor);
b. **works constitution** and **company constitution**;
c. **collective organizations**;
d. tripartite institutions; and
e. the International Labour Office and International Labour Organization (ILO).

Industrial relations at international level in fact have significance for relations between the actors within individual countries only to the extent that they establish universal standards and the multinational organization of capital influences national markets, since there has as yet been little real development in international co-operation by **trade unions**. Lastly, the **labour markets** at individual company, regional and national levels form an important subdivision of industrial relations.

Characterized as it is by a high degree of welfare state regulation and **juridification**, the industrial relations system in the Federal Republic of Germany has different actors and modes of action at almost every level:

a. basically informal: among colleagues or in relation to supervisors;
b. elaborately regulated in the system of **institutionalized representation of interests**: between **works councils** and **management** and between employee and employer representatives on the **supervisory board**;
c. under the conditions of **collective bargaining autonomy**: between employers or **employers' associations** and trade unions;
d. regulated in the case of institutionalized tripartite bodies (*e.g.* **social security**) and informal in the case of *ad hoc* tripartite

181

bodies (*e.g.* **concerted action**): between employers' and employees' associations and the appropriate state authorities.

424. INDUSTRIELLER KONFLIKT — INDUSTRIAL CONFLICT: Term denoting the clash of interests, and resultant disputes of varying intensity, between different individuals, groups and organizations in the **industrial relations** system. Industrial conflict may centre around differences in values and objectives, and relationships in terms of status, power and distribution. Depending on the onlooker's theoretical viewpoint and position, industrial conflicts are perceived either as disruptive to the proper functioning of society or as providing an impetus for social change and progress. They exist at every level of industrial relations, with localized conflicts even within the separate groups of actors. Like any other disagreement, they are affected by emotional tensions between the actors concerned and by various outside influences.

In the interests of the uninterrupted flow of goods and services, efforts are made at establishment and company level to keep industrial conflict to the unavoidable minimum. Conflicts arise at this level mainly as a result of structural conditions, *e.g.* hierarchies, discrepancies between status, powers and responsibility or informal manifestations of authority and subordination. Against this background, management concepts such as the functional application of **corporate cultures** seek to avoid the segmentation of individuals or groups and thereby prevent inherent conflict from taking root. Beyond this level, the potential areas of industrial conflict in the overall structure of industrial relations in the Federal Republic are separated to a relatively rigid degree. General disputes about the distribution of resources (essentially, working hours and pay) are assigned exclusively to the **parties to collective agreements**. On the other hand, disagreement regarding direct terms and conditions of employment is handled within the formalized context of the **works constitution**. In this connection, the purpose of imposing on **works council** and **employer** the obligation of **co-operation in good faith** is to release the parties at establishment level from the traditional clash of interests between capital and labour.

425. INDUSTRIEVERBANDSPRINZIP — PRINCIPLE OF INDUSTRIAL ORGANIZATION: The overwhelming majority of trade unions in the Federal Republic are organized on an industry basis, *i.e.* their function is to represent the interests not of particular occupations but of the employees working in a given industry or branch of activity. For example, IG Metall, which is the largest individual union, is not a union of manual metalworkers alone (**occupational union**) but an industrial union whose membership also includes all other employees working in the metal industry.

This principle of industrial organization, which is enshrined in the standing rules of the **German Federation of Trade Unions** (**DGB**), has the advantage of concentrating the system of bargaining to a very considerable extent, since it counteracts excessive overlap in the bargaining jurisdiction of different unions, *i.e.* **conflict between collective agreements**, and eliminates the necessity of separate groupings for manual workers, white-collar workers and career public servants ("Beamte"), *e.g.* the Public Services, Transport and Traffic Union (ÖTV), a combined organization uniting all three groups.

426. INFORMATIONSRECHTE DES BETRIEBSRATS — INFORMATION RIGHTS OF THE WORKS COUNCIL: The elementary form of **participation rights of the works council**. The works council's performance of its functions and exercise of the **consultation rights** and **co-determination rights of the works council** are usually preceded by the disclosure of information by the employer. To this end the employer is required to provide information in good time, together with the necessary documents. The works council may, as necessary, enlist the aid of experts for the purposes of safeguarding and using its information rights.

427. INFORMELLE REGELUNGEN — INFORMAL RULES: A component aspect of **industrial relations** closely connected with, and occasionally in conflict with, **institutionalized representation of interests**. Informal rules cover all interrelations and patterns of behaviour which are inaccessible to formal generalized agreements and hence also to the organized collective efforts of the **works council** and **trade unions**. They preserve a limited scope for individual worker autonomy even in the face of collective regulation by **management**, and hence may also reduce **industrial conflict**. They also ensure that the establishment runs as smoothly as possible, by filling gaps in planning and making up for deficiencies in control. With the increasing complexity of the manufacturing process in the application of **new technologies**, informal rules are assuming steadily growing importance. Consequently, employers are seeking to influence the basis and mechanisms of such rules through corresponding **corporate cultures**.

428. INHALTSFREIHEIT — FREEDOM OF CONTRACTUAL CONTENT: Although the principle of **freedom of contract** also applies in labour law, it is subject to a number of constraints for the protection of the economically weaker party, *i.e.* the employee. For instance, because of the **favourability principle** a provision in an individual **contract of employment** diverging from the regulation laid down in a **collective agreement** or **works agreement** is valid only if the employee thereby acquires more or improved rights. A provision in the individual contract may not diverge from collectively agreed provisions to the employee's disadvantage even if the employee has consented to this. The same applies in respect of statutory regulations on **employee protection** which are not discretionary for the parties to the contract of employment. If the content of a particular contract is in fact lawful in these respects, it is subject only to a special procedure for **control of contractual content** by the Labour Courts.

429. **INHALTSKONTROLLE — CONTROL OF CONTRACTUAL CONTENT**: To protect the **employee**, the **Labour Courts** examine the content of contracts of employment to check not only whether it constitutes a breach of the law or is contrary to public policy but also whether it is contrary to natural justice. The courts apply this procedure to the examination of standard terms and conditions, *i.e.* contracts which are concluded routinely in the same form with a large number of employees. They have not as yet used it to examine contracts of employment negotiated individually. Collectively agreed provisions, *i.e.* both **collective agreements** and **works agreements**, are subject to examination by the courts as regards the legality of their conclusion and their compliance with the rules of law applicable to them. The Federal Labour Court holds that works agreements are also, like standard terms and conditions of employment, subject to examination by the courts to check whether they are contrary to natural justice, whereas collective agreements, given the well-defined social function of the collective bargaining parties, are not.

430. **INNERBETRIEBLICHE WEITERBILDUNG — IN-SERVICE TRAINING**: Further training aimed at extending existing **skills** or acquiring new ones associated with the company's needs within an existing employment relationship. Despite regular adjustment of the content of **vocational training relationships** to altered market conditions, such development training is assuming ever-growing importance, with instruction in non-occupational aspects such as the ability to communicate and co-ordinate and other social skills as an increasingly significant component. In addition to careful analysis of the needs to be met and the employees who should participate, the success of such training programmes depends in large measure on a **corporate**

culture that stimulates a company "training climate". Also, both programmes and methods need to be subjected to constant review and improvement.

A number of recent **collective agreements** provide for continuous in-service training, in some cases during time made available by (voluntary) reductions in working hours.

The implementation of in-service training is subject to a **co-determination right of the works council**.

431. **INSOLVENZ — INSOLVENCY**: See **bankruptcy, composition**.

432. **INSOLVENZSCHUTZ — PROTECTION IN THE EVENT OF INSOLVENCY**: In the event of inability to pay on the part of the person or body responsible for pension payments, *i.e.* either the **employer** or a **pension or benevolent fund**, protection is provided for **employees'** entitlements to **occupational pensions** and for non-forfeitable **occupational pension expectations** of such payments. This protection is provided through the **Pension Security Association** (PSV), which takes the place of the pension-provider and assumes responsibility for guaranteeing pension payments, to the amount for which the pension-provider was liable. This also includes future increases, if the **assurance of an occupational pension** contained an adjustment clause to this effect. The conditions under which protection comes into effect are: the institution of **bankruptcy** proceedings; a **composition** either ordered by the court or arranged out of court; liquidation of the pension-provider without bankruptcy proceedings on the grounds of insufficient assets; or the cessation or reduction of payments by the pension-provider in cases of financial need established by the court. Protection cannot be claimed in cases of abuse where the real purpose of providing assurance of a pension was to pass on responsibility for pension entitlements to the PSV.

433. **INSTITUTIONALISIERTE INTERESSEN-VERTRETUNG — INSTITUTIONALIZED REPRESENTATION OF INTERESTS**: In the Federal Republic **industrial relations**, like most other areas of society, exhibit a high degree of **juridification**. The various mechanisms for the representation of **employees'** interests are typical examples, particularly **co-determination** and the **works constitution**. Both are safeguarded by law and provide what for a **market economy** may be considered relatively numerous opportunities for participation by the workforce and the **trade unions**.

At the same time the pattern of institutionalized representation of interests has an integrating effect, as witness, for example, the

peace obligation throughout the lifetime of **collective agreements** and the prohibition of **strike** action in the context of the works constitution. The very fact that the **works council** is established by law as a body representing employees in its own right, independent of the unions, is a clear indication of this dual function. The works council is positioned between the workforce and the employer, towards whom it is required to maintain **co-operation in good faith**; it provides management with a democratically authorized and in most cases stable opposite number. In large and medium-sized companies in particular, works councils are accepted and their participation rights are in principle granted duly and comprehensively, albeit not always voluntarily, by the employer. Empirical studies have also demonstrated that institutionalized protection of employees and their rights to have a voice in shaping the course of events enables restructuring measures, *e.g.* the introduction of **new technologies**, to proceed more smoothly.

The practical form which **social partnership** at establishment level normally takes does, however, meet with some criticism. Since the mid-1970s in particular, independent union members and other employees have stood as rival candidates in **works council elections** against the lists supported by the member unions of the **German Federation of Trade Unions** (DGB). Despite this, approximately 80 per cent. of all seats on works councils are occupied by members of a DGB union. It is uncertain what effects there will be on the system of institutionalized representation within the establishment as a result of the **representative bodies for executive staff** recently established by law and the changes made to the conditions of eligibility for election to the works council.

The unions have a direct presence within the establishment in the form of their **union workplace representatives**. However, the second mainstay of the unions, next to **collective bargaining autonomy**, is unquestionably the works council, which in the future is likely to become even more important. Given the difference in their basic nature and hence in the interests that characterize them, growing disagreement between these two forms of employee representation is not impossible.

434. **INTERESSENAUSGLEICH — RECONCILEMENT OF INTERESTS**: Procedure aimed at reconciling the viewpoints of the **employer** and the **workforce** in the event of a proposed **substantial alteration to the establishment** (Works Constitution Act §§ 111 f.) and also **bankruptcy** and composition. An agreement reached in this way has valid effect only if it is in writing and is adopted by the works council by formal resolution.

The procedure involves weighing the respective interests against each other and agreeing, for example, on whether the major change envisaged should be carried out at all, and if so the extent and timing of the change and the necessary **human resource planning** and organization of work. Detailed arrangements for the subsequent implementation of the changes are then subject to the **co-determination right of the works council**. If the employer and works council fail to agree on a reconcilement of interests, they may call on the Director of the Land Employment Office to mediate. Should they not wish to do so, or should mediation prove unsuccessful, they can refer the matter to the **establishment-level arbitration committee**, although its decision will not be binding on them. In cases where the employer makes no attempt to arrive at an agreed reconcilement of interests or without compelling reason fails to abide by one, employees who are dismissed or suffer economic disadvantage as a result may claim the corresponding **compensation for job loss**. A "**social plan**" can be drawn up regardless of whether or not a reconcilement of interests has been sought.

435. **INTERNATIONALE ARBEITSORGANISATION — INTERNATIONAL LABOUR ORGANIZATION**: The International Labour Organization (ILO) was founded in 1919. Most UN member countries belong to it; the Federal Republic was admitted on application in 1951.

Its main bodies (the General Conference, the Governing Body and the International Labour Office) have their headquarters in Geneva. The International Labour Office collects and processes information relevant to the international regulation of living and working conditions for employees and drafts Conventions, which are then laid before the General Conference. ILO Conventions have the nature of legislation proposals which pass into law only when ratified by member countries. The Federal Republic has so far ratified more than 60 Conventions, *e.g.* on benefits payable for **accidents at work** and **occupational illnesses** and for old age and invalidity, on equal treatment of nationals and aliens in the social security system, on various aspects of **protection against technical hazards at work** and on paid **annual holidays** and **educational leave**.

436. **INTERNATIONALES ARBEITSRECHT — INTERNATIONAL LABOUR LAW**: International labour law constitutes a law on the choice of laws, *i.e.* it establishes rules for dealing with cases where there is a conflict of labour laws because they involve a foreign element. These cases arise both in the employment of **foreign workers** and in the employment

of German workers abroad. A subsidiary problem is where there has been agreement on electing a legal domicile abroad, which normally signifies agreement to accept foreign labour court procedure. As regards the conflict of laws aspect, a distinction has to be made as follows. For private-law **individual labour law**, the prevailing legal opinion is that it is primarily a matter of the wishes of the parties to the contract of employment (subjective criterion). They are in principle free to choose which rules of law shall apply. Otherwise, the principles of private international law apply. If it is agreed that foreign law is to have valid effect, this must be applied as a matter of principle. If, however, the foreign law concerned falls short of German **collective labour law** in terms of social protection such an agreement is invalid wherever it is contrary to *ordre public* (*i.e.* public policy). This is so if application of the foreign law is by its very nature contrary to the interests of the community *(contra bonos mores)* or to the purpose of a German statute.

Lastly, the term also covers internationally agreed labour law. This mainly comprises **European Community law** and other treaties. It also includes numerous **ILO** Conventions signed and ratified by the Federal Republic. In addition, on November 23, 1973 the Federal Republic assented by statute to the UN International Treaty on Economic, Social and Cultural Rights of December 19, 1966 that was signed in New York on October 9, 1968.

437. INVESTIVLOHN — INVESTED PAY: Component of pay which is not paid to the employee but deposited with the company itself or outside funds and invested in production-financing assets. The unions are sceptical of this form of financial participation for employees. They argue that it involves a double risk for employees, namely, both job loss and financial loss in the event of bankruptcy, and that it is used by employers as a pretext for offering low pay increases.

An initial agreement on invested pay was concluded in the construction industry in 1965 by collective agreement, stipulating that 9 pfennigs per hour from the employer and 2 pfennigs per hour from the employee should be deposited in a savings account. This was superseded by subsequent collectively agreed provisions on **capital-forming payments**. Nowadays, the only form in which invested pay arrangements are found is in voluntary employee share ownership schemes.

J

438. **JOB SHARING**: An arrangement for dividing one or more **jobs** between several employees. The purpose of this form of **part-time work**, as sanctioned by law under the Improvement of Employment Opportunities Act (§ 5), is to ensure that the shared jobs are permanently staffed. The individual tasks involved may either be divided equally between all the job sharers or broken down functionally into skilled and ancillary tasks.

Most employees who are employed in a job-sharing context are part of a **work group** formed by the employer, and less commonly are members of a **self-constituted employee group**. As a rule, therefore, they have no legal relationship with each other, nor do they have joint and several liability for the work performance due. In principle the individual job sharers decide their own working hours between themselves. If one of them is unable to work, the others cannot be called on to act as replacements unless this is agreed for the particular case, there are urgent operational requirements and they can reasonably be expected to undertake the additional work. If one job sharer leaves, as a general rule the employer cannot use this fact to justify **termination** of the **employment relationships** with the others. The wording of the Act indicates that departures from the minimum terms and conditions laid down therein for job sharing are permissible under a **collective agreement** provided they are in the employees' favour.

439. **JUGENDARBEITSSCHUTZ — YOUTH EMPLOYMENT PROTECTION**: Juveniles (*i.e.* individuals under the age of 18) who are in employment as **employees, homeworkers** or **persons treated in law as similar to an employee** or are in a **vocational training relationship** or similar relationship are covered by special protective provisions, mostly grouped in the 1976 Youth Employment Protection Act (Jugendarbeitsschutzgesetz). Some of these provisions date back to regulations that have existed since the middle of the 19th century.

In principle the employment of juveniles under the age of 15 is prohibited, but exemptions are allowed if they are in a vocational training relationship or employed on light work, and always provided that it does not involve prohibited **child employment**. Juveniles aged 15 and over may be employed, but only to a restricted extent: their working hours may not exceed 8½ hours per day and 40 hours in a week, and they may work on only five days in a week but not (with certain exceptions) on Saturdays, Sundays or public holidays. They have a statutory **annual holiday** entitlement of 25-30 **working days**, according to age. **Vocational trainees** who are required to attend vocational training school must be released from work for the time during which they receive instruction and for examination of their work. Juveniles are guaranteed longer breaks, longer uninterrupted rest periods between each working day and more leisure time than other employees. They may not be employed on work that is too arduous for them, dangerous or unhealthy, or on a **piecework** or **payment by results** basis, and they may not work underground. Exceptions are allowed if the purpose of their training involves such employment or if they have been trained specifically for such activities, provided they are under expert supervision. **Employers** previously convicted for serious offences against certain criminal laws or against the regulations on youth employment protection are prohibited from employing juveniles. The **Labour Inspectorate** can specify additional restrictions on and exemptions from the regulations and in the event of contraventions can declare further **employment bans**.

The employer is required to ensure that juveniles are employed in jobs appropriate to their abilities and to give them proper warning of any hazards, and may not inflict corporal punishment on them. Juveniles must be medically examined before and one year after the commencement of their employment, and the employer must obtain a certificate testifying their physical fitness for the work they are to perform. Contraventions of the regulations on youth employment protection are punishable by fine or imprisonment.

440. JUGEND- UND AUSZUBILDENDENVERTRETUNG — REPRESENTATIVE BODY FOR YOUNG WORKERS AND TRAINEES: An organ of the **works constitution** that must be elected in all establishments regularly employing at least five employees under the age of 18 or vocational trainees under the age of 25 (Works Constitution Act §§ 60 ff.). Its responsibilities correspond to those of the **works council** in matters specific to young employees and trainees; it is, however, entirely dependent on the works council as regards taking any practical action and must be allowed the appropriate initiative. It must be provided with all the necessary documents by the works council, with the exception of trade and business secrets. It has its own co-determination rights and rights to make claims in the courts under the **"Beschluss" procedure**. It may hold meetings and send representatives to works council meetings. Except for the right to leave of absence from work, its members have the same rights as works council members. There is a special regulation covering the case where the **vocational training relationship** comes to an end. If the employer does not wish to continue employing a **vocational trainee** who is a member of the representative body,

190

this must be indicated in writing three months before the vocational training relationship expires. If the trainee concerned demands admission to the status of an open-ended employment relationship, a corresponding contract is deemed to be created. However, the employer is then entitled to have the non-existence or cancellation of the employment relationship established by court decision, if the necessary grounds exist.

All employees under the age of 18 and all vocational trainees under the age of 25 may participate in elections for the representative body; voting is by direct secret ballot, according to the majority principle. All individuals under the age of 25 by the date of the election are eligible to be elected. The electoral board is appointed by the works council or, if the council declines to do so, by the Labour Court on application. Elections are normally held between October 1 and November 30. The term of office is two years.

Corresponding bodies under staff representation law in the public sector exist, in accordance with the principle of the **hierarchical representation body**, at the **staff council**, **general staff council** and **main staff council** levels (Federal Staff Representation Act §§ 57 ff., 64).

441. **JURISTISCHE PERSON — LEGAL PERSON**: The law distinguishes between a natural and legal person. A natural person is any human being, with legal capacity commencing from the time of birth. A legal (artificial) person is an association of people or special-purpose fund (*e.g.* a foundation) that is recognized by law as having legal personality. It differs from other associations of people in that it possesses legal capacity and can appear before the courts as plaintiff or defendant ("Parteifähigkeit", *i.e.* capacity to be a party in court). A legal person is separate and distinct in law from its members and from their number or changeover. It is an independent legal entity and is in principle protected by **basic rights**. Its particular name is also protected by law against unauthorized use by third parties. It has the capacity to act and can thus acquire rights and create obligations with binding effect. It does this through its organs, which in the sphere of private-law labour relations are, depending on the **form of company**, the **shareholders' meeting** or **company general meeting**, the **supervisory board**, the **management board** or a **managing director**. It is recognized in **case law** that a legal person is liable for unlawful conduct on the part of its organs and must pay damages where appropriate.

There is a difference between a private-law and public-law legal person. The society or association (Verein) is regulated in the Civil Code as the basis of legal personality under private law.

Other civil-law societies are the private limited company (GmbH), the registered co-operative society (eG), the public limited company (AG) and the partnership limited by shares (KGaA), all with their legal basis founded in separate statutes. Otherwise, in the absence of special regulations the provisions of the Civil Code and the Commercial Code are applied to supplement them. The state also can avail itself of a private-law legal person in executing its functions.

Public-law legal persons exist by virtue of recognition under public law and can be established only by statute or by an act of sovereignty (**act of administration, executive order**) on the basis of a statute.

K

442. **KALTE AUSSPERRUNG — "COLD" LOCK-OUT**: If work is interrupted in an establishment as a result of industrial action elsewhere, according to the doctrine of **"works risk"** the fact that it becomes impossible to employ them means that employees lose their entitlement to remuneration; that is to say, the employees must sustain the loss of remuneration if the cause originates from their own sphere. Since in the case of such interruptions employees lose their entitlement to remuneration even though they are not directly involved in the strike, the unions talk of a "cold" lock-out by the employer.

443. **KAMPFBETEILIGUNG VON BESONDEREN ARBEITNEHMERGRUPPEN — PARTICIPATION IN INDUSTRIAL ACTION BY PARTICULAR EMPLOYEE GROUPS**: All employees in an establishment may in principle participate in a strike, irrespective of their function. This also applies to members of the **works council** and **staff council** and to employee representatives on the **supervisory board**. **Vocational trainees** are in general deemed only to have the right to participate in brief **token strikes** of fixed duration, even if the issue concerned is vocational training pay. **Executive staff** are generally denied the right to strike, on the grounds of their special function as representatives who act on behalf of the employer.

444. **KAMPFPARITÄT — BALANCE OF BARGAINING POWER**: See **industrial action, lock-out**.

445. **"KAPOVAZ"**: Acronym standing for "kapazitätsorientierte variable Arbeitszeit", *i.e.* capacity-related variable **working time**. It denotes a special form of variable working hours under which the **employee** is used only as and when the **employer**'s demand for labour so dictates. (The term "Bedarfsarbeitsverhältnis" is also used, *i.e.* supply employment relationship.) The Improvement of Employment Opportunities Act (§ 4) lays down minimum terms and conditions for "KAPOVAZ" as a special form of **part-time work**. The contracting parties are required to specify in advance the amount of working time due over a given period. The employer is then free to call on this agreed time allowance according to need, provided that the employee is given four days' prior notice. If the parties do not specify any particular arrangement, the legal assumption is that the agreed working time is at least 10 hours weekly, for which remuneration is also payable. The performance of work must not be demanded at unreasonable times. In addition, if it has not been regulated otherwise the employer must employ the employee for at least three consecutive

hours on each occasion, but in any case pay the corresponding remuneration. The actual timing of such work is subject to the **co-determination right of the works council**.

The wording of the Act indicates that departures from the minimum terms and conditions laid down therein for "KAPOVAZ" are permissible under a **collective agreement** provided they are in the employee's favour.

446. **KERNZEIT — CORE TIME**: See **flexitime**.

447. **KETTENARBEITSVERTRÄGE — CONSECUTIVE SHORT-TERM CONTRACTS**: Term used to indicate a chain of **fixed-term employment relationships**, with a new contract commencing as the previous one expires. As a general principle, a succession of directly consecutive contracts is not unlawful; the validity of the fixed term set for each individual contract is governed by the principles laid down on the matter. There is, however, a presumption that setting a fixed term in the case of such consecutive contracts cannot be substantively justified.

448. **KINDERARBEIT — CHILD EMPLOYMENT**: Child employment is subject to narrow restrictions in the Federal Republic. The employment of children, *i.e.* individuals under the age of 14 or below the statutory school-leaving age (the vast majority of 15-year-olds), is in principle prohibited. The only exemption is employment for the purposes of occupational therapy or in the context of practical work experience during compulsory full-time education. Provided children are aged over 13, between 0800 and 1800 hrs they may be employed, by way of exception:

a. by the persons having legal custody of them, *i.e.* usually their parents, in their own agricultural enterprise for up to three hours per day;

b. with the permission of the persons having legal custody of them, by third parties during harvesting for up to three hours per working day;

c. in delivering newspapers, for up to two hours per working day;

d. in helping in sports activities, for up to two hours per day.

In addition, the supervisory authorities, usually the **Labour Inspectorate**, may authorize the employment of children in connection with particular theatrical performances and musical events.

Despite these narrow limits, child employment is as widespread as ever. Recent estimates indicate that some 10 per cent. of all children aged between 10 and 15 are employed, mainly in newspaper delivery and agriculture, in 20 per cent. of these cases doing work that is in contravention of the law.

449. **KINDERBETREUUNG — CHILDCARE**: Childcare outside the family is provided during very limited hours by kindergartens, crèches and nurseries run by local authorities, Religious Communities and charitable institutions or on a private basis. Workplace childcare facilities are provided only in a few cases; support for working parents is confined to **childcare leave** and **parental leave**. In 1989 there were 102,000 kindergarten places in the Federal Republic, and nursery places were available for only 2 per cent. of children under the age of two.

450. **KINDERGELD — CHILD BENEFIT**: A social security benefit provided under family policy and paid directly by the relevant local **Employment Office** or the **public sector employer** within the **public service**. It amounts to 70 Deutschmarks monthly for the first child, 130 for the second, 220 for the third and 240 for each additional child thereafter. It is paid for legitimate, legitimated, adopted and illegitimate children and stepchildren whom the recipient of the benefit cares for in his or her household or predominantly maintains. It is payable for children over the age of 16 only if they are in full-time education or vocational training and do not already receive vocational training pay of 750 Deutschmarks per month. From the age of 27, it is still payable only if the child concerned is on compulsory military or community service, etc. or has not obtained a university or college place.

In principle child benefit is payable only for children within the purview of the Federal Child Benefit Act (Bundeskindergeldgesetz). Exceptions are allowed for EC nationals, Austrian and Turkish nationals, refugees and stateless persons, who also receive child benefit for children living outside Federal Republic territory. The European Court of Justice has ruled that this applies even if child benefit is not being paid by the EC Member State concerned simply because it has not been claimed. Conversely, Germans employed in the countries named above also receive child benefit there for their children living within Federal Republic territory in accordance with the legislation of the country concerned.

451. **KIRCHEN — CHURCHES**: See **Religious Communities**.

452. **KIRCHLICHE MITARBEITERVERTRETUNG — ECCLESIASTICAL STAFF REPRESENTATION BODY**: Establishments associated with the Christian **Religious**

Communities are not covered by the Works Constitution Act and therefore do not have **works councils**. In the organizational sphere of the Protestant and Roman Catholic Churches in the Federal Republic agreements were reached on the introduction of ecclesiastical staff representation bodies which have functions similar to those of works councils but less extensive rights overall, particularly in Roman Catholic establishments.

453. **KIRCHLICHES ARBEITSRECHT — ECCLESIASTICAL LABOUR LAW**: There are more than 500,000 employees of the Churches, their subdivisions and the institutions (mostly charitable) associated closely or less closely with their religious aims. Owing to the special legal status of the **Religious Communities**, as compared with the regulations applicable for secular employers these employees are covered by a modified form of **labour law** which is extensively accommodated to the specific interests of ecclesiastical employers, in many respects at the expense of their employees' interests. Holders of ecclesiastical office are not covered by labour law at all, and employees of employers associated with the Churches lack the protection of important sections of collective labour law. Forms of **industrial action** are regarded as irreconcilable with the special nature of ecclesiastical employment and therefore as unlawful. The only allowance made for the **freedom of association** of employees is the fact that the representation of their interests by **trade unions** is permitted, *i.e.* employees of ecclesiastical establishments may join trade unions and the unions are able to have a presence within the establishment at least through their members who are employed there. However, they have scarcely any means of pursuing these members' interests. The conclusion of **collective agreements** is rejected totally by the Roman Catholic Church and extensively by the Protestant Church. Ecclesiastical establishments are exempt from the application of the Works Constitution Act. Instead of the normal mechanisms for adjusting employer/employee interests under collective law, both of the major Churches have introduced systems of their own. For Protestant establishments, labour law committees jointly composed of employer and employee representatives issue guidelines on the framing of contracts of employment. For Roman Catholic establishments, a similar function is performed by committees for the regulation of employment contract law. For the purposes of employee representation as under the **works constitution, ecclesiastical staff representation bodies** have been introduced in both Churches.

Individual labour law is in principle binding on ecclesiastical employers as it is on other employers. Modifications are, however, introduced in instances which the Churches themselves perceive as touching on their religious identity. This is a particular problem if employees' conduct within the employment context, but above all outside it, is contrary to the teachings of the Church without this having any direct connection with their actual work. According to the **Federal Constitutional Court**, which strongly favours the Churches in its rulings, in such cases the latter's interests must be protected largely to the exclusion of employees' rights. Consequently, employees whose religious or moral views differ from official Church doctrine have to face the likelihood of being dismissed if they let their opinions be known.

454. **KNAPPSCHAFT — MINEWORKERS**: See **health insurance fund**.

455. **KOALITION — COLLECTIVE INDUSTRIAL ORGANIZ-ATION**: Term used to refer to **trade unions** and **employers' associations**; in having "working and economic conditions" defined as their specific functional sphere (Basic Law, Article 9(3)) they are both distinguished from other associations that are formed in virtue of general freedom of association. Only collective industrial organizations and the individual employer possess the **capacity to conclude collective agreements** (Collective Agreements Act § 2(1)). According to the identifying characteristics developed by case law, the only associations recognized as having collective industrial organization status are those which:
a. have voluntary membership;
b. follow the principles of **democratic decision-making** in their collective policy decisions;
c. possess the necessary autonomy;
d. satisfy the criterion of **independence from the opposing side**;
e. have embraced the **purpose of a collective industrial organization**, *i.e.* seek to safeguard and improve working and economic conditions;
f. possess the power to exert pressure and counterpressure on their collective bargaining counterparts, although this does not necessarily imply being willing to engage in **industrial action**.

The principal function of collective industrial organizations is to bring about an effective regulation of working life through the conclusion of **collective agreements**. In addition, they advise and support their members and play a part in the context of the **works constitution** and **co-determination** at company level. They also participate, in many ways, in **legislation** and public administration by the authorities.

456. KOALITIONSFREIHEIT — FREEDOM OF ASSOCIATION (RIGHT TO ORGANIZE): In guaranteeing general freedom of association in its Article 9(3), the Basic Law guarantees every individual the right to form a **collective industrial organization,** to participate in the formation of one, to join an existing one, to choose between several in deciding to join one, to remain a member of one and to decide to withdraw from membership of one ("positive" freedom of association). Constitutional protection is also given to **"negative" freedom of association,** *i.e.* the right of the individual not to join a collective industrial organization. The Basic Law here protects not only the right of the individual to join with others in forming organizations but also the organizations as such (collective freedom of association). This incudes a **guarantee of existence** and **guarantee of activity.**

All agreed arrangements that restrict the individual right to organize are invalid (Basic Law, Article 9(3, subparagraph 2)). Examples of such invalid arrangements are provisions in the individual contract of employment placing the employee under an obligation not to join a trade union, or **closed shop clauses** whereby an employer undertakes to hire only employees who are union members. The right to organize also gives individual members the right to take an active part in respect of their collective industrial organization. This includes, for example, the right of union members to publicize the union within the establishment.

457. KOALITIONSZWECK — PURPOSE OF A COLLECTIVE INDUSTRIAL ORGANIZATION: Defined as the safeguarding and improvement of working and economic conditions. In order to operate legitimately within this sphere, a collective industrial organization must acknowledge that it is bound by the current law on collective bargaining and see as its function the conclusion of **collective agreements** to improve the economic and social situation of its members. Its regulatory powers as protected under the Constitution relate only to matters which serve this purpose.

458. KOLLEKTIVES ARBEITSRECHT — COLLECTIVE LABOUR LAW: The area of **labour law** which regulates collective relations between employers and employees and their results. In particular, it covers the **works constitution** and **staff representation,** the **right to organize** and **collective bargaining autonomy.**

459. KOMMUNALVERBAND — ASSOCIATION OF MUNICIPALITIES: Name given to the public-law entities (**legal person**) which are the units of administration ranking between a **municipality** and a Land Government. They are independent authorities, in some cases with a directly elected representative body called the "Kreistag" (district council). Their powers extend geographically over a "Landkreis" (district) and the municipalities within it. The district council elects a "Landrat" (district council chairman) who is responsible for administration of the district. In other respects, these associations of municipalities are organized differently in the district structures of the individual Länder. Their powers are derived partly from **statutes** and partly from delegation by the municipalities. These latter responsibilities mainly relate to matters concerning the municipalities within their district which need to be regulated above individual municipality level. The associations of municipalities have powers of self-government as regards their statutory responsibilities and can issue **byelaws**.

460. **KOMMUNE — MUNICIPALITY**: A local administration area which, like the Federal Government and the **Länder**, is a public-law territorial authority. By virtue of sovereign jurisdiction derived from the state, it is the smallest organizational unit of the state and entitled to administer its own affairs within its local boundaries. Some municipalities cover a comparatively small geographical area and are akin to the English parishes. Others, however, are large-scale authorities covering an entire city such as Frankfurt.

461. **KONKURRIERENDE GESETZGEBUNGSKOMPETENZ — CONCURRENT LEGISLATIVE POWERS**: In so far as **legislative powers** in a given field are not assigned exclusively either to the Federation or to the **Länder**, they both have the right to enact **legislation**. The conflict arising from this situation is regulated by the principle of concurrent legislative powers as laid down in the **Constitution**. This stipulates that the Länder may legislate in a given field so long as the Federation makes no use of its regulatory powers. They lose this authority as soon as the Federation regulates the same matter comprehensively and exhaustively by statute. The Federation is permitted to do this only if there is an imperative need for the matter to be regulated uniformly throughout the Federal Republic. Earlier Land laws on the matter cease to have effect in such cases, while any new Land laws enacted in the face of existing concurrent Federal law are null and void.

In practice, the main factor involved is the need to preserve legal and economic unity and in the labour-law context to preserve uniform living conditions. Concurrent legislative powers mainly

199

cover the organization of the judicial system, procedural law, criminal law, etc. Other notable examples are **pay** and pensions in the **public service**. They also cover the regulation of most **taxes**.

462. **KONKURS — BANKRUPTCY**: In the event of a debtor's inability to pay, on their own petition or the petition of one of their creditors they can be declared bankrupt by the district court. This is to ensure that the debtor's assets, which are insufficient to settle all debts, are distributed fairly. If an employer is declared bankrupt, employees' claims are treated beforehand or enjoy a preferential position in a priority ranking of provable debts as laid down by law. Thus, first priority is given to the remuneration of employees who are employed by the official receiver or trustee subsequent to the bankruptcy judgment. After this, priority ranking is given to arrears of pay for the six or twelve months immediately preceding the bankruptcy judgment, compensatory payments arising from non-competition covenants and payments from an occupational pension scheme.

It frequently happens, however, that bankruptcy is not even declared because there are no assets, or that the assets are so small that no money or insufficient money is available for claims to arrears of pay. For the protection of employees the legislators have therefore provided the regulations on **bankruptcy non-payment benefit** and protection in the event of insolvency for payments from **occupational pension schemes**.

Under a draft statute from the Federal Ministry of Justice, the regulations on bankruptcy and on **composition** may be combined in a single law on insolvency.

463. **KONKURSAUSFALLGELD — BANKRUPTCY NON-PAYMENT BENEFIT**: If a company is declared bankrupt or a **bankruptcy** petition is rejected on grounds of insufficient assets (or the company's operation is shut down without a bankruptcy petition), the employees affected receive a special benefit from local Employment Offices to offset outstanding pay entitlements for the last three months of the employment relationship (Employment Promotion Act §§ 141a ff.). The payment they receive corresponds to their net pay for the period concerned. It is financed from a levy payable by all employers which is collected by the **Occupational Health and Safety Agencies**. In the context of the steeply rising number of company failures, mainly since the mid-1980s, this benefit has proved to be one of the most important means of providing security for employees, since in most cases there were no assets, or only negligible assets, available for distribution. By making provision for the bankruptcy

non-payment benefit, which was incorporated into the Act as early as 1975, the legislators have enacted the terms of the corresponding EC Directive.

464. KONSULTATIONSPFLICHT — DUTY TO CONSULT (PUBLIC SECTOR): An obligation on **public-sector department heads**, in all matters on which the **staff council** has at least a consultation right, to provide the council with timely and comprehensive information concerning measures aimed at changing the *status quo* (Federal Staff Representation Act § 72). If the staff council fails to comment within seven working days, its assent is presumed. Thus, in the public sector the duty to consult guarantees the staff council a comprehensive right to timely information and goes beyond the scope of the **information rights of the works council** in the private sector.

465. KONZERN — GROUP (OF COMPANIES): A group consists of two or more **companies**, each independent in law, which are joined under uniform direction by a controlling company. It is the commonest form in which companies are associated, and in a pre-existing group of companies can also be constituted as such outside company law. In **labour law**, the significance of such corporate groups lies in the fact that the employees of all the group's member companies are counted towards the statutory minimum number required for co-determination. Special regulations exist for group parent and member companies falling within the scope of the 1951 Coal, Iron and Steel Industry Co-Determination Act (Montan-Mitbestimmungsgesetz) and 1956 Co-Determination Amendment Act (Mitbestimmungsergän-zungsgesetz), and for cases where the entire number of employees in the group is below the minimum number required. There is a distinction between compulsory co-determination and optional opportunities for employee participation under the **works constitution**. The **company works councils** or individual establishment-level **works councils** of the member companies of a group can decide to form a **group works council** for the group as a whole.

466. KONZERNBETRIEBSRAT — GROUP WORKS COUNCIL: An organ of the **works constitution** which may be established by the **company works councils** or establishment-level **works councils** of a group of companies (Works Constitution Act §§ 54 ff.). It is responsible for dealing with matters which concern the **group** as a whole or several of its member companies and which cannot be regulated by individual company or establishment-level works councils or need to be regulated uniformly for the entire group. Only the group works council can conclude special **works agreements** that apply throughout the group. Its other powers, the formation of committees and the conduct of its business follow the corresponding regulations laid down for the company works council.

467. KONZERTIERTE AKTION — CONCERTED ACTION: Term used to refer to the procedure which, under the 1967 **Stability Act**, must be introduced by the **Federal Government** in situations where the goals stated in the Act (**"magic square"**) are under threat. It consists in making available to the "social partners" (**employers' associations, trade unions**) and territorial authorities guideline data based on an overview of the state of the economy. This is then used as a working basis for concerted efforts to overcome the crisis. For the **parties to collective agreements**, therefore, this can mean that guideline figures are proposed for bargaining policy. Such a procedure actually occurred in the 1970s when, in particular, the Federal Government and national representatives of the employers' associations and trade unions sought to harmonize their policies in joint discussions.

Among other reasons, the steady rise in unemployment from 1975 onwards and controversy regarding company-level **co-determination** led to the breakdown of concerted action at the end of the 1970s.

Concerted action also exists as an institution in the health sector, where its purpose is a joint effort by all the major parties involved to control costs.

468. KRANKENGELD — SICKNESS BENEFIT: In the event of incapacity for work due to illness, members of a statutory **health insurance fund** receive sickness assistance. This comprises health care, *i.e.* reimbursement of the cost of medical treatment and drugs and medicines, and sickness benefit. Since the function of sickness benefit is to offset loss of earnings, it is not paid so long as the employee is receiving **sick pay** from the employer. It amounts to 80 per cent. of the gross remuneration lost as a result of incapacity for work, subject to a ceiling equivalent to net remuneration, and is subject to a time limit of 78 weeks in respect of the same illness within any period of three years.

Sickness benefit is also payable for days off to nurse a sick child (see **day's leave for sick-nursing**).

469. KRANKENKASSE — HEALTH INSURANCE FUND: A health insurance institution which collects contributions from insured individuals and employers and grants payments in the event of illness. At present there are almost 1,300 in existence, divided into statutory public, guild, seafarers' and **company health insurance funds** and mineworkers' and white-collar workers' health insurance funds (an approved alternative fund, *i.e.* "Ersatzkasse", see **social security obligation**) and private health insurance funds.

The public, company and guild funds are independent self-administered bodies, run by elected employee and employer representatives in the members' representatives' meeting and the management board on a strictly joint basis. In the mineworkers' funds employees are over-represented in a ratio of two to one, and in the white-collar workers' funds the organs are composed exclusively of insured persons' representatives.

470. KRANKENPFLEGETAG — DAY'S LEAVE FOR SICK-NURSING: If nobody else is able to care for the child, parents have an entitlement to leave of absence from work in order to nurse sick children under the age of 12 (10 days in each case), and to **sickness benefit** during this period. For single parents the entitlement is 20 days. As regulated in **Social Security Code V**, the entitlement is limited to a total of 25 working days respectively within a given year. Consequently, from the third child onwards such days off can only be taken on a shared basis. Some **collective agreements** improve the entitlements, for example by stipulating that the employer will make up the difference between sickness benefit and net pay or by raising the age limit for the children concerned to 14.

471. KRANKENVERGÜTUNG — SICK PAY: One of the exceptions to the principle that entitlement to **wage** or **salary** exists only in return for work performed. It allows for the paramount importance of **remuneration** to the employee. Nowadays, this entitlement to the **continued payment of remuneration** in the event of incapacity for work caused by illness is recognized for almost all employees. **Manual workers** are covered by the Continued Wage Payment Act, and there is provision for **white-collar workers** in the Civil Code (§§ 617 f.); in addition, there are special statutory provisions establishing entitlements for particular employees.

The general rule is that entitlement to sick pay commences at the start of the employment relationship, for a period of illness of up to six weeks; thereafter, employees receive **sickness benefit**. In principle the employee is able to reassert this entitlement in full on every occasion of incapacity for work caused by illness, but the entitlement remains limited to a total of six weeks if during one bout of illness another occurs. There is a new entitlement to sick pay on each occasion that a previously suffered illness occurs again. However, if an employee's illness caused by the same underlying medical condition recurs within 12 months, they are only able to claim sick pay for up to six weeks in all, unless in the meantime they have been fit for work for six months. There is no entitlement to sick pay if the employee has acted in a manner "grossly contrary to the conduct expected of a reasonable person in their own interests", *i.e.* where the illness is judged to be self-inflicted.

The amount of sick pay is determined by the **loss-of-pay principle**.

At present, there is still no entitlement to sick pay for manual workers who are in a fixed-term employment relationship lasting 1-4 weeks which is not a probationary period, or for manual workers whose normal working time does not exceed 10 hours per week or 45 hours per month. Following a decision by the Federal Constitutional Court, this less favourable treatment of manual workers as compared with white-collar workers may cease in the future.

472. KRANKENVERSICHERUNG — HEALTH INSURANCE: One of the branches of **social security**, administered by **health insurance funds**. Its structural feature, particularly in the case of statutory health insurance, is the acceptance in many respects of shared liability for funding equal cover for all. For instance, contributions are graduated according to **gross pay**, members' contributions also provide entitlement to non-contributory cover for their family members who are not economically active, and "good" and "bad" risks are accepted without differentiation. In contrast to this, private health insurance funds carry out a risk assessment and, where appropriate, raise the contribution concerned. For some years now the trend has been for the contributors who remain with the statutory Public Health Insurance Funds (AOK) to be pensioners, the unemployed and individuals with a comparatively low income or no income. As a result, the contributions have to be increased to cover the costs borne, and in many cases the contributions levied by Public Health Insurance Funds are now higher than those for private funds or approved alternative funds ("Ersatzkassen"). The average contribution rate is at present 12.3 per cent. in western Germany and 12.8 per cent. in eastern Germany.

473. KRANKHEIT — ILLNESS: For the purposes of labour law, the concept presupposes an illness in the medical sense which constitutes the basis of a limitation of the employee's ability to perform, *i.e.* incapacity for work. An illness in the medical sense is taken to mean an abnormal physical or mental condition which manifests itself in external symptoms and can be diagnosed by a doctor.

The question of whether an illness exists within the meaning of labour law has to be judged from the circumstances in each particular case, especially the nature and severity of the condition and the type of work performance due. Even alcoholism and drug addiction are regarded as an illness for the purposes of labour law, although the existence of entitlement to the continued payment of remuneration in such cases is a matter of controversy.

474. **KRANKHEITSBEDINGTE KÜNDIGUNG — DISMISSAL ON GROUNDS OF ILL HEALTH: Termination** of an **employment relationship** by the employer because of illness on the part of the employee (Protection Against Dismissal Act § 1) is the commonest instance of dismissal on grounds of personal capability. The concept of illness is given wide interpretation: it also includes psychosomatic conditions and addictions. Normally, dismissal on grounds of ill health is conceivable only as an ordinary termination with notice. And it can only be considered, as a last resort, in the case of particularly serious and long-lasting illnesses or frequent short bouts of illness and a prolonged decline in performance.

An additional requirement is an unfavourable medical prognosis for the long term and evidence furnished by the employer demonstrating that the deficient work performance received from the employee because of illness is causing particularly serious economic or organizational difficulties and that these business interests outweigh the interests of the employee (whose need for protection is increased by the fact of being ill) in continuing to be employed. In assessing the extent of the burden borne by the employer as a result of the illness in question, considerable importance is attached to the employee's length of service with the employer effecting dismissal.

475. **KRANMELDUNG — NOTIFICATION OF ILLNESS**: If employees are prevented by illness from rendering their work performance as due under the employment contract, they must inform the employer of this without delay, and hence normally during the initial working hours on the first working day of their illness (*e.g.* in accordance with the Continued Wage Payment Act § 3). This may be done in person, by telephone or (provided in this way it can still take place without delay) in writing. There is no obligation to provide information on the nature of the illness or its symptoms. Employees need only notify the employer that it prevents them from working and indicate how long this is likely

to last. Normally, on the third day of their illness at the latest employees must also present a **certificate of incapacity for work** to the employer. Failure to provide notification may, in the case of repeated breach of the duty to notify the employer (as one of the employee's secondary duties under the contract of employment), lead to a formal warning or dismissal.

476. KÜNDIGUNG — TERMINATION: A unilateral declaration of intent by one contracting party to the other to the effect that the contractual relationship is to be ended at a specified time. It takes effect when it is received by the contracting partner.

Unless provisions in the contract of employment or a collective agreement regulate otherwise, no special formalities need be observed in terminating an employment relationship. It can even be done orally. Except in cases of **dismissal for variation of contract** its validity may not, however, be made dependent on certain conditions. A distinction is made between ordinary **termination with notice**, by which the employment relationship is ended when the **period of notice** expires, and **summary termination**, which brings about immediate cancellation of the employment relationship. Termination by the employer is unlawful if it contravenes one of the regulations of **protection against dismissal** or a contractual restriction of the right to terminate and the employee then invokes these grounds.

Provided no contractual restriction has been agreed, termination by the employee is unreservedly lawful if due notice is given. Termination by the employee without notice is subject to the same rules as those for summary dismissal by the employer.

477. KÜNDIGUNGSFRIST — PERIOD OF NOTICE: The period of time that must elapse between notification of **termination** being received by the contracting partner and the date on which a contract ends. If the terminating party fails to comply with the due date for giving notice, the termination does not take effect until the next possible termination date.

For employment relationships of **white-collar workers**, the statutory period of notice is six weeks before the end of the calendar quarter (Civil Code § 622(1)). Longer periods of notice are stipulated for older white-collar workers, according to their continuous length of service in the same establishment subsequent to their 25th birthday: three months after at least five years' service, four months after eight years, five months after ten years and six months after twelve years. In each case notice must be given at the end of the calendar quarter (White-Collar Workers' Protection Against Dismissal Act § 2). Years of employment in the establishment prior to their 25th birthday are not included in the calculation.

For employment relationships of **manual workers**, the period of notice is two weeks. This increases to one month after five years' continuous length of service, two months after ten years and three months after twenty years, notice being given in each case at the end of the month (Civil Code § 622(2)). Years of employment in the establishment prior to their 25th birthday are not included in the calculation.

The **Federal Constitutional Court** has ruled that this differential treatment of manual workers and white-collar workers as regards the statutory period of notice is unconstitutional. The legislators are required to enact new regulations on the statutory period of notice for both groups of employees by June 30, 1993. Until then, all disputes of rights relating to the period of notice are being deferred.

Regulations diverging from the statutory period of notice, even to the disadvantage of the employee, may be adopted by **collective agreement**.

478. **KÜNDIGUNGSSCHUTZ — PROTECTION AGAINST DISMISSAL**: A system of restrictions on the lawfulness of **termination** of existing employment relationships by the employer. Its most important element is the statutory protection provided; in addition, restrictions on dismissal may be imposed by **collective agreement** and the **contract of employment**. The general rules of statutory protection against dismissal are in the Civil Code and the Protection Against Dismissal Act (Kündigungsschutzgesetz). Special regulations for particular groups of employees are contained in the special legislation applicable to them. The Labour Courts play a very important part in the development of protection against dismissal through interpretation of its abstract rules and direct application of them to specific cases.

The purpose of protection against dismissal is, on behalf of employees, to maintain their job and hence their means of livelihood in a framework that is judged to be socially and economically justifiable. This is achieved by the fact that, in cases where the employer has no reasonable cause to dismiss or the cause is not sufficiently serious, on application from the employee who has been dismissed the court declares the dismissal to be null and void.

As a general criterion, the Protection Against Dismissal Act is applicable only if the employee was employed in an **establishment** or **public sector establishment** regularly employing more than five employees (not counting **vocational trainees** and "**marginal**" **part-time workers**) and worked there without interruption for longer than six months. Employment relationships which do not meet this criterion can be terminated

by the employer without any justifying reason. Otherwise, the employment relationship may be terminated by the employer with valid legal effect only by way of three exceptions:
1. **dismissal on grounds of personal capability** or **ill health**;
2. **dismissal on grounds of conduct**;
3. **redundancy**
(Protection Against Dismissal Act § 1). Alongside this, there is the possibility of dismissal by **summary termination** for special reasons (Civil Code § 626).

For any dismissal it must be the case that, when a detailed assessment is made to weigh the interests of the particular parties concerned against each other, the employer's interest in cancelling the employment relationship outweighs the employee's interest in continuing it. Although systematic guidelines for typical circumstances of dismissal have been developed in case law, there are no fixed rules on the weighting of opposing interests. The **proportionality principle** must always be observed. Accordingly, dismissal is the last resort in cases where employers are unable to use a less drastic remedy such as a **transfer**, **warning** or **dismissal for variation of contract** as a way of protecting their legitimate interests.

In establishments where there is a **works council** or **staff council**, this protection against dismissal as provided under individual labour law is supplemented by collective-law provisions (Works Constitution Act § 102, Federal Staff Representation Act § 79). Under these provisions, the employer must inform the works council or staff council of a proposed dismissal, specifying the reasons, and give it the opportunity of stating its position on the matter. If the employer pronounces a dismissal before the council has responded or before a set period has elapsed of one week in the case of ordinary dismissals with notice and three days in the case of summary dismissals, the dismissal is invalid irrespective of whether or not it is lawful in other respects. The works council or staff council has the right to object to a dismissal if it contravenes one of the agreed company guidelines on personnel policy, if the employee could continue to be employed in a vacant job in the same establishment or another establishment of the same company, or if re-training or further training which the employer could reasonably be expected to provide or amendment of the contract of employment (subject to the consent of the employee concerned) would make continued employment possible. An objection by the works council or staff council has no direct effect on the validity of a dismissal. However, if a dismissed employee then makes an application to the courts for protection against dismissal an objection issued by the works council or staff council, if deemed by the court to be justified, means that without any further assessment of the interests involved the court rules the dismissal to be unfair. An objection also secures for the employee the right to **continued employment during dismissal proceedings**.

A higher degree of protection against dismissal than this general protection is provided for:

a. members of works councils and staff councils and of **representative bodies for young workers and trainees** and **for disabled employees**;
b. **vocational trainees**;
c. **disabled persons**;
d. pregnant women, mothers (**maternity protection**) and employees on **childcare leave**;
e. employees on compulsory military or community service;
f. members of the European Parliament, **Federal Parliament**, Länder Diets, district councils and municipal councils.

Homeworkers, on the other hand, have less protection against dismissal than the general level provided.

In all cases, for a dismissal to be ruled invalid the employee must make an **application for protection against dismissal** to the court within the due time limit (Protection Against Dismissal Act §§ 4,7,13).

The effectiveness of this system for protection against unfair dismissal is open to question. Only about 9 per cent. of applications made to the courts by dismissed employees lead to their reinstatement. This means that, in terms of preserving jobs, the statutory protection is effective in less than 1 per cent. of all dismissals. It is characteristic of such applications, and in fact encouraged by the labour court procedure itself, that a high proportion of them end in settlements, both in court and out of court, which normally result in the employment relationship being cancelled in return for compensation. In addition, even if the employee wins the case there is statutory provision for the court then to dissolve the employment relationship and order the payment of **compensation for job loss**. Essentially, therefore, protection against dismissal operates not as a barrier to dismissal but as a mechanism which compels employers to state rational grounds to justify dismissals and, if this justification is unsuccessful, secures material compensation for the employees concerned but not the retention of their job.

479. KÜNDIGUNGSSCHUTZKLAGE — APPLICATION FOR PROTECTION AGAINST DISMISSAL: If employees wish to contest the **termination** of their employment relationship, they must bring a legal action against the employer applying for a declaratory judgment that the employment relationship was not cancelled by the dismissal. Material jurisdiction for disputes concerning unfair dismissal lies with the **system of labour courts**.

209

If the employee is invoking absence of substantial reason in the case of a **summary termination**, or lack of social justification or improper application of **social criteria for redundancy** in the case of an ordinary **termination with notice**, the application must be made to the court within three weeks of receiving notification of dismissal; otherwise, the dismissal has valid legal effect irrespective of its lawfulness (Protection Against Dismissal Act §§ 4,7,13). Only in cases of special hardship may the court afterwards admit a belated application. Once the time limit has expired, an application for protection against dismissal can only be based on other grounds, such as failure to consult the **works council** or contravention of special protective legislation. In certain cases employees are entitled to **continued employment** in their old job while the legal action is proceeding.

If the court rejects the application by final judgment, this establishes, without possibility of appeal, that the employment relationship was cancelled by the dismissal. If it allows the application by final judgment, this establishes, without possibility of appeal, that the employment relationship was not cancelled by the dismissal. In certain cases the court, having ruled the dismissal to be invalid, may then dissolve the employment relationship and order the employer to pay **compensation for job loss**.

In cases where employees have entered into a new employment relationship while the legal action was proceeding, if their application is successful they are free to choose between continuing the new or the old employment relationship. If they opt for the new one, they must inform their previous employer of the fact within one week. If they decide to continue the one that was terminated, they must end the new employment relationship as quickly as the due **period of notice** allows and then resume work in the old establishment. In this latter case they are entitled to be paid remuneration for the period as if they had not entered into a new employment relationship, despite not having continued to work after the dismissal. Deductions will, however, be made from the amount owing to them, to allow for the sum they have received from **unemployment insurance** or earned from employment elsewhere or could have earned by accepting suitable employment.

480. **KURZARBEIT — SHORT-TIME WORKING**: A temporary reduction of normal working hours in an establishment, or complete cessation of work for a specified (usually very brief) period, which is necessitated by a lack of orders. Short-time working (also referred to as ''Feierschichten'') accompanied by a corresponding reduction in pay may not be imposed unilaterally by the employer. It may be introduced in the establishment only

if it has been allowed for under a **collective agreement** or **works agreement** or with the assent of the employees affected. Even then, the **co-determination right of the works council** must be observed. In order to preserve jobs and enable the establishment to keep its trained workforce together, such employees are paid a short-time allowance from **Federal Employment Service** funds. This allowance amounts in principle to 63 per cent. or 68 per cent. (for employees with at least one child) of the net remuneration which they would have earned under normal circumstances in the hours not worked (Employment Protection Act §§ 63 ff.).

Owing to the special conditions prevailing in eastern Germany, for this region the maximum duration for payment of the short-time allowance has been extended for a stipulated period of 18 months. In addition, some collective agreements provide that, during short-time working, employers will make up pay to 92 per cent. of the original net remuneration. Some of the short-time workers in eastern Germany are employed in so-called **job creation companies**.

481. **KURZARBEITERGELD — SHORT-TIME ALLOWANCE**: See **short-time working**.

L

482. **LADENSCHLUSS — SHOP CLOSING HOURS**: The statutory regulation of hours of opening or trading for retail outlets in which goods are offered for sale to the general public. Apart from a number of exceptions (*e.g.* pharmacies, bakeries, newsstands or bookstalls, petrol stations, shops at railway stations and airports), shops must be closed on Sundays and public holidays, until 0700 and from 1830 hrs on weekdays and until 0700 and from 1400 hrs on Saturdays. Special regulations apply to the first Saturday in the month (closing time no later than 1800 hrs in winter and 1600 hrs in summer) and to "late-night opening" on Thursdays (closing time no later than 2030 hrs).

   The actual timing of working hours within these limits is subject to a **co-determination right of the works council**. A **works agreement** which does not allow full use to be made of the maximum hours of opening is lawful. Hours of opening may also be regulated by **collective agreement**; the Federal Labour Court has ruled that this does not constitute a contravention of the law on cartels or competition.

483. **LAG**: Land Labour Court (Landesarbeitsgericht). See **system of labour courts**.

484. **LANDESARBEITSGERICHT — LAND LABOUR COURT**: See **system of labour courts**.

485. **LANDESBEAMTE — CAREER PUBLIC SERVANTS AT LAND LEVEL**: All career public servants ("Beamte") who are not **federal career public servants** or career public servants at municipal level and whose **public sector employer** is one of the **Länder of the Federal Republic**. Together with career public servants at municipal level, they are subject to the career public service law of the particular Land concerned, although this is largely identical in content with federal career public service law (**appointment of career public servants, career public servants, career public service relationship, disciplinary law for career public servants, oath of service, pay of career public servants, strike by career public servants**). In other respects they are subject either directly or indirectly to the provisions of the Career Public Service Framework Act (Beamtenrechtsrahmengesetz).

486. **LAUFBAHN — CAREER BRANCH**: Categories in the career public service each grouping together offices or posts involving the same kind of activity and requiring the same level of general education and qualifications. The principle of the career branch

is regulated in the Career Public Service Framework Act (**career public service relationship**) and the Federal and Länder Career Regulations ("Laufbahnverordnungen"). According to this principle, appointments may normally only be made to the lower-level posts within a particular branch. The branches are distinguished from each other in two respects: firstly as regards occupational considerations and education and training, and secondly as regards groupings with their different general job requirements.

487. **LEHRE — APPRENTICESHIP**: See **vocational training**.

488. **LEICHTLOHNGRUPPEN — LIGHT-WORK PAY GRADES**: Where pay grades are specified in a **collective agreement**, they frequently include so-called "light-work" pay grades. These typically cover jobs which demand little physical effort on the part of the worker and which are therefore deemed by the courts to justify a correspondingly lower level of pay. The jobs in these low-pay grades are occupied almost exclusively by women. A constant watch must therefore be kept on whether they result in a contravention of **anti-discrimination laws**. This may be so even in the case of a regulation that turns out to apply exclusively or predominantly to women. Any unequal treatment for these low-pay grades must be justified by practical reasons.

489. **LEIHARBEITGEBER — TEMPORARY WORKER'S EMPLOYER**: Viewed strictly in terms of contract law, it is the **lessor**, *i.e.* the entrepreneur who hires out employees as temporary workers to third parties, who is in the first instance their employer. In reality, however, in the **hiring-out of labour** the lessor's authority as an employer is confined to making the arrangements with the third party who is to be the lessee. As far as the actual work is concerned, for all practical purposes the lessee then assumes the position of employer for the period of hiring-out and exercises the employer's right to issue instructions. In functional terms, therefore, the lessee is the employer. The legislators have, nevertheless, chosen to stress the contract law aspect: the lessor is deemed to be the temporary worker's employer.

If a lessor who practises the hiring-out of temporary workers as a business ("Leiharbeit" or "Zeitarbeit") places them at the disposal of a lessee without possessing the necessary licence, the contract between the lessor and lessee is void. For the protection of the employees who have been hired out as temporary workers, in this case the law assumes a notional employment relationship between the employee and the lessee. Also, if the lessor/lessee

213

contract becomes void during the hiring-out period the notional employment relationship is assumed to exist from that time onwards. The employee is therefore safeguarded against the contractual risk between lessor and lessee.

Under social security law, there is an obligation in the first instance on a temporary worker's employer, *i.e.* the lessor, to register them with the appropriate social security institution for the purposes of checks and controls. The social security contributions payable by the lessor become the liability of the lessee as direct guarantor.

By 1989, the number of agencies in business in the Federal Republic to hire out employees as temporary workers had risen to around 4,700.

490. **LEISTUNGSLOHN — PAYMENT BY RESULTS**: Payment system under which pay is not directly related to the amount of time actually worked, as in the case of **time-based pay**, but is determined by the employee's measurable performance, particularly the quantity and quality of work performed. The main problem lies in calculating the amount fairly. The commonest forms of payment by results (PBR) are **piecework** and **incentive bonus systems**.

The introduction of PBR systems is subject to the **co-determination right of the works council**.

491. **LEISTUNGSSTÖRUNG — TEMPORARY NON-PERFORMANCE**: Situation where, in a contractual relationship, performances are not rendered as specified under the terms of the contract.

The various forms of temporary non-performance are **impossibility of performance**, default and defective performance. Impossibility of performance denotes a situation where it is not possible for anybody to render the performance due under the contract. Impossibility is equated here with inability. The obligor is recognized as being unable to render performance of the contract. If it is impossible for employees to render the work performance due, special rules apply to their entitlement to remuneration. The civil-law criteria are altered by the doctrine of "**works risk**".

Defective fulfilment of the work performance leads to liability for damages on the part of employees, but their entitlement to remuneration remains unaffected. Default is a rare occurrence in the context of the employment relationship. This is because it presupposes that, although performance due under the contract has not been rendered in due time, it can still be rendered subsequently. In an employment relationship, once there has been an omission of performance it is usually impossible to repair the omission, so that it then becomes a case of impossibility of performance. This also applies to the most important instance of default, *i.e.* **employer's non-acceptance of the work performance**.

As a general rule, in cases of temporary non-performance employees lose their entitlement to remuneration only where this is through fault on their own part or where fault on someone else's part is imputable to them.

492. **LEITENDE ANGESTELLTE — EXECUTIVE STAFF**: A separately defined category of members of the workforce who perform (some of) the functions of an employer or entrepreneur (Works Constitution Act § 5(3)). This entails a certain polarization of interests between them and other **employees**. According to the Act, executive staff are individuals who possess independent authority to engage and dismiss employees within the establishment or one of its departments or have been invested with full power of attorney or **commercial power of attorney** (which is not confined to purely routine matters). Also included in this category are individuals who regularly perform managerial functions which in terms of their importance and consequence are on a par with the authority and powers mentioned. This is the case if the sphere of activity for which they have responsibility, basically without following directions from others, is important to the existence and development of the company or an establishment. In addition, the classification covers individuals who, although not performing a line management function, exert an important influence on management decisions in a central staff capacity.

If it is uncertain whether a particular individual should be classed as a "Leitender Angestellter" on the basis of these criteria, their annual salary may be used as a yardstick, at a level of around 118,500 Deutschmarks. On the other hand, **white-collar workers exempt from collectively agreed terms** are not normally also classed as executive staff. The provisions of the **works constitution** do not apply to executive staff; their interests are represented by separate **representative bodies for executive staff**. There are also special regulations as regards **protection against dismissal** and pay for **overtime**. Executive staff are frequently subject to a **restraint on competition**.

493. **LOHN — WAGE**: "Lohn" is a term used ambiguously in German labour law. For instance, in the case of continued **payment of remuneration** ("Lohnfortzahlung") or **earnings tax** ("Lohnsteuer") it refers to pay or **remuneration** in general,

including additional payments and occupational pensions. In the stricter sense, however, it refers only to the basic wage earned by a **manual worker**, normally paid weekly, fortnightly or monthly. It corresponds to the **salary** of a **white-collar worker**.

Wages are in principle calculated as **time-based pay**, according to the number of hours worked, or on a **payment by results** basis, according to the work result. In contrast to the general trend towards eliminating differentiation between white-collar and manual workers in labour law, this is not yet the case as regards remuneration; pay agreements which cover all employees in a given industry are still the exception. **Payment of remuneration** is in principle effected in cash, but cashless methods of payment are also becoming widespread.

494. **LOHN-PREIS-SPIRALE — WAGE-PRICE SPIRAL**: Term used in the economic policy debate to describe a process whereby an increase in pay levels, particularly collectively agreed rates, results in an upward adjustment of prices, since they take effect as a component of costs. The opposing argument assumes that pay increases are made necessary by previous price rises. Irrespective of the causal connection, it is generally acknowledged that the collective bargaining parties are not obliged to take account of these circumstances. Even the **Stability Act**, which states price stability as an aim, stipulates only that the parties should be given guideline figures; it does not bind them to such figures.

495. **LOHN- UND GEHALTSABZÜGE — DEDUCTIONS FROM PAY**: These mainly arise from the employer's obligations under public law to hold back **earnings tax**, Church tax where applicable and the **social security contributions** payable by employees and to pay them over to the tax office and **social security** collecting agencies. The amount of such deductions is determined by the employee's gross pay and marital status. Tax and other social contributions amount at present to approximately 35 per cent. of gross income.

496. **LOHN- UND GEHALTSTARIFVERTRAG — PAY AGREEMENT**: Collective agreements which fix rates of pay for **time-based pay** and **piecework** systems. Pay grades are defined on the basis of the type of work done, and a specified rate of pay is assigned to each. In some cases it is customary to regulate only the pay of one middle pay grade (*e.g.* for a skilled worker) as the so-called standard rate ("Ecklohn"). The rates of pay for the other grades are then determined as percentages of the standard rate. Pay agreements normally have a fixed term of 1-2 years.

497. LOHNAUSFALLPRINZIP — LOSS-OF-PAY PRINCIPLE: Principle applied for the purposes of **continued payment of remuneration**. It serves to quantify the **remuneration** payable where pay is due from the employer to the employee although no work is performed. The amount that must be paid is what employees would have earned if they had been working during the period concerned. In practical terms, this is gauged from a comparable employee in the same establishment. Difficulties arise in cases where a **payment by results** system has been agreed.

498. LOHNFORTZAHLUNG — CONTINUED PAYMENT OF REMUNERATION: Owing to the dependence of the employee on **remuneration**, in certain cases an obligation is imposed on the employer by statute, collective agreement, works agreement or the individual contract of employment to continue paying it although the work performance due from the employee has not been rendered. Instances which give rise to this obligation are, in particular, incapacity for work due to **illness** (Continued Wage Payment Act §§ 1 ff., Civil Code §§ 616 f.), **prevention from working** for personal reasons (Civil Code §§ 616, 629), leave of absence in the context of **maternity protection** and **"works risk"**, but also **employer's non-acceptance of the work performance** and activities associated with the **works council**. The amount payable is calculated according to the **loss-of-pay principle**.

499. LOHNGLEICHHEIT — EQUAL PAY: Principle deriving from the principle of **equal rights** which decrees that male and female employees employed by the same employer should not be paid differently for the same work or work of equal value. It encompasses the whole of remuneration inclusive of allowances, fringe benefits provided by the employer and **occupational pension scheme** payments. For the purposes of determining what constitutes work of equal value, various methods of evaluation have been developed which can be used to classify jobs systematically on the basis of the physical and mental demands made on the employee. In cases where discriminatory treatment is established by the courts, the members of the group discriminated against can claim retrospective restitution of equal treatment, in so far as the employer is unable to prove that the differentiation is based on material grounds unrelated to gender. For example, it is lawful to grant male employees pay supplements for **night work**, which is prohibited for female employees because of an **employment ban**, but not to pay different levels of basic pay. Despite these rules, in many establishments women are still disadvantaged in terms of remuneration, mainly as a result of forms of **indirect discrimination**. This is because women, while there is formal observance of the principle of equal pay, are nevertheless denied access to better paid **pay grades** by arbitrary demarcations defended on the grounds of allegedly biological differences in performance. The legal instruments to enable women to advance from lower pay grades, in which they are over-represented, into higher pay grades are inadequate.

500. **LOHNGRUPPE — PAY GRADE**: The **remuneration** of employees is generally governed by the collectively agreed pay grade into which the job they do is classified. These pay grades are normally regulated in general pay agreements. Each grade brackets together a list of the required skills for employees in various occupations, and all employees to whom these apply are assigned to one and the same pay grade and earn the corresponding specified remuneration. By virtue of the **favourability principle**, rates of pay in excess of these collectively agreed rates are perfectly in order and very common in practice.

501. **LOHNPFÄNDUNG — ATTACHMENT OF EARNINGS**: If an employee fails to fulfil his or her payment obligations towards third parties, the latter must in principle be able to obtain by court order the right of recourse to the employee's **remuneration** for the settlement of such debts, since entitlement to remuneration often constitutes an employee's single notable asset. For precisely the same reason, however, employees must also be protected to ensure that a high level of attachment of their earnings in this way does not threaten their livelihood. Consequently, although attachment of earnings is possible as a general principle, employees must be left with a proportion of their remuneration which is exempt from attachment and may not be touched. This attachment threshold is fixed according to the employee's family circumstances and is regulated in the Code of Civil Procedure.

In addition, certain elements of remuneration such as expense allowances, some **pay supplements** and a proportion of any Christmas bonus are always non-attachable.

502. **LOHNRÜCKFORDERUNG — RIGHT TO RECLAIM PAY**: For employees, **remuneration** normally constitutes their most important asset; since they are under an obligation to render the work performance in advance of receiving payment for it, they must consequently be able to rely on the fact that, once they have earned entitlement to remuneration, as a matter of principle they are protected from having to pay it back.

No right exists in law for the employer to reclaim remuneration after an employment relationship has been declared void. Instead, in such cases the courts presume the retrospective validity of a *de facto* **employment relationship**. However, a right to reclaim payments made by mistake is possible, unless employees have already, in ignorance of the mistake, incurred expenditure which they would not have incurred had it not been for the unexpected extra earnings. In such cases the employer can, however, claim a substitute. If employees realize that a mistake has been made in the payment of remuneration to them, they are under an obligation to draw attention to it.

Payments from the employer over and above the wage or salary may be granted subject to a proviso that they must be paid back in part or in full if the employee should terminate the employment relationship within a certain time limit, if they have been granted not in respect of work already performed but with a view to the employee's future employment. This is the case with training grants and in some cases also **special bonuses**.

503. **LOHNSTEUER — EARNINGS TAX**: A form of income tax which is levied on earnings from work as an employee. It is deducted at source by the employer and must be paid over to the tax office by the tenth day of the following month. The basis for calculation is gross pay, minus any tax-exempt allowances entered on the earnings tax card.

504. **LOHNSTEUERKARTE — EARNINGS TAX CARD**: This is issued by the competent authority of the **municipality** in which the **employee** had his or her main place of residence or was living on September 20 of the preceding year, and is normally sent to them by October 31 of the current year to cover the coming year. Otherwise, the card is issued on application. Entered on the card are the employee's marital status, Taxation Class, together with the number of children to be taken into account in the case of Taxation Classes II-IV, and religious denomination.

The earnings tax card forms part of the **employment documents**. If the employee is at fault in failing to present it in due time, the **employer** must deduct earnings tax as for Class VI. The employer is required, on pain of liability for damages, to fill in the card in the prescribed form and by the prescribed date at the end of each calendar year or when an **employment relationship** comes to an end.

505. **LOHNZAHLUNG — PAYMENT OF REMUNERATION**: **Wages** and **salaries** must be paid in cash, but cashless methods of payment are possible by agreement. In principle it is **gross pay** that must be paid. **Net pay arrangements** are also possible, or semi-formal works agreements on **payment in kind**. In the

219

latter case the **ban on the truck system** must, however, be observed. In rendering the performance due from them under the contract, employees are subject to an obligation to render performance first; thus, remuneration is paid weekly, fortnightly or monthly for work already done (Civil Code § 614). Regulations on when remuneration is to be paid are usually stated in **pay agreements**, but often in the contract of employment as well.

506. LOHNZUSCHLAG — PAY SUPPLEMENT: If work involves particularly difficult conditions, it is normally agreed in a **collective agreement** or **works agreement** or the **contract of employment** that the employee should receive a pay supplement, in most cases calculated as a percentage of basic pay. Determining the amount is simpler in the case of **time-based pay** than under a **payment by results** system. In practice, common forms of pay supplement are "dirty money" ("Schmutzzulage", *i.e.* pay supplement for working in dirty conditions), a piecework premium, and a premium for working **overtime** or on public holidays. In addition, there are various benefits such as allowances relating to employees' families and children.

M

507. MAGISCHES VIERECK — "MAGIC SQUARE": A term relating to economic policy which has its origin in the **Stability Act** of 1967. It signifies the four main aims towards which the economic policy of the Federal Government and the Länder should be directed: price stability, a high level of employment, balance of payments equilibrium, and steady and adequate economic growth. The equal status of all four aims in the context of economic and fiscal policy led to their being dubbed the "magic square". In practice, however, there is general agreement that these are planning precepts which to a large extent cannot be forced through and which economic policy-makers have so far failed to translate into long-term reality.

508. MAK-WERTE — MAC VALUES: The German acronym stands for "maximale Arbeitsplatzkonzentration", *i.e.* maximum allowable concentration (MAC) in the workplace (of, for example, toxic substances). For the purposes of **protection against technical hazards at work**, some 600 substances and their MAC values are listed officially every year. The values refer to a healthy employee for an average working week of 40 hours, but are not unreservedly applicable for pregnant women (**maternity protection**). Their observance is monitored by the **Labour Inspectorate** and the **Occupational Health and Safety Agencies**.

509. MANAGEMENT: Generic term indicating the sphere of activity which exercises directive functions in establishments, companies and other social systems through planning and decisions on policy-making and the implementation of these by means of instructions and controls. Modern German management, which originally developed from the "scientific management" of **Taylorism**, makes use of various management methods. *Management by objectives* works by defining operational goals for all organizational levels and leaving the choice of action to be taken to attain these goals largely to those being managed, thereby (it is hoped) stimulating their motivation to perform. Controls are maintained by making comparisons of target figures with actual figures. *Management by exception* adopts this process and then delegates routine tasks to subordinate staff members, but here giving them total responsibility. This leaves management free to concentrate on problems which really require its active attention. *Management by system* seeks, by systematizing and standardizing administration activities, to ensure the smoothest possible co-ordination of tasks in this growing field. The purpose of all such techniques in company and **personnel management** is, by incorporating collaborative elements (*management by motivation*), to improve the performance of the members of the organization concerned and ensure the adaptability of this organization to changes in environmental conditions. In industry, the so-called **new production concepts** are an example. In large enterprises in particular, management relies on co-operation with the **works council** within the scope of **informal rules** and **institutionalized representation of interests**. Management normally includes the members of the executive **company organs** and other individuals who, without themselves being **company members**, by virtue of a contract of employment play an influential part in operating the business with far-reaching discretionary authority. **Labour law** applies to these **executive staff** only to a limited and correspondingly modified extent.

510. **MANKOHAFTUNG — DEFICIT LIABILITY**: Form of **employee liability**, developed by the Federal Labour Court in its judgments, for damage arising for the employer from the fact that shortfalls and deficits occur in stocks of goods and cash holdings placed in the employee's charge. Deficit liability is excluded if its enforcement would be unfair *(contra bonos mores)*, would violate the principle of loyalty and good faith or would be contrary to the employer's **duty of care**. The general limitations on employee liability must also be observed. An employee who is held liable on the grounds of deficit is indebted to the employer for the purchase price of the missing goods.

511. **MANTELTARIFVERTRAG — FRAMEWORK AGREE-MENT ON EMPLOYMENT CONDITIONS**: Collective agreement containing regulations on conditions of employment which extend beyond remuneration. These regulations range in scope from norms on **working time**, pay supplements for **overtime, night work** and **shiftwork** and **leave**, to preconditions for dismissal and **periods of notice**. Most framework agreements on employment conditions run for a term of several years.

512. **MARKTWIRTSCHAFT — MARKET ECONOMY**: See **social market economy**.

513. **MASSENENTLASSUNG — COLLECTIVE DISMISSAL**: In the case of collective dismissals, establishments normally employing more than 20 employees must follow a special procedure under **protection against dismissal** as regulated in the Protection Against Dismissal Act (§§ 17,18). The purpose of this procedure is not directly to assist the continuance of individual **employment relationships**, but to ensure that the employment authorities are given early warning of impending collective

dismissals and hence have enough time to make arrangements to avoid dismissals and place employees in other jobs. The legal definition of collective dismissal is a situation where, within a given period of 30 days, the employment relationships of a relatively large number of employees are actually terminated by the employer by way of ordinary **termination with notice**. The precise number of dismissals necessary to meet the definition depends on the size of the establishment; the figure lies between around 10 and 25 per cent. of the workforce for medium-sized establishments and decreases with increasing size of establishment. The dismissal of at least 30 employees is always deemed in law to constitute collective dismissal.

An employer who is planning collective dismissals must inform the **works council** of the fact at an early stage and consult with the council on whether and how the measures envisaged can be avoided or mitigated. The employment authorities must also be alerted. The employer is required to inform the Head of the relevant Land Employment Office without delay if discernible changes suggest that collective dismissals are likely within the next 12 months. Before actually proceeding with collective dismissals, the employer must notify the local Employment Office; they may not take effect until a period of one month has elapsed after this notification. The Employment Office can reduce this period or extend it to a maximum of two months, during which time it can authorize the introduction of **short-time working**.

514. **MASSENPRODUKTION — MASS PRODUCTION**: The manufacture of identical products in large quantities under a system which has a low level of flexibility in manufacture. The production facilities are normally specialized and automated for recurring work cycles. The main principle is the achievement of a reduction in unit costs without loss of quality. Owing to the high set-up costs for production plant and stocks, traditional mass production using line systems allowed relatively little adaptability to changes in market conditions. Furthermore, the predominance of monotonous tasks fragmented into minimal job content imposed particular stresses on employees. In recent years, the possibilities offered by **new production technologies** and the calls being made for a **humanization of work** have led to the application of so-called **new production concepts**, which free mass production from the principles of **Taylorism** to at least some extent.

515. **MASSREGELUNGSVERBOT — BAN ON DISCIPLINARY TREATMENT**: The ban on disciplinary treatment which was

incorporated into the Civil Code (§ 612a) in 1980 by a statute implementing EC Directives prohibits *de facto* and *de jure* discriminatory treatment of employees through agreements and measures on the part of the employer because of the lawful exercise of a right by these employees, such as bringing a legal action against the employer or expressing an opinion that is not in breach of a contractual obligation. The employee concerned must prove that it is in fact because of the exercise of a right that he or she has suffered disadvantageous treatment. If this is proved, the measures are declared invalid or annulled. This also applies to **termination** of the employment relationship, even if the employer was able to justify it on other grounds.

Many **collective agreements** also contain bans on disciplinary treatment. In this case their function is to restore industrial peace after labour disputes and prohibit the discriminatory treatment of employees (usually regardless of whether or not their conduct was lawful) for having participated in a **strike**.

516. **MEHRARBEIT — OVERTIME EXCEEDING MAXIMUM WORKING HOURS**: Term referring specifically to hours of work done in excess of statutory maximum **working time** (48 hours per week at present). The stipulation that such overtime may be done on no more than 30 days in a given year is laid down under the provisions on **restrictions on working hours**, and the obligation to do it is governed by the contract of employment. As a general rule, it attracts special **overtime premium pay**. The arrangement of such overtime is subject to the **co-determination right of the works council**.

Career public servants ("Beamte") are in principle required to work overtime exceeding statutory working hours without being paid, but must be granted time off in lieu. There are exceptions to this, for example, in the case of hospitals and other areas of activity where compelling reasons make it impossible to grant time off.

As distinct from such overtime in excess of statutory maximum working hours, ordinary **overtime** covers any hours of work done in excess of a particular establishment's normal working hours.

517. **MEHRARBEITSVERGÜTUNG — OVERTIME PREMIUM PAY**: As a general principle, in cases of **overtime exceeding maximum working hours** an employee is entitled to overtime premium pay. By the application of a **pay supplement** it is usually at least 25 per cent. higher than the pay which the employee could have earned if the work had been done in normal **working time**. Employees can claim overtime premium pay even if such overtime was prohibited by statute or collective agreement. No

entitlement exists if the overtime exceeding statutory working hours is done to enable employees to catch up on work that has not been done through their own fault.

518. **MEINUNGSFREIHEIT — FREEDOM OF OPINION**: See **basic rights, duty of loyalty, employee rights, third-party effect of constitutional rights.**

519. **MIKROELEKTRONIK — MICROELECTRONICS**: Branch of electronics characterized by miniaturization which has developed into a key technology. The advancing miniaturization of microelectronic components (hardware) and, in particular, the multifarious form of control possible with the aid of mathematical programs (software) allow universal application. The impact of microelectronics not only includes all **new technologies**, **rationalization** and the stimulation of new areas of use but also extends, for example, to employees' **skills** and to **work organization**. For instance, "chip" manufacture itself demands specialist knowledge and painstaking care and the smoothest possible production process, and the result has been an expansion of fully continuous **shiftwork**. The main qualitative feature of microelectronics, in addition to the integration of different fields, lies in the trend towards a shift in the focal points of economic activity. With products that employ microelectronics, the value added element lies less in the material sphere of craft skills than in the intellectual sphere of mental skills.

The risk areas of electronic data processing are the misuse of data, which **data protection** seeks to prevent, and the danger of loss of data through technical and operator faults.

520. **MINDERHEITENSCHUTZ — PROTECTION OF MINORITIES**: Principle applying in **works council elections**, the composition of the **works council executive committee** and the release of **works council members** from work which ensures that the groups present in the establishment receive due consideration. The minimum number of representatives of a group on the **works council** is fixed by statute. In order to fulfil the quorum requirements for works council elections, a list of nominations must be supported by one twentieth of those members of the relevant group who are eligible to vote in the case of **group-based election**, and otherwise by one twentieth of all those employees eligible to vote. Every trade union that has at least one member in the establishment may also make nominations: here, the list need only be signed by two union officers who are the union's authorized representatives. If it is not represented on the electoral board, the union is also entitled

to send an employee belonging to the establishment as a non-voting delegate to the board. As regards the composition of works council executive committees, their additional members alongside the works council chairperson and vice-chairperson are appointed from among the body of works council members in accordance with the majority principle and the principles of proportional representation and the d'Hondt counting system. Each group to which more than one tenth of the works council members belong (subject to a minimum of three) elects its own representatives and also removes them. This does not, however, necessarily mean that every group actually has a seat on the committee. In a vote based on proportional representation, certain members of the works council executive committee may be removed by only a three quarters majority in the works council. Where there is only one nomination, majority voting applies. The selection of members for release from work is also based on proportional representation. If, however, there is only one nomination or if only one works council member is to be granted such release, majority voting is used.

521. **MINDESTARBEITSBEDINGUNGEN — MINIMUM CONDITIONS OF EMPLOYMENT**: A number of protective statutes in the sphere of labour law lay down statutory minimum conditions to be observed in the formation of employment relationships (although there is, in fact, no statutory regulation of pay in the Federal Republic). However, in areas where there are no **collective agreements** because **trade unions** and **employers' associations** do not exist for the branch of activity concerned or have too small a membership to exert any influence on the fixing of terms and conditions of employment, subject to certain provisos conditions of employment may be stipulated within the scope of the 1952 Statutory Definition of Minimum Employment Conditions Act (Gesetz über die staatliche Festsetzung von Mindestarbeitsbedingungen), if this is necessary in order to meet the essential social and economic needs of employees. Recourse to the Act is permissible only where the regulation of employment conditions has not already ensued from the official extension of a collective agreement. Mainly in the interests of **collective bargaining autonomy**, the powers conferred by the Act on the **Federal Minister for Labour and Social Affairs** to decree minimum conditions of employment have so far never been used.

522. **MITARBEITERBETEILIGUNG — FINANCIAL PARTICIPATION (BY EMPLOYEES)**: Term referring to the participation of the employees of a company in its equity capital

or profits. Employees frequently acquire shares in equity capital by way of investment made possible by **capital-forming payments** or profit-sharing schemes.

523. MitbestErgG: Co-Determination Amendment Act (Mitbestimmungsergänzungsgesetz 1956). See **co-determination in the coal, iron and steel industry**.

524. MitbestG: Co-Determination Act (Mitbestimmungsgesetz 1976). See **co-determination**.

525. MITBESTIMMUNG — CO-DETERMINATION: The concept of co-determination refers to two distinct levels and forms of employee participation: co-determination at establishment level by the works council (see next entry on **co-determination rights of the works council**) and co-determination above establishment level, on the **supervisory board** of companies, which is the main subject of this entry. At this level, co-determination is regulated by three statutes for different sectors of the economy and sizes of company. The system which provides the most extensive form ("parity co-determination") is **co-determination in the coal, iron and steel industry**, governed by the 1951 Coal, Iron and Steel Industry Co-Determination Act (Montan-Mitbestimmungs-gesetz). Companies in other industries with between 501 and 1,999 employees are covered by the corresponding provisions of the Works Constitution Act of 1952 (Betriebsverfassungsgesetz), under which employee representatives occupy only one third of seats on the supervisory board. Lastly, the 1976 Co-Determination Act (Mitbestimmungsgesetz) covers all standard forms of company normally employing more than 2,000 employees. This provides for equal numbers of representatives from the employee side and the company side on the supervisory board, which consists of 12, 16 or 20 members according to the size of the company. However, the procedure for electing the chairperson of the supervisory board stipulates that, if a second ballot is necessary, the chairperson is elected by the shareholders' representatives while the employee representatives may elect only the vice-chairperson. This is crucial since decisions by the supervisory board require a simple majority vote. In the event of a tie, the chairperson has two votes in the second ballot and hence can give the casting vote in favour of the shareholders' side. For all practical purposes, this means that the shareholders' side is always over-represented by one vote.

The employee representatives are elected either by direct election by the workforce if they so wish, or otherwise indirectly by a secondary body of delegates elected by the workforce. The shareholders' representatives are elected by the appropriate **shareholders' meeting** or **company general meeting**.

Historically, participation at company level dates back as far as the 1920 Works Councils Act (Betriebsrätegesetz). In terms of the history of ideas it covers a broad spectrum, ranging from catholic social theory via radical democratic to socialist perspectives. The Works Councils Act itself already provided a right for the works council to send a member to the supervisory board. Following the system established in the coal, iron and steel industry in 1951 and that introduced under the "works constitution" in 1952, the 1976 Co-Determination Act laid down a new form of participation at company level which was more extensive than the 1952 system, although the parity co-determination prevailing in the coal, iron and steel industry was still not achieved. In this respect the emphasis here again is more on acquiring additional information, without the ability to exert a real influence.

The 1976 Co-Determination Act was passed in the face of strong resistance from the **employers' associations**. Their **constitutional appeal** against the Act was rejected by the Federal Constitutional Court in 1979.

As regards the form of co-determination to be applied in the **European Company** (Societas Europea, or SE), there are three variants available. The first is modelled closely on practice in the Federal Republic and the Netherlands, and the second corresponds to the French system. The third variant provides minimum conditions for co-determination; here, the form of co-determination can be agreed between management and employees as they choose, but employee representatives must be informed and consulted on the company's business situation at least every calendar quarter. As a general principle the nature of co-determination is, however, governed by the provisions on the matter in the Member State in which the SE is located.

526. **MITBESTIMMUNGSRECHTE DES BETRIEBSRATS — CO-DETERMINATION RIGHTS OF THE WORKS COUNCIL**: The most far-reaching form of the **participation rights of the works council**. With the establishment of general collective rules as its objective, co-determination covers participation in arrangements on health and safety at work, voluntary and obligatory co-determination and the formal adoption of a **reconcilement of interests** and a **"social plan"** in the event of a **substantial alteration to the establishment** (Works Constitution Act §§ 87 ff., 111 ff.). The works council's co-determination rights also include the involvement of the council in deciding on the design of staff application forms,

methods of appraisal and **guidelines for personnel selection, in-service training** and individual staff measures (engagement, grading and re-grading, transfer, dismissal) (§§ 94 f., 96 ff., 99, 102). As a general principle, the right of co-determination is exercised through a **works agreement** or **semi-formal works agreement** in the case of collective measures, and through a corresponding decision by the works council in the case of matters relating to individual staff. In individual matters, a decision by the courts may take the place of the council's assent. The works council's co-determination rights must be observed even in urgent cases.

The area of obligatory collective co-determination encompasses matters connected with: **works rules; working time** in the establishment, including **breaks, short-time working** and **overtime**; the actual method of payment used for **remuneration**; the arrangement of general principles on annual holidays and the preparation of the holiday roster; the introduction and use of technical devices for monitoring employees' conduct and performance; accident prevention and health protection; the form, structure and administration of fringe benefits; the provision and withdrawal of company-owned housing; matters connected with remuneration arrangements within the establishment and principles and systems of remuneration; the fixing of performance-related rates of pay; and the principles underlying the company suggestions scheme for employees' **suggestions for improvements**. On these matters, the **employer** cannot take any action without the agreement of the works council, and indeed either side can take the initiative in such matters. Consequently, the works council can even require the company to accept rules on these matters by referring to the **establishment-level arbitration committee**. In collective matters, the decision of this arbitration committee can take the place of voluntary agreement between employer and works council. As a rule, the co-determination rights of the works council are confined to formal regulatory conditions of employment and, as regards company fringe benefits and performance-related rates of pay, to participating in the "how" after the employer has made a decision on the "whether". This restriction of the council's rights of co-determination is a result of the fact that statutes and **collective agreements** take precedence over the exercise of these rights.

With the introduction of **new production technologies** and **new production concepts**, and terms in collective agreements which assign the practical implementation of regulations on working hours to the parties at establishment level, the co-determination rights of the works council have steadily increased in importance. These rights can be extended by collective agreement.

527. **MitbG**: Coal, Iron and Steel Industry Co-Determination Act (Montan-Mitbestimmungsgesetz 1951). See **co-determination in the coal, iron and steel industry**.

528. **MITTELBARE DISKRIMINIERUNG — INDIRECT DISCRIMINATION**: Term indicating discriminatory treatment of certain groups of people which does not rest directly on membership of the group but ostensibly refers to other criteria which in fact affect a disproportionately large number of members of the group, and thus contravenes **anti-discrimination laws**.

It is particularly common in the form of indirect discrimination against women, especially in contravention of the principle of **equal pay**. This mainly happens where certain groups of employees (*e.g.* part-time workers) which, because of the predominant pattern of role distribution in society, contain far more women than men, are excluded, without any material reason or on some alleged ground, from payments granted by the employer to the remainder of an establishment's workforce. According to the case law of the **system of labour courts**, in line with the European Court of Justice, such forms of differentiation are permissible only within narrow limits. The courts require the employer to prove that the differentiation is in the material interests of the company, that its motive is not differential treatment on grounds of sex, and that it is appropriate and necessary to the achievement of the objective in view. This case law has created a relatively effective remedy against particularly arbitrary acts by employers; at the same time, its overall impact on them is limited. The mechanisms which lead to the over-representation of women in certain subordinate and hence inevitably poorly paid jobs lie outside its scope.

529. **MITWIRKUNGSRECHTE DES BETRIEBSRATS — CONSULTATION RIGHTS OF THE WORKS COUNCIL**: The rights of the **works council** to be consulted and express its views which give it the opportunity to play a part in decisions made by the employer. This form of participation, or its omission, has no effect on the legal validity of a measure taken by the employer, since providing the works council with information is not a mandatory precondition. The works council's right to be consulted must be observed, for example, in matters involving the provisions of the works constitution which serve to protect **employee rights, protection against dismissal, protection against technical hazards at work** and the design of working methods, workflows and workplaces, **job advertisements** and **guidelines for personnel selection, in-service training**, the activities of the **economic committee** and the preparation of a **reconcilement of interests** and a "**social plan**".

(The term "Mitwirkung" is sometimes used loosely to mean "participation".)

530. **MONTAN-MITBESTIMMUNG — CO-DETERMINA-TION IN THE COAL, IRON AND STEEL INDUSTRY**: Term denoting the system incorporating the most extensive form of **co-determination**. It is confined to the **coal, iron and steel industry**; its operation is also extended to **group** parent companies which are not active in this industry themselves but whose subsidiary companies within the coal, iron and steel industry produce at least 20 per cent. of the group's net output or employ more than 2,000 employees. Its foundation in law derives from the Coal, Iron and Steel Industry Co-Determination Act (MitbG) of May 21, 1951 as amended on December 19, 1985 and the Co-Determination Amendment Act (MitbestErgG) of August 7, 1956 as amended on December 20, 1988.

It incorporates down special provisions on the composition of the supervisory boards of the companies concerned. These boards normally consist of 11 members, and the number can be increased to 15 or 21 in companies where the nominal capital is correspondingly higher. In all cases, half of the members represent the employees and half represent the shareholders (hence the term **"parity co-determination"**), and there is also one additional member. Each side chooses its own candidates. The trade unions and works councils propose their nominated candidates to the **shareholders' meeting** for election; this is purely a formality and the meeting must confirm their nominations. The additional member, who is needed to act as a casting vote, must be elected by the shareholders' meeting on the proposal of the majority of both factions on the supervisory board. The company's management board must include one member who is responsible for personnel matters, the so-called employee director, who may not be elected against the majority vote of the employees' side on the supervisory board. In companies to which this system is extended under the Co-Determination Amendment Act, the supervisory board consists of 15 members, *i.e.* seven members each for the employees' and employer's sides plus one additional member. Four of the employee representatives must be employed in establishments belonging to the group member company, and must comprise three manual workers and one white-collar worker. The employee representatives are elected by the secondary election procedure, and an employee director must be appointed in this case also.

531. **MONTANINDUSTRIE — COAL, IRON AND STEEL INDUSTRY**: Sector deemed to include all public limited

companies, limited liability companies and cost-book companies (form of company specific to the mining industry) possessing their own legal personality (**legal person**) which employ more than 1,000 employees and carry on their main activity in the extraction of coal and lignite or iron ore and in the dressing, coking, carbonization or briquetting of these materials, and whose establishments are subject to the supervision of the mining authorities. In addition, it covers companies in the iron and steel producing industry which are listed by name in the Allied Industrial Deconcentration Act (Entflechtungsgesetz) of May 16, 1950 and continuing to be operated either as individual registered companies or in some other form. Their group member companies are also included, provided their main activity is in the extraction or preparation of basic materials or iron and steel production.

532. **MUTTERSCHAFTSGELD — MATERNITY ALLOWANCE**: See **maternity protection**.

533. **MUTTERSCHUTZ — MATERNITY PROTECTION**: Special provisions for mothers and expectant mothers who are in an **employment relationship**, **homeworkers** or equated with homeworkers, but not for other **persons treated in law as similar to an employee**. They are codified in the 1968 Maternity Protection Act (Mutterschutzgesetz).

To enable protective measures to be taken, expectant mothers must inform their employer of their pregnancy and the expected date of their confinement, and the employer in turn must notify the appropriate authorities of the **Labour Inspectorate**. As a rule, expectant mothers are not required to make their pregnancy known before entering into employment.

Maternity protection comprises protection against hazards, job protection and protection of remuneration. Protection against hazards includes the obligations imposed on employers to adapt the workplace to the health needs of women before or shortly after their confinement, and not to allocate dangerous and physically arduous work to them, together with certain restrictions on their employment. During a period of six weeks prior to their confinement pregnant women are released from their obligation to perform work. After their confinement, mothers may not be employed for a period of at least eight weeks. If after this their capacity to work is still impaired, the employer must take this into account in the allocation of work. Nursing mothers must be granted the necessary time off for this purpose. After the protected period has ended, women have the choice of taking **childcare leave** and (if provided for by collective agreement) **parental leave**.

232

Job protection takes the form of an absolute ban on dismissal. Any **termination** of the employment relationship by the employer is invalid if the employer knew of the pregnancy at the time of dismissal or is informed of the pregnancy within two weeks of pronouncing dismissal. This ban on dismissal ends four months after the woman's confinement. Only in special cases where the employer is undergoing unusually severe difficulties is dismissal lawful as an exception, with the permission of the authorities.

Mothers must not suffer any financial disadvantage during pregnancy and the protected period. They are therefore entitled to be paid maternity pay equivalent to the average income earned prior to pregnancy irrespective of how much work is performed during this period, in so far as they are not entitled to be paid maternity allowance from statutory health insurance or the state authorities. Such an entitlement exists during the protected period (from six weeks before until eight or twelve weeks after the confinement), but is less than the normal average income. The employer is required to make up the difference. Mothers covered by statutory **health insurance** are also entitled to other maternity benefits, mainly health care.

N

534. **NACHTARBEIT — NIGHT WORK**: As defined by statute, **working time** that lies between 2200 and 0600 hrs. More detailed regulations are frequently laid down by **collective agreement**. A special collectively agreed **pay supplement** is normally paid to compensate for night work; this is sometimes smaller if the work is done as part of regular **shiftwork**. The arrangement of night work is subject to the **co-determination right of the works council**.

535. **NACHTEILSAUSGLEICH — RECONCILEMENT OF DISADVANTAGE**: See **reconcilement of interests**.

536. **NATURALVERGÜTUNG — PAYMENT IN KIND**: Any **remuneration** which is not in the form of money. Examples of such non-pay benefits include board and lodging, work clothing, etc. The **ban on the truck system** does not exclude payment in kind. If employees cannot reasonably be expected to accept payment in kind, or if such acceptance is actually impossible, the employer must pay them the sum of money which they would have needed to spend to procure on the open market what was provided as payment in kind.

    Associated **deductions from pay** are calculated on the basis of the current market value of the payment in kind, which the Federal Government fixes annually by executive order. Tax is not payable in respect of amenities which either do not constitute a counter-performance (*i.e.* remuneration in respect of work performed) or, while being gainful to the employee, are granted predominantly in the company's self-interest. This category covers, for example, subsidized meals, the payment of telephone bills and company-owned holiday homes.

537. **NEBENTÄTIGKEIT — SECOND JOB**: The performance of services under a contract carried on in addition to the main occupation and in return for payment, or spare-time employment for private profit of the **employee**. A second job may be arranged in the form of a **contract of employment, contract for services** or jobbing contract. Carrying on a second job is lawful provided that no restrictions to the contrary are imposed by the contract of employment or a collective agreement, that it does not substantially impair the employee's capacity to work and that there is no conflict with the (main) employer's interests from the point of view of competition. Also, it may not be done during **leave** or incapacity for work because of **illness**. To the extent that taking a spare-time job results in the statutory **maximum working hours** being exceeded, any contractual obligation

constituting the excess working time is null and void. The employee may, however, claim remuneration for work already performed in accordance with the principles of the *de facto* employment relationship.

Where a second job is being carried on unlawfully and a formal warning from the employer has had no effect, the employer may pronounce **dismissal on grounds of conduct**. In the **public service** there are special regulations under which official permission is necessary before taking a second job. Individuals employed in the public service may be required to assume the functions of a subsidiary post ("Nebenamt").

538. **NEBENTÄTIGKEITSVERBOT — PROHIBITION OF SECOND JOBS**: As a general principle, employees are allowed to take on a second job. This may in fact be prohibited under the terms of a **contract of employment**, **works agreement** or **collective agreement**, but only in so far as the second job can have some actual effect on the employee's work performance as due under the contract of employment.

Employees in the **public service** must always obtain special permission to carry on a second job; the remuneration earned from a second job may in some cases also be counted as part of the **pay of career public servants**.

539. **NEGATIVE KOALITIONSFREIHEIT — "NEGATIVE" FREEDOM OF ASSOCIATION**: The right of the individual not to be obliged to join an association, *e.g.* a collective industrial organization such as a **trade union**. It does not prohibit recruitment activities to attract new members or the grant of internal benefits for members, such as the provision of **strike pay** by the unions. It does, however, prohibit the exertion of unfair pressure on non-members, for instance by denying them privileges that are not purely internal to the organization; one such example is a **differential treatment clause** in a collective agreement under which privileges granted by the employer are reserved for union members only. It is also unlawful to make it unreasonably difficult to resign from membership; a period of notice of resignation exceeding six months is deemed to be too long.

540. **NETTOLOHNVEREINBARUNG — NET PAY ARRANGE-MENT**: As a general principle, the **remuneration** due to the employee from the employer is a gross sum, *i.e.* **gross pay**. However, if the parties to the contract of employment have agreed on a net pay arrangement, the employer's obligation is to pay the employee the agreed net pay and over and above this

to pay taxes and social security contributions to the authorities. These **deductions from pay** are calculated on the basis of the hypothetical gross pay to which the employee would have needed to be entitled in order to earn the net pay in question. In such cases the employer also pays the employee's share of social security contributions.

541. **"NEUE BEWEGLICHKEIT"**: Term (literally, "new mobility") referring to a strike strategy developed by the unions in the early 1980s whereby, as a warning during the process of collective negotiations, the form of brief strikes traditionally known as "token strikes" are systematically organized on a rotating basis in different establishments within a collective bargaining area.

The Federal Labour Court has ruled that, in accordance with the criteria governing token strikes, such strikes are still lawful when they form part of this highly developed "new mobility" strategy (in which context they are referred to as "**warning strikes**").

542. **NEUE PRODUKTIONSKONZEPTE — NEW PRODUCTION CONCEPTS**: Ideas on the redesign of the industrial manufacturing process in terms of both greater integration of production flows and closer adaptation to employees' **skills** and **motivation to work**. Such approaches include the fullest possible exploitation of the potential for flexibility offered by **new production technologies**, universal efforts to shape the flow of materials towards reducing throughput times, and the reduction of holding and storage costs by means of demand- or consumption-driven production flows ("just-in-time", "kanban"). These approaches not only alter manufacturing processes and logistics at establishment level, so that **mass production** in its traditional sense no longer really exists, but also have impacts outside the establishment, particularly on suppliers. They are also important to the strike tactics of the trade unions, for example in the "**neue Beweglichkeit**" strategy, and with respect to the impartiality of the **Federal Employment Service**. These new production concepts go some way towards meeting all kinds of demands for the **humanization of work** in terms of the employee's situation and **work organization**. They are based on the knowledge that the limited use of individual capacity that is inherent in **Taylorism** actually forfeits significant potential for productivity. In contrast to such wastage, they recognize that in the skills and occupational sovereignty of the worker, and the corresponding design of jobs as non-fragmented entities, there lie productive forces ready to be exploited. New

production concepts are often linked with forms of **corporate culture**. So far, however, the practical implementation of these ideas, which are along the lines of the Japanese style of **management**, has failed to make headway against the individualistic basis of Western patterns of work organization and, in the Federal Republic, against the system of **institutionalized representation of interests**.

543. NEUE PRODUKTIONSTECHNOLOGIEN — NEW PRODUCTION TECHNOLOGIES: Term mainly encompassing, in addition to the use of **biotechnology and chemical technologies**, manufacturing techniques controlled with the aid of **microelectronics (process innovations)**. Computer controlled and assisted systems are now used at almost all levels of production, with varying degrees of interconnection. They include: CAD (computer aided design); CAE (computer aided engineering); CAM (computer aided manufacturing, incorporating both CAD and CAE); CAP (computer aided planning, in some cases linked with CAD, CAE and CAM, for the compilation of work and industrial schedules and production data and control commands for numerically controlled NC and CNC machines); PPS (production planning systems); and CIM (computer integrated manufacturing, *i.e.* the integrated computer aided control of the technical manufacturing process incorporating all computer aided techniques and other flexible production planning, manufacturing and logistic transport systems). CIM represents the goal of the "factory of the future", in which large numbers of variably programmable industrial robots carry out the flexible production of different products in different batch sizes and in which humans perform only supervisory, control and monitoring tasks.

New production technologies bring with them a wide range of possibilities for **rationalization**, and hence the threat of job losses. At the same time they offer, often in conjunction with so-called **new production concepts**, opportunities for more "rounded" job design, since in many cases these machines allow manual follow-up control and indeed, owing to the flexibility needed, are often designed for this. This raises the **skill** levels demanded of employees. The **works council** must be informed of any plans to introduce new production technologies and consulted regarding the resultant impact on employees and the nature of their work.

544. NEUE TECHNOLOGIEN — NEW TECHNOLOGIES: Generic term conventionally used to denote operating procedures fed from various individual techniques. The connecting link between the individual techniques concerned is normally **microelectronics**, in its turn a combination of physical devices (hardware) and control programs (software). The characteristic feature of new technologies (NT), as exemplified by **biotechnology and chemical technologies**, **office communications technology** and **new production technologies**, is the integration of what have up till now been separate work stages. The very term "technology", with its original transferred meaning of the application of science in the sense of systematic knowledge about all areas of life, points to the cross-linking that is the particular feature of NT and, in addition, a growing awareness of how the application of science is linked with the environment, society and culture.

545. NEUTRALITÄT DES STAATES — IMPARTIALITY OF THE STATE: Principle which imposes on the welfare state legislators the obligation to maintain impartiality in relation to the **collective industrial organizations** and their spheres of autonomy specifically during **labour disputes**. Accordingly, **unemployment insurance** also must be administered impartially in the event of industrial action. Under the Employment Promotion Act § 116(1), employees who participate directly in industrial action or are directly affected by **lock-out** have their entitlements to **unemployment benefit** and **short-time allowance** suspended. For employees who are without work or on short time through the indirect effect of industrial action elsewhere, the regulations are as follows:

a. Indirectly affected employees who are outside both the industry and the region covered by the **collective agreement** to which the industrial action relates always receive unemployment benefit or short-time allowance; only indirectly affected employees who belong to the industry and the region concerned lose these entitlements.

b. Indirectly affected employees who belong to the industry concerned but are outside the region concerned normally receive unemployment benefit or short-time allowance. The exceptions are defined by statute.

Entitlement to benefits is suspended only in the event of "industrial action by proxy" ("Stellvertreterarbeitskampf"), *i.e.* if the dispute is being conducted on a representative basis for also changing the employment conditions of the indirectly affected employees, so that those without work must be deemed to be participating. This is the case only subject to the strict precondition that those indirectly affected will also share in the results achieved.

The question of whether a particular case constitutes industrial action by proxy is decided by the Impartiality Committee (Neutralitätsausschuss), which is composed of three trade union representatives and three employers' representatives from the management board of the Federal Employment Service. The trade unions and employers in their capacity as associations may appeal directly to the **Federal Social Security Court** against the Committee's decisions. The employees affected may appeal to the local Social Security Court against the decision of the local **Employment Office** regarding their claim for benefits.

546. **NICHTZULASSUNGSBESCHWERDE — NON-ADMISSION PETITION**: See **appeal on a point of law, "Beschluss" procedure appeal, judicial review application**.

547. **NORMALARBEITSVERHÄLTNIS — TYPICAL EMPLOYMENT RELATIONSHIP**: The typical employment relationship is understod to mean full-time employment for an indefinite period of time. It represents the outcome, for the present, of decades of collective efforts to narrow down the employer's total power of disposal over labour that prevailed in the early days of industrialization as a result of free labour markets and to make the general conditions of work measurable. A means to this end was the **collective agreement**. Since then, modern **labour law** and **social security law** have been founded on the basic principles of full-time work and continuous length of service. The "typical" or "normal" model also furnished companies with a reliable basis for calculation and with equal terms of competition on the labour market. The mesh of rules and minimum conditions deriving from this typical model, and the impression stamped by it on other types of employment relationship, provide the backdrop to current demands for more use of "atypical" forms of working, *i.e.* **flexibilization**.

548. **NOTARBEITEN — EMERGENCY WORK**: Work which must be done whatever the circumstances and which is exempt from the limitations of **maximum working hours**. Emergency work may be brought about by emergencies, *i.e.* by unusual, unforeseeable and suddenly occurring events which necessitate immediate intervention, and by extraordinary instances, *i.e.* by unforeseen, temporary circumstances beyond the employer's control whose consequences cannot be rectified in any other way. It also arises when work that has been started needs urgently to be completed since otherwise the work result would be endangered or disproportionate damage would ensue and the employer cannot reasonably be expected to take some other precautionary action. Only a small number of employees may

ever be called upon to perform emergency work at any one time.

A distinction is made between emergency work in the strict sense and the **maintenance of essential supplies and services** during industrial action.

O

549. ÖFFENTLICHER DIENST — PUBLIC SERVICE: Any activity within the context of a public-sector relationship contract of service with an authority of the Federal Government or the Länder, a **municipality** or **association of municipalities**, or some other **legal person** under public law. The legal relationships of Ministers, judges and military personnel are also included. In the stricter sense, the term means the contract of service of **career public servants** ("Beamte") and of **manual workers** and **white-collar workers** employed under public law. In the case of **career public servants** this is governed by the legal provisions on the **career public service relationship**, while other white-collar workers are covered by the National Agreement for Public Sector White-Collar Workers (BAT) and manual workers by collective agreements at Federal, Land and municipality level.

In 1989 there were 4.62 million people (excluding military personnel) employed in the public sector. Of these, 1.84 million were career public servants including judges, 1.74 million were white-collar workers and 1.04 million were manual workers. Women represented 42.2 per cent. of this total, over 18 per cent. of them in **part-time work**.

550. ÖFFNUNGSZEITEN — HOURS OF OPENING: See **shop closing hours**.

551. ORDENTLICHE GERICHTSBARKEIT — SYSTEM OF ORDINARY COURTS: Branch of jurisdiction consisting of the civil and criminal courts at district, Land and Higher Land levels and the Federal Court of Justice (BGH). With the exception of the BGH, depending on the area of law, value of any claim involved and matter in dispute they can all be courts of first instance, with the result that it can be either simply a two-instance or a three-instance process of law. Legal costs are payable for actions before the ordinary courts, and (with the exception of family cases) the parties are permitted to represent themselves only before the district courts.

Civil actions are dealt with by the ordinary courts only if they are not assigned to some other branch of jurisdiction, *e.g.* the **system of labour courts**. Accordingly, matters from the field of labour relations which they hear are those concerning:
a. the lawfulness of an expulsion of union members;
b. particular disputes between employer and employee or the collective bargaining parties which are not directly connected with the employment relationship and therefore not assigned to the Labour Courts;

    c. disputes arising from the sphere of **co-determination**, in so far as they do not concern the election of employee representatives to the supervisory board or (other than for just cause) their removal.

Apart from this, the ordinary courts deal with all criminal offences on the part of employers or employees. The parties to the employment contract can render themselves liable to prosecution in a number of ways, for example if an employer misappropriates social security contributions after deducting them at source or if employees take into their personal possession tools and materials that have been made available to them. Penal provisions are found not only in the Penal Code but also in a great deal of secondary labour legislation.

552. ORDENTLICHE KÜNDIGUNG — TERMINATION WITH NOTICE: Literally, "ordinary" termination, *i.e.* termination when an **employment relationship** is ended after the due **period of notice** has expired (as opposed to "extraordinary" or summary termination, for which there must be specific just cause). **Employees** have the unreservedly lawful right to terminate their employment relationship in this way by simply giving the due period of notice. **Employers**, on the other hand, may terminate employment relationships in this way only as permitted by the provisions on **protection against dismissal**.

553. ORDNUNGSFUNKTION DES TARIFVERTRAGES — NORMATIVE FUNCTION OF COLLECTIVE AGREEMENTS: The third major function (in addition to protection and the preservation of industrial peace) of **collective agreements** concluded at trade union and employers' association level, which are referred to as association-level agreements. The application of such agreements within the establishment results in standardized **contracts of employment**, with predictable staff costs and uniform regulation of labour relations within the establishment.

554. ORDNUNGSPRINZIP — SUPERSEDENCE PRINCIPLE: Within their area of application, a **collective agreement** and a **works agreement** apply to contracts of employment like a law, and hence form a unified normative order. Consequently, in accordance with the supersedence principle if two collective agreements or works agreements with overlapping scope follow each other consecutively the more recent regulation supersedes the earlier one, regardless of whether it is more favourable for the employee or not. The only exception is if the earlier agreement specified that special payments were to be granted on a permanent basis. Nor can existing acquired rights or non-forfeitable occupational pension expectations be encroached upon by **collective agreement** or works agreement.

555. **ORGANISATIONSKLAUSELN — CLOSED SHOP CLAUSES**: Clauses imposing on employers covered by a **collective agreement** the obligation to employ only trade union members. In some cases their effect extends beyond this by prohibiting the engagement of all employees who do not belong to the particular trade unions that have participated in the agreement (so-called "beschränkte Organisationsklauseln", *i.e.* limited or pre-entry closed shop).

Such clauses were not unusual in the days when the unions were still having to fight for recognition. The principle of the closed shop is not unknown in other countries as well. It is unlawful in the Federal Republic to agree closed shop arrangements, since they contravene the principle of **freedom of association**. For the same reason, all measures aimed at ousting particular employees from the establishment because they belong to a different union are also contrary to law.

556. **OVG**: Higher Administrative Court (Oberverwaltungsgericht). See **system of administrative courts**.

P

557. **PARITÄTISCHE MITBESTIMMUNG — PARITY CO-DETERMINATION**: See **co-determination**.

558. **PARLAMENTSVORBEHALT — RESERVATION OF PARLIAMENTARY POWERS**: A special case of **reservation of statutory powers**; it determines for which matters regulation by **executive order** is sufficient. According to the "Wesentlichkeitstheorie" (essentiality theory) developed by the **Federal Constitutional Court**, the main criterion is how important a particular rule is for the community at large and the individual citizen. "Essentiality" is not a hard and fast legal concept, but an indeterminate one: the more seriously the citizen's constitutional rights are affected or threatened or the more important the consequences are for the community at large and the more controversial a nexus of problems is in public opinion, the narrower and more exact the legislative regulation needs to be. Consequently, with crucial issues, conferring powers by statute as provided for under the **Constitution** for an authority to regulate a matter by executive order is too indeterminate. The reservation of parliamentary powers requires that such matters be regulated directly by Parliament within the context of the formal legislative procedure. Only matters of less importance may be delegated to authorities for regulation by executive order.

559. **PAUSE — BREAK**: An interruption of work. In the case of short breaks for the employee's personal needs or operational stoppages for technical reasons, remuneration is payable. However, scheduled breaks for rest in accordance with the relevant **regulations on working hours** or as laid down by collective agreement or works agreement do not count as part of **working time**. These are intended for relaxation and eating meals, and as far as possible suitable rooms not too far from the workplace must be provided for the purpose.

In principle, for working time in excess of 6 hours male employees must be granted one 30-minute or two 15-minute breaks. In the case of female employees, there must be a break of at least 20 minutes for working time in excess of 4½-6 hours, 30 minutes for working time of 6-8 hours, 45 minutes for working time over 8 hours and 1 hour for working time over 9 hours. If daily working time is 8½ hours, this break may be shortened to 30 minutes if the purpose of extending working time on some days is to enable work to end earlier on the working day before a non-working day. Young employees must be allowed a break of 30 minutes for working time of more than 4½-6 hours and 1 hour for working time of more than 6 hours.

The scheduling of breaks within a shift is subject to the **co-determination right of the works council**.

The legal provisions on breaks stipulate merely minimum conditions. According to ergonomic findings, these are insufficient; depending on job content and working conditions, during each shift there should be 1-5 breaks lasting 2-15 minutes. The relaxation value is greatest at the start of a break. Consequently, in the case of stressful activities it is most beneficial to have a large number of short breaks. A period of 45 minutes must be allocated for the midday break or break for a main meal, so that after eating the employee still has some 20 minutes left for pure relaxation.

560. **PENSIONS- UND UNTERSTÜTZUNGSKASSEN — PENSION AND BENEVOLENT FUNDS**: Institutions independent in law for the administration of **occupational pension schemes** for one or more companies. In the case of pension funds, insured employees possess a legal claim to the pension payments assured. The fund is financed by the employer, but the employees entitled to a pension may be required to contribute. Pension funds, like commercial insurance companies, are subject to the insurance supervisory authorities. In the case of benevolent funds, on the other hand, insured employees do not have a definite legal claim to a specified payment. However, protection against the reduction or cancellation of **occupational pensions** is essentially the same as in the case of other forms of **assurance of an occupational pension**. Employees may not be required to contribute. Benevolent funds are not subject to the insurance supervisory authorities. They have full discretion in deciding on the investment of their assets, which may also be loaned to the fund's pension-paying company at appropriate rates of interest.

561. **PENSIONS-SICHERUNGS-VEREIN — PENSION SECURITY ASSOCIATION**: The institution (referred to as the PSV) which provides **protection in the event of insolvency** for pension entitlements arising from **occupational pension schemes**. It is an independent body in law, founded by the Confederation of German Employers' Associations, the Confederation of German Industry and the Association of Life Insurance Companies (Verband der Lebensversicherungsunternehmen). The members of its organs include, in addition to representatives of the member companies, life insurance company representatives and employee representatives. Under the Improvement of Occupational Pension Schemes Act (Gesetz zur Verbesserung der betrieblichen Altersversorgung), all

employers who guarantee pension payments are required, within three months of granting **assurance of an occupational pension**, to inform the PSV of the fact and become contributing members of it. The scale of their contributions depends on the nature and scale of the sums they have assured. Since the legal relationship between the PSV and its members is subject to public law, any disputes fall within the jurisdiction of the **system of administrative courts**. If a member company becomes insolvent, the PSV takes the place of the company as pension-payer. Disputes with employees who have pension entitlements fall within the jurisdiction of the **system of labour courts**.

In 1989 the PSV had some 35,000 members and made payments to some 180,000 pension claimants.

562. **PERSONALAKTE — PERSONAL FILE**: Collection of written documents maintained by the employer concerning an **employee**'s relevant personal information and employment-related conduct. It may contain, for example, job application documents, recruitment questionnaires, medical certificates, appraisals of performance and conduct, and records of disciplinary sanctions and warnings. The keeping of such records is a lawful limitation of the **right of self-determination over personal data** of the employees concerned. They do, however, have the right to inspect the files concerning them and may demand that any inaccurate data which could prejudice their career prospects be corrected. They may also demand that their own comments be added to their file.

The employer must store personal files in such a way that no unauthorized access to them is possible. Special problems arise in connection with the storage of personal data in computerized **personnel information systems**. This rapidly spreading form of personnel administration is subject to specific regulations on **data protection**.

563. **PERSONALEINSATZ — LABOUR UTILIZATION**: The deployment of employees in particular areas of activity for the purpose of achieving the best possible performance of tasks. It forms part of **human resource planning** and, in addition to the regular occupancy of jobs, also includes making arrangements for cover during leave and illness. Where necessary, a number of supernumerary staff are held in reserve for this.

564. **PERSONALFRAGEBOGEN — RECRUITMENT QUESTIONNAIRE**: See **application form, human resource planning**.

565. PERSONALFÜHRUNG — PERSONNEL MANAGEMENT: The process of managing the employees of a company in accordance with the principles and needs of **human resource planning and personnel policy**.

566. PERSONALHOHEIT — AUTHORITY TO APPOINT AND DISMISS STAFF: See **public sector employer**.

567. PERSONALINFORMATIONSSYSTEM — PERSONNEL INFORMATION SYSTEM: A computerized system for processing data concerning the personal circumstances, characteristics or behaviour of employees. The collection, storage, processing and disclosure of data are subject to the corresponding provisions of **labour law** and **data protection**. Under these provisions, the storage and transfer of personal data are permitted if this is necessary to the performance of the employment relationship. They are also lawful if protection of the legitimate interests of a third party so requires and legitimate interests of the employee concerned are not thereby prejudiced. In such cases, any detrimental information about the employee may only ever be communicated in so far as it could also be found in a **reference**. The individuals concerned must be given details of the personal data about themselves being stored and the users to whom data has been disclosed. Data that can be proved to be inaccurate must be erased, and data that is possibly inaccurate must be prohibited from use or destroyed, if it relates to health matters, criminal offences or political and religious views. Personal data must also be erased if its storage was unlawful or has become unnecessary. The significance of data and its accuracy becomes evident where personnel information systems are used for more than purely administrative and payroll purposes. In the context of **human resource planning** and **personnel management** such systems are used in undertaking so-called profile matches for particular tasks and skills in order to identify the most suitable employee for a given job. They are also used in applying **social criteria for redundancy** in cases where redundancies are necessary. In the absence of any regulation by statute or collective agreement, these systems, which are deemed to be technical devices for monitoring employees' conduct and performance, are subject to the **co-determination right of the works council**. There is a right to information and consultation in general before their installation. There is also a right to co-determination in the drawing-up of general guidelines and design of recruitment questionnaires for the purposes of establishing the database for such systems.

568. PERSONALPLANUNG — HUMAN RESOURCE PLANNING: Process concerned with forecasting the future labour requirements of a company or establishment in both quantitative and qualitative terms. It is subject to the **participation rights of the works council**, which thus prevents the council's **co-determination rights** concerning individual staff measures from being undermined by previous general policy decisions about which it knows nothing. The works council can also take the initiative with proposals of its own on the matter. Human resource planning, which may be influenced by particular **personnel management** approaches, includes the planning of, for example, **labour utilization** and availability, staff development, staff structure and staff costs. It therefore has an effect on the hiring and dismissal of employees and arrangements for **in-service training**. The means whereby its objectives are translated into reality include **job advertisements** to activate the company's internal labour market and recruitment questionnaires and assessment criteria. Questionnaires serve to provide the employer with a picture of the employee's personal circumstances and abilities. Their content and the definition of assessment criteria are subject to the co-determination of the works council. These criteria are guidelines for the evaluation of an employee's performance and conduct. In many cases data obtained in this way is stored and processed in **personnel information systems**. Guidelines on hiring, transfers, re-grading and dismissal are also important in human resource planning. Known as guidelines on personnel selection, in establishments normally employing up to 1,000 employees they may be introduced only with the agreement of the works council and in establishments with more than 1,000 employees the council can insist on their introduction; they have considerable influence on **personnel selection**. Modern human resource planning seeks to cope with the altered circumstances brought about by structural change by decoupling the development of a company's labour supply from short- or medium-term fluctuations in labour requirements and to focus on building up a body of staff for the long term which is relatively unchanging in number and with continually rising skill levels. This corresponds (contrary to narrow interpretations of the idea of **flexibilization**) to a perception of the employment relationship as a long-term legal relationship and to the trend in recent collective agreements towards gearing pay more closely to skills than to job requirements. (The term ''manpower planning'' is also sometimes used.)

569. PERSONALPOLITIK — PERSONNEL POLICY: Term denoting the background to and changing basic principles of

human resource planning and personnel management.

Since the early 1970s, adjustment to **structural change** and far-reaching efforts towards greater flexibility in labour relations have brought sweeping changes in personnel policy. Whereas in the 1960s there was still a tendency to gear labour capacity to peak workloads, the approach subsequently adopted, even in buoyant sectors of the economy, was to scale down labour requirements as unobtrusively as possible and adjust them to the average workload. This is one of the reasons why even an upturn in the economy can no longer have the effect of massively reducing **unemployment**. Current personnel policy is an expression of the moves towards **flexibilization** which are a reaction against the economic and social structures of the heyday of Taylorized mass production. The relevant legislation and case law, bargaining policy and **co-determination** have moved responsibility for staffing matters right into the top-level management and management board of companies and at the same time increasingly set limits to a purely profit-oriented personnel policy. In addition to a greater degree of primary utilization of labour without increasing direct costs, personnel policy is now much concerned (also as a result of **new production concepts**, for example) with tapping hitherto neglected abilities and influencing the attitude of the employee to his or her job.

It is still not possible to foresee what impact personnel policy will ultimately have on the collective representation of employees, and especially the **trade unions**. On the one hand, it may be associated with a weakening of the unions. On the other hand, it is probable that the highly skilled employees on whom personnel policy is focused will also have special demands to make regarding their conditions of employment and will also articulate this. Furthermore, the unions' scope of activity is only gradually changing. They will continue to be responsible for fixing collectively agreed minimum standards for existing forms of work. Although this does not alter the fact that the emphasis is shifting from **collective bargaining autonomy** to "establishment autonomy" (Betriebsautonomie), it still means that the unions fix the framework within which **works councils** are able to shape conditions of employment within a given company to its employees' needs. In addition, despite the criticism levelled at the **juridification** of relations within the establishment there is something to be said for the argument that institutional safeguards are an essential precondition if employees are to be expected to welcome moves towards greater flexibility. Lastly, even management is unlikely to see any advantage in eliminating the existing functional division between the different institutions that represent the balance in **industrial conflict**; any curtailment of union powers would not simply afford companies more scope for holding the initiative, but would in fact open up the way for all kinds of social conflict to penetrate the sphere of employment within the establishment. And the current provisions on **works agreements** actually restrict the possibility of encroaching on the regulatory scope of collective agreements. Nevertheless, in practice **establishment-specific bargaining** and case law are evincing an expansion of the scope for regulation at establishment level.

570. **PERSONALRAT — STAFF COUNCIL**: The equivalent in the public sector of the **works council** in the private sector. A staff council must be formed in every **public sector establishment** with at least five employees including **career public servants** ("Beamte"), **white-collar workers** and **manual workers**. Its legal basis lies in the Federal Staff Representation Act (Bundespersonalvertretungsgesetz) and the staff representation laws of the individual Länder.

In terms of the individuals concerned, the composition of the staff council is determined by the outcome of **staff council elections**. The statutory regulations, however, stipulate that every employee group with a presence in a public sector establishment must have at least one representative on the staff council. The actual number of such representatives depends on the total number of members of the group. The size of the staff council itself is calculated on the basis of the number of people employed in the public sector establishment concerned. The term of office is normally four years.

The internal structures of the staff council are laid down by law. It must elect an executive board which includes at least one representative of every group present in the council, each group electing its own board member. The staff council also elects the chairperson and a vice-chairperson. The chairperson represents the council in the context of the decisions it takes. These are arrived at by an absolute majority vote of the members present. The costs of the staff council's activities are borne by the public sector establishment; this includes reimbursement of travel expenses, accommodation facilities and office staff where applicable. In public sector establishments with more than 300 employees, staff council members are granted full-time release from work.

The activities of the staff council consist essentially in exercising its participation rights, in which it is required, together with the **public-sector establishment head**, to maintain amicable **co-operation in good faith**. Its participation rights are structured along similar lines to those under the **works constitution** in the private sector, with information and consultation rights mainly in personnel matters, and co-determination rights in the context of social matters. In all these areas the staff council reaches its decisions by formal resolution. In cases where a matter to be decided concerns only one of the employee groups represented, that group alone is involved in reaching the decision. The council can also exercise its co-determination rights in concluding an **establishment agreement** with the head of the public sector establishment. If it proves impossible to come to an agreement, the matter can be referred to the **establishment-level arbitration committee**.

In all cases, the precondition for the exercise of participation rights is that the public sector establishment concerned should possess the authority to regulate the matters in question. Furthermore, if no agreement can be reached authority passes to the next-higher administrative level and the **hierarchical representation body** associated with it.

571. **PERSONALRATSWAHL — STAFF COUNCIL ELECTION**: The **staff council** is elected by direct secret ballot. All employees in the **public sector establishment** who are aged 18 or over are eligible to vote (Federal Staff Representation Act §§ 13 ff.). All those employees eligible to vote who have belonged to the sphere of activity of their top-level administrative authority for six months and have been employed in the **public service** for one year are eligible for election. The electoral procedure depends on whether joint or group-based election applies.

Elections are normally held every four years between March 1 and May 31. The staff council must form an electoral board consisting of three electors and its chairperson. If the council has failed to appoint an electoral board by six weeks before the term of office expires, this duty passes to the relevant **public-sector establishment head** on application from at least three electors or from a trade union with a presence in the establishment concerned.

If the staff council consists of only a single member there is a direct election or, where there are several candidates, proportional representation voting. If the staff council consists of several members and there are members of various employee groups in the establishment concerned, the manual workers, white-collar workers and career public servants ("Beamte") elect their own group representatives themselves on a proportional basis, unless every group has opted by majority vote in favour of a joint election. Those elected are the candidates with the proportionally largest number of votes per group or overall.

The electoral procedure for the higher-level staff representation bodies is almost identical: in this case all employees belonging to the sphere of activity of the corresponding authority are eligible to vote.

572. **PERSONALRESERVE — SUPERNUMERARY STAFF**: See **labour utilization**.

573. **PERSONALVERSAMMLUNG — GENERAL STAFF MEETING**: The public sector equivalent of the **works meeting** as provided for under the works constitution in the private sector (Federal Staff Representation Act §§ 48 ff.). It consists of all the employees in the **public sector establishment** concerned, is presided over by the chairperson of the **staff council** and is not open to the public. The staff council must convene a general staff meeting on a regular basis once every six months and present a report on its activities. The council may convene a general staff meeting at the behest of the **public-sector establishment head** concerned, and must do so if a quarter of the employees who are entitled to vote so request; the subject they wish to be discussed is then included on the agenda. If the six-monthly frequency is not maintained, a trade union that has members in the public sector establishment concerned may also insist that a general staff meeting be held. The meeting takes place during working hours, without loss of **remuneration** or **pay of career public servants**. The general staff meeting can submit proposals to the staff council and adopt a formal opinion regarding its decisions, but may discuss only matters directly affecting the establishment or its employees, particularly collectively agreed pay, career public servants' pay and social matters. It may be attended in an advisory capacity by a representative of any trade union that has members among the employees and a representative of the employers' association to which the establishment belongs. The head of the establishment may also attend, and is required to do so if the meeting has been convened at his or her behest.

574. **PERSONALVERTRETUNG — STAFF REPRESENTA-TION (BODY)**: The internal co-determination body for employees in the **public service**; to that extent it corresponds to the **works council** in the private sector. But whereas the latter may, subject to certain preconditions, be formed in any establishment, a staff representation body may be elected only in what is formally classed as a **public sector establishment**. Its statutory regulation is founded in the Federal Staff Representation Act and the staff representation laws of the individual Länder.

Staff representation in the public sector also differs from the

works constitution in the private sector in terms of its organizational structure. Mainly because the system of state administration is structured according to different levels (lower, intermediate, upper and top level public authorities), the system of staff representation is hierarchical. The organ of co-determination under staff representation law is the **staff council**. Owing to the link with public service law, disputes arising in staff representation law are dealt with by special panels within the **system of administrative courts**.

Lastly, in the public sector the limits of co-determination are defined in accordance with different legal criteria. Substantively, of course, the main emphasis of consultation and co-determination rights lies in social and personnel matters. But whereas the limits of co-determination under works constitution law in the private sector tend to be imposed by entrepreneurial freedom as guaranteed under the Constitution, for the purposes of legal judgments in the context of co-determination under staff representation law in the public sector the determining factor lies in the provisions of the Constitution relating to the organization of the state. There is general agreement in case law that the limits of the co-determination and consultation rights of the staff representation body are imposed by the core area of state jurisdiction and the functioning of the state apparatus. This means that a true right of co-determination is excluded in areas where the public service employer is directly responsible to Parliament as the representative of the sovereign people, since the staff representation body has not been duly elected by the latter. It is also excluded in areas where there is a danger of prejudice to the functioning of the state and the core area of state jurisdiction is therefore affected.

575. **PERSONENBEDINGTE KÜNDIGUNG — DISMISSAL ON GROUNDS OF PERSONAL CAPABILITY: Termination with notice** or **summary termination** of an employment relationship by the employer which is justified by a circumstance relating to the employee's personal attributes (Protection Against Dismissal Act § 1). Such grounds have their origin in particular permanent personal characteristics and abilities; examples include lack of vocational, physical or mental aptitude for the work in question, advanced age and serious illness (dismissal on grounds of ill health). The dividing line between **dismissal on grounds of conduct** and on grounds of personal capability is fluid.

Employment relationships covered by **protection against dismissal** may be lawfully terminated on grounds of personal capability if the employer's interests in cancelling the relationship outweigh the employee's interests in maintaining it. Since in this

253

case the employees concerned are in particular need of protection, the requirements applied in weighing up the interests are especially rigorous in comparison with the case of dismissal on grounds of conduct or **redundancy**.

In weighing up the respective interests consideration must be given, in the employee's favour, to whether the impairment of performance being asserted as justification for dismissal has occurred in the course of employment in the establishment. It is particularly important, in observance of the **proportionality principle**, to examine whether on the basis of the employee's abilities he or she can continue to be employed in a different vacant job in the establishment or elsewhere in the company. If this is so, possibly after re-training or further training which the employer could reasonably be expected to arrange or after amendment of the contract of employment, and if the employee agrees to this, dismissal is almost always unlawful.

576. **PERSÖNLICHKEITSRECHT — RIGHT TO PRIVACY OF THE INDIVIDUAL**: The general right to individual privacy guarantees the inviolability of an individual's immediate personal sphere of existence. It embraces, for example, their honour, good character and public reputation, the right to their own physical appearance and their own name, and their intimate personal life. The concept was defined by the case law of the Federal Constitutional Court and Federal Court of Justice, as derived from the guarantees of human dignity and personal liberty, and ranks as a **basic right**.

The purpose of the general right to individual privacy is to provide more flexible and comprehensive protection than that guaranteed by the traditional fundamental freedoms. Its protective scope is therefore not rigidly defined, and it is open to further development. In 1983, for example, the Federal Constitutional Court derived from it the **right of self-determination over personal data**.

Since its protective scope is wide-ranging, exercise of the general right to individual privacy frequently gives rise to conflicts with the interests of third parties, particularly the freedom to express their opinion. In the event of its unjustified infringement the individual concerned is entitled, irrespective of whether such infringement is on the part of organs of the state or of private persons, to claim eradication of the consequences of the infringement and abstention in the future from the wrongful act concerned. In serious cases (gross defamation, for example) they are also entitled to be paid compensation for pain and distress ("Schmerzensgeld").

577. **POLITISCHER STREIK — POLITICAL STRIKE**: As distinct from a **strike** intended to impose the aims of a collective agreement, a political strike is directed not against the employer but against Parliament or the Government; the intention is that the latter, in order to avoid damage to the national economy as a whole, will thereby be prevailed upon to take a particular form of action, *e.g.* to pass a law. Since they are not directed at aims that can be regulated by collective bargaining, political strikes are deemed to be contrary to law.

578. **PRAKTIKUM — WORK EXPERIENCE**: Period of work familiarization which may be part of general education (*e.g.* higher education), in which case the individual concerned (the "Praktikant") is neither covered by the provisions of labour law nor liable to **social security** contributions. It may, however, also be in the context of a legal relationship with the employer similar to a conventional vocational training relationship. This term does not apply to trainees who are undergoing training with the specific view of employment in the same establishment.

579. **PRÄMIE — BONUS**: Payments made by the employer to the employee as a reward for loyal service or work performed. The payment of bonuses is normally at the employer's own discretion, although the principle of **equal treatment** must still be observed. There is a distinction between bonuses and the **incentive bonus system**, which is a form of **payment by results**.

580. **PRÄMIENSYSTEM — INCENTIVE BONUS SYSTEM**: The most widespread form of **payment by results** next to **piece-work**, which it resembles. In addition to basic pay, employees receive a percentage which may be related to the quality and quantity of the work result they have achieved. This performance related system differs from piecework in that the increase in earnings is not directly proportional to the increase in quantitative output, not least because quality is a major factor.

581. **PROBEARBEITSVERHÄLTNIS — PROBATIONARY EMPLOYMENT RELATIONSHIP**: Arrangement whereby the employer and employee have the opportunity to test whether they themselves, their contracting partner and the job in question come up to expectations and long-term collaboration seems possible.
    Although a probationary period is compulsory only in the case of a **vocational training relationship**, such an arrangement is normally agreed between the parties to a contract of employment. It may be agreed both as a **fixed-term employment relationship** and as an open-ended employment relationship. Setting a fixed

term to an employment relationship for the purpose of a mutual trial period is lawful in principle, but firstly this purpose must constitute the content of the contract and secondly the duration of the fixed term must be in proportion to the requirements associated with the job in question. Consequently, as a general principle the probationary period may not exceed four months for "easy" work and six months for more difficult jobs. Usually, however, a probationary period is agreed within an open-ended employment relationship. In such cases, the effect of the probationary period is that until it expires the required periods of notice are reduced to the minimum, *i.e.* one month for **white-collar workers** and two weeks for **manual workers**, in each case up to the end of a calendar month, unless the relevant collective agreement provides otherwise. After the probationary period has been completed, the open-ended probationary employment relationship automatically turns into a normal employment relationship.

582. **PRODUKTIONSWEISE — MODE OF PRODUCTION**: The mode of production is embodied in the prevailing economic system, in the Federal Republic in that of the **social market economy** and, as in the other developed Western countries, characterized by industrial capitalism. Principal features are the separation of home from workplace caused by the factory system, and the division of society into those who own the means of production and those who must sell their labour in order to survive. Wage-earning workers perform their work subject to someone else's control and (according to Marxian terminology) are thereby exploited, *i.e.* the value of the services rendered or products manufactured is greater than the wages paid to them. The antagonistic division into capital and labour is in this view the basis of **industrial conflict**. In has, however, been lessened in many respects in the process of the development of industrial capitalism, particularly through the activity of the **trade unions**, and the influences have shifted to some extent in the course of **structural change**.

583. **PRODUKTIVE WINTERBAUFÖRDERUNG — PROMO-TION OF WINTER CONSTRUCTION**: See **winter assistance for the construction industry**.

584. **PRODUKTIVITÄT — PRODUCTIVITY**: Coefficient used in economics as a measure of the productiveness of production. It is the ratio of output to the input of one factor, either labour or capital. Productivity can be increased by means of **process innovations**, higher utilization of capacity and improved **work**

organization. It is normally the guide figure for **collective bargaining** on pay increases, **reduction of working hours** and other areas of regulation affecting costs.

585. **PRODUKTZYKLUS — PRODUCT CYCLE**: Prototype description of the sales curve of a commodity from its launch on the market through the phases of growth, maturity and stagnation. The product cycle influences the **structural change** of industries. Its tendency to become shorter necessitates a particular flexibility of manufacture which is being sought through, for example, **new production concepts**.

586. **PROKURA — COMMERCIAL POWER OF ATTORNEY**: A limited form of power of attorney. It confers normally unlimited power to act as an authorized signatory for a principal judicially and extra-judicially in all matters involved in running a commercial business or legally constituted **form of company**, but not in real property transactions unless they are expressly included. It is granted and cancelled by the owner of a commercial business or the owner's representative, and by the **management board** or **managing director** of a legally constituted form of company. Sole signatories (Einzelprokurist) exercise their authority alone, while joint signatories (Gesamtprokurist) do so in conjunction with other signatories. Conferral and dispossession of commercial power of attorney must be formally notified for entry in the Commercial Register. Its grant and cancellation have no effect in terms of labour law on the existence of the **employment relationship**. Also, authorized signatories are not necessarily **executive staff**.

587. **PROVISION — COMMISSION**: If employees are paid commission, they are entitled to a certain percentage of the gross value of certain transactions. These may be any transactions concluded in a particular sphere, but they are usually transactions which the employees themselves have concluded or arranged. Commission is therefore also typical of **commercial representatives**. It is deemed to be **remuneration**. Although employees who earn their remuneration partly or even wholly in the form of commission are able to increase it by working harder, as in the case of **payment by results**, commission should not be equated with the latter.

588. **PROZESSVERTRETUNG — REPRESENTATION IN COURT**: State in which a third person acts for one of the parties in a lawsuit; in principle anybody may have themselves represented by other persons possessing the capacity to appear

in court, but representation by lawyers is prescribed for particular court procedures of the various **systems of jurisdiction**.

In the rules of **labour court procedure**, representation for the "**Urteil**" and "**Beschluss**" **procedures** is regulated as follows. In the first-instance Labour Courts the parties may both appear on their own behalf and be represented. In addition to representation by a lawyer, representatives of **trade unions** or **employers' associations**, or of groupings of such organizations, may also act for them. In the Land Labour Courts there must be representation by lawyers or such union and association representatives, and in the Federal Labour Court only lawyers may appear for the parties concerned.

For proceedings in the system of finance courts, the parties may represent themselves in all instances. In the systems of social security courts and administrative courts they may represent themselves in the courts of first instance and in the Land Social Security Courts and Higher Administrative Courts. Otherwise, there must be representation by suitably qualified persons.

589. **PSV**: Pensions-Sicherungs-Verein (**Pension Security Association**).

Q

590. **QUALIFIKATION — SKILL**: Competence or aptitude for a particular type of work or employment. It encompasses qualifications acquired both in general and higher education and also in the context of a **vocational training relationship**, in many cases updated and developed through **in-service training**. The number and nature of recognized occupations requiring training are constantly adjusted to the needs of the economy. Skills have a major influence on the occupational mobility of employees, and their importance is growing. **New production concepts**, for example, rely not only on employees' occupational proficiency as such but also on their skills in a broader sense, *i.e.* a general intellectual flexibility and problem-solving ability. This has resulted in the fact that even for jobs which require training from scratch only employees who have completed their vocational training are used. The trend is towards a general rise in skill levels, and this is also having the effect that the key positions in the establishment as regards the effectiveness of strikes are shifting to the technicians and engineers.

Classification into **pay grades** is frequently based on skill characteristics, with differentiation according to qualifying accomplishments, *i.e.* vocational training completed, and specific task descriptions of the particular job or area of production concerned. The shift in work content towards monitoring, anticipation of errors and elimination of faults which is occurring with new production concepts makes such a skill-based system of pay and grading more appropriate than the payment by results that has been common in the context of mass production. Not least because of its significance for grading purposes, the maintenance of skill levels is one of the aims of **protection against rationalization**. Since skills are also linked with the continuous practice of an occupation, **unemployment** is accompanied by a progressive "de-skilling" which, as the duration of unemployment becomes longer, can result in the individuals affected becoming unemployable. The Federal Employment Service seeks to overcome this danger by means of employment promotion measures, for example **job creation schemes** or re-training.

591. **QUALITATIVE TARIFPOLITIK — QUALITATIVE BARGAINING POLICY**: Policy which seeks to tie in calls for **humanization of work** and **protection against rationalization** with collective agreements. The trade unions in the Federal Republic are pursuing on principle the strategy of active structural change. This involves co-operating in creating the necessary conditions for the growth of new industries and endeavouring

259

to mitigate the effects on employees in stagnant sectors and to safeguard the terms already achieved when companies are carrying out adjustment measures. The formative elements have been present in collective agreements since the end of the 1970s, but their translation into reality often comes to nothing because they are confined to regulations at establishment level, there is a lack of co-ordination between agreements on pay, human resource planning and skill levels, and the powers of the works councils are insufficient. As yet, there has been no inclusion in collective agreements of a **human- and environment-centred technology strategy**.

592. **QUALITÄTSSICHERUNG — QUALITY ASSURANCE**: The condition of an article as regards its fitness for purpose, *i.e.* its quality, is of crucial importance during the manufacturing process and for its marketability. On the assumption that deviations in quality from the established standard are due to chance occurrences (*e.g.* connected with employees' efficiency or differences of interpretation in materials testing), considerable efforts are therefore devoted, particularly in mass production, to reducing these contingencies with the aid of **new technologies**. Use is made, for example, of computer aided quality assurance (CAQ), which was developed for the purpose, and attempts are made to minimize sources of error by means of automation and correspondingly improved forms of **work organization**. Quality assurance is particularly important in **new production concepts** which aim to eliminate buffer stocks of materials and stockpiling of products, in the manufacture of **microelectronics** and in **biotechnology and chemical technologies**. In these areas adherence to an established quality standard frequently results in shiftwork and work on Sundays.

593. **QUOTIERUNG — QUOTA SYSTEM**: A form of "positive action" which is a politically and legally controversial instrument of the **advancement of women**, introduced into the debate in recent years, with the purpose of eliminating existing situations of discrimination against women. It involves the introduction of quota regulations for Government and political party offices and for posts in the **public service** but also to some extent in **trade unions** and the private sector.

Models of the quota system provide either that a certain percentage of a certain number of posts must be reserved exclusively for women, or that (where there are both male and female applicants available) for certain posts female applicants must be given preference over male applicants. In 1988, for example, the Social Democratic Party introduced a variant of the first model whereby men and women must each have at least 40 per cent. representation among officials in office and candidates for public offices. And some Länder use moderate variants of the second model for the allocation of posts in the public service under which, for instance, although allocation continues to be based primarily on applicants' skill level and degree of need, where these are equal preference must be given to female applicants. On the basis of the **welfare state principle**, such contraventions of the principle of **equality before the law** have been held by the Administrative Courts to be lawful if a corresponding statutory regulation exists. At present, however, there is a case pending before the Federal Constitutional Court in which the compatibility of quota systems with the **Basic Law** is being examined.

R

594. RAHMENGESETZ — FRAMEWORK STATUTE: In addition to legislation on the basis of **exclusive legislative powers** and **concurrent legislative powers**, the Federal Parliament is able to enact framework statutes in accordance with its framework legislative powers. It is permitted to do this only in matters where there is a need for uniform regulation throughout the Federal Republic. It may not, however, regulate a matter exhaustively by framework statutes, but merely lay down a framework within which the regulation of details must be left to the legislative bodies of the Länder. So long as the Federal legislature makes no use of these powers, the Länder possess full authority for legislation.

595. RAHMENTARIFVERTRAG — GENERAL AGREEMENT ON PAY GRADES: Wage and salary grading systems are usually regulated specially by general agreements on wage and salary grades. These normally define between five and seven wage grades for **manual workers,** and for **white-collar workers** five or seven salary grades and three to four supervisor grades. They specify the characteristics with which an activity must comply in order for the employee to be entitled to the corresponding pay. Owing to the abstract nature of the descriptions given, there is frequently still room for decision-making in the actual classification of a particular activity. Such agreements may also contain provisions on methods of pay determination and the practical details of pay calculation, such as fixing the standard times allowed per unit of output in the case of **piecework.**

As a rule, general agreements on pay grades are concluded for a term of several years since, unlike the fixing of pay levels, the matters they regulate do not need to be adjusted all that frequently.

596. RANDBELEGSCHAFT — PERIPHERAL WORKFORCE: See **labour market.**

597. RATIONALISIERUNG — RATIONALIZATION: Process aimed at the improvement of existing circumstances in the establishment, as manifested in greater technical and economic efficiency. It is made possible by process innovations such as the use of more versatile equipment and general-purpose materials and by more highly skilled employees and appropriately adjusted forms of **work organization.** Often, it is also the outcome of reciprocally induced standardization and automation of production. An important part in regularization through the establishment of uniform standards is played by **rationalization associations.** Rationalization has a vitally important influence on the nature and volume of human labour. Firstly, it frequently leads to its elimination or devaluation, and is therefore significant as regards **redundancies**; to offset disadvantages for employees there are arrangements for **protection against rationalization** at **collective agreement** level and **"social plans"** at establishment level. Secondly, the rationalized production process demands higher **skill** levels on the part of employees. Recently, in addition to increased efficiency in the strict sense the improvement of quality in the context of **quality assurance**, as an integral element of **new production concepts**, for example, has been gaining growing importance as another of the objectives of rationalization. The trend in rationalization is not merely shaped by the actual potential technologically available, but must be seen as the outcome of a complex process in which divergent user interests and motives for rationalization underlie alternative forms of technology selection and their application (**technology impact analysis**). Nevertheless, the indications are that the introduction of new technologies is turning the trend away from *ad hoc* rationalization as applied to individual functions, and towards systemic rationalization. The **economic committee** must be provided with information on any rationalization programmes. If rationalization results in a major alteration to the establishment, negotiations must be carried out with the works council on a reconcilement of interests and a "social plan".

598. RATIONALISIERUNGSKURATORIUM DER DEUTSCHEN WIRTSCHAFT — BOARD FOR RATIONALIZATION OF THE GERMAN ECONOMY: An association (referred to as the RKW) with 8,000 members within which the Federal Government and the Länder, employer and employee representatives and academics co-operate with the aim of improving the performance of the German economy in terms of technological, economic, social and environmental considerations by means of advisory services, further training and provision of information. The RKW has five specialist advisory committees in the fields of labour and social management, business management, technology, packaging and construction and so far is represented by Land groups in all the western Germany Länder and Berlin. In addition to employers and **trade unions**, the Federal Government and the Länder concerned, which contribute virtually half of the total budget, are represented on the executive board.

599. RATIONALISIERUNGSSCHUTZ — PROTECTION AGAINST RATIONALIZATION: The first examples of moves to offset **rationalization**-induced disadvantages for employees on a **collective agreement** basis were in the 1960s, when regulations were agreed in various branches of industry providing for re-training wherever possible, extended **periods of notice** and financial compensation for the individuals concerned in the event of job loss or phased compensatory payments in the event of downgrading to lower **pay grades**. Whereas in the beginning rationalization measures were still in conformity with the mutual interests of employers and employees, *i.e.* the long-term and conflict-free utilization of available labour on the one hand and material remuneration on the other, from the mid-1970s onwards disagreements at collective bargaining level began to intensify as a consequence of far-reaching restructuring processes and altered demands on labour. Since then trade union demands, partly in connection with **qualitative bargaining policy**, have focused on the protection of employment levels, the maintenance and upgrading of skill levels and the shaping of employment conditions with emphasis on the **humanization of work**. Recently, however, there has also been evidence of a broadening of the regulatory scope of collective agreements and of **works council** participation rights extending beyond the traditional areas. This ranges from regulations on the protection of employment as regards pay levels, and arrangements on work organization, to provisions aimed at securing a direct influence on technological and organizational changes, or at least subjecting them to some measure of control. The employers' side, which is resisting this, justifies its attitude not only with economic considerations but also on the grounds that the opportunities for control over investment provided by "Rationalisierungsschutzabkommen" (rationalization protection agreements) contravene the principles of the **social market economy** and the Basic Law.

The functions fulfilled by such agreements at collective level are in many cases covered at establishment level by the "**social plan**".

**600. RATIONALISIERUNGSVERBAND —
RATIONALIZATION ASSOCIATION**: Associations which promote rationalization measures, usually through the collection and definition of standards and uniform types (DIN, *i.e.* German Standards Institute), in which they are released from the obligation normally imposed by the laws on competition to declare their recommendations and indications as non-binding, or through the financing of long-term rationalization investment. One of the most prominent examples is in coal mining.

The "Coal Mining Rationalization Association" (Rationalisierungsverband des Steinkohlebergbaus) has as its members all operators of collieries with an annual output of at least 100,000 tonnes. Forms of assistance are normally financed from members' contributions.

601. RECHT AUF ARBEIT — RIGHT TO WORK: See **freedom of occupation, promotion of employment**.

602. RECHT AUF INFORMATIONELLE SELBSTBESTIM-MUNG — RIGHT OF SELF-DETERMINATION OVER PERSONAL DATA: A separate and specific form of the general **right to privacy of the individual**, covered by the guarantees of human dignity and personal liberty (**basic rights**). It guarantees individuals the freedom to decide for themselves whether data concerning their person may be disseminated.

The concept of such a right was defined by the Federal Constitutional Court in 1983. The background to this ruling was the extraordinarily rapid increase in the capacity and spread of electronic data processing, which meant that an unlimited quantity of personal data could be stored and then accessed at any time and at any place. These systems, particularly when linked with others, make it possible to build up a comprehensive picture of any individual within a matter of seconds, without their knowledge. The awareness that any act can be recorded and stored without restriction as an item of data can exert enormous pressure to conform on potential subjects and hence limit their personal liberty, and therefore constitutes a threat to democratic freedom of thought and speech. Furthermore, as the technology becomes increasingly powerful there is a corresponding increase in the possibilities of misuse and the inherent sources of error. If incorrect data, data taken out of context or inaccurate data is stored over a lengthy period in instantly retrievable form in an information system that can be accessed by a large number of users, the implications are totally different from what they would be if the information were contained in documents in a conventional filing system.

The Federal Constitutional Court therefore guaranteed every individual the right of self-determination over the disclosure and use of data concerning their person. This right is, nevertheless, limited by legitimate interests of the state or third parties: if a particular purpose (such as bringing criminals to justice) necessitates storage without the knowledge or consent of the individuals concerned, this is lawful. The user in question must, however, be empowered to carry out such storage by a statute which regulates clearly the preconditions and extent of storage and which observes the **proportionality principle**, *i.e.* encroaches on this right of self-determination only to the extent necessary to achieve the purpose intended by the legislators. Data collected on such a basis must be used strictly as designated, *i.e.* data stored for a particular purpose may not be used for other purposes for which storage is subject to different legal criteria. The right of self-determination over personal data is guaranteed by the provisions on **data protection**.

603. **RECHTSBESCHWERDE — JUDICIAL REVIEW APPLICATION**: The **remedy at law** in the **"Beschluss" procedure** against decisions by the Land Labour Courts and also, in the form of a **direct judicial review application**, against decisions by the first-instance Labour Courts. Such applications are heard by the Federal Labour Court. Since the proceedings do not constitute a rehearing, the decision forming the basis of the application may not be examined as to questions of fact, but purely as to questions of law. Such an application may be lodged only if leave to do so has been granted by the Land Labour Court or if a non-admission petition against refusal of such leave has been successful. A judicial review application is the equivalent in the "Beschluss" procedure of an **appeal on a point of law** in the **"Urteil" procedure**, and is admissible in the same cases.

604. **RECHTSFORTBILDUNG — FURTHER DEVELOPMENT OF THE LAW**: Term indicating the adjustment of existing law to new needs and developments in society. It comes about as a result of additions or amendments made to codified law by the legislators, but above all through **case law**, particularly where whole areas have been left without regulation by the legislators. Precisely because of its inherent momentum, **labour law** undergoes constant recasting and adjustment, since broad areas of it need to be adjusted as soon as possible to the realities of economic and social policy. Supplementary **judge-made law** is an important **source of law** in the sphere of labour law.

605. **RECHTSMITTEL — REMEDY AT LAW**: The constitutional guarantee of comprehensive protection of legal rights against decisions and acts of the Federal Government, Länder and other territorial authorities, their administrative agencies and public-law institutions, the courts of law and all other entities under public law (**legal person**) is effected through various remedies at law. In its strict sense, the term "Rechtsmittel" refers only to appeal against judicial decisions; for procedure in administrative matters, an appeal is referred to as "Rechtsbehelf".

When a judicial appeal or administrative appeal is lodged, the result is that the decision becomes legally non-valid or the legality of an actual act is examined. The way in which this occurs is that, on the strength of an administrative appeal or judicial appeal, the decision of a state or public-law institution is inspected by the latter itself or by a higher-ranking public authority or first- or higher-instance courts. There are only a few exceptions to the principle of comprehensive protection of legal rights: examples include a number of acts to institute legal proceedings and the decisions of the **Federal Constitutional Court**. Likewise, no appeal is possible against last-instance decisions, in so far as they do not involve any contravention of **basic rights**.

The various legal and administrative remedies available are regulated by the particular rules of procedure of the individual **systems of jurisdiction** or the legislation concerning encroachment on the legal position of the individual or concerning guarantee of benefits. Guidance for individuals on the corresponding remedies is provided by **instructions on right of appeal**. In the broadest sense, remedies include **appeal**, **"Beschluss" procedure appeal**, **non-admission petition**, **appeal on a point of law**, **direct judicial review application**, and **direct appeal on a point of law**, objection and protest in tax and administrative matters, the mechanisms for temporary protection of legal rights (distraint order, **interlocutory injunction** or court order) and remedies in the context of **enforcement of judgment** (*e.g.* objection, third-party objection and petition to cancel enforcement order). In addition to effecting one of these remedies it is also possible, subject to certain conditions, to re-institute fresh proceedings.

The question of which remedy is available in the context of **labour court procedure** is governed firstly by whether a case is dealt with in the **"Urteil" procedure** or **"Beschluss" procedure** and secondly by the instance in which a particular decision has been issued. In the "Urteil" procedure, appeal against decisions of the first-instance Labour Courts (ArbG) is lodged with the relevant Land Labour Court (LAG) or as a direct appeal on a point of law with the Federal Labour Court (BAG), and against decisions of the LAG as an appeal on a point of law with the BAG. In the "Beschluss" procedure, appeal against the first-instance ArbG is lodged with the relevant LAG or as a direct judicial review application with the BAG, and against decisions of the LAG as a judicial review application with the BAG.

606. RECHTSMITTELBELEHRUNG — INSTRUCTIONS ON RIGHT OF APPEAL: In the **labour court procedure**, procedure under the **Social Security Code** and before the **social security courts**, procedure in administrative matters and administrative court procedure and tax matters, written information indicating the appropriate **remedy at law** available must be issued to individuals to whom a decision is addressed by the state or some other public-law legal person, its administrative agencies or institutions. These instructions contain details on the time limit for lodging an appeal and the authority with which it should be lodged, together with information on other formal preconditions. The statutory period within which appeal is allowable does not commence until the correct instructions have been issued; in general, the form of appeal concerned may be lodged within one year from when the decision is delivered.

In the specific case of procedure in administrative matters, these instructions are called "Rechtsbehelfsbelehrung".

607. RECHTSPRECHUNG — CASE LAW: The decisions of the labour courts, particularly the **Federal Labour Court**, are of paramount importance in labour matters. **Judge-made law** as shaped by court decisions, in part via **further development of the law** and legal **interpretation**, supplements areas which have been left unregulated by **legislation** or have been regulated only in the form of general clauses.

608. RECHTSQUELLEN — SOURCES OF LAW: The question of sources of law arises in general where a natural circumstance of life has to be assessed judicially or a conflict in the field of labour relations is to be resolved at law. In the broad sense, a source of law is any directive provision which is recognized by the members of a particular sphere of the legal system as generally binding and which, when occasion arises, is also enforced against individuals. In the Federal Republic sources of law are the **Constitution, statutes,** unwritten customary law, law derived from **further development of the law**, and in some areas also **judge-made law**. In the case of **labour law**, additional sources are **collective agreements**, **works agreements**, in special circumstances **semi-formal works agreements** and, lastly, the individual **contract of employment**.

Sources of law alone do not, however, suffice to determine what is ultimately lawful in the individual case; abstract principles need to be transformed into social reality by way of an effective set of procedures for applying the law.

609. RECHTSSTREITIGKEIT — DISPUTE OF RIGHTS: Term used to refer to disputes in which the matter at issue is the question of whether the preconditions exist for the application of an existing rule of law with legal effect. If the parties or participants are asserting concrete claims, this constitutes a dispute of rights. For disputes relating to the law on the works constitution, a distinction is made between disputes of rights and

disputes of interest. Disputes of rights are decided by the **system of labour courts**, while disputes of interest are decided by the **establishment-level arbitration committee**.

610. RECHTSVERORDNUNG — EXECUTIVE ORDER: A law in the substantive sense, with authority derived from a statute, ranking in hierarchical terms between a formal **statute** and an **act of administration**. In contrast to a formal statute, although an executive order contains an abstract regulation universally applicable to a large number of individual cases it does not come into being via a formal legislative procedure, which in accordance with the principle of the distribution of powers is required for the promulgation of generally binding legal provisions. The **Constitution** does, however, make provision for the Executive to be empowered to promulgate executive orders, subject to observance of the **reservation of parliamentary powers**.

A statute conferring powers to promulgate executive orders must define the content, purpose and extent of the authorization thereby granted. It must be possible for the individual citizen to ascertain in which cases and with which intent such authorization may be utilized, and the permitted content of the executive orders to be promulgated. An executive order, in its turn, must state the basis on which it is authorized. It is also possible to make the promulgation of executive orders subject to the assent of the **Federal Council** or **Federal Parliament**. Also, an executive order, like a statute, must be announced in the Federal Law Gazette (Bundesgesetzblatt) or in the Law Gazette or Official Gazette of the individual Land concerned. If a lawsuit depends on the validity of an executive order, the court concerned must examine this as an incidental issue. Otherwise, direct control by the courts is possible only to a limited extent; even an examination of individual executive orders by the **Federal Constitutional Court** is not permissible. Executive orders play a significant part in practice, and their coverage is more extensive than that of regulation by formal statutes.

611. REGELUNGSABREDE — SEMI-FORMAL WORKS AGREEMENT: Synonym of **Betriebsabsprache**.

612. REGELUNGSKOMPETENZ DER TARIFVERTRAGS-PARTEIEN — REGULATORY POWERS OF THE COLLECTIVE BARGAINING PARTIES: See **limits of bargaining powers**.

613. REGELUNGSSTREITIGKEIT — DISPUTE OF INTEREST: In the sphere of labour law, a distinction is made between **disputes of rights** and disputes of interest. In a dispute of interest, the matter at issue may be both whether a regulation or measure should be adopted at all, and also how the content of a regulation or measure should be shaped. This category includes, in particular, disputes which are based on the exercise of a right of co-determination by the **works council** (dispute of interest relating to the law on the works constitution). They are decided not by the labour courts but by the **establishment-level arbitration committee**.

614. **REGIERUNGSVORLAGE — GOVERNMENT BILL**: A draft of a proposed statute which the Federal Government submits first to the **Federal Council** for comment and then to the **Federal Parliament** for adoption.

615. **REHABILITATION**: Term covering measures aimed at helping physically, mentally or psychologically disabled employees to be absorbed into the work process.

Primary responsibility for such measures lies with the **Federal Employment Service**. It promotes the integration into working life of disabled persons or individuals for whom disablement is impending, by means of programmes for vocational training and further training, the payment of maintenance allowances and the grant of training subsidies for employers. It is also able to award employers loans and grants for the improvement, enlargement and equipping of workplaces for disabled persons (Employment Promotion Act §§ 56 ff.).

616. **RELIGIONSGEMEINSCHAFTEN — RELIGIOUS COMMUNITIES**: A Religious Community, or Church, is an organization constituted as a single entity with a particular theological creed which differentiates it from other Religious Communities and serves as the basis for its own doctrine. Religious Communities generally have the status of public-law entities. They do not, however, possess sovereign authority and are organizationally separate from the state (as they already were during the time of the Weimar Republic). Within narrow limits the corporate Religious Communities are, nevertheless, authorized by the state to exercise individual sovereign powers, mainly the levy of taxes from their members. The Basic Law guarantees all Religious Communities the right to order and administer their affairs independently within the limits laid down by law and to confer tenure of their offices without intervention from the state. This autonomy for the Religious Communities in their capacity as organizations is the parallel to the **basic right** of freedom of faith which is guaranteed to every individual. It has considerable

significance as a protective right against state intervention in their internal organization, *i.e.* above all where the Religious Communities regulate matters which they themselves perceive as part of their religious practice in relations between their individual institutions or with their members in the capacity of members of the Religious Communities. By virtue of the case law of the Federal Constitutional Court, however, this autonomy also has importance where the Religious Communities, their subdivisions or institutions belonging to them or associated with their religious aims engage in activities governed by private law. Their employment of **employees**, in particular, is governed by extensive special regulations (**ecclesiastical labour law**) as distinct from general **labour law**.

617. **RENTE — STATUTORY PENSION**: See **statutory pension scheme, statutory retirement pension**.

618. **RENTENVERSICHERUNG — STATUTORY PENSION SCHEME**: The majority of gainfully active individuals working as employees, and some of those working on a self-employed basis, are subject to obligatory insurance under the statutory pension scheme. The protection provided covers **total disability**, **occupational incapacity**, retirement and death of the insured persons. The **statutory retirement pension** is paid from the age of 65 onwards in the normal case, but in certain cases earlier than this. For example, women, **disabled persons** and the unemployed are entitled to an early retirement pension from the age of 60 onwards; apart from that for disabled persons, however, these exceptions are to be abolished within the next few years. If the insured person dies, there are entitlements to a widow's or widower's pension and to an orphan's pension for children still attending school or undergoing vocational training.

The existence of these entitlements is subject to the completion of a **qualifying period**. The amount of the pension is graduated according to the income of the insured person and the duration of the insurance period. Depending on their own income, survivors receive between 40 and 60 per cent. of the pension entitlement of the insured person who has died. In 1986 the average monthly pensions were 1,600 Deutschmarks for manual workers and 1,900 Deutschmarks for white-collar workers; average pensions for women were almost one third lower than those for men. Pensions are adjusted regularly in line with economic trends.

Owing to the trend in the population structure, particularly the decline in the birth rate since the 1960s and the rise in life expectancy, the costs of the statutory pension scheme will continue to increase steadily in the foreseeable future. They are financed in equal proportions from contributions paid by the insured persons and by their employers, plus sizeable subsidies from the public authorities from time to time. The institutions which administer the scheme are various funds established at Federal and Länder level. Disputes relating to such insurance are dealt with by the **system of social security courts**.

619. **REVISION — APPEAL ON A POINT OF LAW**: The **remedy at law** in the "Urteil" **procedure** against appeal judgments by the Land Labour Courts (LAG) and also, in the form of a **direct appeal on a point of law**, against judgments by the first-instance Labour Courts. Such applications are heard by the Federal Labour Court (BAG). In addition to serving the interests of the parties, the remedy of appeal on a point of law promotes the consistency of court decisions and hence the security of justice.

Such an application does not enable the appeal judgment to be re-examined as to questions of fact, but purely as to questions of law. It may be lodged only if leave to do so has been granted by the Land Labour Court or if a non-admission petition to the Federal Labour Court against refusal of such leave has been successful. It must be admitted if the dispute is of fundamental importance or if in its decision the Land Labour Court has diverged from that of a higher court. If no decision has as yet been issued by a higher court on the point of law at issue, the appeal must also be admitted if the decision diverges from another decision by a Land Labour Court. The equivalent remedy in the "Beschluss" **procedure** is the **judicial review application**.

Appeal on a point of law is also available in proceedings before the ordinary, finance, social security and administrative courts in accordance with the relevant rules of procedure.

620. **RICHTERRECHT — JUDGE-MADE LAW**: Term referring to legal principles developed by **case law**. It also applies to examples where the courts initiate **further development of the law** or interpret statutory provisions.

In labour law, many areas such as the law on **industrial action** and **employee liability** are not regulated at all by statute, while in others there are general clauses which need to be supplemented by court decisions. As the court of highest instance the Federal Labour Court is of paramount importance in shaping judge-made law.

621. **RICHTLINIE — DIRECTIVE**: Term mainly denoting what are called administrative regulations ("Verwaltungsvorschriften"). It refers to separate general instructions emanating from

a public authority to a lower-ranking authority or from a superior official to subordinate staff (**career public servants, manual workers** and **white-collar workers** in the **public service**). Their effect is therefore purely internal. Although they are binding and hence constitute legal principles, since they do not have external effect they do not count as **laws.**

Legal instruments adopted by the EC Commission for the purposes of harmonization of the laws of Member States are also referred to as Directives.

622. **RUHEGELD — OCCUPATIONAL PENSION**: The benefit payable from an **occupational pension scheme** to employees who have left the establishment. Entitlement and amount depend on the nature of the **assurance of an occupational pension** on the part of the employer. Since its function is a supplementary one, it usually starts at the same time as the pension payable from the **statutory pension scheme**, *i.e.* usually from the age of 65 onwards and (if provision of an invalidity pension has also been guaranteed) in the event of occupational incapacity or total disability.

Employers are under an obligation to check every three years to see whether current pension payments should be adjusted to changes in the cost of living. Their decision on the matter is discretionary; it may not, however, be made arbitrarily but must give due consideration to the interests of the pensioners concerned. In normal cases, this gives rise to an obligation to adjust pensions in line with economic trends, which those entitled to the pension can enforce in the labour courts. The yardstick for adjustment is the change in the cost-of-living index for a four-member employee household with an average income. The adjustment need not be more than the growth in the real earnings paid to active employees, even if the rise in the cost of living actually exceeds this. It may be partly or wholly omitted if it would impose an excessive burden on the company. This becomes a possibility if the rise in pension costs exceeds the company's expected capital growth and earnings yield.

Once the payment of an occupational pension has commenced, entitlement may be revoked or reduced only in exceptional cases. One possible example is serious violation by the pension recipient of obligations deriving from the **retirement pension relationship**, such as taking up employment in competition with the former employer despite the existence of a non-competition covenant. Economic difficulties for the company may constitute justification for discontinuing or reducing pension payments subject to the same conditions as those for reductions in the assurance of an occupational pension. In carrying out the reconcilement of interests necessary in such cases, however, special priority is given to the interests of pension recipients whose entitlements have already been earned in full.

623. **RUHESTANDSVERHÄLTNIS — RETIREMENT PENSION RELATIONSHIP**: Where an employer guarantees an employee who leaves the establishment payments from an **occupational pension scheme**, after the **employment relationship** that existed between the two comes to an end it is replaced by the retirement pension relationship. This places the employer under an obligation to pay the **occupational pension** guaranteed. The employee who is entitled to receive the pension must protect the employer against avoidable damage. This entails, in particular, claiming payments from the **statutory pension scheme** that can be allowed for in fixing the occupational pension, and informing the employer of this. The employer and employee may also agree on a covenant imposing a **restraint on competition** during the retirement pension relationship.

624. **RUHEZEIT — REST PERIOD**: Period of free time between the end and the resumption of a day's work. Its duration is 11 hours as the general rule, 13 hours for young employees and 10 hours in special cases. It is permissible for employees to be on-call and on **stand-by** during the rest period.

S

625. **SABBATICAL — SABBATICAL LEAVE**: An arrangement whereby **working time** is reduced by several months or a year under annual working time arrangements in the context of permanent employment relationships. It enables employees to pursue their own interests, participate in vocational or personal educational and training courses or carry on some other activity for personal benefit or charitable purposes. Training and charitable activities are supported and promoted by companies in some instances. In Germany the **employment relationship** is basically suspended during sabbatical leave, and so there is a cessation of remuneration and of entitlement to **continued payment of remuneration** in the event of **illness**. However, employees retain their entitlements to incidental benefits which are related to the existence of the employment relationship or their continuous **length of service**. A proportionate reduction of **leave** is permissible only if a **collective agreement** so provides. For calculating sick pay or holiday pay which has to be based on average earnings during the period immediately preceding the event that gives rise to entitlement, it is best to assume the income that could theoretically have been earned during sabbatical leave. Otherwise, the recommended procedure is to agree on a uniform distribution of benefits over the entire year. This also ensures continuous payment of the employer's share of **social security contributions**. If the employer concludes corresponding annual working time contracts with a large number of employees, this is subject to the **co-determination right of the works council**.

626. **SABOTAGE**: Deliberate damage to or destruction of materials, machinery and the products of work. It constitutes a breach of the contract of employment and justifies dismissal by **summary termination**. It may also be deemed a criminal offence. Sabotage is therefore not a lawful form of **industrial action**.

627. **SACHBEZÜGE — NON-PAY BENEFITS**: See **payment in kind**.

628. **SAISONARBEITSVERHÄLTNIS — SEASONAL EMPLOYMENT RELATIONSHIP**: If employment relationships are entered into for the purpose of meeting additional requirements for the duration of the season in a seasonal establishment, these are **fixed-term employment relationships**. The seasonal increase in the amount of work arising constitutes justification in law for setting a fixed term to the contract of employment.

275

629. SAISONBETRIEB — SEASONAL ESTABLISHMENT: Establishments in which, although work is carried on throughout the year, the number of employees is regularly subject to seasonal fluctuations for reasons associated with the weather, their sales or their location. For example, hotels and restaurants in health spas and holiday resorts, gravel and sand pits and stone quarries are deemed to be seasonal establishments. To enable these establishments to adjust quickly to periodically recurring changes in their staffing requirements, they are exempted from the provisions of **protection against dismissal** on collective dismissal (Protection Against Dismissal Act § 22).

630. SATZUNG — STANDING RULES: Term referring, in general, to the written set of basic rules of a legally constituted association of people. In private law, such rules exist in the case of associations and registered **forms of company** (where they are usually called "articles of association" in English). In this sphere they are established by legal act.

In public law, the term refers to what are called "byelaws" in English, *i.e.* the delegated right of certain public-law entities, such as **municipalities** or **associations of municipalities**, to regulate their own affairs within the context of their jurisdiction. This power to make byelaws is an expression of the right of self-administration (**legislation**) and must be authorized by statute. For municipalities, the power to make byelaws is regulated in the Local Authority Codes (Gemeindeordnungen) of the various Länder. The byelaws of municipalities, associations of municipalities and public-law entities are law in the substantive sense. They are subject to examination as part of the control procedure carried out by the **system of administrative courts**. By appropriate authorization in Federal or Land law, the power to make byelaws may also be extended to areas beyond the regulation of strictly local matters. In such cases a municipality, for example, is also able to issue an **executive order** instead of a byelaw.

631. SCHADENSERSATZANSPRUCH — ENTITLEMENT TO DAMAGES: If **employees** culpably fail to render the performance due from them, the **employer** is able to claim damages from them for non-performance of contract. This entitlement includes recovery of the damage that has been caused to the employer because it was necessary to cancel the **employment relationship,** and where applicable also the profit that has been lost. This entitlement to damages is to be distinguished from the compensation arising from **employer** or **employee liability**.

632. SCHICHT — SHIFT: The span of time between the start and end of **working time**, including **breaks**. In the coal-mining industry it corresponds to working time.

633. SCHICHTARBEIT — SHIFTWORK: System whereby work is performed in the same job by several employees who succeed each other, over a period of time longer than the **working time** of one individual. It permits forms of operation that require uninterrupted working, allows full utilization of capital-intensive plant and takes place in two or more **shifts**. In the case of fully continuous shiftwork, it involves special inconveniences such as **night work** and unusual **maximum working hours**. Since shiftwork also imposes burdens on employees in terms of health and the social disadvantages resulting from their unnatural rhythm, it attracts special **pay supplements** and a shorter **working week** than that for other employees is agreed by **collective agreement** for the employees concerned. Other models which seek to mitigate the burdens of shiftwork combine it with **flexitime** and/or **part-time work**.

The introduction of shiftwork is subject to the **co-determination right of the works council**.

634. SCHIEDSGERICHT — ARBITRATION TRIBUNAL: Subject to certain conditions regulated in the Labour Courts Act (Arbeitsgerichtsgesetz), instead of the **system of labour courts** labour-related cases can also be decided by arbitration tribunals with exclusive jurisdiction. These tribunals must be composed of equal numbers of employee and employer representatives, and may also include impartial members.

An arbitration tribunal arrangement is lawful only for disputes between the collective bargaining parties arising from a **collective agreement** or concerning its existence, and for disputes arising from the **employment relationships** of members of the acting profession and the film-making industry, performing artistes and seafarers whose employment relationships are governed by a collective agreement containing an arbitration tribunal arrangement. **Joint dispute resolution agreements** also often contain regulations on the establishment of an arbitration tribunal.

In proceedings before an arbitration tribunal the parties are first given an oral hearing, and the tribunal can take evidence, etc. The proceedings end with a settlement or with an arbitration award for which the reasons must be set forth. An appeal may be made to the Labour Court against the award. A compulsory **enforcement of judgment** arising from the award is possible only if the President of the Labour Court responsible for dealing with the application declares it to be enforceable.

277

635. SCHIFFSBESATZUNG — SHIP'S CREW: Special regulations apply to ship's crews, according to whether the ship in question is a seagoing or inland waterways vessel: for example, the Seafarers Act (Seemansgesetz) and the Inland Shipping Act (Binnenschiffahrtsgesetz). The provisions of the **works constitution** and **co-determination** also apply, *mutatis mutandis*, to maritime shipping companies which operate merchant fleets and have their registered head office in the Federal Republic. Under these provisions the ships of such a company are combined to form a maritime establishment. If the necessary criteria are met, a maritime works council can then be elected for such establishments (Works Constitution Act § 116). For individual ship's crews normally including at least five crew-members entitled to vote, an **on-board representation** can be elected (Works Constitution Act § 115).

636. SCHLECHTWETTERGELD — BAD-WEATHER ALLOWANCE: See **winter assistance for the construction industry**.

637. SCHLICHTUNG — JOINT DISPUTE RESOLUTION: If the negotiations of the collective bargaining parties for the conclusion of a new **collective agreement** have failed to achieve any result, a joint dispute resolution procedure normally commences which is aimed at adjusting the clash of interests and preventing the outbreak of **industrial action**. This process, sometimes inappropriately translated into English as "arbitration", may involve the use of techniques of conciliation and/or mediation. Even if industrial action has already started, the procedure can offer a way of seeking to reach a compromise and hence an end to the dispute. This is referred to as "besondere Schlichtung" (special joint dispute resolution). A distinction is made between such joint dispute resolution established by agreement between the parties ("vereinbarte Schlichtung") and dispute resolution by a state authority ("staatliche Schlichtung"), which is used only as a last resort. Joint dispute resolution is employed for disputes of interest concerning a collective agreement to be concluded in the future, but not for disputes of rights, which may be decided only by the courts. Joint dispute resolution as provided for by collective agreement or by law has consequential effects on the lawfulness of industrial action: the imposition of an obligation on the parties to carry out a joint dispute resolution procedure means that the **peace obligation** deriving from the previous collective agreement is prolonged.

278

638. SCHLICHTUNGSVEREINBARUNG — JOINT DISPUTE RESOLUTION AGREEMENT: In order to avoid **industrial action**, the collective bargaining parties may establish joint dispute resolution boards to which they refer their disputes of interest. These boards established by agreement are given precedence over the statutory conciliation or arbitration procedure. Arrangements for joint dispute resolution may be included as clauses in collective agreements or form a separate agreement. There are no differences of opinion as to their lawfulness, since the possibility of industrial action is not entirely ruled out.

Joint dispute resolution agreements exist in most industries. They are based on a model which the German Federation of Trade Unions and the Confederation of German Employers' Associations recommended their members to adopt. The agreed procedure may be initiated on the application of either or both of the parties. More recent agreements also provide that it should commence automatically following the breakdown of negotiations. A joint dispute resolution agreement places the collective bargaining parties under an obligation to make efforts to resolve their dispute before starting to engage in industrial action.

A joint dispute resolution board established by collective agreement is composed of members representing the parties involved, together with an impartial chairperson. If the board fails to arrive at a compromise proposal, or if its proposal is not accepted by both sides, the joint dispute resolution procedure is deemed to have been exhausted unsuccessfully, the peace obligation ceases to exist and industrial action may commence. If, on the other hand, the parties agree on a compromise in the joint dispute resolution procedure, the compromise achieved is regarded as constituting a new collective agreement.

639. SCHUTZFUNKTION DES TARIFVERTRAGES — PROTECTIVE FUNCTION OF COLLECTIVE AGREEMENTS: The central purpose of a collective agreement is to protect the individual employee against the economically stronger employer as far as the fixing of terms and conditions of employment is concerned. Collective agreements prevent employers from being able to dictate such terms and conditions unilaterally and thereby help to place the two sides on an equal footing. This protective function takes precedence over the other two functions of collective agreements, namely, the preservation of industrial peace and their **normative function**.

More recently, collective bargaining policy has been concentrated on regulations on **protection against rationalization** and the **reduction of working hours**. Also, there is a discernible

279

trend in current bargaining practice towards a gradual increase in normative provisions on matters connected with the design of workplaces, forms of **work organization** and work procedures. As yet, however, there are only isolated instances where the range of topics covered by collective bargaining policy extends beyond this towards core areas of employer decision-making such as decisions on investment and location, **personnel policy** and **human- and environment-centred technology strategy**.

640. **SCHWARZARBEIT — UNDECLARED EMPLOYMENT**:
The so-called "hidden economy" ("Schattenwirtschaft") costs the state and the social security institutions vast sums of money every year in terms of lost taxes and **social security contributions** as a result of undeclared unemployment (also referred to as "moonlighting" in English). Consequently, under the Control of Undeclared Employment Act (Gesetz zur Bekämpfung der Schwarzarbeit) a fine of up to 50,000 Deutschmarks can be imposed on anyone who acquires significant financial gain through the performance of work or services although they:
1. are in receipt of benefits paid by the **Federal Employment Service** and have not reported the relevant change in their personal circumstances;
2. have not registered their self-employed activity or obtained the requisite operating licence;
3. are carrying on a craft or trade as an established **business** without being registered in the Roll of Craftworkers maintained by the **Chamber of Craft Trades**.
Individuals who acquire significant financial gain from commissioning others to carry on undeclared unemployment are likewise deemed to be acting contrary to public policy. As a means of preventing undeclared employment, a special **social security card** has just been introduced. Also, the relevant authorities are making efforts to exert more intensive control over the **hiring-out of labour**.
The following are not classed as undeclared employment:
a. services rendered in a spirit of goodwill or neighbourliness;
b. work done on own account in the construction of family-owned homes or separately owned dwellings in accordance with the Second Housebuilding Act (Wohnungsbaugesetz) on an unpaid or mutual self-help basis.

641. **SCHWERBEHINDERTER — DISABLED PERSON**:
Classification applying to individuals who have a physical, mental or psychological handicap of at least 50 per cent., irrespective of its cause. (The English term "handicapped person" is also used to denote such classification.) In order to reduce the

disadvantages in working life which such individuals suffer as a result of their handicap, various protective mechanisms have been developed to promote their integration into employment. Individuals with a handicap of at least 30 per cent. may be officially classed as equivalent to disabled if it can be established that they are unable to obtain or retain a job without the benefit of **protection for disabled employees**.

642. **SCHWERBEHINDERTENBEAUFTRAGTER — DISABLED-EMPLOYEE OFFICER**: If **disabled persons** are employed in an establishment, the employer must appoint a special officer for disabled employees. This officer acts as the employer's representative, subject to instructions, in matters relating to disabled persons and has the principal function of monitoring observance of the obligations deriving from **protection for disabled employees**.

643. **SCHWERBEHINDERTENSCHUTZ — PROTECTION FOR DISABLED EMPLOYEES**: To enable **disabled persons** to be integrated into working life, the Disabled Persons Act (Schwerbehindertengesetz) provides special protection for disabled employees. The origins of these regulations date back to the Weimar Republic, where the main purpose was to safeguard the employment opportunities of war victims. Nowadays, protection for disabled employees centres on four main points: an obligation on employers to employ disabled persons; special **protection against dismissal**; special privileges during existing employment relationships; and special provision in relation to the law on the works constitution, in the form of a **representative body for disabled employees**.

The obligation to employ disabled persons applies to all employers who employ more than 16 people. It does not constitute justification for particular disabled individuals to claim entitlement to be employed, but imposes an obligation on employers to employ a certain percentage of disabled persons (currently 6 per cent. of their workforce). All employees employed in the establishment are counted towards the total for the purposes of this calculation; disabled persons who are particularly difficult to absorb into employment may each count as two or three persons. For every job in this obligatory quota that is not duly allocated to a disabled person, an employer must pay a compensatory tax of 150 Deutschmarks per month to the appropriate **Central Agency for the Disabled**. The money is used for the occupational advancement of disabled persons, assistance provided by the Agencies to accompany the integration of disabled persons into an establishment, and a Federal Employment Service compensatory fund established under the Federal Ministry of Labour and Social Affairs. In 1985 approximately one sixth of the obligatory quota of jobs were not duly occupied by disabled persons; and in 1988 approximately 135,000 disabled persons were unemployed.

For the duration of the employment relationship, special regulations apply in favour of disabled employees which go farther than general employee protection. The employer's **duty of care** is extended. Disabled employees have an entitlement, enforceable through the courts, to be employed in a job in which their abilities and knowledge can be utilized as fully as possible and developed, although this does not entitle them to preferential treatment over more highly skilled non-disabled employees. They may refuse to work any **overtime** in excess of the agreed working hours, and have a statutory entitlement to one extra week's **annual holiday**. Disabled employees must be employed under normal pay and employment conditions; pensions or similar benefits related to their handicap must not be counted towards their remuneration. The dismissal of disabled employees is subject to the prior consent of the Central Agency for the Disabled. The Agency has discretionary powers to decide whether such a dismissal is lawful, giving due consideration to the views expressed by the parties concerned, the local Employment Office, the works council and the representative body for disabled employees. In so doing the Agency must weigh the importance in the public interest of absorbing disabled persons into employment, together with the interest of the disabled individual concerned in keeping their job (particularly with regard to the severity of their condition), against, on the other hand, the interest of the employer in making the establishment economically efficient.

644. **SCHWERBEHINDERTENVERTRETUNG — REPRESEN-
TATIVE BODY FOR DISABLED EMPLOYEES**: Under collective labour law, protection for disabled employees is provided in the context of the **works constitution** in the private sector and **staff representation** in the public sector by two institutions. Firstly, the **works council** or **staff council** is charged with the task of fostering the integration of disabled employees in the establishment. Secondly, in establishments normally employing at least five disabled persons these disabled employees can elect a representative body consisting of at least two members (one **employee representative for the disabled** plus a deputy), usually for a term of office of four years.

This representative body provides disabled employees with assistance and advice and represents their interests within the establishment. It has the right to attend, in an advisory capacity, meetings of the works council or staff council and their consultations with the employer, and to hold plenary meetings of disabled employees. The employer must supply it with sufficiently early and comprehensive information, and hear its views, on all matters affecting disabled employees individually or as a group, such as hiring, transfer and dismissal or **termination**. Any decision taken without hearing its views may not be implemented until this omission has been rectified.

Where there is a **company works council** in a company, or a **general staff council** for several **public sector establishments**, the disabled employees elect a company or general representative body which represents their interests in matters that cannot be regulated at individual establishment level and takes on the functions of the individual representative body for disabled employees in establishments which do not have one.

645. **SCHWERPUNKTSTREIK — SELECTIVE STRIKE**: See **partial or selective strike**.

646. **SICHERHEITSBEAUFTRAGTER — SAFETY OFFICER**: Safety officers are the element of the **workplace health and safety arrangements** closest to the actual work procedure. They are employees trained by the **Occupational Health and Safety Agencies** whose principal task is to monitor, in practice, the use of protective devices and observance of the provisions of **protection against technical hazards at work** and to advise the employer on these matters.

In establishments with more than 20 employees the employer, in consultation with the **works council** or **staff council**, must appoint one or more safety officers in accordance with the accident prevention regulations of the Occupational Health and Safety Agencies. If there are more than three safety officers in an establishment, they form a safety committee for the purpose of advising the employer in cases where the establishment does not have a **health and safety committee**.

In the system of occupational health and safety in the Federal Republic, the safety officer performs some of the functions which the EC Directive of June 12, 1989 on the introduction of measures to encourage improvements in the health and safety of workers at work assigns to people whom it describes as employee representatives with a special function in health and safety protection at work.

647. **SOLIDARITÄTSBEITRAG — NON-UNION MEMBERS' LEVY**: Since **non-union members** employed by the employers

bound by a **collective agreement** are almost always treated fully in accordance with its provisions, trade unions have in the past sought to incorporate in collective agreements the obligation on non-union members to pay to the appropriate union concerned, in place of the union membership subscription they save, a special levy as a contribution towards the costs of union activity.

The imposition of such a levy by collective agreement is held to be unlawful, since an agreement between the parties to a collective agreement to oblige third parties to pay levies is not covered by **collective bargaining autonomy**, which as a matter of principle encompasses only members of the organizations concluding the agreement.

648. SONN- UND FEIERTAGSARBEIT — WORK ON SUNDAYS AND PUBLIC HOLIDAYS: See **rest on Sundays and public holidays**.

649. SONN- UND FEIERTAGSRUHE — REST ON SUNDAYS AND PUBLIC HOLIDAYS: On Sundays and statutory public holidays there is a general compulsory rest from work. Under the most important **regulations on working hours** on this matter, work in the producing industries and trades is prohibited on these days for at least 24 hours. Where two such days are consecutive the compulsory rest from work lasts 36 hours, and at Christmas, Easter and Whitsun it lasts 48 hours (Industrial Code §§ 105a ff.). The same applies to **shop closing hours**.

There are exemptions from the rule in the case of particular activities (referred to as "Sonntagsgewerbe", *i.e.* Sunday trades) such as the restaurant trade and musical and theatrical performances. In addition the Federal Government, with the agreement of the Federal Council, may grant exemptions for entire sectors of activity, particularly those in which the very nature of the work means that it cannot be interrupted or postponed. For example, Government Orders to this effect exist for pharmacies, the iron and steel industry and the papermaking industry. Lastly, the Mining Inspectorate and **Labour Inspectorate** can authorize employment on Sundays and public holidays in order to avoid disproportionate expense in the event of unforeseeable requirements. The rule on compulsory rest from work does not apply to individual instances of emergency work and work that cannot be postponed for other reasons. In such cases the employer must maintain a special record of the nature and duration of work done on Sundays and public holidays and the number of employees involved, and keep it available for scrutiny at any time by the Labour Inspectorate.

The manufacture and full utilization of new technologies are frequently associated with an increase in **shiftwork** and hence also with a wish on the part of companies for further exemptions from the rule on compulsory rest on Sundays and public holidays.

Employees are under an obligation to work on Sundays and public holidays only if their **contracts of employment** so provide. If the duration of such work is longer than three hours or if it prevents them from visiting their place of public worship, employees must be granted a rest period of 36 hours on every third Sunday or a rest period from 0600 to 1800 hrs on every other Sunday. The arrangement of permitted work on Sundays and public holidays is subject to the **co-determination right of the works council**.

650. **SOZIAL- UND UMWELTVERTRÄGLICHE TECHNIK-GESTALTUNG — HUMAN- AND ENVIRONMENT-CENTRED TECHNOLOGY STRATEGY**: Concept signifying employee access to decision-making in the process of the development and selection of technologies in the work context. It constitutes an attempt to eliminate the situation where employees play no more than a purely reactive role in the introduction of **new technologies**, the practical implementation of **process innovations** and the manufacture of new products. The organization of such a strategy in the establishment requires, in particular, the appropriate knowledge and an extended degree of co-determination in the workplace. Well-tried models of the strategy exist in Scandinavia, where **trade unions**, in conjunction with scientists and work groups within the establishment, develop and test alternative production techniques on the basis of specific examples and then make them the subject of negotiation in the context of **collective agreements** and **works agreements**. In the Federal Republic, the only instances as yet have been proposals for the conversion of armaments industries and a number of projects on process-related employee participation. The beginnings of such a strategy in practice are also to be found in the **"Work and Technology" Action Programme**. In recent years, the unions have been seeking to exert an influence on the design of technologies mainly in their bargaining policy, by means of agreements on **protection against rationalization** and wider-ranging collective agreements concluded as part of a **qualitative bargaining policy**. In addition, the institution of technology advisory services is intended to provide suggestions and assistance for establishment-level representatives and companies themselves in the design and use of technologies within the establishment.

651. "SOZIALADÄQUANZ": Concept central to the treatment of collective **industrial action** within German labour law, difficult to render precisely in English but perhaps best approximated by "general acceptability". The Federal Labour Court has established that a **strike** is lawful only if it is "generally acceptable" as determined by the following principles:

1. Industrial action may be carried on only between parties possessing the capacity to conclude collective agreements.
2. The purpose of industrial action must be the achievement of aims that can be regulated by collective agreement.
3. Industrial action may not violate basic rules of labour law.
4. Industrial action must satisfy the *ultima ratio* **principle**.
5. Industrial action must observe the rules of fair play.
6. Defensive industrial action against "unacceptable" offensive collective action is "unacceptable".

652. SOZIALAUSWAHL — SOCIAL CRITERIA FOR REDUNDANCY: In the case of **redundancy** effected by ordinary **termination with notice**, the provision of **protection against dismissal** can be described as a two-stage process. The initial obligation to establish the existence of urgent operational requirements is followed by the obligation to select the particular employee to be dismissed on the basis of "social aspects", *i.e.* the job loss must first be established as lawful *in abstracto* and must then be individualized (Protection Against Dismissal Act § 1(3)). In accordance with this principle, the employee selected is the one for whom dismissal will have the least effect. The selection procedure includes all comparable employees in the establishment. Here, "comparable" means employees who are employed in identical jobs or in jobs for which the employee whose former job is being abolished possesses the skills and abilities required. Employees for whom ordinary dismissal with notice is excluded by statute, collective agreement or their contract of employment are exempted.

In the selection procedure, the social circumstances of all comparable employees are weighed against each other in detail. The most important criteria are age, continuous length of service in the establishment and number of dependants. Other aspects are the financial situation and state of health of the employee and their immediate family, and their likely opportunities on the labour market. If, for reasons such as economic or technical requirements, the employer has an interest in retaining particular employees even though on purely social grounds they would be selected for redundancy, this must be taken into account if the reasons are sufficiently important to make the continued employment of the individuals concerned a necessity. Since it is not permissible to evaluate these social criteria on a systematic basis, in practice the selection procedure presents a particular problem in cases of redundancy, which is invalid unless the procedure has been properly followed.

653. **SOZIALE MARKTWIRTSCHAFT — SOCIAL MARKET ECONOMY**: The basic form of economic organization in the Federal Republic is called a social market economy. Like a free market economy, it is an economic system in which the supply of and demand for goods and services, co-ordinated and made consistent with each other by movements in prices, are in principle left to the individual decisions of buyers and sellers. In addition to this an attempt is made, by means of regulatory framework legislation, to prevent restraints on competition resulting from monopolies and cartels (**merger**). And all this is backed by a social policy directed at a socially desirable degree of corrective adjustment of income distribution and at protection of the weaker members of society. In **labour law** there are elements of **economic democracy** in the corresponding regulations of the **works constitution** and **co-determination**. The structural principles of the social market economy are secured in the Basic Law: the principle of the welfare state, the economic system and system of regulating competition, community tasks and the traditional fundamentals such as private ownership, freedom of contract and consumption, freedom of information and association, freedom of settlement and freedom of occupation. Expropriation and nationalization are possible by or in virtue of a statute and in return for compensation. Thus, the Basic Law does not decide in favour of any particular economic system and enables the legislators to pursue any constitutional economic policy which they think suitable.

654. **SOZIALGERICHTSBARKEIT — SYSTEM OF SOCIAL SECURITY COURTS**: The system of jurisdiction which deals with matters relating to **social security**, the Employment Promotion Act (Arbeitsförderungsgesetz) and other functions performed by the Federal Employment Service, war victims' pensions and military pensions, the Disabled Persons Act and the Childcare Payment and Childcare Leave Act, the law on health-insurance doctors and dentists and old-age benefits for the agricultural sector, and with public-law disputes brought before the social security courts in virtue of the Continued Wage Payment Act or special instructions on the process of law.

It is a three-tier system, with first-instance Social Security Courts (SG) and Land Social Security Courts (LSG) as the appeal instance, and the Federal Social Security Court (BSG) for appeal on points of law. The individual panels (or chambers) of the SG have one career judge and two lay judges on the bench; the panels (or senates) of the LSG and the BSG have three career judges and two **lay judges**. No legal costs are payable for proceedings before the social security courts, and the parties are able to represent themselves before the SG and the LSG.

655. **SOZIALGESETZBUCH — SOCIAL SECURITY CODE**: All the various individual legal provisions on **social security** and state social security benefits have not yet been codified into a single consistent collection; so far four Books of the Code exist. Social Security Code (SGB) I contains regulations on the functions of the Code, the individual benefits and institutions and general provisions of the Code as a whole. SGB IV contains general provisions on social security, SGB V contains the provisions on statutory **health insurance** and SGB X regulates the corresponding administrative procedure, the protection of social security data, and co-operation between the social-security benefit institutions and their relations towards third parties. Under the Pension Reform Act (Rentenreformgesetz) of 1989, the regulations of the Reich Insurance Code (Reichsversicherungs-ordnung) on the **statutory pension scheme** were transformed into SGB VI as from January 1, 1992.

Other important legislation in the field of social security law includes the Reich Insurance Code on **accident insurance**, the White-Collar Workers' Insurance Act (Angestelltenversicherungs-gesetz) and Federal Social Assistance Act (Bundessozial-hilfegesetz), and the Employment Promotion Act (Arbeitsförderungsgesetz).

656. **SOZIALPARTNERSCHAFT — SOCIAL PARTNERSHIP**: See **concerted action, institutionalized representation of interests**.

657. **SOZIALPLAN — "SOCIAL PLAN"**: Programme drawn up in the form of a special **works agreement** to compensate or reduce economic disadvantages for employees in the event of a **substantial alteration to the establishment** or in cases of **bankruptcy** and **composition** (Works Constitution Act §§ 111, 112). It resembles a special form of redundancy programme. It has valid effect only if it is in writing and is adopted by the **works council** by formal resolution. If the employer and the works council fail to agree on a "social plan", they may call on the Director of the relevant Land Employment Office to mediate. Should they choose not to do so, or should mediation prove unsuccessful, they may refer the matter to the **establishment-level arbitration committee**, whose decision is binding. In

arriving at its decision the committee must be guided by the actual disadvantages caused and the likely employment opportunities on the labour market for the employees affected, and in fixing the total sum to be made available under the plan must avoid endangering the future existence of the establishment. If the committee exceeds this scope, the employer and the works council may apply to the courts under the **"Beschluss" procedure** to have the plan ruled invalid. There is no obligation to draw up a "social plan" provided that the proposed alteration to the establishment consists solely of dismissals, certain maximum limits in terms of a percentage of the total workforce are not exceeded, or the case involves a newly formed enterprise. However, a **reconcilement of interests** must then be arranged. Departures from the establishment brought about by the employer by means of severance agreements are also deemed to be dismissal. In cases of bankruptcy, employees suffering dismissal receive **compensation for job loss**, up to a maximum of two and a half months' pay, which is given preferential settlement in the bankruptcy proceedings.

658. **SOZIALRECHT — SOCIAL SECURITY LAW**: In recent years the term "Sozialrecht" has increasingly tended to be restricted to the sphere of social security benefits and compulsory insurance under the system of **social security**. It typically comprises the area of law of the **Social Security Code** and the Federal Social Assistance Act (Bundessozialhilfegesetz). Alongside **labour law**, social security law is an instrument of legal policy for effecting welfare-state functions. The two are in fact frequently combined, either cumulatively (*e.g.* **statutory pension scheme** and **occupational pension scheme**) or chronologically (*e.g.* **continued payment of remuneration** and **sickness benefit**). In this respect, the ongoing development of labour and social security law is one of the central elements of a social policy which can only be pursued as a coherent entity. They are, nevertheless, two separate areas of law. Social security law constitutes an independent subject, as evidenced by the separate existence of a **system of social security courts** and a **system of labour courts**. Furthermore, the protective function of social security law covers many individuals who are not employees.

659. **SOZIALSTAATSPRINZIP — WELFARE STATE PRINCIPLE**: An important structural feature of the developed Western, and above all West European industrialized countries. In the Federal Republic it has constitutional status and counterbalances the individualistic regulatory principles of the **basic rights**. It serves to protect the weaker members of society

and imposes on the state the obligation to ensure that such people enjoy, like others, freedom from want, human dignity of life and an adequate share in the general prosperity. Viewed more broadly, it aims at a just and balanced organization of social conditions. The definitions of the welfare state principle are not exclusionary; concrete expressions of it include, for example, the entire field of **social security** and state social security benefits. It also has importance in legal **interpretation**. Industrial relations have particularly close links with the welfare state principle; this is expressed in the responsibility of the state for legislation and the **systems of labour courts** and **social security courts**, social security and social policy, employment administration and labour market policy (**Federal Employment Service**), in the guarantee by the state of the **freedom of association** (right to organize) and in its role in incomes policy and the interrelationship of the social partners with the relevant groups in society, and, not least, in the function of the state as an employer.

660. SOZIALVERSICHERUNG — SOCIAL SECURITY: The statutory system of compulsory insurance in the Federal Republic, with the purpose of providing benefits in the event of **illness, accidents at work, occupational illness, occupational incapacity** and **total disability** as well as maternity, retirement and death. It is financed by contributions from employers, employees and other insured persons, plus subsidies from the Federal Government. This does not apply to contributions for **accident insurance**, however, which are paid by employers alone since this insures a risk devolving on them, namely, the **duty of care**. Social security benefits are not conditional upon means testing, since claimants help to finance them through their own contribution payments and thereby acquire an entitlement to benefits. All employees are subject to compulsory insurance under the system, up to fixed income limits which are based on gross earnings and adjusted regularly (**social security contribution**).

Social security is divided into the following branches: **health** and **accident insurance**, manual workers' pension insurance in accordance with the Reich Insurance Code (Reichsversicherungsverordnung), white-collar workers' insurance under the White-Collar Workers' Insurance Act (Angestelltenversicherungsgesetz) and miners' insurance for mining and subsidiary activities in accordance with the Reich Mineworkers Act (Reichsknappschaftsgesetz). In addition, it includes **unemployment insurance** and old-age benefits for the agricultural sector. Historically, some elements of the social security system date back to **Bismarck's social security legislation**.

661. SOZIALVERSICHERUNGSAUSWEIS — SOCIAL SECURITY CARD: A social security card was introduced in 1989 by the legislature, and came into use in 1991, as a means of exerting better control over illegal employment (**undeclared employment**) and preventing the improper receipt of social security benefits. Every employee receives a card issued by the **statutory pension scheme** on which the employee's name and insurance number are entered. On entering into employment, the employee must present this card to the employer concerned. The employer is required to inform the employment authorities if the card is not presented. In the case of the construction industry, travelling fairground operations, industrial contract cleaning services and employees engaged in the erection and dismantling of trade fairs and exhibitions, *i.e.* branches of activity in which employment in breach of social security and tax laws was widespread in the past, there is an obligation on employees to carry on their person during work a card bearing their photograph. The social security offices and **Employment Offices** are required to call in the card if they are paying out benefits to the employee. In addition, **health insurance funds** may retain the card if the employee is drawing sickness benefit.

662. SOZIALVERSICHERUNGSBEITRAG — SOCIAL SECURITY CONTRIBUTION: The contributions for **health** and **unemployment insurance** and the **statutory pension scheme** payable by the employee represent half of the total contributions that must be paid over to the social security institutions; the employer deducts them from the employee's **gross pay** and must then provide the other half from own resources and pass on the total to the institutions concerned. Depending on the funds to which they belong, the share payable by employees who are liable to pay the above three contributions may amount in all to 19-20 per cent. of their gross monthly pay. **Accident insurance** contributions are paid only by the employer.

However, social security contributions are not necessarily compulsory for an employee. Individuals whose earnings are above the so-called "Beitragsbemessungsgrenze" (income limit for chargeable contributions) may choose whether they will opt to remain in the statutory insurance scheme, insure themselves privately or dispense with insurance protection altogether. This income limit differs in western and eastern Germany. It is based on gross earnings, and as at 1992 is fixed at 81,600 Deutschmarks per year in western Germany and 57,600 Deutschmarks per year in eastern Germany for pension and unemployment insurance, and at 61,200 and 43,200 Deutschmarks respectively for health insurance.

663. **SOZIALVERSICHERUNGSPFLICHT — SOCIAL SECURITY OBLIGATION**: See **social security, social security contribution**.

664. **SPESEN — EXPENSES**: Term customarily used to refer to expenditure incurred by the employee in the performance of work, which the employer is in principle under an obligation to reimburse. Such expenditure includes, for example, the costs of transport to other places to perform work and of **business travel**. Fraudulent claims for expenses constitute sufficient cause for **dismissal on grounds of conduct** and dismissal via **summary termination**.

665. **SPRECHERAUSSCHUSS DER LEITENDEN ANGESTELLTEN — REPRESENTATIVE BODY FOR EXECUTIVE STAFF**: Representative body which may be elected in **establishments** regularly employing at least 10 **executive staff** ("Leitende Angestellte") in accordance with the result of a prior ballot among such staff as to whether one should be formed. The ballot may be subject to a re-vote and the decision taken may be revised. The election is conditional on a corresponding classification procedure carried out by the electoral boards for the election of works councils and representative bodies for executive staff: only executive staff as such are eligible to vote and eligible for election. If an establishment has fewer than 10 employees classed as executive staff, they are counted towards the number employed in the geographically nearest establishment of the same company in which the quorum is met. By the majority vote of all the executive staff in a company normally employing at least 10 executive staff overall, a single company-level representative body for executive staff can be formed with responsibility for all the company's establishments. A general representative body for executive staff must be formed if there are several such bodies at individual establishment level. A group representative body for executive staff can be formed with the agreement of the general representative bodies of the group member companies together employing at least 75 per cent. of the executive staff employed by the group of companies as a whole. The period of office of these representative bodies is four years. Their size depends on the number of executive staff normally employed in the establishment or company concerned. Members of such bodies do not enjoy entitlements to release from work, retention of grading and special **protection against dismissal** comparable to those of **works council members**. Nor do they have access to the actual decision-making process comparable to the **co-determination rights of the works council,**

but they do have the equivalent information and consultation rights.

Up till January 1, 1990 representative bodies for executive staff existed on an optional and informal basis. Their formation is now specifically regulated in the Sprecherausschussgesetz (Formation of Representative Bodies For Executive Staff Act). The fact that the creation of a company-level body allows a representative body to be formed even where the requirement for at least 10 executive staff in a given establishment is not fulfilled, together with the broader classification given to executive staff, suggest that the role of these bodies should be seen as rooted less in the representation of specific interests than in a fragmentation of the workforce in an establishment or company, and of its informal powers and representational strength.

666. SPRUNGRECHTSBESCHWERDE — DIRECT JUDICIAL REVIEW APPLICATION: As a parallel to the **direct appeal on a point of law** in the **"Urteil" procedure**, it is also possible in the **"Beschluss" procedure** to bypass the normal appeal instance, *i.e.* the relevant Land Labour Court, and lodge a **judicial review application** against a decision by the first-instance Labour Court directly with the Federal Labour Court. In addition to requiring the written consent of all participants in the proceedings, such a direct application may be lodged only if leave to do so has been granted by the first-instance Labour Court concerned, either in the actual decision ending the proceedings or by a separate decision. The Labour Court must grant such leave upon request if the dispute forming the basis of the application is of fundamental importance. No **remedy at law** is available to the participants against the refusal of such leave.

667. SPRUNGREVISION — DIRECT APPEAL ON A POINT OF LAW: By way of exception, it is possible in the **"Urteil" procedure** to bypass a normal **appeal** and lodge an **appeal on a point of law** against a judgment by the first-instance Labour Court directly with the Federal Labour Court. Such a direct appeal may be lodged only if the opposing party has consented to this in writing and if the Labour Court, upon request, has granted leave to do so in its judgment or by a subsequent decision. Leave to lodge a direct appeal on a point of law must always be granted if the lawsuit forming its basis is of fundamental importance and concerns **disputes of rights** between **parties to a collective agreement** arising from **collective agreements**, their interpretation or existence. The same applies when at least one party with the capacity to conclude collective agreements is involved in a dispute of rights arising from unlawful action in

293

connection with a **labour dispute** and in the case of questions relating to **freedom of association** (the right to organize). Refusal of such leave by the Labour Court cannot be contested.

Direct appeal on a point of law is also available under the rules of procedure for the ordinary, social security and administrative courts.

668. **STAATLICHE BERUFSAUSBILDUNG — STATUTORY VOCATIONAL TRAINING**: Vocational training is organized as a **dual system**. There is a distinction between **company vocational training** and statutory vocational training, which accompany each other. Statutory vocational training takes place in a **vocational training school** and its emphasis is on teaching **vocational trainees** theoretical knowledge relevant to particular occupations and extending their general education.

669. **STAATLICHE SCHLICHTUNG — STATUTORY DISPUTE RESOLUTION**: Procedure regulated in Allied Control Council Act No. 35 of August 20, 1946 on "Conciliation and Arbitration Procedure in Labour Disputes". It is of only marginal importance in practice, since it is subordinated to **joint dispute resolution** voluntarily agreed between the **parties to a collective agreement**. Consequently, it becomes a possibility only if no joint dispute resolution board has been established by agreement and the issue has been referred to the state authority by one or both parties, or if the agreed joint dispute resolution procedure has been unsuccessful and the parties have then referred the issue to the state authority. The procedure is not compulsory, nor can the eventual decision be declared binding against the will of one of the parties (**compulsory arbitration**).

The outcome of the procedure's first stage before a Land conciliator may take the following forms:
1. the conclusion of a **collective agreement**;
2. agreement between the parties on a voluntary joint dispute resolution procedure before a board established by agreement;
3. agreement between the parties to refer the issue to a state arbitration committee;
4. the breakdown of negotiations.

The decision of the arbitration committee in (3) above is binding only if both parties accept it or have agreed beforehand to accept it. As **acts of administration**, the decisions of the committee may be contested in the **system of administrative courts**.

670. **STAATSVERTRAG — TREATY**: Treaties are international agreements containing regulations whose national implementation requires legislative action. Consequently, treaties on matters relating to legislation by the Federal Government or the Länder

require the assent of the Federal Parliament and, where applicable, of the Federal Council or the Land Parliament concerned via a statute known as a ratification or transformation instrument. Only when it is in the form of such a statute does a provision constitute a **source of law** in terms of labour law. The Länder may conclude treaties with other countries only with the assent of the Federal Government, and with each other within their general sphere of jurisdiction. The ratification of treaties by the Federal Government is performed by the Federal President via an act of assent ("Zustimmungsakt").

671. **STABILITÄTSGESETZ — STABILITY ACT**: Short title used for the Gesetz zur Förderung der Stabilität und des Wachstums der Wirtschaft (Law to Promote Stability and Growth of the Economy) of June 8, 1967, aimed at a special regulatory policy in the context of the **social market economy**. The history behind it is closely linked with the recognition of certain inadequacies of market control mechanisms at times of economic crisis and the resultant need for corrective intervention by the state. The Act is essentially directed at two objectives:
1. co-ordination of the finance policy of the central, regional and local authorities with the monetary and credit policy of the Bundesbank (Federal Bank);
2. extension of the Federal Government's scope for action in relation to the other territorial authorities and autonomous policy-forming groups (*e.g.* **employers' associations** and **trade unions**).

The former was given statutory effect by an amendment of the provisions on public finance laid down in the Basic Law, and the latter by a specification of the machinery for **concerted action**. It was stipulated that economic and financial policy should be guided by the four elements of the **"magic square"** and that the collective bargaining parties should also be involved via concerted action. The main objective was the co-ordination of action taken by all bodies and groups controlling the economic process (so-called "global steering") by means of monetary and credit policy, compensatory finance policy counteracting the effect of the business cycle and complementary structural policy. The latter was intended to supplement global steering as guided by cyclical requirements in promoting the mobility of production factors necessary to its long-term goal, and thus to ensure prolonged adherence to the aims of the "magic square" by means of targeted measures. The instruments of structural policy were mainly subsidies, in the form of either direct (payments) or indirect (tax concessions) allocations from the state to private individuals.

295

Viewed retrospectively, the intended aims have not been achieved. In particular, over wide areas the subsidies have not resulted in the structural change needed, but have sustained and reinforced obsolete structures.

672. **STEUER — TAX**: The most important tax levies in the sphere of labour relations are **earnings tax** or income tax, corporation and trade tax, and turnover or value-added tax. Rates of income tax, which increase linearly, range from 19 per cent. at an annual income of up to 8,153 Deutschmarks for single persons and 16,306 Deutschmarks for married persons, up to 53 per cent. at an annual income of from 120,042 and 240,084 Deutschmarks respectively. Tax-exempt employment- and family-related allowances are claimable, and also mileage allowance. Double taxation agreements between two countries stipulate that taxpayers are taxed either in their country of origin or in the country they are living in, but in any case only once. Forms of official appeal and **remedy at law** in tax matters include objection to a tax assessment, complaint against all other **acts of administration** and action before the **system of finance courts**.

673. **STREIK — STRIKE**: Collective action by a number of employees consisting in the agreed cessation of work, with the intention of resuming work once their stated demands have been successfully achieved in the form of the conclusion of a **collective agreement**. The strike is the most important form of **industrial action** by employees, and nowadays almost the only form customarily engaged in. There is a distinction between an **all-out strike, partial or selective strike** and **general strike** according to the tactics used, and between an **official strike** and an **unofficial strike** according to the basis on which it is organized. In the event of a strike the precept of **"Sozialadäquanz"** and the **proportionality principle** must be observed. This leads to the following consequences: to be valid in law, a strike must be conducted by a trade union, and must pursue an aim that can be regulated by collective agreement; the strike must not violate the **peace obligation** deriving from an existing collective agreement; the union must follow the strike procedure laid down in its standing rules; the strike must represent the last resort as a means of achieving the aim in dispute (see *ultima ratio* **principle, warning strike**); and lastly, the **fairness principle** must be observed.

An unlawful strike gives rise to entitlements to damages and in particular mutual entitlements to a restraining injunction between those involved.

674. STREIKARBEIT — PERFORMANCE OF WORK DURING A STRIKE: In the question of whether work which is not being done because of a **strike** may be allocated to employees who are not participating in the **labour dispute**, a distinction is made between direct and indirect performance of work during a strike. Indirect performance of work during a strike means the continuation of the employee's former work. Employees remain under an obligation to do this, even if it is dependent on work done upstream by strikebreakers, since refusal to do so would constitute participation in the strike. Direct performance of work during a strike refers to the case where employees, as strikebreakers, undertake work not forming part of their normal function which is usually done by the employees who are on strike. Employees who are not on strike may not be compelled to undertake such direct strikebreaking work, since due consideration must be given to solidarity between employees, *i.e.* within the same establishment, and the effectiveness of the strike would be directly impaired.

In the **public service**, on the other hand, in the event of a strike by white-collar and manual workers **career public servants** ("Beamte") may be assigned to jobs affected by the strike. The courts base this view on the close connection between the institution of career public service and the "common good".

The performance of **emergency work** and the **maintenance of essential supplies** and services do not constitute the performance of work during a strike.

675. STREIKBRECHER — STRIKEBREAKER: Also referred to colloquially in English as "scab" or "blackleg". See **performance of work during a strike**.

676. STREIKLEITUNG — STRIKE LEADERSHIP: Under their **union strike guidelines**, for the purposes of conducting a strike the **trade unions** form a central and local strike leadership whose composition varies according to the individual case, particularly the size of the geographical area affected by the strike. The central strike leadership is the body within the union with overall responsibility for conducting the strike; it organizes and supervises the industrial action, keeps the strikers informed and issues information to the general public. The local strike leadership is responsible for the necessary organizational measures within the establishment, such as the deployment of pickets or organization of the **maintenance of essential supplies and services**. Under the law on associations, all union members are obliged to follow the instructions of the strike leadership.

297

677. **STREIKPOSTEN — PICKET**: One of the conventional manifestations of a **strike**. It refers to individuals who station themselves at the entrance to an establishment or company affected by a strike for the purpose of prevailing upon those who wish to continue working to join them in ceasing work. Pickets may not subject strikebreakers to duress and may only employ methods of peaceful persuasion.

678. **STREIKUNTERSTÜTZUNG — STRIKE PAY**: In accordance with its standing rules, a **trade union** which calls a **strike** pays strike pay to its striking members, and in certain cases also to **non-union members**. This is intended to offset the loss of income suffered by employees because they lose their entitlement to remuneration while on strike.

Eligibility to receive strike pay normally commences after three months' **union membership**. In some cases strike pay is not granted during short strikes lasting for no more than three days. As a matter of principle, strike pay is paid only if an employee observes the **union strike guidelines**. No strike pay is granted if a strike is curtailed or extended without the approval of the **strike leadership**, or in the event of an **unofficial strike** by union members.

The actual amount of strike pay received is generally governed by the level of union subscription paid and the duration of union membership; a family supplement is often granted. Strike pay usually amounts to around two thirds of gross earnings.

679. **STRUKTURWANDEL — STRUCTURAL CHANGE**: This term has a number of meanings. At sector level it usually refers to the process whereby, in accordance with the three-sector hypothesis, first the primary sector, *i.e.* agriculture, is supplanted by the secondary sector, *i.e.* manufacturing industry, and this in turn is then overtaken in highly developed societies by the tertiary sector, *i.e.* the provision of services. Not least because of the expansion of public services, the share of the tertiary sector in total employment and gross national product (GNP) has risen above the 50 per cent. mark in all advanced Western countries.

Viewed in terms of individual industries, local structural change or adjustment takes place in several phases in which a structural crisis, the phase of conversion, is characterized by the stagnation and contraction of numerous forms of activity and a simultaneous spread of **new technologies** on the market. This trend, which is related to the **product cycle**, continues with the phase of expansion, *i.e.* the appearance of new competitors. The range of uses of the new products is enlarged, and their manufacture is improved by **process innovations**. The more entrepreneurs who are "chasing" the potential market, the more intensive competition becomes; some suppliers drop out. Signs of market saturation and a downward trend in the marginal utility of **productivity** characterize the phase of maturity, which is then succeeded by the phase of stagnation and decline.

The structural change which is being brought about by **microelectronics**, for example, is characterized by the fact that production is becoming increasingly integrated and that the abilities of employees, over and above their strictly vocational skills, are assuming growing importance.

680. **STÜCKAKKORD — MONEY PIECEWORK**: See **piecework**.

681. **STUFENVERTRETUNG — HIERARCHICAL REPRE-SENTATION BODY**: In the public sector, the concept of **staff representation** includes, in addition to the **staff council**, the principle of the staff representation body at each higher level, in both the Federal administration and the Länder. This hierarchical pattern is necessary in order to match the structures of staff representation to the structure of the administration and its authorities.

The organizational structure of both Federal and Länder state administration is hierarchical. For each tier of administration there is a corresponding "Stufe" or level.

The Federal authorities are divided into central, intermediate-level and lower-level authorities. The central level includes the top-level Federal authorities, *i.e.* in particular the Ministries and the Federal Chancellorship and the top-level authorities directly subject to the Ministries. Below these come the intermediate-level authorities, and below these in turn the lower-level authorities. In each case, the higher authority exercises control over the next-lower authority in terms of departmental function and the law.

Likewise, most of the Länder, with the exception of the city states (*i.e.* Berlin, Hamburg and Bremen) and Saarland and Schleswig-Holstein, also have a three-tier administrative structure.

682. **SUBJEKTIVES RECHT — INDIVIDUAL'S RIGHT**: A subjective right, *i.e.* the scope to exercise a power which is conferred on individual legal entities with respect to other legal entities and objects by law ("objektives Recht") on the basis of the various **sources of law**. It describes the sphere of the individual freedom of the legal entity concerned and their powers as arising from the particular right in question. The various subjective rights (*e.g.* the right of ownership, the right to establish, change or terminate relationships, the right to participate and

299

the right to privacy of the individual) invest their holders with entitlements, *i.e.* the right, to be able to require others to do something or abstain from doing something. In the Federal Republic, with its high degree of juridification, the existence of a subjective right or the assertion of a possible subjective right is a necessary precondition for pursuing individual claims before the courts in any of the systems of jurisdiction. Subjective rights may be either absolute or relative, and their holders may be both natural and legal persons.

683. **SUBVENTION — SUBSIDY**: Term referring to an allocation from the state to support a particular element of economic policy. It may take the form either of a direct subsidy or so-called irrecoverable grant, or of an indirect tax privilege. The background to the allocation of subsidies is a specific economic policy, such as that which has been embodied in the **Stability Act**, for example, and the resultant decision to promote **structural change** and alleviate any hardship that this entails.

684. **SYSTEMATISCHER ARBEITSPLATZWECHSEL — JOB ROTATION**: A form of changed work structuring representing a response to calls for the **humanization of work**. No change is made to the content of the work, but a number of employees alternate with each other in performing different jobs.

T

685. **TANTIEME — SHARE OF PROFITS**: Share of the company's profits paid to an employee. The intention is that employees should identify with the company's economic development and have a direct interest in optimizing it. An employee is entitled to such profit-sharing only if it has been expressly agreed between the parties to the contract of employment. This is more frequently the case with **executive staff** than with other employees. (The French term "tantième" is also used in English.)

686. **TARIFAUTONOMIE — COLLECTIVE BARGAINING AUTONOMY**: The right of the **collective industrial organizations** to regulate terms and conditions of employment on their own responsibility and independently of any influence exercised by the state; more specifically, their right to create an appropriate system of regulation of working life, and to adjust it regularly to current economic and social developments, through the conclusion of **collective agreements**.

The core of this authority is protected by the Basic Law. By law, collectively agreed terms and conditions of employment apply only to members of the organizations concluding the collective agreement in question. In practice, however, they are usually applied to all **employment relationships**.

Thus, it is primarily the **parties to a collective agreement** who create a uniform system of employment conditions covering all establishments within each individual collective bargaining region. For the employees' side, the most important consequence of **freedom of association** (*i.e.* the right to organize) and autonomy of collective bargaining is that, instead of having to deal with the employer on an individual basis in negotiating their terms and conditions of employment, employees are able to unite in forming **trade unions** to negotiate conditions with the employers' side and, where necessary, to impose these by means of **strikes**. In accordance with the Basic Law, collective bargaining autonomy may not be undermined by prohibiting **industrial action** and replacing it by state-imposed arrangements or **compulsory arbitration**.

687. **TARIFBINDUNG — BINDING EFFECT OF COLLECTIVE AGREEMENTS**: In principle, the provisions laid down by a **collective agreement** apply only between the parties to individual contracts of employment who are mutually bound by the agreement. The Collective Agreements Act (Tarifvertragsgesetz) makes an exception for provisions relating collectively to the establishment and to the law on the works constitution. Those deemed to be bound by a **collective agreement** are the members

301

of **parties to a collective agreement** and individual employers who are parties to a collective agreement. **Association-level agreements** apply to employees who are members of the trade union concluding such an agreement and who are employed by an employer who is a member of the employers' association concluding the agreement, and also to these employers. **Company agreements** apply to the employer concluding the collective agreement in question and to his or her employees, provided that they belong to the union concluding the agreement. There is also a binding effect in the case of agreements which have been the subject of the **extension of collective agreements**.

688. **TARIFEINHEIT — EXCLUSIVITY OF COLLECTIVE AGREEMENTS**: Principle whereby only a single **collective agreement** can apply to a given **establishment**: the agreement which takes precedence is that which is the most relevant in terms of the establishments, occupations, personnel and geographical area it concerns (principle of specificity). In cases where it is not possible to determine this precedence for the establishment concerned, the collective agreement which is deemed applicable is the one which covers the most **employment relationships** within the establishment.

689. **TARIFFÄHIGKEIT — CAPACITY TO CONCLUDE COLLECTIVE AGREEMENTS**: The capacity of a **collective industrial organization**, with the agreement of its social counterparts, to regulate matters such as terms and conditions of employment with direct and mandatory effect for the individuals bound by a collective agreement, *i.e.* in the form of a **collective agreement**. On the employees' side this capacity is possessed only by trade unions and their "Spitzenorganisationen" or central organizations (Collective Agreements Act § 2(1.2)); on the employers' side, in addition to the **employers' associations** an individual employer is also able to conclude a collective agreement (Collective Agreements Act § 2(1)). Craft trades associations and guilds also possess the capacity to conclude collective agreements (Craft Trades Code § 54(3) 1, § 82(3)).

The concept is of crucial importance in deciding whether an association of employees possesses trade union status, since the Federal Labour Court has ruled that only collective industrial organizations which fulfil the eligibility criteria for the capacity to conclude collective agreements are trade unions within the meaning of the law.

The Federal Labour Court has established the following minimum criteria which an association of employees must fulfil in order to possess the capacity to conclude collective agreements. Its standing rules must state one of its functions to be the safeguarding of its members' interests in their capacity as employees, and it must have the intention of concluding collective agreements. It must be freely formed, not subject to influence from the opposing side, independent and organized on a basis above individual establishment level, must recognize current law on collective agreements as binding and must possess a measure of social power in terms of its organizational strength and its ability to exert pressure on its social counterpart.

Willingness to resort to **industrial action** is a common but not essential characteristic of the capacity to conclude collective agreements.

The collective industrial organizations have a special procedure before the labour courts available to them ("**Beschluss**" **procedure**, Labour Courts Act §§ 2a (1.3), 97) for declaratory judgments on the capacity to conclude collective agreements. The procedure is initiated at the request of any trade union, association of employees or employers' association provided that they are responsible in terms of the geographical area and occupations concerned.

690. **TARIFFONDS — EMPLOYEE INVESTMENT FUND**: The creation of investment funds for the benefit of employees is proposed by the trade unions as an instrument of policy to promote the formation of capital by employees. In contrast to the **financial participation** of employees in the company itself, this approach concerns the creation of investment funds which are financed from the profits of companies in accordance with some apportionment formula and incorporated in the general banking system. In the mid-1970s the Federal Government considered a scheme for the formation of decentralized investment funds of this kind into which all companies with a given annual profit should pay a proportion of that profit. For constitutional reasons, and because of the onset of economic problems, the scheme was never implemented. Since then such funds have played no real part in policy to promote the formation of capital by employees.

691. **TARIFGEMEINSCHAFT DEUTSCHER LÄNDER — EMPLOYERS' ASSOCIATION OF GERMAN LÄNDER**: See **employers' association**.

692. **TARIFKONKURRENZ — CONFLICT BETWEEN COL-LECTIVE AGREEMENTS**: Conflict deemed to exist where two or more **collective agreements** are applicable to the same

employment relationship within an establishment, with the result that the same subject-matter is regulated by collective agreement more than once. Such is the case only if this employment relationship in an establishment falls within the scope of each of the currently valid collective agreements in terms of the personnel, geographical area, establishments and occupations concerned and if these agreements are also actually applicable by virtue of the **binding effect of collective agreements** or the **extension of collective agreements**. There is a distinction between this situation and the case of a straightforward "plurality" of collective agreements where, although there are two or more collective agreements for a given establishment, they each cover different employees.

In practice, it usually follows from the **principle of industrial organization** that both conflict between collective agreements and a plurality of collective agreements occur only if competing trade unions are active within the same establishment. Where a conflict between collective agreements occurs, the courts have ruled that it should be resolved in accordance with the principle of specificity (Federal Labour Court Decisions No. 2 and No. 11 relating to the Collective Agreements Act § 4).

693. TARIFNORMEN — NORMATIVE PROVISIONS (OF COLLECTIVE AGREEMENTS): In addition to an obligational part regulating the mutual rights and obligations of the parties to the agreement (**peace obligation, duty to exert influence, joint dispute resolution agreement**), a **collective agreement** also contains provisions which apply to all employment relationships with normative effect as if laid down by statute (normative part). As a matter of principle, these normative provisions have direct and mandatory effect on all **employment relationships** bound by the collective agreement, *i.e.* these relationships are automatically invested with the content of the agreement, irrespective of whether a corresponding arrangement has been agreed between employer and employee or whether employer and employee are aware of the collective agreement. Any individually agreed arrangements which are contradictory to the collective agreement are null and void, and are replaced by the collectively agreed regulation. Divergences from the collective agreement are lawful only if they are expressly permitted by the agreement or if they make more favourable provision for the employee (**favourability principle**).

A distinction is made between: normative provisions regulating the content, conclusion and termination of the individual contract of employment; normative provisions relating collectively to the establishment and the law on the works constitution; and normative provisions on joint institutions set up by the parties to the collective agreement (Collective Agreements Act §§ 1(1),4(2)).

The most important of the normative provisions are those regulating the content of the individual contract of employment. Called "Inhaltsnormen", they include all provisions which the parties to the collective agreement intend should regulate the content of employment relationships and cover the entire range of matters that can be the subject of a contract of employment from pay to working hours, aspects of job protection, working conditions, skills, etc. They can also cover matters merely allied to the employment relationship, such as employee liability or time limits for asserting entitlements. Normative provisions on the conclusion and termination of the contract of employment regulate the conditions and formalities for entering into and ending the employment relationship.

Normative provisions relating collectively to the establishment, *e.g.* on **health and safety** and on the maintenance of order within the establishment, mainly in the form of bans on smoking, checks on attendance, inspections at the gate and **disciplinary sanctions**, can be agreed irrespective of whether the employment relationships are bound by the collective agreement or not. Provided that the actual employer is bound by the agreement, such provisions apply to all employees of the establishment.

Normative provisions on matters relating to the law on the works constitution concern the legal position of employees in the establishment, and specifically define or extend the **co-determination rights of the works council**.

Lastly, normative provisions which are of considerable importance in terms of the law on collective agreements are those on joint institutions set up by the parties to the agreement, *e.g.* on wage equalization funds and holiday funds in the construction industry.

For reasons of expediency, in practice **pay agreements** are concluded separately from longer-term **framework agreements on employment conditions**, which are more general. In many cases pay grading systems are specially regulated in **general agreements on pay grades**.

694. **TARIFPARTNER — PARTIES TO A COLLECTIVE AGREEMENT**: Synonym of **Tarifvertragsparteien**.

695. **TARIFREGISTER — REGISTER OF COLLECTIVE AGREEMENTS**: Register maintained by the **Federal Ministry of Labour and Social Affairs** (Collective Agreements Act § 6) which is intended to provide exhaustive information on the

existence and scope of all **collective agreements** concluded. The nature of the details which should be entered in the register is specified by the Collective Agreements Act §§ 6, 11(1) in conjunction with the Implementing Order §§ 14-16.

Registration has no significance in terms of the legal validity of a collective agreement.

696. TARIFVERHANDLUNGEN — COLLECTIVE BARGAIN-ING: Term denoting the process of arriving at a **collective agreement**. Rules on the procedure to be followed in bargaining and the participation of members of the parties to collective agreements are contained in their standing rules or in guidelines issued on the matter.

In practice, bargaining usually proceeds in three stages. In the first stage, the demand made by the **trade union** and the offer from the employers' side are put forward and discussed, if necessary in several rounds of negotiations, and then deliberated on separately by the two sides, each usually in consultation with a collective bargaining committee. If no mutually acceptable outcome can be reached, the negotiating team of one or other side pronounces the breakdown of negotiations, thereby initiating the second stage, namely, the **joint dispute resolution** procedure. This ends with a solution proposed by the impartial conciliator, on which there must again be consultation with the parties to the collective agreement. If the proposed solution is not accepted by one of the parties, the joint dispute resolution procedure must likewise be declared to have broken down. This marks the start of the third stage of bargaining, namely, the preparation and commencement of industrial action.

697. TARIFVERTRAG — COLLECTIVE AGREEMENT: Instru-ment for the regulation of employment conditions and associated economic conditions, as constitutionally guaranteed by Article 9(3) of the Basic Law (**collective bargaining autonomy**) and formulated by the legislature in the Collective Agreements Act (Tarifvertragsgesetz). A collective agreement has two parts: an obligational part, which regulates the rights and obligations existing between the **parties to a collective agreement**, and a normative part, which contains **normative provisions**. The most important of the obligations arising from a collective agreement, namely, the **peace obligation** and the **duty to exert influence**, are deemed to be inherent in the very existence of the agreement. The obligational part of the agreement also includes obligations on the parties which are expressly stated, more particularly the widespread inclusion of **joint dispute resolution agreements**. The nomenclature of the various types of collective agreement that exist is determined by the scope of application of their regulations (**association-level agreements** and **company agreements**) and by their content (**pay agreements, general agreements on pay grades** and **framework agreements on employment conditions**). Other types of collective agreement include agreements on **capital-forming payments** or end-of-year payments, **protection against rationalization** and joint dispute resolution procedures, or **union workplace representatives**.

Collective agreements are of central importance to industrial relations. Some 5,000-7,000 collective agreements are concluded annually, although the majority amend, follow or supplement previous ones. In 1990 approximately 5,000 were concluded for the former Federal Republic of Germany, and approximately 700 for the former German Democratic Republic or newly incorporated Länder of the Federal Republic. From the time when the Collective Agreements Act came into force in 1949 up to the end of 1990 some 245,000 collective agreements were concluded in the Federal Republic.

As at 1990 the number of collective agreements in force was 34,000, made up of some 24,700 association-level agreements and some 8,800 company agreements in the western Länder and some 250 association-level agreements and some 450 company agreements in the eastern Länder. These agreements applied directly to close on 11 million employees, and by virtue of the individual contract of employment their application was extended to 18.5 million employees.

698. **TARIFVERTRAGSPARTEIEN — PARTIES TO A COLLECTIVE AGREEMENT**: Collective agreements may be concluded on the employees' side by **trade unions** and on the employers' side either by **employers' associations** or by individual employers. The central organizations ("Spitzenorganisationen"), *i.e.* federations of employers' associations and trade unions, are also potential parties to collective agreements, but little or no provision is made for this in the standing rules of the individual organizations. Lastly, craft trades associations and guilds may also be expressly invested by statute with the capacity to conclude collective agreements.

699. **TARIFZUSTÄNDIGKEIT — COLLECTIVE BARGAIN-ING JURISDICTION**: Term denoting the authority of collective industrial organizations possessing the capacity to conclude **collective agreements,** as laid down in their standing rules, to conclude agreements applying to specific geographical areas, establishments, occupations and personnel. It constitutes the basis on which the scope of collective agreements is defined. Every

collective agreement concluded must specify its scope of application as deriving from the jurisdiction of the parties to the agreement according to their standing rules; this indicates clearly which employees are directly and compulsorily affected by the agreement in question. Collective bargaining jurisdiction therefore corresponds to the sphere of activity defined in the standing rules of a collective organization for which collective agreements may be concluded.

Autonomy in laying down standing rules is founded in the **freedom of association** as protected by Article 9(3) of the Basic Law. The collective organizations may base their collective bargaining jurisdiction on the **principle of industrial organization** or the **principle of occupational organization**. If it is industry-based, the standing rules may also include subsidiary establishments outside the industry, and may also include or exclude subsidiary establishments involving the same occupations in other industries.

Under the standing rules of the **German Federation of Trade Unions**, its member unions undertake to comply with the organizational regions for collective bargaining and, in the event of overlaps, to follow an arbitration procedure.

Like the capacity to conclude collective agreements, collective bargaining jurisdiction can also be examined before the labour courts in a special **"Beschluss" procedure**.

700. **TAYLORISMUS — TAYLORISM**: System of directing and organizing production developed from the "scientific management" method devised by F.W. Taylor. Rejecting management based merely on practical experience and relative autonomy on the part of the employer, scientific management focused on the systematic analysis of work procedures and movement sequences, so that work could then be fragmented into simple tasks and reallocated. In this way, Taylorism made it possible to control the important factors of the establishment's operation: **management** was able to determine the space-time dimension of the performance of work and its occupational skill elements, fix the ergonomic aspect of the relationship between pay and performance, and influence the basis for the formation of any power on the employees' side. Although intended to be universally applicable, Tayloristic methods were ideally suited to the conditions of industrial **mass production**. Repetitive, rapidly recurring tasks led to calls for a **humanization of work**. Also, Taylorism is inappropriate for meeting the current need to be able to respond flexibly to market changes with the aid of **new technologies**. It is giving way to approaches such as the so-called **new production concepts**.

701. TECHNIKFOLGENABSCHÄTZUNG UND -BEWERTUNG — TECHNOLOGY IMPACT ANALYSIS AND ASSESSMENT: Discipline which seeks, with the aid of various methods (*e.g.* listings of problems, objectives and means), to analyse the effects of technology on different areas of life and to avoid identifiable harmful or unwanted consequences or promote a **human- and environment-centred technology strategy**. At present it comprises three component elements: technological forecasting, impact analysis and policy analysis, in which an attempt is made to take account of imponderables of future developments, particularly as regards the nature of the process of political and economic implementation. This is of special importance in the case of universally applicable technologies (*e.g.* **microelectronics**). The nature and impact of their use depend on how, in a given situation, the available elements are selected and combined with organizational and human-related measures. Since the users concerned are, however, able to anticipate future developments in only an approximate fashion, there is an increased danger that all other considerations will be subordinated to whatever happen to be the dominant interests at the time.

In the past, there was no institutionalized basis for technology impact analysis and assessment in the Federal Republic, and it remained confined to *ad hoc* committees of inquiry. Nowadays, the Federal Parliament Committee for Research, Technology and Technology Impact Analysis has attached to it a corresponding Bureau which is part of a Division of the Karlsruhe Nuclear Research Centre.

Basically, it is only through the attitudes of the actors concerned that technology impact analysis has an effect on the shaping of industrial relations. Nevertheless, the "state of the art" concept has resulted in the introduction into statutes and **technical standards** of a normative entitlement to provision against risk which is linked to more than strictly technical possibilities.

702. TECHNISCHE NORMEN — TECHNICAL STANDARDS: Technical standards do not possess the status of a legal rule, but are usually laid down by a **rationalization association** (*e.g.* **DIN**). They acquire their legal significance where generally recognized technical rules are applied more specifically for the purposes of occupational health and safety and **protection against technical hazards at work**. They also constitute indices of the "state of the art". In the context of more recent legislation, fixed technical requirements are no longer specified in detail; instead, protective aims are laid down, and the normative requirements thereby linked to the movements of technical development. Other standards are determined by the "established scientific findings" concept, which accords with the prevailing body of opinion in a specialist discipline.

Within the European Community there will be uniform technical standards in the future, issued by the European Committee for Standardization (CEN, *i.e.* Comité Européen de Normalisation).

703. **TECHNISCHER ARBEITSSCHUTZ — PROTECTION AGAINST TECHNICAL HAZARDS AT WORK**: Range of provisions intended to protect employees against the hazards in the establishment deriving from technical installations, machinery and materials. They thereby assist the process of the **humanization** of working life.

The earliest of these regulations were developed in the middle of the 19th century in response to the inhumane working conditions during the period of industrialization, which damaged the health, and hence fitness for military service, of the workers to such an extent that Prussia's military capability seemed threatened. **Labour Inspectorate** authorities were set up to monitor observance of the protective provisions concerned.

The areas covered by such regulations are the design and layout of **workplaces** to suit human needs, **safety of equipment** and protection against **dangerous substances**. For the purposes of their implementation, establishments are required to operate particular **workplace health and safety arrangements**. National provisions on occupational health and safety protection are essentially regulated in statutes, in many instances supplemented by Orders issued by the Federal Government and general administrative provisions issued by the Federal Ministry of Labour and Social Affairs. In the case of **protection against accidents**, the **Occupational Health and Safety Agencies** ("Berufsgenossenschaften"), which are independent of the state, also possess powers to make rules and regulations and powers of inspection which basically supplement statutory provisions. The statutory provisions do not regulate all areas in detail; they frequently make reference to "generally recognized technical rules and established ergonomic findings". The purpose of these general clauses is to ensure that the requirements laid down keep pace with technical development.

This particular field is subject to detailed regulation at EC level. There are a number of EC **Directives** on the manufacture and use of products and machines. The so-called Machinery Directive of 1989 will be of particular importance; under its provisions, which are to be transformed into German national law by the end of 1992, in normal cases any machine manufactured within the EC must be automatically licensed for use in any Member State. The former **accident prevention regulations** will then give way to the successive technical standards issued by the European Committee for Standardization (CEN, *i.e.* Comité Européen de Normalisation).

Following a peak in the early 1960s, the number of recorded accidents at work and work-related accidents *en route* has since halved, to approximately 1.6 million in 1989.

704. **TEILAUTONOME ARBEITSGRUPPEN — SEMI-AUTONOMOUS WORK GROUPS**: A form of changed work structuring representing a response to calls for the **humanization of work**. Responsibility is assigned to a particular work group for the performance of a certain task, which is then carried out in accordance with the group's preference within predetermined parameters of organization, time limits and technical conditions. A further development of this form of production, which is frequently allied with production-line manufacture, is the so-called "work island" ("Fertigungsinsel").

705. **TEIL- ODER SCHWERPUNKTSTREIK — PARTIAL OR SELECTIVE STRIKE**: Term referring to the situation where only some of the employees in an establishment or branch of industry affected by strike action actually withdraw their labour (*e.g.* those employees in key positions who by striking bring the whole of production to a halt), or where only individual member employers of an employers' association are subjected to strike action by their employees. In the latter case, such a strategy can cause lasting disruption to the solidarity on the employers' side which is necessary for **association-level agreements**, by intensifying the clashes of interest related to competition between different employers. Any restriction of strike action to certain sections of the workforce (referred to as "Engführung") may upset the balance of bargaining power and constitute justification in law for a **lock-out**.

706. **TEILZEITARBEIT — PART-TIME WORK**: Defined as an arrangement whereby the normal **working week** as agreed under the contract of employment is shorter than that of full-time employees (Improvement of Employment Opportunities Act § 2(2)). Disadvantageous treatment of part-time employees is prohibited; labour law is in principle fully applicable to them. Accordingly, part-timers are entitled to remuneration commensurate with their working hours, to leave, to pay for public holidays, to continued remuneration when they are unavoidably prevented from working, and to the continued

payment of remuneration as generally provided for (Improvement of Employment Opportunities Act § 2(1)). Also, part-timers may not normally be excluded from discretionary fringe benefits that have the nature of remuneration (*e.g.* bonuses). This is, however, permissible in the case of payments which are linked to length of working hours (*e.g.* meal allowance). All entitlements are, however, reduced in proportion to the shorter working hours actually worked. In the context of the **works constitution**, part-timers are treated as equivalent to other employees in every respect; they are also covered by **protection against dismissal**. The question of whether ordinary **overtime** and **overtime exceeding maximum working hours** may lawfully be arranged in the case of part-time work is a matter of controversy. If employees work overtime which is in excess of their individual working hours but still within the normal daily working hours for the establishment concerned or as laid down by law, the courts hold that in principle they have no entitlement to the corresponding **pay supplement**.

The formal establishment in law of the principle of essentially equal treatment for part-time employees has not eliminated the practical problems associated with part-time work. Part-time employees are still predominantly women (approximately 93 per cent.), and highly skilled fields of employment offering corresponding career opportunities are still mostly inaccessible to part-timers. Furthermore, the supply of part-time jobs does not match the demand. Although one in three jobs available in the Federal Republic in 1988 was a part-time job, only one in five employees in the **public service** is part-time, while in manufacturing industry the number of part-time employees is as low as one in 25; yet the level of interest in part-time work is greater than this. Lastly, the fact that part-time employees spend less time in the workplace frequently means that their interests differ from those of full-timers and that they therefore make different claims on the activity of the **works council** and the **trade unions**. The first **collective agreements** to regulate the employment conditions of part-timers more specifically now exist in a number of sectors (*e.g.* chemical industry, retail distribution, metal industry).

If individual employees express a wish to change over to a part-time job, the employer must inform them of any such vacant jobs in the establishment. There is no entitlement to a corresponding **transfer**. Special forms of part-time work include **"KAPOVAZ"**, **job sharing** and annual working time arrangements such as **sabbatical leave**.

The introduction of part-time work is subject to the **co-determination right of the works council**.

312

707. **TELEARBEIT — TELEWORK**: Usually characterized by the fact that work activities are taken out of the establishment and transferred to the homes of **homeworkers**. These workplaces are often linked with the establishment by means of telecommunications technology, most commonly so that fairly straightforward office tasks can be performed in this way. Decentralization into regional offices or external service enterprises is also possible. Since telework offers such a wide variety of possible forms, teleworkers do not necessarily fall into the category of homeworkers and persons treated as equivalent in law to employees, but may also be self-employed persons or employees.

708. **"TENDENZBETRIEB"**: Literally, a "tendential" establishment: term used to refer to an establishment in which, owing to the nature of its particular purpose, the provisions of the **works constitution** are only partly applicable (Works Constitution Act § 118). The category covers all establishments which serve political, religious, charitable, educational, scientific or artistic aims or engage in news reporting and the expression of opinion. The provisions on **economic committees** are inapplicable to such establishments. The **co-determination right of the works council** for the case of a **substantial alteration to the establishment** applies only as far as regulations on the reconcilement of disadvantages are concerned. Alongside this, the provisions of the works constitution apply in principle. However, the co-determination rights of the works council are restricted to measures by the employer which do not enjoy the special protection granted by the Act for such establishments ("Tendenzschutz"). These normally include matters relating to the maintenance of order within the establishment, working hours and pay structure. In the case of individual staff measures, for example the engagement or dismissal of a newspaper editor, the presumption in law is that the interests of the establishment take precedence; the **information** and **consultation rights of the works council** must, however, be observed.

   In institutions belonging to the **Churches** and charitable organizations, differential treatment of individual employees because of their faith may, contrary to the principle of **equal treatment**, be lawful. Moreover, there are no **works councils** in these institutions, but special **ecclesiastical staff representation bodies**.

709. **TREUEPFLICHT — DUTY OF LOYALTY**: One of the **employee**'s subsidiary **obligations under the contract of employment**. It is founded in the fact that employees are accepted

313

into the employer's establishment, that tools and equipment (frequently valuable) are entrusted to their care, and that they become privy to **trade secrets**. It places the employee under an obligation to have regard for the employer's interests, and in particular not to cause damage to the employer. The implied post-contractual **restraint on competition** also derives from the duty of loyalty. Contravention of the duty of loyalty leads to liability for damages. The corresponding obligation on the employer's part is the **duty of care**.

In the case of **career public servants** ("Beamte"), the duty of loyalty extends to the **public sector employer** concerned and to the Constitution of the Federation and, where applicable, the individual Land concerned. Contraventions are dealt with as laid down by **disciplinary law for career public servants**.

710. **TREUHANDANSTALT — TREUHAND AGENCY**: A Federal agency charged with the task of the administration, in the capacity of a trustee, of the publicly owned property of the former German Democratic Republic. Some 95 per cent. of all property was so-called "Volkseigentum" (national property). The task of Treuhand, which was set up at the start of 1990, is essentially to carry out privatization. It has its headquarters in Berlin, plus 15 branch offices.

Because of the low level of competitiveness of most enterprises in eastern Germany, by the end of 1991 only half of the businesses administered by Treuhand had been successfully transferred to private ownership; at the same time, the Agency's costs far exceed its revenue from selling off businesses. This deficit is not the only reason for the controversy which surrounds Treuhand's activities. Another criticism levelled against it is that its privatization policy is leading to a de-industrialization of eastern Germany which makes independent development impossible. As a result, the Agency is also receiving much of the blame for the high level of unemployment.

711. **TRUCKVERBOT — BAN ON THE TRUCK SYSTEM**: Ban first imposed in the 19th century and later incorporated in the Industrial Code (Gewerbeordnung §§ 115, 166 ff.). Its purpose was to abolish the practice of employees being paid by their employer in the form of highly priced goods, in some cases in the form of advance credit, and thereby losing the right of free disposal over part of their remuneration. The sale of motor vehicles to employees is also subject to the ban. Exemptions are specified in the Industrial Code and in an Order issued by the former Reich Ministry of Labour. The ban does not affect an agreed arrangement for **payment in kind**.

U

712. ÜBERARBEIT — OVERTIME: Any hours of work done in excess of the working hours normally worked in the establishment. Overtime must be worked as instructed by the employer if corresponding provision has been made under the individual contract of employment or by collective agreement, or if urgent operational requirements so dictate. It attracts the same rate of pay as normal work, unless **pay supplements** have been agreed under the contract of employment or by collective agreement. However, such supplements frequently become the established custom within an establishment or an industry, with the result that enhanced rates are payable even where there is no special arrangement. The supplement payable depends on the basic pay, usually inclusive of all other pay supplements.

In the case of a five-day week and preparatory and finishing-off tasks to make up for a public holiday falling within it, overtime attracts a supplement if the corresponding collective agreement is based on the five-day week and daily working hours.

For **executive staff**, any overtime worked is deemed to be already remunerated by their normal salary.

The question of whether overtime may be arranged in the context of **part-time work** is a matter of controversy. If employees work overtime which is in excess of their individual working hours but still within the normal (full-time) daily working hours for the establishment concerned or as laid down by law, the courts hold that in principle they have no entitlement to a corresponding pay supplement.

The arrangement of overtime is subject to the **co-determination right of the works council**.

713. ÜBERBETRIEBLICHE MITBESTIMMUNG — CO-DETERMINATION ABOVE ESTABLISHMENT LEVEL: See **co-determination**.

714. ÜBERGANGSGELD — INTERIM PAYMENT: Social security benefit paid during medical or occupational rehabilitation programmes (medical, vocational and supplementary services and programmes for integrating physically, mentally and psychologically disabled persons into employment and society) organized under the **statutory pension scheme** or **accident insurance** or by the **Federal Employment Service**. It is intended to make up for loss of earnings, up to 70-90 per cent. of normal or basic pay.

715. ÜBERMASSVERBOT — PROHIBITION OF DISPROPORTIONATE MEASURES: See **proportionality principle**.

716. ÜBERSTUNDEN — OVERTIME: Synonym of **Überarbeit**.

717. ÜBERSTUNDENVERGÜTUNG — OVERTIME PAY: See **overtime**.

718. ÜBLICHE VERGÜTUNG — RATE FOR THE JOB: If the rate of **remuneration** due from the employer is neither expressly nor impliedly agreed, the employer is liable to pay the employee the rate for the job. This means the rate of pay normally paid for the same or similar work in the locality concerned, taking account of personal circumstances. For employees who are not covered by a collective agreement, it is usually the appropriate collectively agreed rate including pay supplements. The question of which collectively agreed rate is the appropriate one is governed by the nature and extent of the work actually performed by the employee on the employer's instructions.

719. ULTIMA-RATIO-PRINZIP — *ULTIMA RATIO* PRINCIPLE: Principle which has been derived by the courts from the **proportionality principle** and which must be observed in the context of the law on dismissal and on industrial action. It stipulates that **termination** of the employment contract or **industrial action** must represent the last possible means, *i.e.* last resort (*ultima ratio*). A dismissal may not be pronounced, or industrial action may not be initiated, until all reasonable measures or possibilities of reaching an understanding have been exhausted. For example, the parties to a collective agreement must have made an attempt at amicable agreement, which must have been demonstrably unsuccessful. They are also under an obligation to exhaust the available dispute resolution procedures; see **joint dispute resolution agreement**.

720. UNFALLSCHUTZ — PROTECTION AGAINST ACCIDENTS: Viewed generally, all the measures and precautions necessary to avoid an **accident at work** (accident prevention). These are codified in various statutes. The law on protection against accidents therefore forms part of **protection against technical hazards at work** and **safety of equipment**. Under private law, the **duty of care** devolving on **employers** places them under an obligation to protect the life and health of their employees. Under public law, special regulations are laid down respectively in the Commercial Code, the Industrial Code, the Homeworking Act, the Seafarers Act and the Youth Employment Protection Act.

Alongside these regulations there are also the protective provisions dealing specifically with accident prevention issued by the **Occupational Health and Safety Agencies** ("Berufsgenossenschaften") with the authorization of the Federal Ministry of Labour and Social Affairs. These must be observed by both employers and employees. Their observance is supervised by technical inspectors employed by the Agencies. Every establishment with more than 20 employees must also appoint a **safety officer**, who is responsible for helping the employer to ensure that the accident prevention regulations are put into practice and for keeping a constant check on the presence and proper use of protective devices. Contraventions, whether deliberate or resulting from negligence, may incur the imposition of a fine. Wilfully or knowingly removing or modifying protective devices is an offence punishable by fine or imprisonment.

In addition, the operation of a **business** is subject to the provisions on protection against accidents in the Industrial Code (Gewerbeordnung), which, unlike the Agencies' accident prevention regulations, affect only the employer. These require every employer to provide and maintain premises, facilities, machinery and equipment in such a way that employees are protected from danger to life and health, in so far as the particular nature of the establishment allows. Infringement of these Industrial Code provisions, whether deliberate or resulting from negligence, may incur a fine of up to 10,000 Deutschmarks. Any contravention which endangers another person's life or health or valuable property belonging to another person is an offence punishable by a fine or up to one year's imprisonment. Also, continued operation of the business may be prohibited on the grounds of untrustworthiness.

These public-law provisions on accident prevention cannot be modified or avoided via individual contract. If the employer fails to observe them, employees may refuse to render the work performance. Given that they offer their work performance for the case where the provisions are observed, failure by the employer to ensure this constitutes **employer's non-acceptance of the work performance**, and the employer must pay the agreed remuneration even though no work is performed. The **works council** and the **staff council** also have the right and the duty, in general, to keep a check on the observance of accident prevention regulations. They may also conclude **works agreements** and **establishment agreements** with the private sector employer or **public sector employer** on additional protective measures.

Changes to the regulation of protection against accidents are likely to result from the harmonization measures necessary to create the European **internal market**. Important EC-wide regulations are the so-called Machinery Directive and the

317

Directive of June 12, 1989 on the introduction of measures to encourage improvements in the health and safety of workers at work.

721. **UNFALLVERHÜTUNGSVORSCHRIFTEN—ACCIDENT PREVENTION REGULATIONS**: See **Occupational Health and Safety Agencies, protection against accidents**.

722. **UNFALLVERSICHERUNG — ACCIDENT INSURANCE**: The Federal Republic has both a social system of statutory accident insurance and private-law accident insurance.

Social insurance against accidents is a branch of general **social security**. Its primary function is to provide benefits for claimants in the event of an **accident at work** or **occupational illness**. All individuals who are in an **employment relationship**, **service relationship** or **vocational training relationship** are insured. Others covered include **homeworkers, persons carrying on a business from home** and also schoolchildren and students. Accident insurance is financed by employers. The main provisions are curative treatment and forms of **state occupational assistance**, together with supplementary payments. The **Occupational Health and Safety Agencies** are the principal institutions administering this industrial injuries insurance. It is subject to statutory regulation in Book 3 of the Reich Insurance Code (Reichsversicherungsordnung); historically, it dates back to what is known as **Bismarck's social security legislation.**

In addition to the statutory system, there is also a private-law system of accident insurance. This is not a form of social insurance, however, but private insurance covering personal risk and based on a contractual insurance policy.

723. **UNION LEITENDER ANGESTELLTER — ASSOCIATION OF EXECUTIVE STAFF**: An umbrella organization consisting of eight occupational unions from the private sector, in which **executive staff**, specialist personnel and trainee staff in these categories are organized. These member unions of the Association of Executive Staff (ULA) have a total combined membership of 40,000; 20,000 of these members belong to just one union, the Association of Graduate and Executive Staff in the Chemical Industry. Whereas 80 per cent. of scientists in the chemical industry are organized, there are almost no ULA members in small and medium-sized establishments, with the result that average union density is only 8 per cent. Although these unions occasionally conclude **collective agreements**, owing to the special status of executive staff within the establishment a separate judgment has to be made for each union on the extent

318

to which it may be recognized as possessing **trade union** status and hence the **capacity to conclude collective agreements**.

724. **UNMÖGLICHKEIT DER ARBEITSLEISTUNG — IMPOSSIBILITY OF PERFORMANCE**: If employees are unable to render the performance of work due from them, this constitutes a case of impossibility of performance. There are differing consequences as regards their entitlement to remuneration. In the first place, the employer may still be under an obligation, by virtue of a statute or case law, for the **continued payment of remuneration** in such cases. If this is not so, the question of who is answerable for the impossibility of performance must be examined. If the fault lies with the employer the employees' entitlement to remuneration is retained, but if it lies with the employees they lose their entitlement.

In cases where the impossibility of performance is through no fault of either party, the existence of the entitlement to remuneration is decided in accordance with the theory of "**works risk**".

725. **UNTERNEHMEN — COMPANY**: In commercial law and labour law, a company (*i.e.* enterprise) is the totality of all the assets, intangible resources and rights and the organization, including employees, necessary in order to achieve a particular economic objective. Intangible resources include, in addition to the company's reputation (goodwill), its **corporate culture** (company philosophy). The company is run by the **entrepreneur** as its owner or in the form of the responsible **managing director** or **management board**, usually with the assistance of **management**. In terms of the organization of work the company's economic objective is pursued by means of one or more **establishments**; several companies may, however, also have a common establishment. Employees who can no longer be employed in a given establishment must be offered any suitable vacant jobs in other establishments belonging to the company. If a company has several **works councils**, a **company works council** must be formed. Various **forms of company** exist. Depending on their particular structure in terms of company law, this gives rise to differing rights and obligations for the **company members** and **company organs** and also different **company constitutions** and opportunities for **co-determination**. Companies may be transferred by legal transaction resulting in the **acquisition of a company** and may also be amalgamated with others by way of **merger**, possibly leading in specific cases to a **substantial alteration to the establishment**. Companies in the form of a public limited company or partnership limited by shares are able

to form groups and thereby commit themselves, for example, to control or transfer of profits.

Because of their conceptually elastic and multiple demand for labour, even in the form of an individual person companies and entrepreneurs constitute, sociologically, a *de facto* **collective industrial organization**. They are frequently organized in **employers' associations**.

726. UNTERNEHMENSAUFSPALTUNG — COMPANY SPLIT-UP: The transformation of one company into several companies. If, as frequently happens, individual **establishments** or **departments** are separated off from the company and upgraded into independent individual companies, it also constitutes a **company split-up at establishment level**. Where a company split-up is associated with a change in the organization of an establishment, it is an instance of a **substantial alteration to the establishment**, and any change of owner involves **transfer of an establishment**. A company split-up has considerable significance in relation to the preconditions for the formation of a **works council** and the extent of the **participation rights of the works council**, and also as regards the **binding effect of collective agreements** in cases where the company formed as a result of split-up is not a member of an employers' association or joins a new one.

Special aspects arise in the case of eastern Germany under the Law for the Regulation of Unresolved Questions of Property and the Law concerning the Split-up of Companies Administered by the **Treuhand Agency**. In instances of company split-up and company split-up at establishment level and of establishment split-off, the regulations there provide special information rights and a three-month interim mandate for the works council.

727. UNTERNEHMENSAUTONOMIE — COMPANY AUTONOMY: See **basic rights, free enterprise, freedom of occupation**.

728. UNTERNEHMENSFORMEN — FORMS OF COMPANY: Enterprises or companies can be organized in a variety of forms under commercial and company law in the Federal Republic. In addition to the sole proprietorship there are various types of association and company which are established by the conclusion of a contract or deed of association; in this form ("Gesellschaft"), with the exception of the sole proprietorship and the non-incorporated civil-law association (GbR) they must, in addition to other requirements, be entered in the Commercial Register or Co-operative Societies Register.

Partnerships comprise the GbR and the general partnership (OHG), in which the partners need not be natural persons. Unless the deed of association or partnership provides otherwise, the holdings are equal and direction of the business is the joint responsibility of all partners, who are also personally subject to joint and several liability for the partnership's debts and obligations. The limited liability partnership (KG) occupies a halfway position between a partnership and a joint-stock company. Personal liability is restricted to the general partner, while the limited partners are liable only to the value of the capital contribution they have paid in. Partnerships and the KG do not have the status of **legal persons** but the OHG and KG are independent in law within the scope of their activity.

Joint-stock companies (*i.e.* a company limited by shares, or "Kapitalgesellschaft"), into which (unlike partnerships) entry can be effected only by making a cash or non-cash contribution, are legal persons. Within this category, there is a distinction between the registered co-operative society (eG), the private limited company (GmbH), the public limited company (AG) and the partnership limited by shares (KGaA). In the case of the eG, the value of the contribution to capital is usually restricted. The members are not directly liable to debtors, but only with respect to the eG. In the case of the GmbH, the value of the contribution to capital is unlimited and a so-called single-proprietor GmbH is also possible. Liability is limited to the company's assets, which amount to at least 50,000 Deutschmarks. In the case of the AG, holdings are in the form of shares which are in principle freely transferable and frequently bought and sold on the stock exchange. The minimum ordinary capital is 100,000 Deutschmarks. In the case of the KGaA, there is at least one personally liable partner. The rest of the capital is divided into shares. Whereas in the case of the eG each co-operative member normally has only one vote, in the other forms of joint-stock company the influence of the members varies according to the value of their shareholding. Decision-making, conduct of the company's business and representation, and supervision of the conduct of business, are carried out through the **company organs**.

The legal forms of company which are valid for all EC Member States are the European Business Partnership, which is comparable to a German OHG, and the European Company (also referred to as Societas Europea or SE), denoting the concept of a European public limited company. The minimum ordinary capital requirement for SE formation is 100,000 ECU (approximately 206,000 Deutschmarks). The SE is subject to special provisions on **co-determination**.

321

729. UNTERNEHMENSKULTUR — CORPORATE CULTURE: Term used to refer to the basic system of values which influences **personnel management** and employees' **motivation to work** within a **company**. It includes the particular organization culture concerned, *i.e.* the matrix of underlying assumptions developed by a group of people who have acquired considerable shared experience of resolving problems relating to adjustment to the external context and integration within the internal context. Once developed, these assumptions are usually taken for granted and rarely made consciously. In combination with inherited values, traditions (*e.g.* from the founder's generation) and symbols (*e.g.* general image, external and internal prizes and rewards, bonuses, company housing, forms of status) they constitute the corporate culture as a whole. Since every company has its own individual characteristics, the corresponding corporate culture is necessarily unique and pronounced to a greater or lesser degree. It is reinforced by the results achieved, and is therefore not static but undergoes processes of change, albeit slow ones. Although its connection with performance cannot be measured precisely, the corporate culture has assumed continuously increasing importance. Firstly, the management of multinational corporations requires some sense of community of interests between all their employees in different countries and national cultures. Secondly, ever-shorter **product cycles** demand increased efforts to achieve innovation. Experience shows that innovations are achieved by dint of team work and interdisciplinary co-operation, and these depend on more than purely formal organizational principles. And in large companies in particular, the decentralization necessary for this is possible only if informal control mechanisms guarantee stability and continuity. Here, the corporate culture assists collective awareness of individual corporate identity. The development of a particular corporate culture is fostered by way of appropriate **new production concepts**, measures directed at the **humanization of work**, **in-service training**, quality circles, rotation of employees within the company, "transparent" management and, in general, by the retention of a stable workforce. In particular, making **personnel policy** more consistent and controlling the rate of career development reduces personal competitiveness between employees and encourages a co-operative spirit. Alongside the opportunities they offer to employees, the ideas underlying a corporate culture also carry dangers. Based mainly on **informal rules**, they represent a way of undermining the actual basis of **institutionalized representation of interests** for employees in establishments. By its very nature, the corporate culture provides **management** with social mechanisms for reinforcing the internal legitimacy of its control.

322

730. UNTERNEHMENSORGANE — COMPANY ORGANS:
Functional bodies of particular **forms of company** through which
decision-making takes place, business is conducted and the
company is represented, and the **managing director** or
management board is supervised. The obligatory organs of a
private limited company are the **company general meeting** and
the **managing director** and, in the case of statutory **co-
determination**, the **supervisory board**. The articles of association
may make optional provision for the appointment of a supervisory
board, advisory board or board of directors. The company organs
of a public limited company and a registered co-operative society
are the **shareholders' meeting** or general meeting, the
management board and the supervisory board. Although the
members of the company organs are not treated as employees,
those who belong to the board of directors or the management
board may have their legal actions heard in the **system of labour
courts**.

**731. UNTERNEHMENSORGANISATION — COMPANY
ORGANIZATION:** The regulations and structures within a
company which fix the ordered system of decision-making,
powers of authority and responsibilities. The system is usually
hierarchical: different tasks and corresponding decision-making
authority, powers and spheres of responsibility are assigned to
each level and its functionaries, from the **management board**
down through the departmental heads and production managers,
master craftworkers, first-line and other supervisors to the
production workers, ancillary workers or general clerical staff.
In addition to this horizontal organization, there is a vertical
company organization based on different areas of activity (*e.g.*
development, production, sales, administration). Ways of creating
the greatest possible flexibility for enabling a company to adjust
to changed external conditions are provided, for example, by
appropriate methods of **management**, improvement of
information flows (**office communications technology**) and the
establishment of interfaces.

**732. UNTERNEHMENSÜBERNAHME — ACQUISITION OF
A COMPANY:** The succession in title to a company, which takes
place either by legal transaction (sale, exchange, gift or leasing),
because of death (inheritance, bequest), through the
transformation of a sole proprietorship into an incorporated
company, or through **merger**. (The term "takeover", although
applicable, tends to imply a hostile takeover bid.) For the
purposes of **labour law**, the acquisition of a company can lead
to **transfer of an establishment**; in exceptional cases it may also

323

constitute a **substantial alteration to the establishment**. It is, however, significant as regards the **binding effect of collective agreements** on the employer, in cases where the new owner is not a member of an employers' association or belongs to a different one.

733. **UNTERNEHMENSVERFASSUNG — COMPANY CONSTITUTION**: Term used to refer to the body of provisions on the direct and indirect **co-determination** of employees in the company organs, particularly on the **supervisory board** and via the **employee director**.

734. **UNTERNEHMER — ENTREPRENEUR**: Name given in economic theory to the owner (*e.g.* a particular registered **form of company**) or responsible head of a business enterprise. For the purposes of **social security law**, the entrepreneur is the individual on whose account the enterprise or activity is carried on, which means that a worker classed as employed by the entrepreneur does not need to have concluded a valid **contract of employment**. In **labour law**, the entrepreneur and the **employer** may be one and the same person. Under the **works constitution**, it is the entrepreneur or employer or their representative, depending on the particular situation, who is the opposite number of the **works council**. Because of their conceptually elastic and multiple demand for labour, even in the form of an individual person entrepreneurs or enterprises constitute, sociologically, a **collective industrial organization**. They are frequently organized in **employers' associations**.

735. **UNTERNEHMERFREIHEIT — FREE ENTERPRISE**: Concept grouping together the guarantees of autonomy relevant to business enterprise which are provided by the Basic Law. The holders of these rights are individuals or associations of persons who pursue economic objectives on a private basis and on their own responsibility, with the aim of making a profit. The relevant **basic rights** are, first and foremost, **freedom of occupation** and the right of ownership of private property, and also freedom of association and general liberty of action. Freedom of enterprise is merely the sum of the guarantees of these basic rights. Above all, it does not represent any predetermination by the Basic Law of a particular economic system. It does not exclude either the expropriation of individual firms or the nationalization of economically important enterprises, provided that adequate compensation is paid. The Federal Constitutional Court has also rejected attempts to claim that the guarantee of free enterprise makes the existing legal provisions on **co-determination** unconstitutional.

324

The essential significance of free enterprise is that, as a matter of principle, it guarantees a minimum volume of private entrepreneurial activity, prohibits arbitrary state intervention and permits restrictions only for important practical reasons. The greater the degree of intervention, the more rigorously the state is required to justify it.

736. **URABSTIMMUNG — STRIKE BALLOT**: The breakdown of the **joint dispute resolution** procedure does not lead automatically to **industrial action**. A formal decision to call a strike is also necessary. This is frequently preceded by a ballot of the union members who are to participate in the strike. The ballot is not required by law. Every trade union can decide at its own discretion whether it wishes to practise direct or indirect union democracy (**democratic decision-making**). Nor do the **union strike guidelines** drawn up by the German Federation of Trade Unions (DGB) stipulate a compulsory ballot.

The only way in which non-union members are able to have a voice in the matter is by bringing influence to bear on their unionized colleagues. The actual ballot is carried out by free and secret vote. This is followed by the strike decision, which is made by the union's main executive body (it is not bound by the outcome of the ballot). Taking into account factors such as the economic situation, the consequential effects on other branches of the economy and the organizational circumstances, if the executive body has decided to call the strike it instructs the members (usually simultaneously) to stop work.

737. **URLAUB — LEAVE (OF ABSENCE)**: Period during which the employee's contractual obligation to work is suspended for specific reasons. There are statutory entitlements (in some cases under Länder legislation) to **annual holiday, educational leave** and **childcare leave**, which are in many cases increased by collective agreement.

In addition, employees may obtain leave of absence by agreement with their employer. White-collar workers in the **public service** are entitled to such special leave if they demonstrate an important reason for being granted time off and waive their right to remuneration during the period of leave concerned, and if the general operational circumstances permit it.

There are also entitlements to release from work in cases of **illness**, for exercising civic rights (such as standing as a parliamentary candidate), for applying for and exercising office as a member of a **works council** or **staff council**, for coping with urgent personal circumstances and, in cases where the employment relationship has been terminated, for looking for a new job. These latter entitlements do not, however, fall conceptually within the definition of leave entitlements.

738. **URLAUBSGELD — HOLIDAY BONUS**: See **annual holiday, special bonus**.

739. **URTEILSVERFAHREN — "URTEIL" PROCEDURE**: **Labour court procedure** includes both the **"Beschluss" procedure** and the "Urteil" procedure. The latter is used in disputes under labour law between employees and employers arising from the employment relationship, its pre-contractual obligations and its continuing effect; in **disputes of rights** between the parties to a collective agreement or between the latter and third parties arising from collective agreements or from inadmissible action for the purposes of industrial action; or in connection with questions of **freedom of association** (the right to organize). Since the main features of the "Urteil" procedure are the same as those of the normal procedure before the ordinary system of courts in civil proceedings, the provisions of the Labour Courts Act (Arbeitsgerichtsgesetz) essentially make reference to the corresponding regulations of the Code of Civil Procedure. The special features regulated in the Act are connected with the need to arrive at a decision as quickly as possible so that the parties can make further arrangements as required. Other special features include the obligatory preliminary **conciliation hearing** and the regulations on **representation in court** and **legal costs**. The **remedies at law** available under the "Urteil" procedure are **appeal** and **appeal on a point of law** or **direct appeal on a point of law**.

V

740. VERBÄNDERECHT — LAW ON ASSOCIATIONS: The basis of the law on associations is enshrined in the general **freedom of association**, the right to organize collectively and the right to form societies. These give associations extensive autonomy in determining their internal rules and their objectives in a constitutional manner. Owing to the paramount importance of the **parties to collective agreements** in a pluralistic society, efforts are made from time to time to achieve direct statutory endorsement of the autonomy of associations, more particularly of **trade unions**. To date, however, all such efforts have remained unsuccessful.

741. VERBANDSTARIFVERTRAG — ASSOCIATION-LEVEL AGREEMENT: Term used to refer to a **collective agreement** between an **employers' association** and a **trade union**. Nowadays, such agreements are the general pattern. Although the collective bargaining regions (approximately 3,000) are equally divided between individual company and association-level regions, and the 32,000 collective agreements currently valid include some 8,000 company agreements, association-level agreements are of paramount importance in collective industrial relations. They ultimately govern the employment relationships of some 18.5 million employees, whereas only 500,000 employees are covered by company agreements.

742. VERBESSERUNGSVORSCHLÄGE — SUGGESTIONS FOR IMPROVEMENTS: In the case of technical suggestions for improvements by employees for which they cede to the employer a right of exploitation similar to patent or registered design rights, under the Inventions by Employees Act (Gesetz über Arbeitnehmererfindungen) employees are entitled to fair and reasonable compensation if the employer makes use of the suggestion. In the case of other suggestions for improvements (*e.g.* of a clerical or organizational nature) employees are entitled to compensation provided that the employer makes use of the suggestion, that it represents a special contribution from the employee extending beyond normal contractual obligations, and that some significant benefit accrues to the employer from its use.

Independently of these legal entitlements, in many establishments a company suggestions scheme has evolved under which the employer offers sometimes substantial rewards for suggestions for improvements, with the purpose of further rationalization in the establishment, encouraging employee involvement and improving the general establishment culture.

If there is a **works council** in the establishment, the suggestions scheme and the rewards offered are subject to co-determination.

743. **VERDACHTSKÜNDIGUNG — DISMISSAL ON GROUNDS OF SUSPICION**: Even if a criminal act or breach of contract by an employee is not proven, in certain cases the suspicion of such misconduct may justify dismissal, usually by **summary termination**. The stated reason for this ruling is that in certain posts a relationship of trust between employer and employee, untrammelled by legitimate doubts, is absolutely essential.

Such dismissal is, however, lawful only within narrow limits. The suspicion must be strong and substantiated by facts. The employer must have done everything possible to elucidate the matter and must have given the employee a chance to explain their case. The suspicion must be so grave that it suffices in itself to break the relationship of trust necessary to the performance of the **contract of employment** and therefore makes it unreasonable for the employer to be expected to continue the **employment relationship**.

If it later transpires that the suspicion was unfounded, the post-contractual effect of the employer's **duty of care** entitles the employee to reinstatement.

744. **VEREINIGUNG DER KOMMUNALEN ARBEIT-GEBERVERBÄNDE — FEDERATION OF MUNICIPAL EMPLOYERS' ASSOCIATIONS**: See **employers' association**.

745. **VERFAHRENSINNOVATION — PROCESS INNOVATION**: See **rationalization**.

746. **VERFAHRENSKOSTEN — LEGAL COSTS**: Term used to describe the court fees and the costs incurred by the parties, *e.g.* for lawyers, which arise in a court case. In **labour court procedure** they are regulated differently for the **"Beschluss" procedure** and the **"Urteil" procedure** respectively. In the "Urteil" procedure, although court fees are payable the Labour Courts Act (Arbeitsgerichtsgesetz) stipulates that they should be lower than for proceedings in the other systems of jurisdiction and should not fall due until the end of the instance concerned. The Act also greatly restricts the winning party's entitlement to reimbursement of their extra-judicial costs. In the "Beschluss" procedure, no court fees are payable and the **employer** pays the remaining costs if the **works council** is the other interested party. These special rules are intended to ensure that the risk of costs to be incurred is kept low for both sides.

747. **VERFASSUNG — CONSTITUTION**: The Constitution of the Federal Republic of Germany is the Basic Law (Grundgesetz), and each of the Länder also has its own Land Constitution. Constitutional law occupies an important position in all spheres of life and law. The German Constitutions all contain:
1. guarantees of **basic rights** (*e.g.* Basic Law, Articles 1-19);
2. general regulations on the form of government and functions of the Federation (individual Land concerned), the Länder (districts) and the municipalities (*e.g.* Basic Law, Articles 20-37);
3. provisions on the tasks of the Parliaments, Governments and other constitutional entities and their standing with respect to each other (*e.g.* relating to the **Federal Parliament, Federal Council** and **Federal Government** in the Basic Law, Articles 38-69);
4. rules on **legislation** and legislative procedure (*e.g.* Basic Law, Articles 70-82) and on the execution of laws (*e.g.* Basic Law, Articles 83-91B);
5. provisions on judicial authority (*e.g.* Basic Law, Articles 92-104);
6. rules on the finance system (*e.g.* Basic Law, Articles 105-115); and also,
7. in the Basic Law, regulations on defence (Articles 115A-115L). Under its Article 79, the Basic Law may be amended by a majority of two thirds of the members in both the Federal Parliament and the Federal Council. However, no amendment is admissible which would affect the principles (as enumerated in Article 79(3)) of human dignity and of the Federal Republic as a democratic social and federal state.

In cases relating to violation of the Constitution and constitutional rights, the competent or affected institutions or individuals may lodge an appeal with the **Federal Constitutional Court**.

748. **VERFASSUNGSBESCHWERDE — CONSTITUTIONAL APPEAL**: An application to the court which may be lodged against any form of sovereign act on the part of the public authorities (for instance, against a statute or a court judgment), invoking the grounds that it has resulted in a violation of the appellant's **basic rights** or of other similarly important constitutional guarantees. Depending on whether the case concerns basic rights as provided by the Basic Law or by the Constitution of an individual Land, it is decided either by the Federal Constitutional Court or by one of the Länder Constitutional Courts.

If the Constitutional Court allows an appeal, it quashes the decision against which the appeal was directed: statutes which formed the subject of the appeal are declared partly or wholly null and void, or their interpretation is decided in a manner which is compatible with the Constitution and which is to be binding in future; court decisions are frequently referred back to the court concerned for a fresh decision.

Labour law matters which are particularly likely to form the subject of a constitutional appeal are disputes in which appellants invoke basic rights against acts by the public authorities. Examples include decisions by the **Federal Labour Court** which deny an association the **capacity to conclude collective agreements**.

749. **VERFASSUNGSGERICHTSBARKEIT — SYSTEM OF CONSTITUTIONAL COURTS**: One of the systems of jurisdiction in the Federal Republic protected by the Basic Law. It is exercised by the Federal Constitutional Court (BVerfG) and the Constitutional Courts of the individual Länder (for which the name "Staatsgerichtshof" is used in some cases). As laid down in the Basic Law and the Federal Constitutional Court Act, the responsibilities of the BVerfG include delivering judgments on **constitutional appeals**, disputes between constitutional entities, the Federation and the Länder, bans on political parties and the forfeiture of certain basic rights.

The BVerfG consists of two senates, each with eight career judges, half of whom are elected by the Federal Parliament and half by the Federal Council. As a general principle, no costs are payable for proceedings before the BVerfG, but subject to certain conditions a fee of up to 5,000 Deutschmarks may be levied in the case of inadmissible or unsubstantiated applications. In oral hearings, the parties must arrange to be represented by suitably qualified persons.

750. **VERGLEICH — SETTLEMENT**: Term used to refer to a settlement in the form of a "compromise", *i.e.* an agreement by which dispute or uncertainty between the parties concerning a legal relationship is settled by way of mutual concession. Any court proceedings already started are terminated by the compromise, which may constitute a deed of **enforcement**. Disputes under labour law also may be settled by a compromise. When the **"Urteil" procedure** is used, an obligatory preliminary stage is a **conciliation hearing** in which the president of the chamber attempts to bring about a compromise between the parties; other than this, the Labour Court seeks throughout the proceedings to effect an amicable settlement of the case. A compromise may not be agreed if the matter forming the subject

of the dispute has been placed beyond the control of the parties. This is so, for example, with claims arising from the Federal Minimum Annual Holiday Act (Bundesurlaubsgesetz). **Waiver** of existing collectively agreed rights is possible only with the consent of the **parties to a collective agreement**. This also applies when the **"Beschluss" procedure** is used.

The same term also refers to a "composition", *i.e.* an arrangement with creditors whereby the bankruptcy of an insolvent debtor is averted.

751. **VERHALTENSBEDINGTE KÜNDIGUNG — DISMISSAL ON GROUNDS OF CONDUCT**: Termination of an **employment relationship** by the employer which is justified by a circumstance relating to wilful conduct on the part of the employee (Protection Against Dismissal Act § 1). Establishing the differentiation of dismissal on grounds of conduct from **redundancy** is relatively uncomplicated, since grounds relating to conduct must have their origin within the employee's personal sphere of control, whereas the grounds for redundancy must have their origin in economic reasons of the firm. The dividing line between dismissal on grounds of conduct and **dismissal on grounds of personal capability** is, however, fluid. Grounds relating to conduct concern individual acts committed by the employee, whereas grounds relating to personal capability are associated with certain permanent personal characteristics and abilities of the employee.

Grounds relating to conduct include poor performance, refusal to work, contraventions of the rules for maintaining order within the establishment and betrayal of the relationship of trust between employer and employee. Such grounds may be used to justify dismissal both by **summary termination** and by ordinary **termination with notice**. In both cases, it is usually necessary for the employer to have issued a **warning** to the employee before proceeding to pronounce dismissal. In weighing up the respective interests consideration must be given, in the typical case, to the fault on the part of the employee, the extent of any damage caused and other negative consequences of the culpable conduct, the danger of its recurrence and the practical possibility of re-training or transferring the employee, and also the employee's age and continuous length of service within the establishment.

752. **VERHÄLTNISMÄSSIGKEITSGRUNDSATZ — PROPORTIONALITY PRINCIPLE**: Principle which is a characteristic feature of the entire judicial system of the Federal Republic. It has particular significance in the context of the law on dismissal and industrial action. Application of the principle prohibits all

measures which, for the purposes of achieving the aim in view, are inappropriate, unnecessary or disproportionate.

In the case of **industrial action**, for example, this means that such action may not be pitched at destroying the actual means of existence, including making the continued survival of a company impossible. This applies on a subjective level in the sense of the nature of the aim underlying a labour dispute, but it also applies on an objective level where the existence of a number of individual people and enterprises is of importance to society as a whole. Gross disproportion exists, for example, in cases of industrial action in establishments which provide essential services (electricity and water supplies, hospitals), unless provision is made for the population's needs through the **maintenance of essential supplies and services**. On the other hand, damage to the individual (even of a serious kind) normally has to be accepted; otherwise industrial action, a necessary element of **collective bargaining autonomy**, would be made virtually impossible in practice.

Consequently, the proportionality principle entails a process of weighing-up between collective bargaining autonomy and industrial action in terms of their importance for society as a whole and the respective legitimate positions of the parties involved, third parties and the general public. It is the measure used for examining whether the disadvantage caused respectively to the legal position of the employers and employees directly involved in the dispute and of those indirectly affected is disproportionate or not.

753. **VERLEIHER — LESSOR**: Term applied to an employer who hires out employees as temporary workers ("Leiharbeit") to another employer (the lessee) and thus places them under the latter's authority for a specified period in the exercise of the **employer's right to issue instructions**. This is more correctly termed **hiring-out of labour**. See **temporary worker's employer**.

754. **VERLETZTENRENTE — INDUSTRIAL INJURY PENSION**: Pension paid under **accident insurance** for the loss or at least 20 per cent. reduction of earning capacity as the result of an **accident at work** or **occupational illness**. It is granted only if the impairment of earning capacity lasts longer than 13 weeks after the event insured against. In cases of total incapacity, the full pension amounts to two thirds of annual earnings. In cases of reduced earning capacity, a partial pension is paid according to the degree of reduction.

As a provision under **state occupational assistance**, an industrial injury allowance ("Verletztengeld") may also be paid if the victim is unfit for work within the meaning of health insurance (**certificate of incapacity for work**), is not entitled to an industrial injury pension and is not receiving remuneration, unemployment benefit or assistance, or subsistence, short-time or bad-weather allowances.

755. **VERMÖGENSWIRKSAME LEISTUNGEN — CAPITAL-FORMING PAYMENTS**: Payments which are not paid over to employees in freely disposable form but invested on their behalf (*e.g.* savings with building societies and participation in productive assets in the form of shares, certain investment fund certificates or holdings in private limited companies) or used by the employees for specified purposes (*e.g.* the construction or acquisition of their own home). The state encourages this with the **employee savings supplement**. Employees themselves decide on the particular type of investment, within the range of statutory possibilities. Employees have an entitlement to capital-forming payments over and above their remuneration only if provision has been made for these additional payments in a collective agreement, works agreement or individual contract of employment.

756. **VERRECHNUNGSKLAUSEL — OFFSET CLAUSE**: Clause in a **collective agreement** which has the opposite purpose to **actual-pay** and *status quo* **clauses**. Offset clauses are found where collective agreements fix special payments by the employer (special bonuses, etc.) which have in part already been paid formerly on a discretionary basis. These clauses stipulate that the new collectively agreed payments should be offset against the (discretionary) payments granted formerly.

Offset clauses are held by the courts to be invalid, since a collective agreement can fix only minimum, not maximum, levels of pay. A clause in a collective agreement cannot remove an obligation under an individual employment contract to grant certain payments in addition to the current collectively agreed payment. The question of whether a collectively agreed arrangement is to be classed as an offset clause is decided by interpretation in the courts.

757. **VERRECHTLICHUNG — JURIDIFICATION**: Term denoting the process whereby **industrial relations** in the Federal Republic are embedded in a closely knit system of procedural rules and rules allowing or granting rights for the individual. A comprehensive body of regulations has been built up both by legislation and by case law concerning, in particular, **industrial action**, the **works constitution** and **co-determination**. There

nevertheless exists, in the Federal Republic as elsewhere, a certain interplay between progressive juridification and deregulation. This arises from the ambivalence of juridification: for example, with regard to what is politically desirable it has a pacifying effect on strike activity, but with regard to calls for the **flexibilization** of working hours or of protection against dismissal it preserves existing employee positions as already won.

758. **VERSETZUNG — TRANSFER**: If an employee normally employed in a particular job is assigned to a different area of work by the employer on the strength of the **employer's right to issue instructions**, this constitutes a transfer in so far as the new job is expected to last for more than one month or involves a significant change of employment conditions.

Under individual labour law, the precondition for a legally valid transfer is that:
1. the possibility of transfer is reserved (expressly or impliedly) under the contract of employment, and
2. the employee can fairly and reasonably be expected to accept unilateral designation of the nature or location of the work performance.

A transfer to a lower-grade job is unlawful even if the former level of pay is retained. In all cases in which a transfer is ruled out, a **dismissal for variation of contract** is required. There are restrictions on the possibility of transfer in the case of members of the **works council, disabled persons** and pregnant employees. A transfer may be appropriate on grounds of the employer's **duty of care** if the employee is no longer able to render the contractually agreed work performance or as a milder alternative to dismissal.

A **co-determination right of the works council** exists in the case of transfer in establishments normally employing more than 20 employees entitled to vote, and in the drawing-up of **guidelines for personnel selection**.

759. **VERSORGUNGSANWARTSCHAFT — OCCUPATIONAL PENSION EXPECTATION**: Entitlements to payments from an **occupational pension scheme** which have accrued to an employee from an **assurance of an occupational pension** but have not yet fallen due. Under the regulations laid down in the 1974 Improvement of Occupational Pension Schemes Act, such entitlements cannot be revoked, *i.e.* are retained even if an employee leaves the establishment before the occurrence of the event giving rise to the pension, provided that the employee in question has reached the age of 35 and has been covered by the assurance of a pension for 10 years (or for 3 years in the case

of employees with at least 12 years' continuous length of service in the establishment). These qualifying periods are not interrupted by the **transfer of an establishment** or changes (particularly increases and additions) to the pension assurance.

The pension expectation accumulates in proportion to the continuous **length of service** up to the occurrence of the event giving rise to the pension, which is usually at the same time as that for the **statutory pension scheme**. On its occurrence, the employee becomes entitled to an occupational pension equivalent in amount to the expectation that has been accumulated. Corresponding rules also apply to company schemes for invalidity insurance. The time of occurrence of the event giving rise to a pension can be deferred by the stipulation of qualifying (or "waiting") periods. Such periods (which are to be distinguished from the time limits within which entitlements can be revoked) make the employee's claim to receipt of pension payments dependent on a specified minimum length of continuous service in the establishment.

760. **VERSORGUNGSZUSAGE — ASSURANCE OF AN OCCUPATIONAL PENSION**: A commitment by an employer, validly constituted but not yet fallen due, to grant an **occupational pension** in favour of employees employed in his or her establishment through an **occupational pension scheme**. Since there is no statutory obligation on employers to set up an occupational pension scheme, a special legal act of commitment is necessary in order to constitute such an assurance (the grant of which is thus a component of **pay**). The commitment may come into being by way of arrangements agreed in the **contract of employment** (either by explicit regulation or by reference to a pension scheme existing in the establishment), and also by way of a **general undertaking by the employer, custom, works agreement** (although the **works council** cannot enforce it) or **collective agreement** (a form which rarely occurs in the private sector but is important in the public sector) and, in instances of unjustified discriminatory treatment of individual employees or groups of employees, by virtue of the principle of **equal treatment**.

761. **VERTRAGSFREIHEIT — FREEDOM OF CONTRACT**: Although in principle the concept of freedom of contract applies in labour law also, it is subject to numerous constraints. The only aspect which is free from constraints concerns the pure formalities of entering into an employment relationship. Noticeable constraints are imposed by statute, collective agreement, works

agreement and case law as concerns **freedom of contractual content** in particular, but also the **freedom to conclude an employment contract**, since provisions in an individual contract of employment diverging from any such regulations to the employee's disadvantage are invalid.

762. **VERTRAUENSLEUTE — UNION WORKPLACE REPRE-SENTATIVES**: Literally, "trusted" representatives. These are union members who in accordance with the aims of their **trade union** are responsible, independently of the formal structure of employee representation in the establishment (**works council**), for communicating collective bargaining policy to individual employees and keeping the union informed about employees' wishes. They are usually elected by the union members employed within an establishment or department. They may lawfully be granted special protection by collective agreement. In all, there are at present approximately 70 **collective agreements** which contain provisions on protection and assistance for the activity of these informal union workplace representatives, *e.g.* in the metal and printing industries.

763. **VERTRAUENSMÄNNER UND -FRAUEN DER SCHWER-BEHINDERTEN — EMPLOYEE REPRESENTATIVES FOR THE DISABLED**: Representatives who make up the **representative body for disabled employees** within an establishment. Any member of the workforce who is at least 18 years old and has belonged to the establishment for at least six months is eligible for election. These representatives have the same legal status as members of **works councils** and **staff councils**, including special **protection against dismissal** and entitlement to be released from work for the purpose of fulfilling their functions and attending training sessions.

764. **VERTRAUENSVOLLE ZUSAMMENARBEIT — CO-OPERATION IN GOOD FAITH**: Requirement laid down by law which affirms, by formal declaration, co-operation between the employee representation bodies of the **works constitution** and the **employer** in the system of **institutionalized representation of interests**.

765. **VERWALTUNGSAKT — ACT OF ADMINISTRATION**: Defined as "any order, decision or other sovereign measure which is adopted by an authority for the regulation of an individual case in the field of public law and which is intended for direct external effect". Owing to their limitation to individual cases, acts of administration (other than **executive orders**) are not statutes.

The principle of **reservation of statutory powers** makes it necessary for an administrative authority to possess powers conferred by statute in order to function in this way, and the principle of the **precedence of statutes** binds it to the proper nature and purpose of such powers.

An act of administration is at fault if it contravenes current law. In cases of serious fault it is null and void and non-enforceable from the outset. Otherwise, it remains valid in law until it is repealed by the authority which issued it or by the system of administrative courts. If an act of administration ceases to be rescindable or if all attempts at rescinding it have failed, it assumes the force of law and hence becomes enforceable.

The **remedies at law** available against an act of administration are an objection or an application to the courts to rescind or to create an obligation.

766. **VERWALTUNGSGERICHTSBARKEIT — SYSTEM OF ADMINISTRATIVE COURTS**: As distinct from the **systems of social security** and **finance courts** in their capacity as specialist administrative courts, the general system of administrative courts deals with all those measures on the part of the Federal Government, the Länder and the municipalities, and all petitions concerning them, which do not fall within the jurisdiction of such specialist courts or of the **system of ordinary courts**. As regards labour law this includes, for example, the official authorization which is obligatory before a pregnant employee or a **disabled person** may be dismissed (Maternity Protection Act, Disabled Persons Act) and disputes in the context of **staff representation** in the public sector, for which specialist chambers or senates are established.

The chambers of the first-instance Administrative Courts have three career judges and two lay judges on the bench, and in the appeal instance the senates of the Higher Administrative Courts ("Oberverwaltungsgericht" or "Verwaltungsgerichtshof") have three career judges and, in some Länder, also two lay judges. In the legal review instance, the senates of the Federal Administrative Court consist of five career judges. Voidance petitions arising from **byelaws** are lodged directly with the Higher Administrative Courts.

Legal costs are payable for actions before these courts but, other than in the case of the Federal Administrative Court, the parties are permitted to represent themselves.

767. **VERWIRKUNG — FORFEITURE**: In labour law, the prior contractually agreed extinguishment of a claim subject to certain

337

conditions and the belated assertion of a right in breach of what has been agreed.

Rights arising from a **collective agreement** are non-forfeitable. In contrast to the situation regarding other claims by the employee, employers are unable to contend that, since an employee has refrained from asserting a claim over a lengthy period of time, it was permissible for them to assume that the employee would continue to refrain in future from asserting the claim now being acted upon, and that consequently they can no longer reasonably be expected to fulfil the employee's claim. Only in particularly flagrant cases is a defence of fraudulent misrepresentation possible regarding the employee's claim as arising from a collective agreement. The same also applies to rights arising from a **works agreement**. A strict distinction must be made between forfeiture and the consequences of a **time limit**.

768. **VERZICHT — WAIVER**: Waiver by an employee of rights arising from the employment relationship is possible only within narrow limits.

Existing collectively agreed rights may be waived by the employee only in a **settlement** authorized by the **parties to a collective agreement**. The latter's consent is also required for the waiver of collectively agreed rights by the parties to an employment contract in compromises agreed in the courts. The waiver of collectively agreed claims by way of a **quittance acknowledging settlement** is similarly restricted.

769. **VOLLSTREIK — ALL-OUT STRIKE**: Situation where, in accordance with the strategy adopted in a **labour dispute**, either all employers in a given industry have strike action directed against them (with at least all of their unionized employees stopping work) or all employees in a given establishment stop work.

770. **VOLONTÄR — UNPAID TRAINEE**: Within the meaning of commercial law, an individual who performs clerical, technical or agricultural work without receiving any remuneration and also without having been taken on as a **vocational trainee**. (The term "improver" is also used in English.) Owing to the provisions of the Vocational Training Act, the only situation in which an unpaid trainee is conceivable nowadays is where the son or daughter of an entrepreneur is voluntarily learning this occupation in an establishment belonging to another company. A case which is of more practical importance is work as an unpaid trainee editor. This special **vocational training relationship** for editorial staff

is regulated by corresponding **framework agreements** on **employment conditions**.

771. **VOR- UND ABSCHLUSSARBEITEN — PREPARATORY AND SHUTTING-DOWN TASKS**: Tasks necessary for the maintenance of the establishment's operation which cannot be carried out during normal **working time** without causing considerable disruption. To enable them to be done, it is permissible to extend the daily **maximum working hours** to 10 hours. If the daily working hours are longer than 8 hours and the employer cannot be expected to call in personnel from outside the establishment to perform the necessary tasks, working hours may be increased further, up to a maximum of 12 hours.

772. **VORBEHALT DES GESETZES — RESERVATION OF STATUTORY POWERS**: Synonym of **Gesetzesvorbehalt**.

773. **VORGESETZTER — SUPERIOR**: In the **career public service relationship**, the "Amtsvorgesetzter" or superior officer is the person who has the right to issue instructions to **career public servants** in the context of their work activities (as distinct from the "Dienstvorgesetzter", *i.e.* **superior official**). This direct superior is usually the head of the authority or institution in which the career public servant works. In an ordinary contractual **employment relationship**, the "Vorgesetzter" or superior is the person who issues instructions to employees in the performance of their contractual obligations and hence exercises the **employer's right to issue instructions**. In both cases, only a natural person may be deemed to be the superior.

774. **VORRUHESTAND — EARLY RETIREMENT**: See **partial retirement**.

775. **VORSTAND — MANAGEMENT BOARD**: The organ which conducts the business of an association or of the **forms of company** known as a registered co-operative society (eG) and a public limited company (AG) and which has the legal status of representative for the association or company in all external dealings.

The management board runs a public limited company in the role of **entrepreneur** on its own responsibility and is in principle not subject to instructions. In companies which are subject to **co-determination**, one of its members must be an **employee director**. Its internal procedures are regulated by the articles of association and possibly standing orders. Its functions and obligations are determined by law, the articles of association and the resolutions adopted by the **shareholders' meeting**, the requirements for the proper conduct of the business, loyalty to the company, convening and providing information for the company general meeting or shareholders' meeting, briefing the **supervisory board**, and consideration in general of the members or shareholders and employees and the general public.

The board consists of one or more individuals appointed by the supervisory board for five years, with the possibility of reappointment. Appointment to the board is a separate matter from the conclusion of the corresponding **contract of employment**. If an individual ceases to be a member of the board, this does not automatically end the contract. Board members are subject to a **restraint on competition** for the duration of their membership. Since members of the management board are usually not employees, **labour law** has significance for them only in so far as the board assumes the role of **employer** within the meaning of labour law, with the resultant obligations in relation to the employees, the works council and the **economic committee**. In addition, the board members may have their legal actions heard in the **system of labour courts**.

776. **VORSTELLUNGSKOSTEN — COSTS OF ATTENDING FOR INTERVIEW**: Term used to indicate the expenditure and loss of earnings necessarily incurred in participating in a personal interview. The basis of entitlement to reimbursement is a pre-contractual relationship, irrespective of whether a **contract of employment** actually comes into being at a later date. An employer who summons applicants to attend (even when this is intended to be at their own expense) is under an obligation to reimburse their costs (Civil Code § 670). There is no such obligation to reimburse costs where potential employees attend of their own volition in response to a **job advertisement** or on the recommendation of **job placement** services. Such costs include, in particular, expenses incurred for travel, subsistence and overnight accommodation. Loss of earnings must also be reimbursed to the extent that it exceeds the entitlement of potential employees to reimbursement from their former employer for the cost of looking for a new job. Cost of attending for interview may possibly be subsidized by the job placement services as part of employment promotion policy. Under the provisions on **entitlement to damages** on the grounds of non-performance of contract, employers may claim, from employees who have failed to perform their contract, the recovery of interviewing costs incurred in finding a new employee to fill a vacant job.

W

777. **WAHLVORSTAND — ELECTORAL BOARD**: See **staff council election, works council election**.

778. **"WARNSTREIK"**: Term referring to a form of strike which was traditionally used only in isolated instances and known as a "token strike", but which is now important as a more strategic and planned instrument and known as a "warning strike". It denotes a stoppage of work of fixed duration, intended to demonstrate determination on the part of the employees and the **trade union** to resort to further, open-ended strike action to exert pressure as a means of pushing through certain demands.

According to the view of the **Federal Labour Court**, brief warning strikes to back up negotiations during **collective bargaining** after expiry of the peace obligation are lawful if they are called by the appropriate union. More recently, the Court has also ruled that warning strikes, like other strikes, are subject to the *ultima ratio* **principle**. This means that the union must have made a serious attempt to bring the negotiations to a satisfactory conclusion before calling a warning strike. No formal pronouncement of the breakdown of negotiations is necessary. The scale of the stoppage is at the discretion of the union. It is, however, possible for the employers' side to respond with **lock-outs**.

The so-called **"neue Beweglichkeit"** strategy is a special form of the warning strike tactic.

779. **WARTEZEIT — QUALIFYING PERIOD**: As a general rule, the grant of **social security** benefits is subject to the completion of a specified qualifying period (also called a "waiting period") within which certain contributions must be paid or **periods treated as contribution periods** included.

780. **WEGEZEIT — TRAVEL-TO-WORK TIME**: The time it takes the employee to journey to and from home and the place where work is performed. It differs from **business travel** (for which certain conditions are specified) in that it does not count as part of **working time**.

781. **WEHRDIENST- UND ZIVILDIENSTPFLICHTIGE — PEOPLE LIABLE FOR COMPULSORY MILITARY OR COMMUNITY SERVICE**: See **job protection during compulsory military or community service**.

782. **WEIHNACHTSGELD — CHRISTMAS BONUS**: See **special bonus**.

783. WEITERBESCHÄFTIGUNG — CONTINUED EMPLOY-MENT (DURING DISMISSAL PROCEEDINGS): One of the main reasons why **protection against dismissal** is largely ineffective as a form of job protection is the fact that, in most instances, employees do not continue to work in the establishment while the lawsuit for their **application for protection against dismissal** is proceeding, and they are therefore unable to keep up with technical and organizational developments. Consequently, employees frequently lose their job even if their dismissal was invalid, possibly because the employer lodges an **application for dissolution** or because the employees themselves no longer feel confident of being able to continue in the job and so agree to end the employment relationship in the form of a **settlement**. In certain cases, therefore, there is provision for an entitlement to continue to be employed while the legal proceedings are going on. A statutory entitlement exists in establishments with a **works council** or **staff council** if the council has objected to an ordinary dismissal by way of **termination with notice**: in such circumstances, if the employee institutes legal proceedings for protection against dismissal the employer must, if the employee so requests, continue to employ him or her with unchanged terms and conditions of employment until the lawsuit has been concluded by final judgment. Only in cases treated as exceptions is the employer able to obtain release from this obligation by the Labour Court (Works Constitution Act § 102(5); Federal Staff Representation Act § 79(2)). In addition to this statutory entitlement under collective law, in accordance with a more recent view adopted by the **system of labour courts** there is also an entitlement under individual law. The precondition for this latter entitlement is that the employee's interest in continuing to be employed must prevail over the employer's interest in the immediate *de facto* validity of the dismissal. This will not usually be deemed to be so (given that the dismissal is not obviously invalid) unless the dismissal has been ruled invalid by the court, the employer has lodged an appeal against this judgment and there are no special circumstances presenting an obstacle to the employee's continued employment. The practical possibility of exercising this entitlement is hampered by the fact that, in cases of repeat dismissals, the same criterion also applies to the subsequent dismissals; to a large extent, therefore, the employer is able to prevent continued employment. If employees ultimately lose their legal action for protection against dismissal, they have no claim to the original contractually agreed level of remuneration but can demand only recovery of the actual value of the work they have performed during the intervening period, and they have no claim either to **continued payment of remuneration** in the event of illness or to holiday pay (**annual holiday**).

784. **WERKSBESETZUNG — OCCUPATION (OF THE WORKPLACE)**: Synonym of **Betriebsbesetzung**.

785. **WERKSTARIFVERTRAG — COMPANY AGREEMENT**: Synonym of **Firmentarifvertrag**.

786. **WERKSTUDENT — CASUAL STUDENT WORKER**: As distinct from individuals receiving **work experience**, students and schoolchildren are often employed (usually during holidays) not with a view to their training but as casual workers. Students are not required to pay **social security** contributions in respect of such work. If the work is done frequently, this remains the case only if the criteria for **"marginal" part-time workers** are observed.

The same applies, *mutatis mutandis*, to schoolchildren. If they are employed in a work experience context they are not covered by **labour law**.

787. **WERKTAGE — WORKING DAYS**: In principle, the days from Monday to Saturday. In many industries, **collective agreements** do not treat Saturday as a working day for the purposes of calculating working time and leave.

788. **WERKWOHNUNG — COMPANY HOUSING**: Rented accommodation which is connected with an **employment relationship**. There is a distinction between general and job-related company housing, and also "tied" company housing provided under a service tenancy ("Werkdienstwohnung"). In the case of general company housing there is both a contract of employment and a tenancy agreement, the latter being concluded as a consequence of the employment relationship. If the employment relationship comes to an end, the tenancy agreement can be terminated in accordance with the general legal provisions on rented accommodation; exceptions exist in the case of job-related company housing.

There is no separate tenancy agreement in the case of housing provided under a service tenancy. If the employment relationship comes to an end, the accommodation must also be vacated. This does not apply to dwellings which employees have furnished themselves or in which they and their family have maintained an independent household. In such cases the general legal provisions on rented accommodation apply.

A **co-determination right of the works council** exists as regards the introduction of such housing as a company facility, its nature, arrangement and administration, and also its allocation and withdrawal.

343

If the rents charged for company housing are substantially lower than the normal local rates, the difference is classed as a **non-pay benefit**.

789. **WETTBEWERBSVERBOT — RESTRAINT ON COMPETITION**: Obligation on the employee to refrain from practising the same occupation or trade during the employment relationship or for a specified period after it comes to an end. During an **employment relationship** statutory restraint exists only for commercial employees; for all other employees the restraint on competition is implied by their **duty of loyalty**. Once the employment relationship has ended there is in principle no longer any restraint on competition, even if a retirement pension is being paid.

By way of exception, however, a restraint on competition may exist on the basis of a post-contractual duty of loyalty, in cases where competition is improper according to law and by virtue of a contractual covenant. A covenant in restraint of competition ("vertragliches Wettbewerbsverbot") is null and void if it does not provide for compensatory payment from the employer to the employee as a counter-consideration. This is so even if the employee receives an additional payment during the employment relationship, since there is then still no guarantee that the employee will receive the statutory minimum compensation laid down in the Commercial Code. The compensation must be paid monthly for the duration of the covenant, and the annual total must amount to at least half of the annual remuneration that was being paid to the employee when the employment relationship ended. The covenant in restraint of competition may also be agreed as non-binding: the employer cannot derive any rights from a non-binding covenant; the employee has the option of whether or not to adhere to the covenant and claim the compensation.

790. **WILDER STREIK — UNOFFICIAL STRIKE**: According to the view of the Federal Labour Court, a **strike** is lawful only if it is conducted by a **trade union**. A stoppage of work which is neither authorized in advance by the appropriate union nor subsequently taken over by the union is known as an unofficial strike and is deemed unlawful in terms of labour law. (The American term "wildcat strike" is also used.)

791. **WINTERGELD — WINTER ALLOWANCE**: See **winter assistance for the construction industry**.

792. **WINTERHILFEN FÜR DIE BAUWIRTSCHAFT — WINTER ASSISTANCE FOR THE CONSTRUCTION INDUSTRY**: The **Federal Employment Service** promotes year-round employment in the construction industry by granting payments under the scheme for productive promotion of winter construction (Employment Promotion Act §§ 77 ff.) and the bad-weather allowance (Employment Promotion Act §§ 83 ff.). Under the scheme for productive promotion of winter construction, building firms receive assistance such as subsidies towards the cost of buying winter equipment and the increased operating costs caused by weather conditions.

As a special form of **unemployment insurance** benefit, in the event of enforced idleness due to weather conditions during the period from November 1 to March 31 construction workers are paid a bad-weather allowance provided that the following conditions are satisfied:

1. the employment relationship cannot be terminated on the grounds of the weather;
2. there is an entitlement to collectively agreed compensatory wage adjustment for the period from December 25 to January 1;
3. the loss of working time is caused solely and unavoidably by weather conditions (*e.g.* rain, snow or frost despite protective clothing or coverings) or it is technically impossible to carry out work that is being subsidized under the winter promotion scheme;
4. the loss of working time amounts to at least one hour;
5. the employee is in a form of work relationship in the construction industry that is subject to social security contributions;
6. the loss of working time means that no remuneration is received.

The bad-weather allowance amounts to 63 per cent. of the net earnings last received (68 per cent. for claimants with at least one child). If employees were previously working under a payment by results or piecework system, the allowance is calculated on the basis of their average remuneration, excluding overtime supplements, over the 13 weeks immediately preceding the loss of working time.

In addition, winter assistance for the construction industry includes the payment to employees, during the period from December 1 to March 31, of an additional winter allowance of 2 Deutschmarks per hour worked (Employment Promotion Act §§ 80 f.).

793. **WIRTSCHAFTSAUSSCHUSS — ECONOMIC COMMITTEE**: An organ of the **works constitution** which must be

established in companies normally employing at least 100 employees. Depending on the size of company, this committee consists of at least 3-7 members possessing appropriate expertise, at least one of whom must belong to a **works council**. The committee members are elected by the works council or **company works council** by simple majority voting. They do not enjoy the same protection as **works council members**, but must not suffer any disadvantage as a result of their membership. The committee's function is to consult with the employer on economic matters and to communicate such matters to the works council or company works council. Its sphere of responsibility includes, for example, the company's economic and financial position, the production and marketing situation, production and investment programmes, and plans for **rationalization** and any **substantial alteration to the establishment**. The employer must provide the committee with prompt and comprehensive information on these matters, including any necessary documents, provided that such disclosure does not endanger business or trade secrets. Information concerning any repercussions on **human resource planning** must be included. The functions of the economic committee may also be transferred to a **works council executive committee**, which may not be larger than the size specified for an economic committee.

794. **WIRTSCHAFTSDEMOKRATIE — ECONOMIC DEMOCRACY**: The concept of economic democracy, with the aim of achieving employee participation in all decisions affecting them at all levels within the relevant decision-making structures, was developed in Germany by the trade unionist F. Naphtali and the joint employer/employee councils in the coal and potash industries in the period after the First World War and into the Weimar Republic. This concept underlies the aspirations for the establishment of economic and social councils, particularly on the part of the member unions of the **German Federation of Trade Unions**. More recently, the motivation has been to establish councils comprising, as well as employer and employee representatives, consumer and environmental organizations. The idea is that such councils should have the function of advising Parliaments, Governments and administrative authorities on the solution of economic, social and environmental problems (**technology impact analysis and assessment**) and be empowered to intervene in ways including the targeting of investment. The activities of such councils would directly affect policy on investment and subsidies by the public authorities.

Such institutionalized elements of economic democracy as exist are to be found in the participation of employees and their organizations in the context of the **works constitution** and **co-determination**, and also in the decision-making and administrative bodies of employment promotion and **social security**. To date, no more extensive opportunities than this have yet materialized for the **trade unions** to have any say in shaping contextual economic conditions. Examples of **concerted action** practised on the basis of co-operation between the unions, the state and the employers along the lines laid down in the **Stability Act** represent not so much economic democracy as a form of neo-corporatism at informal level.

795. **WIRTSCHAFTSLENKUNG — "STEERING" OF THE ECONOMY**: Term covering all measures by the state directed at giving coherence to the methods and goals of private business and guiding them in accordance with some particular plan for the economy. Numerous forms of intervention are available, ranging from "hard" measures such as the imposition of bans, with or without penal or administrative sanctions for contraventions, to "soft" measures such as the differential imposition of state levies, grant of subsidies and other forms of promotion via government institutions and monetary, credit and foreign-trade policy.

Restrictions on the freedom of the state to choose aims and methods of economic control may arise from the **basic rights** of the people affected. The most relevant rights in this respect are **freedom of occupation**, the guarantee of private ownership and (as regards the differential subsidizing of competitors, for example) the principle of **equality before the law**. Although the mechanisms of steering the economy are regarded by some experts in modern systems theory as inevitably ineffective and by liberal economists as harmful, the use of these measures is on the increase.

796. **WIRTSCHAFTSRECHT — COMMERCIAL LAW**: The entire body of regulations delimiting and controlling independent gainful activity in industry, commerce, craft trades, agriculture, transport and the **professions**. They include, in particular, the provisions on admission to the exercise of occupations and **businesses** and the sphere of state intervention in **"steering" of the economy**. Other elements include the law on restriction of competition, the law on economic organizations and, at international level, the Foreign Trade and Payments Act (Aussenwirtschaftsgesetz). Sometimes also translated as "business law".

797. WIRTSCHAFTSRISIKO — ECONOMIC RISK: The **employer** bears the economic risk, with the result that in all cases where (in contrast to the **"works risk"**) work is technically possible but is not economically viable, the entitlement to remuneration remains unaffected.

798. WOCHENARBEITSZEIT — WORKING WEEK: In principle, with **maximum working hours** of eight hours daily and six **working days**, the working week amounts to 48 hours. In practice, this working week as permitted under the various **regulations on working hours** is less relevant than the working week as regulated by **collective agreement**. In almost all areas of the public and private sectors, working hours have already been reduced by collective agreement to less than a 40-hour week.

799. WOCHENENDARBEIT — WEEKEND WORK: Work on Saturdays and/or Sundays. It is permitted where there is an exemption from **rest on Sundays and public holidays**, and the employee is required to do such work if Saturday counts as a **working day** and there is a corresponding obligation under the contract of employment. More than half of all employees work on Saturdays in the hotel and restaurant trade, food, drink and tobacco businesses, agriculture and forestry, transport enterprises, the railways and the postal services; in the hotel and restaurant trade this also applies to Sundays.

Z

800. **ZEIT-ARBEITSVERTRAG — FIXED-TERM EMPLOY-MENT CONTRACT**: See **fixed-term employment relationship**.

801. **ZEITAKKORD — TIME PIECEWORK**: See **piecework**.

802. **ZEITARBEIT — TEMPORARY WORK**: Also referred to as "Leiharbeit". See **hiring-out of labour**.

803. **ZEITLICHE LAGE DER ARBEITSZEIT — SCHEDULING OF WORKING TIME**: The framework within which, in observance of the **restrictions on working hours**, the distribution of normal working hours for the establishment can be fixed. It is subject to the **co-determination right of the works council**.

804. **ZEITLOHN — TIME-BASED PAY**: Payment system in which a manual worker's **wage** is determined by the amount of time actually worked. When work is not performed, wages are payable only in circumstances where there is statutory provision for the **continued payment of remuneration**. In contrast, white-collar workers receive a specified monthly **salary** which does not depend on actual working time. Time-based pay is the most widely used payment system for **manual workers**; other systems are **piecework** and **payment by results**.

805. **ZEUGNIS — REFERENCE**: When an **employment relationship** comes to an end, the employee is entitled to be provided with a reference, *i.e.* a written testimonial, by the employer (Civil Code § 630). There is a distinction between a purely formal reference and a descriptive reference.

The purely formal reference contains only facts concerning the nature and duration of the employment; it may not contain any more detailed information concerning the employee's performance and conduct or the reason for leaving. If the employee so requests, however, the employer must provide a descriptive reference covering, in addition to the nature and duration of the employment, the employee's performance and conduct in the establishment. The reference must be made with good intent, but at the same time its purpose is to serve as a job-application document and provide information for a third party. It must therefore be truthful. This means that there is scope for discretion in the employer's assessment, associated with the obligation to include facts that are also unfavourable to the employee unless they merely represent isolated lapses.

806. **ZUGANGSRECHT — RIGHT OF ACCESS**: See **union right of access**.

807. **ZURÜCKBEHALTUNGSRECHT — RIGHT TO WITH-HOLD PERFORMANCE**: Right which entitles an obligor to refuse to effect their own performance under a contract until the other contracting partner has effected the performance due from them. The assertion of a right to withhold performance is possible in labour law also; the precondition is that, apart from their own obligation, one of the parties to the contract of employment has a due claim on the other arising out of the **employment relationship**. For example, provided that no obligation exists for **continued payment of remuneration** an employer can withhold pay for the period during which employees, who are under an obligation to effect performance first, have not rendered the work performance due from them. On the other side, employees also can withhold their work performance if, for example, the employer has failed to pay the due **remuneration** in the preceding month or has infringed subsidiary duties under the employment contract such as the **duty of care**. They must then offer their work performance in the event of their claims being met.

If a number of employees together exercise a right to withhold performance, this may constitute a **strike**. To avoid being deemed to be conducting an **unofficial strike**, in such a case the employees must state clearly that they are asserting a right to withhold performance and identify the due claims of individual employees which the employer must specifically meet.

808. **ZUSTIMMUNGSGESETZ — STATUTE REQUIRING ASSENT (OF THE FEDERAL COUNCIL)**: Term used to denote a statute for which, in accordance with the cases enumerated in detail in the **Basic Law**, actual enactment depends on the express assent of the **Federal Council**. All others are **statutes not requiring assent**.

The term ''Zustimmungsgesetz'' is also used with a different meaning, to refer to an instrument of assent whereby the legislative organs of the Federation, Länder, municipalities or associations of municipalities assent to a **treaty**.

809. **ZWANGSARBEIT — FORCED LABOUR**: Except in the case of detention or imprisonment ordered by the courts and the situations of emergency enumerated in the **Constitution, freedom of occupation** may not be restricted by the imposition of forced (*i.e.* compulsory) labour.

810. **ZWANGSSCHLICHTUNG — COMPULSORY ARBITRATION**: An obligation on the **parties to a collective agreement**, if they are unable to arrive by negotiation at a **collective agreement**, to commit themselves to the decision of an independent arbitrator. At the time of the Weimar Republic a statutory system of compulsory arbitration existed from 1924 onwards. The general view is that it proved unsatisfactory. Under current constitutional law, any form of compulsory arbitration is deemed to be an unlawful encroachment on **collective bargaining autonomy**.

811. **ZWANGSVOLLSTRECKUNG — ENFORCEMENT OF JUDGMENT**: The compulsory execution, by authority of the state, of a claim under civil or labour law.

Like decisions in the ordinary system of courts, decisions in the **system of labour courts** are also enforceable by this process. Firstly, final judgments and compromises reached in the "**Urteil**" **procedure** are enforceable. In addition, since under labour law undecided cases which continue for too long are not acceptable, in accordance with the Labour Courts Act non-final judgments are also provisionally enforceable. Provisional enforceability may, however, be excluded in the judgment itself or on appeal, if defendants credibly establish that enforcement would cause them irrecoverable disadvantage. Since the provisions of the Code of Civil Procedure apply to enforcement, a judgment imposing the performance of services arising from a contract of employment or contract for services is not enforceable.

In the context of the "**Beschluss**" **procedure**, final decisions and compromises are enforceable if they impose an obligation on one of the interested parties. Provisional enforceability applies only to decisions of the Labour Courts in disputes relating to pecuniary rights, where this has not been excluded by the court on application from one of the interested parties on the grounds that enforcement would cause them irrecoverable disadvantage.

Enforcement actions can be contested via special **remedies at law**. In the sphere of public law, the execution of claims on the part of the state and other public-law entities is effected by way of the provisions on administration enforcement, including existing **acts of administration**.

812. **ZWINGENDES RECHT — PEREMPTORY LAW**: Term applied to a legal provision which, in contrast to **discretionary law**, is not transactionable, *i.e.* parties participating in the general operation of the law cannot agree between themselves to set it aside *(jus cogens)*. Procedural law falls into this category as a matter of principle. In **labour law**, the concept of unilaterally

351

peremptory law also exists. This occurs in the case of legal provisions whose validity, in accordance with the principles of precedence and **favourability**, cannot be excluded by individual agreement; private arrangements in favour of the employee are excepted.

813. **ZWISCHENMEISTER — HOMEWORK SUBCONTRAC-TOR**: An individual who, without being an **employee**, receives commissions for work from a trader and passes them on to **homeworkers**.

TABLES

TABLE 1

MEMBERSHIP OF DGB UNIONS

Year	Union of Construction and Quarrying Industries				Union of Mining and Energy Industries				Union of Chemical, Paper and Ceramics Industries				Union of Printing and Paper Industries			
	Absolute number		% change from preceding year		Absolute number		% change from preceding year		Absolute number		% change from preceding year		Absolute number		% change from preceding year	
	total	female	total	female	total	female	total	female	total	female	total	female	total	female	total	female
1965	509,725	3,790			444,728	7,293			542,160	97,328			148,592	25,524		
1970	504,230	4,736	1.5	12.9	387,301	4,697	−3.9	−20.6	598,831	100,004	8.4	9.2	148,325	23,403	3.5	2.8
71	511,699	4,821	1.5	1.8	392,571	5,259	1.4	12.0	613,057	103,599	2.4	3.6	150,831	24,791	1.7	5.9
72	520,879	5,067	1.8	5.1	380,831	4,993	−3.0	−5.1	626,771	108,340	2.2	4.6	153,407	29,160	1.7	17.6
73	522,157	6,123	0.2	20.8	377,589	5,287	−0.9	5.9	645,178	113,032	2.9	4.3	160,062	27,412	4.3	−6.0
74	517,902	7,345	−0.8	20.0	374,082	5,579	−0.9	5.5	655,703	116,158	1.6	2.8	164,465	29,051	2.8	6.0
1975	509,422	8,903	−1.6	21.2	378,369	5,970	1.1	7.0	644,271	114,162	−1.7	−1.7	157,985	28,312	−3.9	−2.5
76	504,548	10,983	−1.0	23.4	371,525	5,847	−1.8	−2.1	643,390	114,132	−0.1	−0.0	158,180	29,349	0.1	3.7
77	500,244	12,855	−0.9	17.0	367,602	6,054	−1.1	3.5	651,037	117,278	1.2	2.8	152,256	28,729	−3.7	−2.1
78	517,842	14,265	3.5	11.0	362,148	6,095	−1.5	0.7	650,675	119,045	−0.1	1.5	145,980	27,547	−4.1	−4.1
79	525,591	15,506	1.5	8.7	363,865	6,566	0.5	7.7	657,920	122,129	1.1	2.6	139,069	26,989	−4.7	−2.0
1980	533,054	17,918	1.4	15.6	367,718	6,975	1.1	6.2	660,973	123,680	0.5	1.3	143,970	29,930	3.5	10.9
81	537,737	20,240	0.9	13.0	371,749	6,959	1.1	−0.2	654,633	123,705	−1.0	0.0	151,796	33,730	5.4	12.7
82	530,960	22,419	−1.3	10.8	367,835	7,294	−1.1	4.8	643,079	121,889	−1.8	−1.5	145,271	33,106	−4.3	−1.8
83	523,129	24,265	−1.5	8.2	366,328	7,001	−0.4	−4.0	635,276	120,197	−1.2	−1.4	144,344	32,924	−0.6	−0.5
84	517,016	26,310	−1.2	8.4	360,316	7,095	−1.6	1.3	638,176	119,147	0.5	−0.9	142,334	33,706	−1.4	2.4
1985	507,528	28,681	−1.8	9.0	356,706	7,206	−1.0	1.6	649,569	121,760	1.8	2.2	140,725	32,790	−1.1	−2.7
86	485,055	30,491	−4.4	6.3	355,201	7,402	−0.4	2.7	653,776	125,433	0.6	3.0	143,384	33,888	1.9	3.3
87	475,575	32,772	−2.0	7.5	347,528	7,307	−2.2	−1.3	655,776	126,377	0.3	0.8	145,054	34,816	1.2	2.7
88	468,238	34,459	−1.5	5.1	340,284	7,076	−2.1	−3.2	662,586	127,903	1.0	1.2	150,259	37,161	3.6	6.7
89									664,618	128,995	0.3	0.9				

Table 1 (continued)

MEMBERSHIP OF DGB UNIONS

Year	German Railways Union				Education and Science Union				Horticulture, Agriculture and Forestry Union				Commerce, Banking and Insurance Union			
	Absolute number		% change from preceding year		Absolute number		% change from preceding year		Absolute number		% change from preceding year		Absolute number		% change from preceding year	
	total	female	total	female	total	female	total	female	total	female	total	female	total	female	total	female
1965	433,743	13,800			96,832	36,228			77,039	4,108			128,85	267,762		
1970	413,087	12,707	2.6	1.6	119,738	48,496	6.1	7.4	46,085	1,963	−6.1	−9.1	157,671	77,239	6.2	4.4
71	425,693	13,793	3.1	8.5	124,819	49,265	4.2	1.6	43,403	2,018	−5.8	1.8	171,341	83,014	8.7	7.5
72	434,889	14,872	2.2	7.8	125,745	49,650	0.7	0.8	41,844	1,950	−3.6	−3.4	191,071	92,510	11.5	11.4
73	444,229	19,363	2.1	30.2	132,430	56,756	5.3	14.3	40,009	1,952	−4.4	0.1	210,038	102,323	9.9	10.6
74	455,380	20,970	2.5	8.3	132,106	59,028	−0.2	4.0	39,859	1,948	−0.4	−0.2	236,642	118,105	12.7	15.4
1975	447,914	20,645	−1.6	−1.5	139,294	63,547	5.4	7.6	39,309	1,915	−1.4	−1.7	257,123	129,919	8.7	10.0
76	436,193	19,973	−2.6	−3.3	151,647	71,676	8.9	12.8	39,964	2,216	1.7	15.7	274,783	140,494	6.9	8.1
77	424,740	19,392	−2.6	−2.9	152,706	71,609	0.7	−0.1	40,519	2,430	1.4	9.7	292,158	151,131	6.3	7.6
78	414,195	18,742	−2.5	−3.4	158,734	76,397	3.9	6.7	41,311	2,863	2.0	17.8	314,244	164,730	7.6	9.0
79	407,934	18,746	−1.5	0.0	173,880	85,467	9.5	11.9	42,179	3,323	2.1	16.1	334,036	178,391	6.3	8.3
1980	406,588	23,070	−0.3	23.1	183,793	92,279	5.7	8.0	42,196	4,007	0.0	20.6	351,328	190,974	5.2	7.1
81	401,959	19,901	−1.1	−13.7	187,467	95,669	2.0	3.0	42,618	4,540	1.0	13.3	365,478	201,955	4.0	5.7
82	392,484	19,540	−2.4	−1.8	185,651	95,081	−1.0	0.0	42,632	4,845	0.0	6.7	360,340	201,580	−1.4	−0.2
83	379,534	18,739	−3.3	−4.1	185,490	95,776	−0.1	0.7	42,249	5,137	−0.9	6.0	360,372	203,628	0.0	1.0
84	364,041	18,179	−4.1	−3.0	196,688	93,634	6.0	−2.2	41,915	5,433	−0.8	5.8	363,264	206,892	0.8	1.6
1985	354,180	20,536	−2.7	13.0	194,028	100,536	−1.4	7.8	42,450	5,829	1.3	7.3	371,228	213,784	2.2	3.3
86	351,408	30,382	−0.8	47.9	192,519	100,544	−0.8	0.0	42,865	6,202	1.0	6.4	376,498	218,898	1.4	2.4
87	340,095	31,265	−3.2	2.9	188,861	100,346	−1.9	−0.7	43,253	6,561	0.9	5.8	385,166	226,811	2.3	3.6
88	329,904	31,466	−3.0	0.6	187,422	100,393	−0.8	±0.0	43,479	6,847	0.5	4.4	393,399	233,285	2.1	2.9
89	319,641	31,249	−3.1	−0.7	188,910	102,587	+0.8	+2.4	43,817	7,223	+0.8	+5.5	407,326	246,240	3.5	5.6

TABLE 1 (continued)

MEMBERSHIP OF DGB UNIONS

Year	Timber and Plastics Union				Design Arts Union				Leather Union				Metal Industry Union (IG Metall)			
	Absolute number		% change from preceding year		Absolute number		% change from preceding year		Absolute number		% change from preceding year		Absolute number		% change from preceding year	
	total	female	total	female	total	female	total	female	total	female	total	female	total	female	total	female
1965	137,363	11,168			35,640	8,641			80,327	31,925			2,011,313	214,673		
1970	129,721	10,028	-0.1	-0.2	34,138	8,730	4.0	4.3	62,253	23,657	1.4	0.6	2,223,467	226,951	7.4	8.9
71	129,830	10,009	0.1	-0.2	34,778	8,730	1.9	0.0	59,066	22,363	-5.1	-5.5	2,312,294	245,672	4.0	8.2
72	130,805	11,354	0.8	13.4	35,344	9,194	1.6	5.3	59,155	22,940	0.2	2.6	2,354,975	267,739	1.8	9.0
73	134,817	11,471	3.1	1.0	35,618	4,965	0.8	-46.0	58,860	23,164	-0.5	1.0	2,460,697	302,005	4.5	12.8
74	135,205	11,546	0.3	0.7	36,150	5,583	1.5	12.4	57,600	22,922	-2.1	-1.0	2,593,480	343,302	5.4	13.7
1975	132,054	14,154	-2.3	22.6	36,461	5,730	0.9	2.6	56,458	22,974	-2.0	0.2	2,556,184	337,614	-1.4	-1.7
76	133,248	14,527	0.9	2.6	41,632	6,656	14.2	16.2	54,417	22,656	-3.6	-1.4	2,581,340	340,812	1.0	0.9
77	136,572	15,071	2.5	3.7	41,382	6,629	-0.6	-0.4	54,596	22,987	0.3	1.5	2,624,388	355,621	1.7	4.3
78	145,076	16,635	6.2	10.4	42,109	6,957	1.8	4.9	55,068	23,781	0.9	3.5	2,680,798	379,824	2.1	6.8
79	151,728	18,586	4.6	11.7	44,113	7,304	4.8	5.0	55,266	23,819	0.4	0.2	2,684,509	380,387	0.1	0.1
1980	157,142	20,245	3.6	8.9	45,252	7,493	2.6	2.6	55,689	23,946	0.8	0.5	2,622,267	369,963	-2.3	-2.7
81	160,040	21,339	1.8	5.4	47,072	7,795	4.0	4.0	55,015	23,239	-1.2	-3.0	2,622,069	376,908	0.0	1.9
82	156,453	19,988	-2.2	-6.3	47,925	7,945	1.8	1.9	52,719	23,709	-4.2	2.0	2,576,471	369,273	-1.7	-2.0
83	149,724	19,886	-4.3	-0.5	46,668	7,777	-2.6	-2.1	50,684	22,291	-3.9	-6.0	2,535,644	361,981	-1.6	-2.0
84	147,177	19,633	-1.7	-1.3	29,590	11,249	-36.6	44.6	49,141	21,516	-3.0	-3.5	2,497,733	360,300	-1.5	-0.5
1985	144,653	19,457	-1.7	-0.9	27,019	10,477	-8.7	-6.9	48,725	21,601	-0.8	0.4	2,553,041	374,791	2.2	4.0
86	142,954	19,395	-1.2	-0.3	28,134	10,701	4.1	2.1	48,332	21,249	-0.8	-1.6	2,598,323	386,615	1.8	3.2
87	143,139	19,532	0.1	0.7	28,440	10,784	1.1	0.8	47,659	20,876	-1.4	-1.8	2,609,247	390,978	0.4	1.1
88	144,763	19,906	1.1	1.9	29,613	9,890	4.1	-8.3	46,560	20,245	-2.3	-3.0	2,624,521	396,346	0.6	1.4
89	149,098	21,022	+3.0	+5.6					44,583	19,510	-4.2	-3.6	2,679,237	411,610	2.1	+3.9

TABLE 1 (continued)

MEMBERSHIP OF DGB UNIONS

Year	Food, Drink and Tobacco and Catering Union				Public Services, Transport and Traffic Union (ÖTV)				Police Union			
	Absolute number		% change from preceding year		Absolute number		% change from preceding year		Absolute number		% change from preceding year	
	total	female	total	female	total	female	total	female	total	female	total	female
1965	281,002	87,717			979,226	174,318						
1970	247,163	78,559	1.6	12.7	977,031	172,827	0.8	1.0				
71	244,829	69,998	−0.9	−10.9	993,879	178,956	1.7	3.5				
72	249,668	73,292	2.0	4.7	997,771	184,209	0.4	2.9				
73	251,879	74,693	0.9	1.9	997,771	184,209	0.0	0.0				
74	248,481	73,058	−1.3	−2.2	1,051,098	215,498	5.3	17.0				
1975	248,724	72,805	0.1	−0.3	1,058,525	231,529	0.7	7.4				
76	241,281	71,097	−3.0	−2.3	1,063,675	244,266	0.5	5.5				
77	249,988	73,249	3.6	3.0	1,077,755	257,782	1.3	5.5				
78	252,440	72,336	1.0	−1.2	1,099,396	272,455	2.0	5.7	152,486	8,325		
79	252,854	75,483	0.2	4.4	1,118,747	286,398	1.8	5.1	161,616	9,131	6.0	9.7
1980	253,001	77,873	0.1	3.2	1,149,689	303,090	2.8	5.9	165,900	9,597	2.7	5.1
81	263,114	82,987	4.0	6.6	1,181,460	319,343	2.8	5.5	168,691	12,476	1.7	30.0
82	265,276	85,375	0.8	2.9	1,179,650	328,967	−0.2	2.9	169,092	13,059	0.2	4.7
83	263,525	85,664	−0.7	0.3	1,173,525	335,370	−0.5	2.1	167,572	13,623	−0.9	4.3
84	263,976	87,247	0.2	1.8	1,168,254	341,723	−0.4	1.7	164,874	13,814	−1.6	1.4
1985	267,158	89,694	1.2	2.8	1,179,396	352,561	1.0	3.2	163,590	14,086	−0.8	2.0
86	266,008	90,094	−0.4	0.4	1,198,567	368,137	1.6	4.4	162,552	14,145	−0.6	0.4
87	267,555	91,468	0.6	1.5	1,202,629	380,327	0.3	3.3	158,888	14,188	−2.3	0.3
88	270,506	93,656	1.1	2.4	1,219,986	394,783	1.4	3.8	160,889	14,615	1.3	3.0
89	271,291	95,150	0.3	1.6					161,310	15,386	+0.3	+5.3

Table 1 (continued)

MEMBERSHIP OF DGB UNIONS

Year	German Post and Telecommunications Union — Absolute number		German Post and Telecommunications Union — % change from preceding year		Textiles and Clothing Union — Absolute number		Textiles and Clothing Union — % change from preceding year		DGB — Absolute number		DGB — % change from preceding year	
	total	female	total	female	total	female	total	female	total	female	total	female
1965	331,456	61,545			336,493	184,329			6,574,491	1,030,185		
1970	360,961	72,569	1.8	4.3	302,545	160,494	-2.7	-2.7	6,712,547	1,027,150	3.6	4.4
71	373,184	77,117	3.4	6.3	287,388	151,073	-5.0	-5.9	6,868,662	1,050,488	2.3	2.3
72	390,788	84,597	4.7	9.7	291,605	155,399	1.5	2.9	6,985,548	1,115,266	1.7	6.2
73	400,624	89,434	2.5	5.7	295,565	157,563	1.4	1.4	7,167,523	1,179,762	2.6	5.8
74	419,966	101,497	4.8	13.5	287,641	152,910	-2.7	-3.0	7,405,760	1,284,500	3.3	8.9
1975	419,585	103,374	-0.1	1.8	283,234	151,498	-1.5	-0.9	7,364,912	1,313,021	-0.6	2.2
76	417,642	103,667	-0.5	0.3	286,556	155,607	1.2	2.7	7,400,021	1,353,958	0.5	3.1
77	418,053	104,216	0.1	0.5	286,971	157,610	0.1	1.3	7,470,967	1,402,643	1.0	3.6
78	428,878	109,836	2.6	5.4	290,143	162,516	1.1	3.1	7,751,523	1,482,349	3.8	5.7
79	436,407	115,295	1.8	5.0	293,851	167,312	1.3	3.0	7,843,565	1,540,832	1.2	3.9
1980	450,201	125,264	3.2	8.6	293,766	169,820	-0.0	1.5	7,882,527	1,596,274	0.5	3.6
81	457,605	131,832	1.6	5.2	289,009	168,255	-1.6	-0.9	7,957,512	1,650,773	1.0	3.4
82	456,930	134,470	-0.1	2.0	276,235	160,859	-4.4	-4.4	7,849,003	1,649,399	-1.4	-0.1
83	457,929	136,830	0.2	1.8	263,920	153,181	-4.5	-4.8	7,745,913	1,644,770	-1.3	-0.3
84	455,686	138,128	-0.5	0.9	260,165	150,502	-1.4	-1.7	7,660,346	1,654,508	-1.1	0.6
1985	460,626	142,086	1.1	2.9	258,846	148,756	-0.5	-1.2	7,719,468	1,705,131	0.8	3.1
86	463,152	145,110	0.5	2.1	255,969	146,877	-1.1	-1.3	7,764,697	1,755,963	0.6	3.0
87	463,757	148,249	0.1	2.2	254,417	145,804	-0.6	-0.7	7,757,039	1,788,361	-0.1	1.8
88	471,175	153,434	1.6	3.5	253,493	145,284	-0.4	-0.4	7,797,077	1,826,649	0.5	2.1
89	472,145	155,943	0.2	1.6								

TABLE 2

NUMBER OF EMPLOYEES AND
DGB UNION MEMBERS

(in thousands)

1	2	3	4	5	6	7	8	9
Year	Total working population, all sectors	Employees	% change in Column 3 from preceding year	Members of DGB unions	% change in Column 5 from preceding year	Column 5 as % of Column 3	Unemployed*	% change in Column 8 from preceding year
1970	26,343	21,723	1.7	6,713	3.6	30.9%	97,338	−3.1
71	26,102	21,793	0.3	6,869	2.3	31.5%	146,740	50.8
72	26,861	22,828	4.7	6,986	1.7	30.6%	194,660	32.7
73	27,066	23,045	1.0	7,168	2.6	31.1%	219,271	12.6
74	26,853	22,998	−0.2	7,406	3.3	32.2%	556,981	154.0
1975	25,960	22,264	−3.2	7,365	−0.6	33.1%	1,005,495	80.5
76	25,752	22,234	−0.1	7,400	0.5	33.3%	898,701	−10.6
77	25,884	22,450	1.0	7,471	1.0	33.3%	911,239	1.4
78	26,021	22,681	1.0	7,752	3.8	34.2%	864,274	−5.2
79	26,347	23,066	1.7	7,844	1.2	34.0%	736,809	−14.7
1980	26,874	23,635	2.5	7,883	0.5	33.4%	822.565	11.6
81	26,947	23,790	0.7	7,958	1.0	33.5%	1,256,030	52.7
82	26,774	23,633	−0.7	7,849	−1.4	33.2%	1,820,030	44.9
83	26,477	23,204	−1.8	7,746	−1.3	33.4%	2,134,140	17.3
84	26,608	23,282	0.3	7,660	−1.1	32.9%	2,143,486	0.4
1985	26,626	23,491	0.9	7,719	0.8	32.9%	2,151,577	0.4
86	26,940	23,819	1.4	7,765	0.6	32.6%	2,046,120	−4.9
87	27,083	24,001	0.8	7,757	−0.1	32.3%	2,107,122	3.0
88	27,366	24,305	1.3	7,797	0.5	32.1%	2,099,863	−0.3

* Number as at end of September each year

TABLE 3

TREND IN COLLECTIVELY AGREED AND ACTUAL EARNINGS

(July 1988 to July 1989)

Sector	% rise (July 1989 over July 1988) in the index of average											
	gross hourly earnings of manual workers			gross monthly earnings of white-collar workers			collectively agreed hourly wages of manual workers			collectively agreed monthly salaries of white-collar workers		
	all	male	female	all	male	female	all	male	female	all	male	female
Energy and water supply	5.0	5.1	4.4	2.9	2.9	3.2	3.8	3.8	—	1.4	1.4	1.4
Mining	2.6	2.6	—	2.6	2.4	3.8	2.3	2.3	—	2.0	1.9	2.0
Basic and producer goods industries	4.0	4.0	3.5	3.3	3.4	3.2	3.9	3.9	3.7	2.5	2.5	2.7
of which: iron and steel industry	4.5	4.6	4.9	3.0	3.4	2.2	4.0	4.0	—	1.7	1.7	1.7
chemical industry	4.1	4.1	3.4	3.4	3.4	3.4	3.9	4.0	3.7	2.7	2.7	2.9
Capital goods industries	4.4	4.5	3.8	3.6	3.7	3.4	3.7	3.7	3.8	2.4	2.5	2.4
of which: mechanical engineering	4.6	4.6	3.8	3.9	4.2	3.4	3.8	3.8	3.8	2.5	2.5	2.4
electrical engineering	4.4	4.5	3.9	3.9	3.9	3.7	3.8	3.8	3.8	2.4	2.5	2.3
Consumer goods industries	4.3	4.0	4.1	3.3	3.3	3.4	3.6	3.5	3.7	2.3	2.3	2.2
of which: wood-processing industry	3.6	3.5	4.1	2.9	2.9	3.5	3.3	3.3	3.4	3.0	3.0	3.0
printing industry	4.3	4.2	4.8	3.1	3.3	3.5	3.8	3.8	3.8	2.6	2.7	2.5
leather-processing industry	2.8	2.4	2.8	4.2	4.4	3.6	2.5	2.5	2.5	2.5	2.4	2.5
clothing industry	3.8	3.3	3.7	2.6	2.3	3.2	3.9	3.9	3.9	1.3	1.2	1.3
Food, drink and tobacco industry	3.7	3.7	4.0	3.5	3.5	3.8	3.5	3.7	3.2	2.8	2.7	2.9
Building industry with finishing and ancillary trades	3.3	3.3	—	3.5	3.7	3.8	3.3	3.3	—	3.3	3.3	3.2
Commerce[1]	—	—	—	3.7	3.3	3.9	3.9	3.8	4.1	2.5	2.4	2.5
of which: retail distribution	—	—	—	4.6	3.7	5.0	4.1	4.0	4.3	3.8	3.8	3.8
Overall industry[2]	4.2	4.2	4.1	3.4	3.5	3.4	3.6	3.6	3.7	2.4	2.5	2.4

[1] Including banks and insurance companies: only for white-collar workers
[2] Actual earnings: industry including building and civil engineering with craft trades;
Collectively agreed earnings: manufacturing industries (excluding specialized building and stuccowork, plastering, rendering, joinery, roofing and finishing)
Source: Statistisches Bundesamt, Fachserie 16, Reihe 2.1, 2.2 and 4.3, plus author's own calculations

TABLE 4

PAY, PRICES AND PRODUCTIVITY IN THE ECONOMY AS A WHOLE, 1971-1989[1]

Year	Productivity[2]	Cost of living index[3]	Collectively agreed earnings[4]	Total gross wages and salaries per employee in employment		Total net wages and salaries per employee in employment		Wage ratio (total wage and salary incomes as % of national income)[5]
				in money terms	in real terms	in money terms	in real terms	
1971	+2.3	+5.2	+13.2	+11.3	+5.8	+9.4	+4.0	68.8
1972	+4.4	+5.3	+9.1	+9.2	+3.7	+9.5	+4.0	68.8
1973	+3.9	+6.8	+10.3	+11.2	+4.1	+7.7	+0.8	69.4
1974	+1.6	+6.7	+12.5	+10.9	+3.9	+9.4	+2.5	71.3
1975	+1.3	+6.1	+8.5	+6.4	+0.3	+6.7	+0.6	71.5
1976	+6.3	+4.4	+5.9	+7.0	+2.5	+4.4	0.0	69.8
1977	+3.1	+3.5	+6.9	+6.8	+3.2	+5.7	+2.1	69.8
1978	+2.3	+2.5	+5.6	+5.4	+2.8	+6.4	+3.8	68.8
1979	+2.7	+3.9	+4.8	+5.6	+1.6	+6.1	+2.1	68.5
1980	+0.3	+5.3	+6.7	+6.6	+1.2	+5.0	−0.3	70.0
1981	+0.9	+5.9	+5.5	+4.9	−0.9	+4.4	−1.4	70.8
1982	+1.1	+5.2	+4.0	+4.2	−1.0	+2.9	−2.2	70.1
1983	+3.1	+3.2	+3.3	+3.2	0.0	+3.2	−1.0	68.7
1984	+2.7	+2.4	+2.9	+3.0	+0.6	+1.8	−0.6	67.5
1985	+1.3	+2.1	+2.8	+2.9	+0.8	+1.6	+0.5	66.8
1986	+1.3	−0.2	+3.5	+3.8	+4.0	−4.2	+4.4	65.9
1987	+1.2	+0.1	+3.4	+3.0	+2.9	+1.8	+1.7	66.0
1988	+3.0	+1.0	+2.9	+3.1	+2.1	+3.4	+2.4	65.0
1989[6]	+2.1	+2.8	+2.8	+3.1	+0.3	+2.0	−0.8	64.1

[1]All figures (except for wage ratio) as % change from preceding year
[2]Gross domestic product (1980 prices) per gainfully active person
  Source: Statistisches Bundesamt, Fachserie 18, Reihe 1.1, Table 3
[3]For an employee household with average income
  Source: Statistisches Taschenbuch, Arbeits- und Sozialstatistik (Federal Minister for Labour), Table 6.11
[4]Up to 1983: calculated on a monthly basis including career public servants' pay
  Source: Deutsche Bundesbank (Tarif- und Effektivverdienste)
  From 1984 onward:
  Source: WSI-Tarifarchiv
[5]Structurally adjusted at constant employee figures for 1970
[6]Provisional calculation, as at January 1990

TABLE 5

COLLECTIVELY AGREED WEEKLY WORKING HOURS, 1984-1989

Employees in the whole economy in bargaining regions covering 1,000 or more employees, as %

As at December 31 in	% breakdown[2] of employees by agreed[1] weekly working hours							Average standard weekly working hours	
	less than 37	37	37.5	38	38.5	39	40 or over	in force	agreed
1984	—	—	—	1.4	23.1	0.0	75.4	—	39.6
1985	—	—	0.2*	1.3	36.3	0.1	61.9	—	39.4
1986	—	—	0.3*	1.7	42.9	1.2	53.6	—	39.3
1987	—	22.9	0.2	2.2	24.9	5.2	45.0	—	38.9
1988	1.0	23.6	0.5	2.9	43.5	11.2	17.3	39.0	38.4
1989	1.0	29.1	9.1	6.4	29.5	13.6	11.0	38.5	38.1

*less than 38 hours

[1]The figures refer to the standard weekly working hours **agreed** (last phase in the case of phased reduction of working hours) irrespective of the date of actual entry into force of the agreed reduction; excluding reduction of weekly working hours for individual employment groups.

[2]Basis for calculation: all employees benefiting from agreements concluded for DGB employees = 100. Percentages may not add up to 100 because in individual branches of activity a number of employees have no standard regulation of weekly working hours or have special regulations.

Source: WSI-Tarifarchiv

TABLE 6

COLLECTIVELY AGREED ANNUAL HOLIDAY ENTITLEMENT

Employees in bargaining regions covering 1,000 or more employees (in thousands)[1]

As at December 31, 1989

Sector[2]	Total employees covered	Employees with final entitlement > 30 working days		Average basic entitlement in working days	Average final entitlement in working days	Average mean entitlement in working days
		number	%			
Horticulture, agriculture and forestry	220	2	0.9	21.7	26.5	24.0
Energy and water supply, mining	356	—	—	29.2	30.0	29.6
Basic and producer goods industries	1,163	—	—	29.8	30.0	29.9
Capital goods industries	4,965	1,116	22.5	29.9	30.2	30.1
Consumer goods industries	1,458	116	7.9	29.2	30.0	29.6
Food, drink and tobacco industry	750	111	14.8	22.8	29.7	26.3
Building industry	1,120	—	—	23.5	26.8	25.2
Commerce	2,834	235	8.3	26.6	30.0	28.3
Transport and communications	910	59	6.5	25.5	29.9	27.7
Banking, finance and insurance	617	2	0.3	29.9	30.0	30.0
Private services, non-profit institutions	1,247	166	13.3	23.5	29.5	26.5
Territorial authorities, social security	2,553	32	1.3	26.2	30.0	28.1
Whole economy	18,193	1,839	10.1	27.3	29.8	28.6

[1]Since no official employment statistics based on bargaining regions are available, the employees falling within the scope of collective agreements have to be estimated from numerous sources; as a rule the figures also include vocational trainees and, where no other sources exist, refer to employees in employment relationships subject to social security.

[2]The delimitation of bargaining regions does not always coincide with the delimitation of sectors in the official statistics; allocation is based on the preponderance of the individual bargaining regions.

Source: WSI-Archiv

TABLE 7

COLLECTIVELY AGREED WEEKLY AND ANNUAL WORKING TIME

Employees in bargaining regions covering 1,000 or more employees (in thousands)[1]

As at December 31, 1989

Sector[2]	Total employees covered	Standard weekly working time in hours		Working days per year[3]	Collectively agreed annual working time in hours[4]
		agreed	in force as at December 31, 1989		
Horticulture, agriculture and forestry	220	39.6	39.9	224.2	1,791.1
of which: agriculture	76	40.0	40.0	224.6	1,796.8
Energy and water supply, mining	356	39.1	39.5	212.4	1,685.0
of which: energy and water supply	156	38.1	39.2	218.5	1,725.3
mining	200	39.8	39.8	207.7	1,653.5
Basic and producer goods industries	1,163	38.5	38.7	219.1	1,713.7
of which: iron and steel industry	170	36.5	36.5	219.1	1,601.6
chemical industry	700	39.0	39.0	219.0	1,732.0
Capital goods industries	4,965	37.1	37.3	219.0	1,639.1
of which: metal-processing industry	3,697	37.0	37.0	218.9	1,625.4
metalworking trades	959	37.5	38.4	219.5	1,687.9
Consumer goods industries	1,458	37.9	38.5	219.5	1,706.4
of which: wood-processing industry	172	37.2	37.6	218.7	1,676.5
leather industry	166	37.0	37.0	219.0	1,626.0
printing industry	57	39.1	39.9	221.0	1,768.2
textiles and clothing industry	373	38.5	39.0	219.6	1,727.9
Food, drink and tobacco industry	750	38.8	39.4	222.7	1,766.5
Construction industry	1,120	39.2	40.0	224.3	1,794.2
of which: building	876	39.0	40.0	224.8	1,798.7
Commerce	2,834	38.0	38.5	221.4	1,706.1
of which: wholesale distribution	1,042	38.5	38.5	220.1	1,695.0
retail distribution	1,566	37.5	38.5	222.3	1,711.8
Transport and communications	910	38.9	39.3	220.4	1,738.8
of which: German Federal Railways	114	38.5	39.0	219.0	1,719.2
German Federal Postal Administration	209	38.5	39.0	219.0	1,719.2
private transport services	366	39.3	39.8	222.3	1,770.3
Banking, finance and insurance	617	38.5	38.8	218.5	1,706.7
of which: banks	376	38.9	38.9	218.9	1,717.1
insurance companies	241	37.9	38.7	218.0	1,690.6
Private services, non-profit institutions	1,247	39.4	39.6	222.5	1,766.0
of which: hotels and restaurants	460	40.0	40.0	223.5	1,788.4
Territorial authorities, social security	2,553	38.5	39.0	218.9	1,717.4
of which: Federal Government, Länder, municipalities	2,226	38.5	39.0	219.0	1,719.2
Whole economy	18,193	38.1	38.5	220.1	1,704.2

[1]Since no official employment statistics based on bargaining regions are available, the employees falling within the scope of collective agreements have to be estimated from numerous sources; as a rule the figures also include vocational trainees and, where no other sources exist, refer to employees in employment relationships subject to social security.

[2]The delimitation of bargaining regions does not always coincide with the delimitation of sectors in the official statistics; allocation is based on the preponderance of the individual bargaining regions.

[3]Standard basis of calculations: 250 potential working days per year, minus average annual holiday entitlement plus other days off per year.

[4]Collectively agreed annual working time

$$= \frac{\text{number of collectively agreed working days per year}}{5} \times \text{collectively agreed weekly working time}$$

[5]Excluding private passenger transport, shipping, port and warehousing businesses.

Source: WSI-Tarifarchiv

TABLE 8

STRIKES AND LOCK-OUTS

Year	Strikes[1]		Lock-outs[2]		Strikes and lock-outs
	Employees participating	Working days lost	Employees affected	Working days lost	
	(in thousands)				
1960	17	38	—	—	38
1961	21	65	0.5	2	68
1962	79	451	0.1	34	54
1963	101	878	216	968	1,846
1964	6	17	—	—	17
1965	6	49	—	1	49
1966	196	27	—	0.2	27
1967	60	390	—	—	390
1968	25	25	—	0.1	25
1969	90	249	—	—	249
1970	184	93	—	—	93
1971	334	2,599	202	1,884	4,484
1972	23	66	—	—	66
1973	179	545	—	—	545
1974	250	1,051	—	—	1,051
1975	36	69	—	—	69
1976	117	412	52	122	534
1977	34	24	—	—	24
1978	299	2,548	188	1,733	4,281
1979	63	405	15	78	483
1980	45	128	—	—	128
1981	253	58	—	—	58
1982	40	15	—	—	15
1983	94	41	—	—	41
1984	399	2,921	172	3,565	5,617
1985	78	35	—	—	35
1986	116	28	—	—	28
1987	155	33	—	—	33
1988	34	42	—	—	42
1989[3]	176	151	—	—	151

[1]Including simultaneous lock-out
[2]Without simultaneous losses through strikes
[3]Estimate
Source: Statistisches Taschenbuch, Arbeits- und Sozialstatistik (Federal Minister for Labour and Social Affairs), Table 3.4

TABLE 9

GROSS WAGE AND SALARY RATIO AND EMPLOYEE RATIO, 1960-1990[1]
(%)

Year	Gross wage and salary ratio[2]		Employee ratio[4]
	actual	structurally adjusted[3]	
1960	60.1	65.0	77.2
1965	65.3	67.3	80.9
1970	68.0	68.0	83.4
1975	73.1	71.5	85.3
1976	71.8	69.8	85.7
1977	72.4	69.8	86.2
1978	71.4	68.8	86.6
1979	71.5	68.5	87.0
1980	73.5	70.0	87.4
1981	74.4	70.8	87.5
1982	73.8	70.1	87.3
1983	71.6	68.7	87.1
1984	70.3	67.5	87.1
1985	69.8	66.8	87.2
1986	69.1	65.9	87.4
1987	69.0	65.7	87.5
1988	67.7	64.5	87.6
1989	67.4	64.1	87.7
1990[5]	66.2	62.8	87.9

[1]Federal territory incl. Berlin (West)

[2]Gross income from wages and salaries as a percentage of national income

[3]The influence of variation in the employee ratio on income distribution is eliminated. For this wage and salary ratio, the employee ratio (number of employees as a percentage of the total gainfully active population) for 1970 (83.4%) is kept constant over all years. It thus answers the following question: what percentage of national income would gross wages and salaries represent if the 1970 employee ratio were still valid today?

[4]Number of employees as a percentage of the total gainfully active population (national concept)

[5]Forecast by DIW (German Institute for Economic Research), in: DIW-Wochenbericht 1-2/1990

Source: Statistisches Bundesamt, 1989 (Erste Ergebnisse der Sozialproduktsberechnung, January 1989) and DIW-Wochenbericht 1-2/1990, own calculations

Formula for structurally adjusted wage and salary ratio q:

$$q = \frac{Wj/Aj}{Vj/Ej} \times \frac{A_{70}}{E_{70}}$$

W = income from wages and salaries
V = national income
A = number of employees in employment
E = totally gainfully active population
j = current year, 70 = 1970

TABLE 10

STRUCTURE OF UNEMPLOYMENT, 1974-1989

Year	Unemployment rate		foreign workers	Proportion of total unemployed, as %[1]									Average duration of unemployment in months
	total	women		young persons aged under 20	young persons aged 20-25[1]	older persons aged 55-59[1]	older persons aged 60-65[1]	part-time job-seekers	without vocational qualifications	with impaired health	disabled persons	unemployed for longer than 1 year	
1974	2.6	3.1	2.9	3.6[1]	3.3	2.5	2.9	5.8	54.3	23.5		6.6	4.5
1975	4.7	5.4	6.8	6.2[1]	6.5	4.2	4.9	9.3	58.1	20.2	2.8	11.0	6.0
1976	4.6	5.8	5.1	4.6[1]	6.0	5.2	5.1	10.6	52.3	24.8	4.4	20.3	7.4
1977	4.5	6.0	4.9	4.7	6.2	5.6	4.8	11.6	53.2	26.8	5.0	21.2	7.9
1978	4.3	5.8	5.3	4.3	5.8	5.6	5.3	11.5	54.4	29.4	6.3	20.3	8.6
1979	3.8	5.2	4.7	3.3	4.5	5.7	6.5	10.8	53.3	33.9	8.3	19.9	8.3
1980	3.8	5.2	5.0	3.2	5.1	5.5	9.1	10.4	54.0	32.3	8.2	12.9[2]	7.6
1981	5.5	6.9	8.2	4.9	8.5	6.6	11.9	8.8	54.8	26.0	7.2	13.0[2]	7.4
1982	7.5	8.6	11.9	7.7	11.5	7.8	10.7	9.8	51.8	21.0	6.4	17.9[2]	8.5
1983	9.1	10.1	14.7	9.1	13.3	9.6	9.4	10.1	50.8	19.8	6.3	24.9[2]	9.2[2]
1984	9.1	10.2	14.0	7.9	12.9	11.4	9.5	9.8	49.4	19.5	6.5	28.8[2]	10.5[2]
1985	9.3	10.4	13.9	8.1	11.5	11.7	9.2	9.0	49.7	19.0	6.2	31.0[2]	11.6[2]
1986	9.0	10.5	13.7	7.4	10.5	10.9	8.1	8.8	50.8	19.9	6.0	31.9	12.5
1987	8.9	10.2	14.3	6.6	9.9	12.2	9.6	8.6	50.5	20.0	6.1	31.9	13.0
1988	8.7	10.0	14.7	6.6	8.5	12.7	10.8		48.8	22.2	6.2	32.6	13.6
1989	7.9	9.4	12.2	42.1[1]	6.8	12.7	10.9		47.2	24.1	6.6	31.4	13.6

[1] As at September each year

[2] These figures were revised in 1985. Up till then, a brief interruption (up to 13 weeks) of unemployment did not count as ending classification as "unemployed". Since 1985, even brief interruptions are counted as ending unemployment

Source: BfA (Federal Employment Service), Amtliche Nachrichten

BIBLIOGRAPHY

BIBLIOGRAPHY

Adamy, W. and Steffen, J. (1985): *Handbuch der Arbeitsbeziehungen [Industrial Relations Handbook]*, Bonn

Bergmann, J., Hirsch-Kreinsen, H., Springer, R. and Wolf, H. (1986): *Rationalisierung, Technisierung und die Kontrolle des Arbeitsprozesses [Rationalization, Mechanization and Control of the Work Process]*, Frankfurt am Main/New York

Endruweit, G., Gaugler, E., Staehle, W.H. and Wilpert, B. (eds.)(1985): *Handbuch der Arbeitsbeziehungen [Industrial Relations Handbook]*, Berlin/New York

Falke, J., Höland, A., Rhode, B. and Zimmermann, G. (1981): *Kündigungspraxis und Kündigungsschutz in der Bundesrepublik Deutschland [Dismissal Procedures and Protection Against Dismissal in the Federal Republic of Germany]*, Forschungsbericht des Bundesministers für Arbeit und Sozialordnung, 2 vols, Bonn

Fitting, K., Auffarth, F., Kaiser, H. and Heither, F. (1990): *Betriebsverfassungsgesetz, Handkommentar [The Works Constitution Act, A Quick-Reference Commentary]*, 16th edn., Munich

Fitting, K., Wlotzke, O. and Wissmann, H. (1978): *Mitbestimmungsgesetz [The Co-Determination Act]*, 2nd edn., Munich

Gemeinschaftskommentar zum Kündigungsschutzgesetz und zu sonstigen kündigungsschutzrechtlichen Vorschriften [Joint Commentary on the Protection Against Dismissal Act and Other Protective Legal Provisions Against Dismissal] (1989), Redaktion Friedrich Becker und Gerhard Etzel, 3rd edn., Neuwied

Grunsky, W. (1990): *Arbeitsgerichtsgesetz, Kommentar [The Labour Courts Act, A Commentary]*, Munich

Hagemeier, Ch., Kempen, O.E., Zachert, U. and Zilius, J. (1990): *Tarifvertragsgesetz, Kommentar für die Praxis [The Collective Agreements Act, A Practical Commentary]*, 2nd edn., Cologne

Halbach, G., Mertens, A. and Wlotzke, O. (1989): *Übersicht über das Recht der Arbeit [A Survey of Labour Law]*, 3rd edn., Bonn

Hanau, P. and Adomeit, K. (1988): *Arbeitsrecht [Labour Law]*, 9th edn., Frankfurt am Main

Jacobi, O. and Mueller-Jentsch, W. (1990): "West Germany: Continuity and Structural Change", in: G. Baglioni and C. Crouch (eds.), *European Industrial Relations: The Challenge of Flexibility*, London, Sage, pp. 127-53

Markovits, A. (1986): *The Politics of West German Trade Unions*, Cambridge, Cambridge University Press

Maydell, B.v. and Kannengiesser, W. (eds.) (1988): *Handbuch Sozialpolitik [Social Policy Handbook]*, Weinsberg

Müller-Jentsch, W. (1986): *Soziologie der industriellen Beziehungen [The Sociology of Industrial Relations]*, Frankfurt am Main/New York

Müller-Jentsch, W. (1987): *Zukunft der Gewerkschaften [The Future of the Trade Unions]*, Frankfurt am Main/New York

Neumann, L.F. and Schaper, K. (1984): *Die Sozialordnung der Bundesrepublik Deutschland [The Social System of the Federal Republic of Germany]*, 3rd edn., Bonn

Schaub, G. (1989): *Arbeitsrechtshandbuch [Labour Law Handbook]*, 6th edn., Munich

Söllner, A. (1987): *Grundriss des Arbeitsrechts [A Compendium of Labour Law]*, 9th edn., Munich

Streeck, W. (1984): "Co-determination: The Fourth Decade", in: B. Wilpert and A. Sorge (eds.), *International Perspectives on Organizational Democracy*, London, John Wiley & Sons, pp. 391-422

Weiss, M. (1980): *Betriebsverfassunsgesetz [The Works Constitution Act]*, 2nd edn., Baden-Baden

Weiss, M. (1987): *Labour Law and Industrial Relations in the Federal Republic of Germany*, Deventer

Wiedemann, H. and Stumpf, H. (1977): *Tarifvertragsgesetz [The Collective Agreements Act]*, 5th edn., Cologne

ENGLISH INDEX

References are to entry numbers. This index is to be used in conjunction with the list of main entries at the front of this volume.

373

375

380

GERMAN INDEX

References are to entry numbers. This index is to be used in conjunction with the list of main entries at the front of this volume.

389